DR. JANG'S
SAT* 800
MATH WORKBOOK
NEW EDITION

2022

Simon Jang and Tiffany T. Jang

*SAT is a registered trademark of the College Board, which was not involved in the production of, and does not endorse, this book.

Jang, Simon.
    Dr. Jang's SAT 800 Math Workbook New Edition 2022 / Simon Jang and Tiffany T. Jang
    415 p. 28 cm.
1. SAT (Educational test) — Study guides. 2. Mathematics — Examinations — Study guides. 3. Mathematics / Study & Teaching. 4. Study Aids / SAT. 5. Redesigned SAT
378.1664 – dc23

ISBN-13: 9781081191467

www.DrJang800.com

*SAT is a registered trademark of the College Board, which was not involved in the production of, and does not endorse, this book.

Table of Contents

How This Book Can Help You

This is the 2022 edition of our New SAT math workbook. For more than 20 years, we have taught math to students in both the high school and the private setting. One thing we noticed throughout our years of teaching is that there is a lack of good learning material for students of any level studying for the math section of the SAT exam. To remedy this, we have produced this book. It contains all the material you need to know to get a great score. Through our years of teaching, we have reached the conclusion that anyone can get an excellent math score on the SAT in a short period of time provided that he or she focuses on the content required for the test and the skills to tackle the questions quickly and easily.

Required Content Knowledge
In this book, we divide the required content knowledge into four chapters based on the guideline provided by the College Board for the 2016 redesigned SAT Math:

- Chapter One: Heart of Algebra
- Chapter Two: Problem Solving and Data Analysis
- Chapter Three: Passport to Advanced Math
- Chapter Four: Additional Topics in Math

Within each chapter, we explore all necessary sub-concepts in depth and provide numerous practice questions mimicking those on the actual SAT.

The problems and techniques in this book will help train and prepare students for the redesigned math section of the new SAT. The breakdown of topics in this book reflects the topics emphasized on the new SAT. Working on the problem solving skills sections will help students build a strong sense of intuition for solving problems and making educated guesses.

Problem Solving Skills
Within each concept section, the problems are grouped into three difficulty levels:

- Easy
- Medium
- Hard

The critical thinking advices, answers, and detailed explanations are located to the right of the problems. Students can refer to the answers easily but can also cover the page if they want to attempt the problem on their own

1500+ Practice Problems and 10 Mock Tests
In addition to a thorough overview of materials, this book provides over 1500 practice problems for you to reinforce your understanding of the material and pinpoint the weak areas you need to improve on. There are some parts of questions needed to be answered without a calculator, of which the symbol of a

no-calculator sign, 🚫, has been added at the end of questions. For other questions, without a no-calculator sign, acceptable calculators are allowed.

The ten SAT Math mock tests located at the back of book closely mimic the actual exam and provide more even practice. By taking these mock exams with a timer under test-like conditions, students will be even more prepared to master the real test.

More SAT Practice Questions Just Like the Real Test
We published this 4th edition to more adequately reflect what students will see on the actual test. We cannot thank you, our readers, enough for giving us feedback and bringing to our attention many ways we were able to improve our mock tests to better simulate those on the actual exam. We will always continue to improve in order to help you be as prepared as possible for the new SAT Math exam.

Based on student and teacher feedback, we have also rearranged questions in the problem solving skill section to more accurately reflect their difficulty levels and revised the concept overview sections to more closely cover what will be on the new SAT Math exam.

About the Authors

Dr. Simon Jang and Mrs. Tiffany Jang have been teaching in public high schools and in their own private tutoring studio for more than 20 years. They have developed a unique and proven SAT Math learning system that suits the students' needs and helps them efficiently prepare for the Math section of the SAT. Over the years, their innovative methods and effective teaching materials have benefitted not only their students' scores, but also their students' endeavors in college and beyond.

Dr. Jang received a Ph.D in Chemical Engineering from New York Polytechnic University. He worked as a software developer before he became a high school teacher. He has been teaching math, physics, and chemistry in New Jersey public high schools for many years. He has dedicated his spare time to developing innovative and effective methods of teaching high school math, chemistry, and physics in his established tutoring studio.

Tiffany Jang earned a Master's degree in Library and Information Sciences from the University of Wisconsin-Madison and a Master's degree in Computer Science from the New Jersey Institute of Technology. After several years of teaching high school math, now she is working as a school librarian in the New Jersey public school system.

They have spent years developing innovative teaching methods and effective learning materials. Their methods can both introduce a new student to the subject and remedy a student's weaknesses to help them efficiently prepare for the SAT Math exam.

Acknowledgements

We would like to acknowledge the help and support from our daughters, Jennifer and Justine, both of whom study Mathematics at the Massachusetts Institute of Technology, as well as the countless students over the years who have provided feedback on our system. Special thanks to our parents back in Taiwan for their help and support as well. Without the help of everyone around us, this enormous project would never even have been conceptualized.

About the SAT Math Test

What Content Knowledge Is Included

According to the College Board, a nonprofit organization that administers the Scholastic Assessment Test (SAT*), mathematics in the new SAT, launched in March 2016, covers content knowledge up to Algebra II. The new SAT Math increases emphasis on critical thinking, problem solving, and data analysis skills.

Four areas of math will be focused on the new SAT Math:
- Heart of Algebra (33%)
- Problem Solving and Data Analysis (29%)
- Passport to Advanced Math (28%)
- Additional Topics in Math (10%)

How the Test Is Organized

The SAT Math exam lasts a total of 80 minutes with two portions of test, Math Test – Calculator and Math Test – No Calculator. Within each portion, SAT Math questions range from easy to hard, with the easier problems at the beginning and the more difficult ones at the end. There are 58 questions, 78% of which are four-option multiple choice questions and 22% are grid-in response questions. Here is the breakdown of the redesigned SAT Math content specifications:

New SAT Math Testing Time (80 minutes)	38 questions with calculators	55 minutes
	20 questions without calculators	25 minutes
Types of Questions (58 questions)	45 multiple choice with 4 options	78%
	13 grid-in questions	22%
Content Areas	Heart of Algebra • Analyzing and fluently solving linear equations and systems of linear equations • Creating linear equations and inequalities to represent relationships between quantities and to solve problems • Understanding and using the relationship between linear equations and inequalities and their graphs to solve problems	19 questions 33%
		17 questions

Content Areas	Problem Solving and Data Analysis ■ Creating and analyzing relationships using ratios, proportions, percentages, and units ■ Representing and analyzing quantitative data ■ Finding and applying probabilities in context	29%
	Passport to Advanced Math ■ Identifying and creating equivalent algebraic expressions ■ Creating, analyzing, and fluently solving quadratic and other nonlinear equations ■ Creating, using, and graphing exponential, quadratic, and other nonlinear functions	16 questions 28%
	Additional Topics in Math ■ Solving problems related to area and volume ■ Applying definitions and theorems related to lines, angles, triangles, and circles ■ Working with right triangles, the unit circle, and trigonometric functions	6 questions 10%

As mentioned above, the SAT Math Test has two portions. One is a 25-minute No-Calculator portion with 20 questions. The other is a 55-minute calculator portion with 38 questions. Here is the breakdown of the content specifications in each portion:

No-Calculator Portion

	Number of Questions	% of Test
Total Questions:	20	100%
Multiple-Choice	15	75%
Grid-in	5	25%
Content Areas:	20	100%
Heart of Algebra	8	40%
Passport to Advanced Math	9	45%
Additional Topics in Math	3	15%
Testing Time	25 minutes	

Calculator Portion

	Number of Questions	% of Test
Total Questions:	38	100%
Multiple-Choice	30	79%
Grid-in	8	21%
Content Areas:	38	100%
Heart of Algebra	11	29%
Problem Solving and Data Analysis	17	45%
Passport to Advanced Math	7	18%
Additional Topics in Math	3	8%
Testing Time	55 minutes	

How the SAT Is Scored

On the new SAT, test-takers will **not be penalized** for incorrect answer in multiple choice questions. The redesigned SAT will be administered both in print and by computer. The top score will return to 1600, which includes the 800 points from the math section and 800 points from the evidence-based reading and writing.

What to Do before the Test
- Get a good night's sleep.
- Have your photo ID, admission ticket, No. 2 pencils, erasers, watch, and a scientific or graphing calculator ready the night before.
- Have a nutritious but not too filling breakfast.
- Be there 15 minutes before the test is expected to start.

What to Be Aware of during the Test
- Read the questions completely and carefully.
- Solve the easy questions with caution; careless mistakes tend to occur when solving easy questions too confidently.
- Don't struggle on one question for too long. Mark the question and work on it at the end.
- Check the scantron frequently to make sure the bubbles are filled in correctly and on the right question number.

About SAT Math Problem Solving Strategies

Two Types of Math Questions on the SAT
- 45 multiple-choice questions
- 13 grid-in questions

Strategies and Some Shortcuts to Solving SAT Math Questions

When taking a math test, you have to think mathematically. To think mathematically, you must become familiar with some keywords and their definitions or mathematical equivalents:

- Even Integer: $2n$
- Odd Integer: $2n + 1$
- Order of Operation: Follow the PEMDAS Rules
- Union, Intersection, and Venn diagram
- GCF (Greatest Common Factor) and LCM (Least Common Multiple)
- Prime Numbers
- Common Denominator
- Multiplying and Dividing Exponents
- Percent and Percent Change
- Ratio and Proportion: Direct Proportion and Inverse Proportion
- Average, Sum, Median, and Mode
- Rate
- Probability of an Event
- Parallel Lines and Their Transversals
- Triangles and Special Triangles
- Interior and Exterior Angles of a Triangle
- Polygons
- Area of Geometric Figures

Read questions carefully and underline or circle the most important key points, such as "average," "sum," "maximum," etc. so that you can catch the scope of the question quickly. One of the most important aspects that you must get used to in SAT Math test is the reading comprehension feature. You will need excellent reading comprehension skills to translate word problems into math problems.

Pay attention to hints in the questions that you can use to decide whether or not to use shortcuts to solve the problem. Do not use shortcuts without understanding the question first. Certain types of example questions can be easily solved by shortcuts. Some examples are shown below.

Shortcuts

1. Plugging in Easy Numbers: If a question is along the lines of "which of the following must be true or must NOT be true," and the answer choices contain variables, you can try to assign an easy number to the variable to find the answer.

   Example 1: If X, Y and Z represent consecutive positive odd integers, which of the following is NOT true?
   a) $X + Y + Z$ is an odd integer
   b) $X + Y$ is an even integer
   c) $\frac{Z - X}{2}$ is an even integer
   d) $\frac{X + Y}{2}$ is an odd integer

   This question looks complicated, but if we plug in, X = 1, Y = 3, and Z = 5, you will find out that only answer (d) is not true. Of course, make sure that the numbers you plug in satisfy the requirements. 1, 3, and 5 are obviously consecutive positive odd integers.

   Example 2: If $|x| < 1$, which of the following is the greatest?
   a) 2
   b) $1 - x$
   c) $1 + x$
   d) $2x$

   Instead of solving this inequality, you can easily find the right answer (a) by plugging in a value of x that satisfies the inequality. If we plug in $x = \frac{1}{2}$, we see that the answer (a) is the greatest.

   Example 3: The figure below shows a square and a right triangle. What is the area of shaded region?

   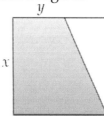

   a) $\frac{x(x + y)}{2}$
   b) $\frac{(x^2 + y^2)}{2}$
   c) xy
   d) $2xy$

To find the answer fast, we can plug in $x = 5$ and $y = 3$. If we do this, the shaded region has area $5^2 - \frac{1}{2}(2)(5) = 20$. Only (a) gives an equivalent answer.

2. In geometry, when you are given a set of parallel lines and possibly a transversal, many times the degree of two angles end up being congruent or supplementary. Many times you can tell which one is which just by looking at the graph (but this is not always the case and sometimes graphs are not drawn to scale).

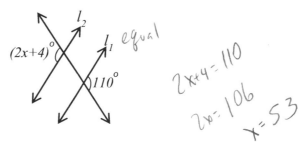

l_2

l_1 equal

$(2x+4)^\circ$

110°

$2x+4 = 110$

$2x = 106$

$x = 53$

Example 4: In the figure above, if $l_1 \parallel l_2$, what is the value of x?
   a) 45
   b) 53
   c) 57
   d) 60

Since we have two parallel lines and a transversal, there are only two different types of angles here: angles with degree equal to 110° and angles supplementary to 110°. By just looking at that graph, we can tell, $2x + 4 = 110$, so $x = 53$. Answer is (b).

3. Sometimes if you can't solve the problem mathematically, you can still use logic to eliminate the answer choices. The more answer choices you can eliminate, the higher the probability of you answering a question right.

Example 5: John can complete a job in 20 minutes. Bob can complete the same job in 40 minutes. If they work together, approximately how many minutes will it take them to complete the job?
   a) 60 minutes
   b) 40 minutes
   c) 30 minutes
   d) 15 minutes

not the average

use logic lol

If they work together, the job should be completed faster than 2 Bobs and slower than 2 Johns. The only reasonable answer should be between 10 to 20 minutes. Answer is (d).

Example 6: Sam drove to work at an average speed of 50 miles per hour from her house and then returned along the same route at an average speed of 40 miles per hour. If the entire trip took her 2.25 hours, what is the entire distance, in miles, for the round trip?

    a) 90
    b) 100
    c) 120
    d) 125

In this problem, since distance = time × speed, the entire distance is between 40 × 2.25 and 50 × 2.25 miles. The reasonable answer is 100 miles, answer (b).

4. Take advantage of your calculator during the calculator portion of the test. Learn to use a calculator efficiently by practicing. As you approach a problem, focus on how to solve that problem and then decide whether the calculator will be helpful. Using a calculator may help to prevent you from careless mistakes and save you some time performing calculations. However, a calculator will not solve a problem for you. You must understand the problem first. Keep in mind that every SAT Math question can be solved without a calculator and some questions can be solved faster mentally than with a calculator.

Example 7: What is the average (arithmetic mean) of 192, 194, and 196?
    We can get the answer, 194, without using a calculator since the median of three consecutive odd integers is also the average.

5. When applicable, use the plug–and–chug technique to solve a question backwards. This method works best when you see simple numbers as answer choices. Plug the numbers from the answer choices into the question until you find the right one. Plug–and–chug is sometimes faster than setting up an equation.

Example 8: Together, Ken, Justin, and Tiff have read a total of 65 books. Justin read 3 times as many books as Ken and Tiff read 3 times as many books as Justin. How many books did Ken read?
    a) 12
    b) 9
    c) 7
    d) 5

Plugging and chugging this question is faster than setting up an equation. You can start with plugging in the number from choice (c) and notice that the number 7 is too big, so you pick a smaller number, (d), to plug in. Thus you arrive at the right answer, (d).

6. Working backwards can sometimes help you organize your thoughts in order to solve a word problem. First, identify what the question is asking. Then, ask yourself what data you might need. Finally, look for the data you need from the question, and use it to solve the problem.

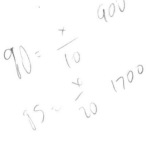

Example 9: On an Algebra exam, class A has 10 students taking the test and an average score of 90. Class B has 20 students taking the test and an average score of 85. What is the average score of all the students in both class A and B?
- By reading the last sentence, we know the question is asking for the average of all the students.
- In order to answer this question, we will use the formula to find averages:

$$Average = \frac{Total\ Score}{Number\ of\ Students}$$

- The total number of students is 10 + 20 and the total score is 10 × 90 + 20 × 85.
- Finally, set up an equation to solve this problem.

$$\frac{10 \times 90 + 20 \times 85}{10 + 20} = 86.666$$

7. Most of the word problems can be translated from English into mathematical expressions by following a few guidelines:

a. Keywords in the problem can help translating the words into algebraic expressions. For instance, the words "greater than," "more," and "increase" indicate addition and "less than," "fewer," and "decrease" indicate subtraction. "2 times" refers to multiplying a number or a variable by 2, and "is" indicates equality in an equation. If the question mentions finding "a number" without specifying the value of the number, assign a variable for that number and then solve for the value of the variable.

b. When dealing with percent problems, the following keywords usually translate to the following actions:
   - Percent in decimal form → divide by 100
   - Decimal in percent form → multiply by 100
   - 'is' → =

- 'of' → ×
- 'what' or 'a number' (the value you are solving for) → x

Examples:	Solutions:

i. What is 15% of 60?   i. $x = \frac{15}{100} \times 60 = 9$

ii. 20% of what number is 16?   ii. $\frac{20}{100} \times x = 16$

                                               $x = 80$

iii. What percent of 20 is 5?   iii. $\frac{x}{100} \times 20 = 5$

                                              $x = \frac{5 \times 100}{20}$

                                              $x = 25\%$

    c. If a geometry question is given in words, make a sketch and label points according to the question. It becomes easier to find the answer once you have drawn your own sketch.

8. It's okay to trust their geometric figures unless when it is stated that the figure is not drawn to scale. You may estimate the answer based on the figure itself if you cannot solve the problem or you run out of time. If it is stated that the figure is not drawn to scale, you may redraw the figure based on the data presented.

Know Some Tricks about Grid-in Questions
- Grid in only one digit per column.
- There is no penalty for wrong answers, so answer all the grid-in questions.
- There are no negative answers.
- Mixed numbers need to be changed to improper fractions. (Grid in $\frac{3}{2}$ instead of $1\frac{1}{2}$. $1\frac{1}{2}$ is not acceptable and will be read as $\frac{11}{2}$.)
- Either fraction or decimal form is acceptable.
- Decimals can be rounded or truncated but answers rounded to fewer digits than space available will be marked wrong.
  - The answer $\frac{16}{21}$ should be entered as .761 or .762 (note: $\frac{16}{21} = 0.7619$), but not 0.76.
  - Don't add a 0 in the far left column except when the answer is 0.
- Don't waste time rounding your decimal answer.
- Don't waste time to reduce fractions.

About the Diagnostic Test in This Book

This diagnostic test contains 58 questions on topics that are most frequently found on the SAT Math test. The purpose of the diagnostic test is to allow you to measure your level of proficiency and identify your weakest areas.

It is important that you take this diagnostic test to find out your weakest areas and then study those areas accordingly. All the questions in the diagnostic test are on a medium to hard level on the actual SAT. So if you quite comfortable with some of these questions, you should be able to do well on SAT Math test in those areas. If you have no idea how to solve a question, you should leave a mark on the question and spend more time studying that area in the future.

After taking the diagnostic test and checking the solutions, group each question based on your confidence level when you were solving it:
1. Low: Questions that you skipped or had absolutely no idea how to solve.
2. Medium: Questions that you may be able to solve but are not completely familiar with and/or made careless mistakes on.
3. High: Questions that you are very confident and you know how to solve.

For the topic areas you have confidence low, you need to read through the concept overviews on each section, try to understand them, and do questions from easy to hard on the problems solving skills sections. Remember, only after recognizing your problem areas, you can tackle them by lots of practices.

For those areas that you have medium confidence in, you may quickly glance at the concept overviews to see if there are some concepts or tricks that you don't know and then jump straight to the medium and hard level practice problems.

If you still have time after dealing with low and medium confidence questions, you can focus on the hard-level questions of the topics you have high confidence in. By doing so, you will improve your skills across the board and become a master of the SAT Math test. Practice makes perfect!

SAT Math Diagnostic Test

Evaluating Algebraic Expressions

1. If $z = \frac{12x^4}{y}$, what happens to the value of z when both x and y are doubled?
   a) z is multiplied by 32.
   b) z is multiplied by 16.
   c) z is multiplied by 8.
   d) z is doubled.

Evaluating Variables in Terms of Another

2. A right circular cylinder with radius 3 and height 7 has a volume v. In terms of v, what is the volume of the right circular cylinder with radius 3 and height 14?
   a) $v + 7$
   b) $7v$
   c) $5v$
   d) $2v$

   $v = \pi r^2 h$
   $v = \pi \cdot 63$
   $\frac{14}{9}$ ... 126

Solving Equations

3. A litter of milk can fill up 3 large cups or 5 small cups. If there are 12 large cups and 10 small cups, about how many litters of milk will be needed to fill up all the cups?
   a) 6
   b) 4
   c) 3
   d) 2

Solving Linear Equations

4. If a linear function passes through the points $(1, s)$, $(3, t)$ and $(5, 10)$, what is the value of $2t - s$?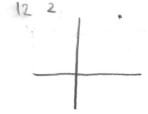
   a) 2   12   2
   b) 4
   c) 8
   d) 10

Solving Quadratic Equations

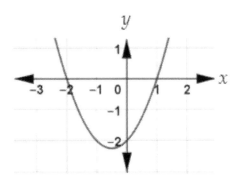

5. Which of the following equations best describes the curve in the figure above?
   a) $y = x^2 - 2$
   b) $y = x^2 + x - 2$
   c) $y = x^2 + x + 2$
   d) $y = x^2 + x$

Solving Systems of Equations

6. There is $180 of cash in John's pocket. John only has 10 and 20 dollar bills. If John has a total of 13 bills, how many 20 dollar bills are in his pocket?

   5

Solving Inequalities

7. If $x < 5 < \frac{1}{x-1}$, then x could be which of the following?
   a) 5
   b) 1
   c) $\frac{7}{6}$
   d) $\frac{10}{3}$

   $x < 5$ $5 < \frac{1}{x-1}$

Word Problems

8. Six erasers cost as much as 3 pencils. If Matt bought one eraser and one pencil for $1.50, how much does one pencil cost in dollars?
   a) 0.25
   b) 0.50
   c) 0.75
   d) 1.00

   6 e   3 P
   x   1 P

Rate Word Problems

9. Sam drove from home at an average speed of 50 miles per hour to her working place and then returned along the same route at an average speed of 40 miles per hour. If the entire trip took her 2.25 hours, what is the entire distance, in miles, for the round trip?

    1 hr   30

    1w   40

    a) 90
    b) 100
    c) 120
    d) 125

Percent Word Problems

10. A store sells a certain brand of TVs for $550 each. This price is 25 percent more than the cost at which the store buys one of these TVs. The store employees can purchase any of these TVs at 20 percent off the store's cost. How much would it cost an employee to purchase a TV of this brand?

    a) $352
    b) $330
    c) $413
    d) $440

Ratio and Proportion Word Problems

11. A recipe of a cake for 8 people requires 1.2 pounds of flour. Assuming the amount of flour needed is directly proportional to the number of people eating the cake, how many pounds of flour are required to make a big cake for 240 people?

    a) 20
    b) 26
    c) 30
    d) 36

Unions and Intersections of Sets

12. For an end of the year party, Mrs. Scott ordered 40 slices of pizza for her class. Among those slices of pizza, 16 were topped with mushroom and 14 were topped with chicken. If 15 slices contained neither mushroom nor chicken, how many slices of pizza must be topped with both mushroom and chicken?

    a) 3
    b) 5
    c) 7
    d) 9

Ratios, Proportions, and Rates

13. If y is inversely proportional to x and y is equal to 12 when x is equal to 8, what is the value of y when $x = 24$?

    a) $\frac{1}{6}$
    b) 4
    c) 1
    d) $\frac{1}{4}$

14. If y is directly proportional to x and y is equal to 40 when x is equal to 6, what is the value of y when $x = 9$?

    a) 40
    b) 45
    c) 50
    d) 60

15. Freddy's family owns two different types of cars, a sedan and an SUV. The sedan has gas mileage of 25 miles per gallon, and the SUV has gas mileage of 20 miles per gallon. If both cars use the same amount of gasoline and the sedan travels 100 miles, how many miles does the SUV travel?

Percents

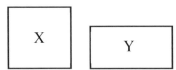

16. Two rectangles X and Y are shown above. If the width of rectangle Y in the figure below is 25 percent less than the width of rectangle X and the length of rectangle Y is 25 percent greater than the length of rectangle X. What is the area of rectangle Y compared to the area of rectangle X?
    a) The area of rectangle Y is 25 percent less than the area of rectangle X.
    b) The area of rectangle Y is 6 percent less than the area of rectangle X.
    c) Both rectangles have the same area.
    d) The area of rectangle Y is 6 percent greater than the area of rectangle X.

Averages

17. Which of the following could be the sum of 8 numbers if the average of these 8 numbers is greater than 9 and less than 10?
    a) 85
    b) 83
    c) 82
    d) 79

Data Analysis

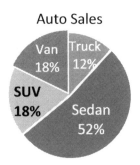

Auto Sales

18. The pie graph above represents the automobiles that were sold by a dealer in 2010, according to their records. If the dealer sold 40 more Sedans than all others combined, how many automobiles did it sell altogether?

Counting Rules

19. A school will send a team of one math teacher and two science teachers to work on a project. If the school has 5 math teachers and 6 science teachers, how many of such teams are possible?

Probability

20. A bag contains red, blue, and green marbles. The probability of pulling out a red marble randomly is $\frac{1}{4}$ and the probability of pulling out a blue marble randomly is $\frac{1}{5}$. Which of the following could be the total number of marbles in the bag?
    a) 10
    b) 12
    c) 18
    d) 20

Sequence Patterns

486, 162, ...

21. In the sequence above, each term after the 1ˢᵗ term is $\frac{1}{3}$ of the term preceding it. What is the 5ᵗʰ term of this sequence?

Symbol Functions

22. For all numbers j and k, Let $ be defined by $j\$k = j - k + 3$. What is the value of $(3\$6)\ \$2$?
    a) 0
    b) 1
    c) 2
    d) 3

Logic

23. Helen threw a fair six sided dice 5 times. Each throw showed a different number according to the following rules:

    The first roll was greater than 5.
    The second roll was less than 3.
    The third roll was 4.
    The fourth roll was the same as the first roll.
    The fifth roll was an even number.

    Which of the following must be true?
    a) Helen could have rolled a 6 more than three times.
    b) Helen could have rolled a 5 only one time.
    c) Helen rolled more even numbers than odd numbers.
    d) Helen rolled 3 at least once.

Factors and Multiples

24. What is the greatest three-digit integer that has the factors 10 and 9?

    a) 100
    b) 900
    c) 955
    d) 990

25. Which of the following must be a factor of x if x is a multiple of both 9 and 12?
    a) 8
    b) 24
    c) 27
    d) 36

Fraction Operations

26. If $x = -\frac{1}{2}$, what is the value of $\frac{1}{x} - \frac{1}{x+1}$?
    a) –4
    b) –2
    c) 4
    d) 2

Algebraic Factoring

27. If $x^2 - y^2 = 15$, and $x - y = 3$, what is the value of $x + y$?
    a) 1
    b) 3
    c) 5
    d) 10

Functions

28. The quadratic function f is given by $f(x) = ax^2 + bx + c$, where a and c are positive real numbers. Which of the

following is the possible graph of

$f(x)$?

a)

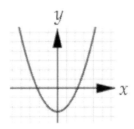

b)

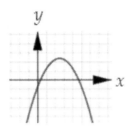

c)

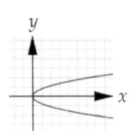

d)

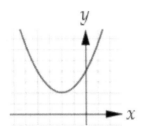

Complex Numbers

29. Which of the following is the expression $\frac{3-2i}{4+3i}$ equivalent to?

a) $\frac{12-4i}{7}$

b) $\frac{6+17i}{25}$

c) $\frac{6-10i}{7}$

d) $\frac{6-17i}{25}$

30. If $3 - 2i$ is a root of $2x^2 + ax + b = 0$, then $b = ?$

a) 7.5
b) –7.5
c) 26
d) It cannot be determined.

Quadratic Functions and Equations

31. Which of the following could be a graph of the equation $y = ax^2 + bx + c$, where $b^2 - 4ac = 0$?

a)

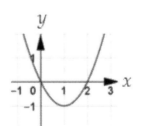

b)

c)

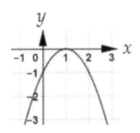

d)

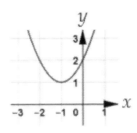

32. A baseball is hit and flies into a field at a trajectory defined by the equation $d = -1.2t^2 + 100$, where t is the number of seconds after the impact and d is the horizontal distance from the home plate to the outfield fence. How many seconds have passed if the ball is 50 meters away from the outfield fence ?
    a) 3.78
    b) 4.33
    c) 5.12
    d) 6.45

Polynomials

33. What is the remainder when $2x^4 - 3x^3 + 4x^2 - 5x + 6$ is divided by $x - 3$?
    a) 108
    b) 96
    c) 87
    d) 75

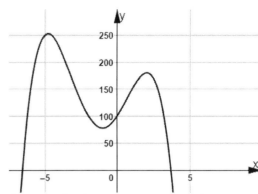

34. The graph above represents the function $y = -x^4 - 5x^3 + 14x^2 + 40x + c$. Which of the following could be the value of c? 🚫
    a) -100
    b) -7
    c) 4
    d) 100

Exponent Operations

35. If $8 = a^y$, then $8a^2 = ?$
    a) a^{y^2}
    b) a^{y+2}
    c) $8a^y$
    d) a^{8y}

Roots and Radical Operations

36. If $x^{\frac{3}{2}} = \frac{1}{27}$, then what does x equal?
    a) -9
    b) -3
    c) $\frac{1}{9}$
    d) $-\frac{1}{9}$

37. $\frac{2}{(x+y)^{-\frac{2}{3}}} = (x+y)^{-\frac{1}{3}}$, which of the following must be true?
    a) $x = 0$
    b) $\sqrt{x+y} = 2$
    c) $\sqrt{x+y} = \frac{1}{2}$
    d) $x + y = \frac{1}{2}$

Lines and Angles

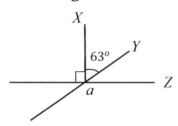

38. What is the value of a in the figure above?

Parallel Lines and Their Transversal

39. In the figure below, $\overline{AB} \parallel \overline{CD}$ and $\overline{CD} \perp \overline{BC}$. What is the value of $x + y$?

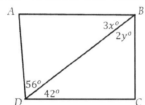

a) 21
b) 34
c) 36
d) 38

Triangle Interior and Exterior Angles

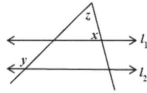

40. In the figure above, if $l_1 \parallel l_2$, what does z equal in terms of x and y?
    a) $x - y$
    b) $y - x$
    c) $180° - y + x$
    d) $180° - x - y$

Special Triangles

41. In the figure below, AB = 2. What is the length of AD?

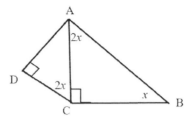

a) $\sqrt{3}$
b) 1
c) $\frac{1}{2}$
d) $\frac{\sqrt{3}}{2}$

Similar Triangles

42. In the figure below, point D is the mid-point of $\overline{AB}$ and point E is the mid-point of $\overline{AC}$. If AB = 10, AC = 12, and DE = 7, what is the perimeter of quadrilateral DBCE?

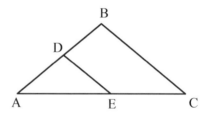

a) 29
b) 30
c) 31
d) 32

Areas of Triangles

43. In the figure below, the area of the shaded region is 26 square units. What is the height of the smaller triangle?

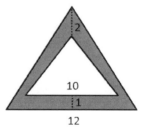

Triangle Inequality Theorem

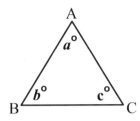

Note: Figure not drawn to scale.

44. The triangle above is isosceles and $a <$ b. Which of the following must be FALSE?
    a) AB = BC
    b) BC = AC
    c) AC = AB
    d) $a = c$

Polygons

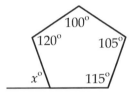

Note: Figure not drawn to scale.

45. The figure shown above is composed of five straight line segments, what is the value of x?

46. In quadrilateral ABCD, $m\angle A = m\angle B = 128°$, and $m\angle D$ is 10° less than 5 times of $m\angle C$. Find $m\angle D$.

Areas of Polygons

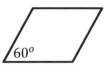

47. If the parallelogram above has side lengths all equal to 12, what is the area of this parallelogram?
    a) 72
    b) $72\sqrt{2}$
    c) $72\sqrt{3}$
    d) 144

Segments of a Circle

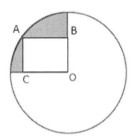

48. In the figure above, rectangle ABOC is drawn in circle O. If OB = 3 and OC = 4, what is the area of the shaded region?
    a) $6\pi - 3$
    b) $\frac{25\pi}{4} - 12$
    c) $25\pi - 12$
    d) $\frac{25\pi}{4} - 3$

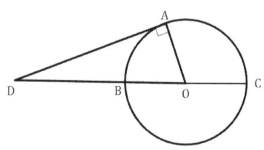

49. Point O is the center of the circle in the figure above. If DA = 12 and DB = 8, what is the area of the circle?

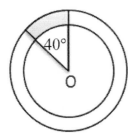

50. In the figure above, O is the center of the two circles. If the bigger circle has a radius of 5 and the smaller circle has a radius of 4, what is the area of shaded region?
    a) 3π
    b) 2π
    c) π
    d) $\frac{2}{3}\pi$

Cubes

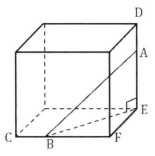

51. The cube shown above has edges of length 3. If $\overline{CB} = \overline{AD} = 1$, what is the length of $\overline{AB}$?

Volumes and Surface Areas

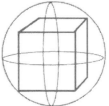

52. A cube is inscribed in a sphere as shown in the figure above. Each vertex of the cube touches the sphere. If the diameter of this sphere is $3\sqrt{3}$, what is the volume of the cube?
    a) 8
    b) 27
    c) 36
    d) 48

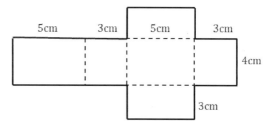

53. If the figure above is folded along the dashed lines, a rectangular box will be formed. What is the volume of the box in cubic centimeters?
    a) 15
    b) 20
    c) 40
    d) 60

Coordinate Geometry

54. Which of the following is the equation of a parabola whose vertex is at (–3, –4)?
    a) $y = (x + 3)^2 - 4$
    b) $y = (x - 3)^2 + 4$
    c) $y = (x - 4)^2 - 3$
    d) $y = x^2 - 4$

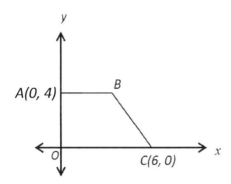

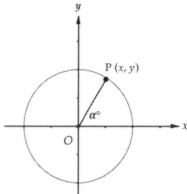

55. In the xy-coordinate plane, AB is parallel to the x-axis. If AO = AB, what is the area of quadrilateral ABCO?
    a) 12
    b) 16
    c) 18
    d) 20

56. If the center of the circle defined by $x^2 + y^2 - 4x + 2y = 20$ is (h, k) and the radius is r, then $h + k + r = ?$

57. On the unit circle above, if the values of sine and cosine of the angle $\alpha°$ are equal, what is the sum $x + y$?
    a) $2\sqrt{2}$
    b) $\sqrt{2}$
    c) $\frac{\sqrt{2}}{2}$
    d) $\frac{\sqrt{2}}{3}$

58. The graph of $y = 3cos\,(2x) + 3$ intersects the y–axis at what value of y?
    a) 3
    b) 6
    c) 9
    d) 0

Trigonometric Functions

Diagnostic Test Answer Keys

1. c	2. d	3. a	4. d	5. b	6. 5	7. c	8. d	9. b	10. a
11. d	12. b	13. b	14. d	15. 80	16. b	17. d	18. 1000	19. 75	20. d
21. 6	22. b	23. c	24. d	25. d	26. a	27. c	28. d	29. d	30. c
31. c	32. d	33. a	34. d	35. b	36. c	37. d	38. 153	39. d	40. b
41. d	42. d	43. 8	44. b	45. 80	46. 85	47. c	48. b	49. 78.5	50. c
51. 4.12	52. b	53. d	54. a	55. d	56. 6	57. b	58. b		

Diagnostic Test Answer Explanations

1. Answer: (C)

$$\frac{12(2x)^4}{(2y)} = 2^3 \left(\frac{12x^4}{y}\right)$$

2. Answer: (D)

$v = \pi (3)^2 \times 7$

$v_2 = \pi (3)^2 \times 14$

$\frac{v}{v_2} = \frac{\pi(3)^2 \times 7}{\pi(3)^2 \times 14} = \frac{1}{2}$

$v_2 = 2v$

3. Answer: (A)

12 large cups need 4 litters and 10 small cups need 2 litters.

The amount of milk needed:

4 + 2 = 6 litters

4. Answer: (D)

The line segment connecting the first two points must have the same slope as the line segment connecting the last two points.

$\frac{10 - s}{5 - 1} = \frac{10 - t}{5 - 3}$

$\frac{10 - s}{4} = \frac{10 - t}{2}$

$40 - 4t = 20 - 2s$

$4t - 2s = 20$

$2t - s = 10$

5. Answer: (B)

From the graph, there are two roots, −2 and 1.

$y = (x + 2)(x - 1) = x^2 + x - 2$

6. Answer: 5

Let x be the number of $20 bills and y be the number of $10 bills.

$x + y = 13, y = 13 - x$

$20x + 10y = 180$

$20x + 10(13 - x) = 180$

$130 + 10x = 180$

$10x = 50$

$x = 5$

7. Answer: (C)

$5 < \frac{1}{x - 1}, \frac{1}{5} > x - 1$

$1 < x < \frac{6}{5}$

8. Answer: (D)

Let the price of one eraser be x and the price of one pencil be y. The price of 6 erasers = the price of 3 pencils.

$6x = 3y, x = \frac{1}{2}y$

The Price of One Eraser = $\frac{1}{2}$ the Price of One Pencil.

$x + y = 1.50$

$\frac{1}{2}y + y = 1.50$

Solve for y to get the price of one pencil $1.00.

9. Answer: (B)

Let one trip have x miles.

$Time = 2.25 = t_1 + t_2 = \frac{x}{50} + \frac{x}{40}$

$2.25 = x(\frac{1}{50} + \frac{1}{40})$

$x = 50$

Total Distance = 2 × 50 = 100

10. Answer: (A)

Store's Cost × (1 + 25%) = 550

Store's Cost = $\frac{550}{1.25}$ = 440

20 percent off the store's cost:

440 × (1 − 0.2) = 352

11. Answer: (D)

$\frac{8\ People}{1.2\ Pounds} = \frac{240\ People}{x\ Pounds}$

$8x = 1.2 \times 240$

$x = 36$ pounds of flour

12. Answer: (B)
Use Venn diagram: Mushroom ∪ Chicken = Total – (No Mushroom ∩ No Chicken)
= Mushroom + Chicken – (Mushroom ∩ Chicken)
Mushroom ∪ Chicken = 40 − 15 = 16 + 14 − (Mushroom ∩ Chicken)
25 = 30 − (Mushroom ∩ Chicken)
Mushroom ∩ Chicken = 5

13. Answer: (B)
$8 \times 12 = y \times 24$
$y = 4$

14. Answer: (D)
$\frac{40}{6} = \frac{y}{9}$
$y = 60$

15. Answer: 80
Small car uses $\frac{100}{25} = 4$ gallons
SUV Miles $= 4 \times 20 = 80$ miles

16. Answer: (B)
Let X's width be w and length be l. Then Y's width is 0.75w and length is 1.25l.
Area of Y = 0.75w × 1.25l = 0.9375wl = 93.75% of area of X.
100% − 93.75% = 6.25% (less)

17. Answer: (D)
Sum = Number of Elements × Average
$9 \times 8 < Sum < 10 \times 8$
$72 < Sum < 80$

18. Answer: 1000
Solve this problem using proportions.
There were 4% (52% − 48%) more Sedans sold than all other cars combined.
4% : 40 = 100% : x
x = 1,000 cars

19. Answer: 75
This is combination. The number of ways to select m objects from n objects ($n \geq m$), where order does not matter:
$C_m^n = \frac{n!}{m!(n-m)!}$
Math: $C_1^5 = 5$
Science: $C_2^6 = 15$
Total number of arrangements:
$5 \times 15 = 75$

20. Answer: (D)
The total number of marbles should be a common multiple of 4 and 5.
The LCM of 4 and 5 is 20, so the total number of marbles has to be a multiple of 20.

21. Answer: 6
The Fifth Term $= 486 \times (\frac{1}{3})^4 = 6$

22. Answer: (B)
Find the 3$6 first.
3$6 = 3 − 6 + 3 = 0
0$2 = 0 −2 + 3 = 1

23. Answer: (C)
List of results: 6, less than 3, 4, 6, even.
Only (c) could meet all the conditions.

24. Answer: (D)
Find the greatest number that ends in 0 and where the sum of the digits is divisible by 9.

25. Answer: (D)
The LCM of 12 and 9 is 36.

26. Answer: (A)
$\frac{1}{-\frac{1}{2}} - \frac{1}{-\frac{1}{2}+1} = -2 - 2 = -4$

27. Answer: (C)
$x^2 - y^2 = (x - y)(x + y)$
$3(x + y) = 15, x + y = 5$

28. Answer: (D)
A positive value of a will make the quadratic function's graph open upward and a positive value of c will show that the function has a positive y-intercept.

29. Answer: (D)
Rationalize the denominator.
$\frac{3-2i}{4+3i} \times \frac{4-3i}{4-3i} = \frac{(3-2i)(4-3i)}{16+9} = \frac{6-17i}{25}$

30. Answer: (C)
If (3 − 2i) is a root of the quadratic equation, then its conjugate (3 + 2i) is also the root of the equation.
The product of the roots is $\frac{b}{2}$; the sum of the roots is $-\frac{b}{a}$.
$(3 - 2i)(3 + 2i) = 13 = \frac{b}{2}$
$9 - (-4) = 13 = \frac{b}{2} \rightarrow b = 26$

31. *Answer: (C)*
    The discriminant, $b^2 - 4ac$, of a quadratic equation reveals the type of its roots.
    When $b^2 - 4ac = 0$, the quadratic equation two equal, real roots.
    - When $b^2 - 4ac > 0$, the quadratic equation has two unequal, real roots.
    - When $b^2 - 4ac < 0$, the quadratic equation has no real roots.

32. *Answer: (D)*
    $50 = -1.2t^2 + 100$
    $t = 6.45$

33. *Answer: (A)*
    Remainder Theorem states if a polynomial $P(x)$ is divided by $x - r$, its remainder is $P(r)$.
    $P(3) = 2 \times 3^4 - 3 \times 3^3 + 4 \times 3^2 - 5(3) + 6 = 108$

34. *Answer: (D)*
    c is the y-intercept which is equal to 100.

35. *Answer: (B)*
    $8a^2 = a^y \times a^2 = a^{y+2}$

36. *Answer: (C)*
    $x^{\frac{3}{2}} = \frac{1}{27}$
    $x = (\frac{1}{27})^{\frac{2}{3}}$
    $\frac{1}{27} = 3^{-3}$
    $x = (3^{-3})^{\frac{2}{3}} = 3^{-2} = \frac{1}{9}$

37. *Answer: (D)*
    $\frac{2}{(x+y)^{-\frac{2}{3}}} = (x + y)^{-\frac{1}{3}},$
    $2 = (x + y)^{-\frac{2}{3}}(x + y)^{-\frac{1}{3}} = (x + y)^{-1}$
    $x + y = \frac{1}{2}$

38. *Answer: 153*
    $a + (90 - 63)° = 180°$
    $a = 153°$

39. *Answer: (D)*
    $3x = 42$
    $x = 14$
    $2y + 42 = 90$
    $y = 24$
    $x + y = 14 + 24 = 38$

40. *Answer: (B)*
    $y = x + z$ (exterior angle theorem and corresponding angles)
    $z = y - x$

41. *Answer: (D)*
    $2x + x = 90°$
    $x = 30°$
    These are two special 30−60−90 right triangles.
    $AB = 2$
    $AC = \frac{1}{2} \times 2 = 1$
    $AD = \frac{\sqrt{3}}{2} \times AC = \frac{\sqrt{3}}{2}$

42. *Answer: (D)*
    Point D is the mid-point of $\overline{AB}$ and point E is the mid-point of $\overline{AC}$, so $\frac{AD}{AB} = \frac{AE}{AC} = \frac{1}{2}$
    Therefore, $\triangle ADE \sim \triangle ABC$ by SAS Similarity theorem
    $AB = 10$
    $DB = 5$
    $\frac{1}{2} = \frac{DE}{BC}$
    $DE = 7$
    $BC = 14$
    $EC = \frac{1}{2}AC = 6$
    Perimeter of $DBCE = 5 + 7 + 14 + 6 = 32$

43. *Answer: 8*
    If h is the height of smaller triangle, then the height of the big triangle is $h + 3$.
    Area of Big $\triangle$ – Area of Small $\triangle$ = 26
    $\frac{1}{2}(h + 3) \times 12 - \frac{1}{2}h \times 10 = 26$
    $6h + 18 - 5h = 26$
    $h = 8$

44. *Answer: (B)*
    If $a < b$, then $BC < AC$.

45. *Answer: 80*
    The sum of all interior angles of a pentagon is
    $(5 - 2) \times 180 = 540°$.
    $540 = 120 + 100 + 105 + 115 + (180 - x)$
    $x = 80$

46. *Answer: 85*
    $A + B + C + D = 360°$
    $128° + 128° + 5x - 10° + x = 360°$
    $x = 19°$
    $5x - 10° = 85°$

47. Answer: (C)

Area = Base × Height = $12 \times 12 \times \frac{\sqrt{3}}{2} = 72\sqrt{3}$

48. Answer: (B)
    OA is the radius of the circle and the shaded area is the area of the quarter circle minus the area of the rectangle.
    Radius = $\sqrt{OB^2 + OC^2} = \sqrt{3^2 + 4^2} = 5$
    Shaded Area = Area of $\frac{1}{4}$ Circle – Area of Rectangle = $\frac{1}{4}(\pi \times 5^2) - 4 \times 3 = \frac{1}{4} \times 25\pi - 12 = \frac{25\pi}{4} - 12$

49. Answer: 78.5
    $DA^2 + OA^2 = OD^2$
    $12^2 + r^2 = (8 + r)^2 = 64 + 16r + r^2$
    $r = 5$
    Area = $\pi \times 5^2 = 78.54$

50. Answer: (C)
    Area = $\frac{40}{360}(\pi \times 5^2 - \pi \times 4^2) = \pi$

51. Answer: 4.12
    $BF = 2$
    $EF = 3$
    $EA = 2$
    $AB = \sqrt{EA^2 + EB^2} = \sqrt{EA^2 + BF^2 + EF^2}$
    $AB = \sqrt{2^2 + 2^2 + 3^2} = \sqrt{17} = 4.123$

52. Answer: (B)
    Let x be the length of one side of the cube.
    Diameter of Sphere = Diagonal of Cube
    Diagonal of Cube = $\sqrt{x^2 + x^2 + x^2} = x\sqrt{3}$
    $\sqrt{x^2 + x^2 + x^2} = 3\sqrt{3}$
    $x\sqrt{3} = 3\sqrt{3}$
    $x = 3$
    Volume of Cube = $3^3 = 27$

53. Answer: (D)
    After folding, the height of the box will be 3 cm, the length will be 5 cm, and the width will be 4cm.
    Volume = 3 cm × 4 cm × 5 cm = 60 cm³

54. Answer: (A)
    The equation of a parabola with vertex (h, k) is y = (x − h)² + k.
    (h, k) = (−3, −4)
    $y = (x + 3)^2 - 4$

55. Answer: (D)
    This is a trapezoid of whose area is equal to $\frac{1}{2}$ (AB + OC) × OA.
    Area = $\frac{1}{2}$ (4 + 6) × 4 = 20

56. Answer: 6
    Rewrite the equation in standard form.
    $x^2 + y^2 - 4x + 2y = 20$
    $(x^2 - 4x + 2^2) + (y^2 + 2y + 1^2) = 20 + 2^2 + 1^2 = 25$
    $(x - 2)^2 + (y + 1)^2 = 5^2$
    The center of circle is (2, −1) and the radius is 5.
    $h + k + r = 2 - 1 + 5 = 6$

57. Answer: (B)
    In the first Quadrant, only when $\alpha = 45$, $\cos(\alpha°) = \sin(\alpha°) = \frac{\sqrt{2}}{2}$
    For a unit circle:
    $x = y = \frac{\sqrt{2}}{2}$
    $x + y = \sqrt{2}$

58. Answer: (B)
    The graph of y = 3cos (2x) + 3 intersects the y–axis at x = 0.
    $y = 3\cos(2 \times 0) + 3 = 3\cos(0) + 3$
    $= 3 \times 1 + 3 = 6$

Chapter 1   Heart of Algebra

I.   ALGEBRAIC EXPRESSIONS

A.   EVALUATING ALGEBRAIC EXPRESSIONS

CONCEPT OVERVIEWS

Variables
A variable is a letter or symbol that represents a value that is usually unknown or subject to change. An **algebraic expression** is made up of one or more **terms**. For instance, the expression $x^2 + 4x + 4$ is made up of three terms: x^2, $4x$, and 4, with x being the variable. The **coefficient** of a term is the constant in front of the variable and is multiplied by the variable. The **base** of a term is another name for the variable.

To raise a number to the nth power is the same as multiplying n copies of that number. The **power** of a term is the number to which the variable or the base has been raised. For instance, 3^2 has a power of 2. To evaluate it, $3^2 = 3 \times 3 = 9$. The **exponent** is the same as the power.

Like Terms
Terms that share a base and the same power are called like terms. For instance, the terms x, $3x$, and $8x$ are like terms because these terms all have the same base, x, and the same exponent (the exponent is one because it is not explicitly stated). The terms $3x$ and $3x^2$ are **unlike terms**, because the variables have different exponents.

Addition and Subtraction of Algebraic Expressions Consist of Combining Like Terms
To add like terms, combine them by adding their coefficients, for example, $3x + 4x = 7x$. To subtract like terms, subtract their coefficients, for example, $9a^2 - 6a^2 = 3a^2$.

Multiply and Divide Terms with Same Base
To **multiply** terms with same base, multiply the coefficients of the terms and add the exponents: $(3b^4)(2b^3) = 6b^7$. To divide terms with same base, divide the coefficients of the terms and subtract the exponents: $\frac{15x^5}{5x^2} = 3x^3$.

-   The **reciprocal** of a number x is equivalent to $\frac{1}{x}$ where x is not 0.
-   To divide by a fraction term is the same as multiplying by its reciprocal. For instance: $\frac{x^5}{\frac{1}{x^2}} = x^5 \times x^2 = x^7$

Distributive Law

Use the **distributive law** when multiplying algebraic expressions with more than one term. The distributive law states that in order to get rid of the parentheses, each element within the parentheses should be multiplied by the term outside.
Examples:

$$A (B + C) = AB + AC$$
$$A (B - C) = AB - AC$$

- Rules for removing the parentheses: if there is no coefficient in front of the parentheses and simply a +, remove the parentheses. This is equivalent to distributing +1. If the sign before the parentheses is −, change the sign of every term inside and take away the parentheses. This can be thought of as distributing −1.
  For instance, $x^2 - (-2x^2 + 3x - 1) = x^2 + 2x^2 - 3x + 1 = 3x^2 - 3x + 1$

- Use **FOIL** to multiply a binomial by another binomial

$$(a + b)(c + d) = ac + ad + bc + bd$$

Example: $(x + 3)(x - 1) = x^2 - x + 3x - 3 = x^2 + 2x - 3$

To multiply two polynomials consisting of three or more terms, multiply each term in the first polynomial by each term in the second polynomial.

$$(a + b + c)(x + y + z) = ax + ay + az + bx + by + bz + cx + cy + cz$$

Example: $(x^2 + x + 1)(2x^2 - x - 1)$
$$= 2x^4 - x^3 - x^2$$
$$+ 2x^3 - x^2 - x$$
$$+ 2x^2 - x - 1$$
$$= 2x^4 + x^3 - 2x - 1$$

Evaluate an Expression
To evaluate an expression by substitution is to replace a variable by its value and then perform the calculations.

Example: Evaluate $x^2 + 3x + 5$ when $x = -1$
Solution: Substitute x with -1, so $(-1)^2 + 3(-1) + 5 = 1 - 3 + 5 = 3$.

Problem Solving Skills

Easy

1. If $x = 4y$ and $y = 2$, what is the value of $5x$?
    a) 4
    b) 10
    c) 20
    d) 40

    y = 8

    Answer: (D)
    Plug y = 2 into the first equation.

    x = 4(2) = 8
    5x = 5(8) = 40

2. If $x + 2y = 5$, what is the value of $x + 2y - 5$?

    0

    Answer: 0
    x + 2y = 5
    (x + 2y) −5 → 5 − 5 = 0

3. If $x + y = 8$, $y = z - 3$, and $z = 1$, then what is the value of x?
    a) 10
    b) 3
    c) −8
    d) −6

    Answer: (A)
    If z = 1, then y = 1 − 3 = −2.

    x + (−2) = 8
    x = 10

4. If $f(x) = \frac{2-x^2}{x}$ for all nonzero x, then $f(1) = ?$
    a) 1
    b) 2
    c) 3
    d) 4

    Answer: (A)
    Plug x = 1 into the function.
    $f(1) = \frac{2 - (1)^2}{1} = \frac{1}{1} = 1$

5. Which of the following is not equal to $6x^2$?
    a) $2x^2 + 4x^2$
    b) $2x + 4x$
    c) $(2x)(3x)$
    d) $(6x)(x)$

    Answer: (B)
    2x + 4x = 6x ≠ 6x²

6. If $ab + 3b = a - 2c$, what is the value of b when $a = -2$ and $c = -1$?

    −2b + 3b = −2 + 2
    b = 0

    Answer: 0
    Plug a = −2 and c = −1 into equation.
    (−2)b + 3b = −2 − 2 × (−1)
    −2b + 3b = 0 → b = 0

7. If $x = y(y - 2)$, then $x + 3 = ?$
    a) $y^2 - y$
    b) $y^2 - 3y$
    c) $y^2 - 2y + 2$
    d) $y^2 - 2y + 3$

    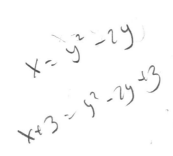

    Answer: (D)
    Use Distribution Law.
    FOIL: x = y(y − 2) = y² − 2y
    x + 3 = y² − 2y + 3

Medium

8. If $\frac{x}{2} = 0$, what is the value of $1 + x + 2x^2 + 3x^3 =$? Ⓧ

    a) 2
    ⓑ 1
    c) 0
    d) 3

    Answer: (B)
    $\frac{1}{2}x = 0$
    $x = 0$
    $1 + 0 + 2(0)^2 + 3(0)^3 = 1$

9. If $x = 3$, $y = 5$, what is the value of $2 \times (\frac{x}{y})^2 \times y^2$?

    a) 5
    b) 10
    c) 15
    ⓓ 18

    $2\left(\frac{9}{25}\right)^{\xi} \cdot 25$

    Answer: (D)
    $2 \times (\frac{3}{5})^2 \times 5^2 = 18$

10. $f(x) = \frac{x^3 - 5}{x^2 - 2x + 8}$, then what is $f(3)$?

    a) 0
    ⓑ 2
    c) 4
    d) 6

    $\frac{27-5}{9-6+8} = \frac{22}{11}$

    Answer: (B)
    $f(3) = \frac{3^3 - 5}{3^2 - 2(3) + 8} = \frac{22}{11} = 2$

11. If $\frac{x+y}{z} = 9$, $\frac{x}{y} = 8$, and $\sqrt{x} = 4$, what is the value of z?

    a) 1
    ⓑ 2
    c) 3
    d) 4

    $x=16 \ y=2$

    Answer: (B)
    If $\sqrt{x} = 4$, then $x = 4^2 = 16$.
    $\frac{x}{y} = \frac{16}{y} = 8 \rightarrow y = 2$
    $\frac{16+2}{z} = 9 \rightarrow z = 2$

12. If $z = \frac{12x^4}{y}$, what happens to the value of z when both x and y are doubled?

    a) z is multiplied by 32.
    b) z is multiplied by 16.
    ⓒ z is multiplied by 8.
    d) z is doubled.

    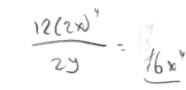
    $\frac{12(2x)^4}{2y} = \frac{16x^4}{2y}$
    $2y$

    Answer: (C)
    $\frac{12(2x)^4}{(2y)} = 2^3 \times \frac{12x^4}{y}$

13. If one soft drink costs \$0.40 and one burger cost \$2, which of the following represents the cost, in dollars, of S soft drinks and B burgers? Ⓧ

    a) S × B
    b) 0.8(S × B)
    c) 2.4(B + S)
    ⓓ 2B + 0.4S

    Answer: (D)
    Total = $2 \times B + 0.4 \times S$

14. The table below gives values of the quadratic function $f(x)$ at selected values of x. Which of the following defines $f(x)$?

x	0	1	2	3
$f(x)$	5	7	13	23

   a) $f(x) = x^2 + 5$
   b) $f(x) = x^2 + 1$
   c) $f(x) = 2x^2 - 5$
   d) $f(x) = 2x^2 + 5$

Answer: (D)
Plug in $x = 0$ and $x = 1$ to try out until the answer found.

(d) $2(0)^2 + 5 = 5$
   $2(1)^2 + 5 = 7$

15. If $x = -5$ and $y = 3$, what is the value of $x^2(2y + x)$?
   a) –275
   b) –75
   c) –25
   d) 25

$25(6-5)$

Answer: (D)
$(-5)^2 \times (2 \times 3 + (-5)) = 25$

Hard

16. If $(x + y)^2 = 49$ and $(x - y)^2 = 29$, what is the value of xy?
   a) 2
   b) 5
   c) 6
   d) 10

$x^2 + 2xy + y^2 = 49$
$x^2 - 2xy + y^2 = 29$
_____
$4xy = 20$

Answer: (B)
$(x + y)^2 - (x - y)^2 = (x^2 + y^2 + 2xy) - (x^2 + y^2 - 2xy) = 4xy$
$49 - 29 = 4xy$
$xy = 5$

Questions 17 – 18 refer to the following information:
   The Doppler effect is the change in frequency of a wave while its source is moving. The Doppler effect formulas shown below are used to calculate the frequency of sound as a result of relative motion between the source and the observer.
   If the source is moving toward an observer at rest, the change of observed frequency can be calculated by:

$$f_{observed} = f_{original} \left(\frac{v_{sound}}{v_{sound} - v_{source}} \right)$$

If the observer is moving toward the sound and the source moving closer to the observer, the change of frequency can be calculated by:

$$f_{observed} = f_{original} \left(\frac{v_{sound} + v_{observer}}{v_{sound} - v_{source}} \right)$$

$f_{observed} =$ observed frequency
$f_{original} =$ frequency of the original wave
$v_{sound} =$ speed of the sound
$v_{observer} =$ speed of the observer
$v_{source} =$ speed of the source

17. Standing on the side walk, you observe an ambulance moving toward you. As the ambulance passes by with its siren blaring, you hear the pitch of the siren change. If the ambulance is approaching at the speed of 90 miles/hour and the siren's pitch sounds at a frequency of 340 Hertz, what is the observed frequency, in Hertz? Assume the speed of sound in air is 760 miles/hour.
    a) 302
    b) 324
    c) 386
    d) 419

Answer: (C)
The source is moving toward an observer at rest.
$$f_{observed} =$$
$$f_{original}\left(\frac{v_{sound}}{v_{sound} - v_{source}}\right)$$
$v_{observer} = 0\ miles/hour$
$v_{source} = 90\ miles/hour$
$v_{sound} = 760\ miles/hour$
$$f_{observed} = 340 \times \left(\frac{760}{760 - 90}\right)$$
$$= 386\ Hertz$$

18. If you are driving a car at the speed of 30 miles/hour while an ambulance is approaching to you at the speed of 60 miles/hour, what is the observed frequency of the siren, in Hertz? Assume that the ambulance sounds at a frequency of 340 Hertz and the speed of sound in air is 760 miles/hour.
    a) 362
    b) 384
    c) 409
    d) 439

Answer: (B)
The observer is moving toward the sound.
$$f_{observed} =$$
$$f_{original}\left(\frac{v_{sound} + v_{observer}}{v_{sound} - v_{source}}\right)$$
$v_{observer} = 30\ miles/hour$
$v_{source} = 60\ miles/hour$
$v_{sound} = 760\ miles/hour$
$$f_{observed} = 340 \times \left(\frac{760 + 30}{760 - 60}\right)$$
$$= 383.7\ Hertz$$

19. If a and b are consecutive odd integers, where $a > b$, which of the following is equal to $a^2 - b^2$? Ⓝ
    a) 4
    b) $2a - 2b$
    c) $2b + 4$
    d) $4b + 4$

Answer: (D)
If a and b are consecutive odd integers and a > b, then a = b +2.

$a^2 - b^2 = (a + b)(a - b)$
$= (b + 2 + b)\ (b + 2 - b)$
$= 2(2b + 2)$
$= 4b + 4$

20. Which of the following expressions must be negative if $x < 0$? Ⓝ
    a) $x^4 - 2$
    b) $x^3 - 3$
    c) $x^4 - 3x^2 - 1$
    d) $x^6 + 3x^2 + 1$

Answer: (B)
If x < 0, then the result of an odd power of x is negative and the result of an even power of x is positive.

B. EVALUATE ONE VARIABLE IN TERMS OF ANOTHER

CONCEPT OVERVIEWS

One Variable in Terms of Another
An equation that contains two variables can be written so that the value of one variable is given in terms of the other. For instance, $y = 3x + 3$ is an equation with two variables, x and y, in which the value of variable y is written in terms of the other variable x. The value of y is $3x + 3$.

Steps to Evaluate One Variable in Terms of Another
1) Combine like terms.

2) Isolate the terms that contain the variable you wish to solve for.

3) Move all other terms to the other side of the equation.

4) Divide all terms by the desired variable's coefficient to calculate the variable in terms of the other.

Example: If $4a + 8b = 16$, what is the value of a in terms of b?
Solution: $4a = 16 - 8b$, Isolate $4a$ on one side of the equation, move $8b$ to the other side of the equation and change the sign of $8b$ to negative.
$a = 4 - 2b$, after dividing all terms by 4, the value of a in terms of b is $4 - 2b$.

Problem Solving Skills

Easy

1. If $2x + y = x + 5$, what is y in terms of x?
   a) $5 - x$
   b) $x + 5$
   c) $1 - 5x$
   d) $1 - 2x$

   $y = -x + 5$

   Answer: (A)
   Isolate the terms that contain the variable you wish to solve for and then move all other terms to the other side of the equation.
   $2x + y = x + 5$
   $y = x + 5 - 2x$
   $y = -x + 5$

2. If $5x \neq 4y$ and $2y = 5z$, what is the value of x in terms of z?
   a) z
   b) $2z$
   c) $3z$
   d) $4z$

   $\frac{5}{2}x = 5z$
   $x = 2z$

   Answer: (B)
   Substitute 2y with 5z in the first equation.
   $5x = 2(2y) = 2(5z) = 10z$
   $x = 2z$

3. If x is $\frac{3}{4}$ of y, y is $\frac{2}{3}$ of z, and $z > 0$, and then what is x in terms of z?
   a) $\frac{3}{4}z$
   b) $\frac{1}{2}z$
   c) $\frac{1}{4}z$
   d) $2z$

   Answer: (B)
   $x = \frac{3}{4}y = \frac{3}{4}\left(\frac{2}{3}z\right)$
   $x = \frac{1}{2}z$

4. If $xy^3 = z$, $z = ky^2$, and $ky \neq 0$, which of the following is equal to k?
   a) xy
   b) $\frac{x}{y}$
   c) $x - 1$
   d) $x + y$

   Answer: (A)
   $xy^3 = z = ky^2$
   $k = \frac{xy^3}{y^2} = xy$

Medium

5. If $x^{-1}y = 5$, what does y equal in term of x?
   a) $-5x$
   b) x
   c) $-x$
   d) $5x$

   Answer: (D)
   $x^{-1} = \frac{1}{x}$
   $x^{-1}y = 5$
   $\frac{y}{x} = 5 \rightarrow y = 5x$

6. If $x = y^2$ for any positive integer x, and if $z = x^3 + x^4$, what is z in terms of y?

    a) $y^2 + y^3$
    b) y^3
    c) $y^6 + y^3$
    d) $y^6 + y^8$

Answer: (D)
Replace x with y^2.

$z = (y^2)^3 + (y^2)^4 = y^6 + y^8$

7. The price of green tea leaves is D dollars for 5 ounces and each ounce makes x bottles of green tea drink. In terms of D and x, which of the following expressions shows the cost of making 1 bottle of green tea drink?

    a) $5Dx$
    b) $\dfrac{5D}{x}$
    c) $\dfrac{5x}{D}$
    d) $\dfrac{D}{5x}$

Answer: (D)
$D = 5 \text{ ounces} \times \dfrac{x \text{ Bottles}}{\text{Ounce}} \times$
$\text{Price of One Bottle}$

$\text{Price of One Bottle} = \dfrac{D}{5x}$

Hard

8. A right circular cylinder with radius 3 and height 7 has a volume v, In terms of v, what is the volume of the right circular cylinder with radius 3 and height 14?

    a) $v + 7$
    b) $7v$
    c) $5v$
    d) $2v$

Answer: (D)
$v = \pi(3)^2 \times 7$
$v_2 = \pi(3)^2 \times 14$
$\dfrac{v}{v_2} = \dfrac{\pi(3)^2 \times 7}{\pi(3)^2 \times 14} = \dfrac{1}{2}$
$v_2 = 2v$

9. If $x = 2y^2 + 3y + 4$ and $z = -y + 1$, what is x in terms of z?

    a) $2z^2 - 7z - 9$
    b) $2z^2 - 7z + 7$
    c) $2z^2 + 7z + 9$
    d) $2z^2 - 7z + 9$

Answer: (D)
Plug in $y = 1 - z$ to the first equation and then apply FOIL method and the distributive law.
$x = 2(1 - z)^2 + 3(1 - z) + 4$
$x = 2z^2 - 7z + 9$

II. Solving Equations

A. Solving Equations

Concept Overviews

Definition of Equation
An **equation** is a statement that two expressions are equal. The both sides of the equation are equal. The key of solving for a variable in the equation is to isolate the variable on one side and everything else on the other side of the equal sign.

Opposite Operations
To isolate variables, use operations that are opposite to the existing operations in the equation in order to move variables or numbers between both sides of an equation and keep the two sides equal.

Using opposite operations is very important for solving an equation. Some pairs of opposite operations include + verses − , × verses ÷, and square verses square root.

Problem Solving Skills

Easy

1. If $-3x + 8 = -2x - 7$, what is the value of x?
    a) 15
    b) 3
    c) −3
    d) −15

Answer: (A)
Isolate x on one side of equation and use opposite operations.
$-3x + 8 = -2x - 7$
$-3x + 8 - 8 + 2x$
$= -2x - 7 - 8 + 2x$
$-x = -15 \rightarrow x = 15$

2. If $x^3 + 6 = x^3 + y$, then $y = ?$
    a) −6
    b) −3
    c) 6
    d) 3

Answer: (C)
Definition of equation. Both sides of the equation are equal.

$x^3 + 6 = x^3 + y$
$y = 6$

3. If $3x + 2 = 5$, what is the value of $3x - 6$?
    a) −1
    b) −2
    c) −3
    d) 1

Answer: (C)
Subtract 8 on both sides.

$3x + 2 - 8 = 5 - 8 = -3$
$3x - 6 = -3$

4. If $a^2 - 1 = b^3$, and $2a = 6$, which of the following could be the value of b? 🚫

    a) –1
    b) 0
    c) 1
    d) 2

Answer: (D)
$2a = 6$
$a = 3$
$3^2 - 1 = b^3$
$8 = b^3 = 2^3$
$b = 2$

5. If $m^2 + 8 = 39$, then $m^2 - 7 =$?

    a) 31
    b) 29
    c) 26
    d) 24

Answer: (D)
$m^2 + 8 = 39$
$m^2 = 31$
$m^2 - 7 = 31 - 7 = 24$

6. If $3(x + 5) = 18$, then what is the value of x?

    a) 1
    b) 3
    c) 6
    d) 9

Answer: (A)
Divide both sides by 3.
$3(x + 5) = 18$
$x + 5 = 6$
$x = 1$

7. If $(0.0010) \times y = 10$, then $y = $?

    a) 0.01
    b) 0.001
    c) 100
    d) 10000

Answer: (D)
Divide both sides by 0.001.
$(0.0010) \times y = 10$
$y = \frac{10}{0.001} = 10000$

8. If $3(x + y)(x - y) = 30$ and $x - y = 5$, what is the value of $x + y$?

    a) 1
    b) 2
    c) 3
    d) –1

Answer: (B)
$3 \times 5 \times (x + y) = 30$
$x + y = 2$

Medium

9. If $\frac{x}{3} = \frac{3x}{z}$ and $z \neq 0$, what is the value of z? 🚫

    a) 9
    b) 6
    c) 4
    d) 3

Answer: (A)
Apply cross multiplication.
$\frac{x}{3} = \frac{3x}{z}$
$\frac{1}{3} = \frac{3}{z}$
$z = 3 \times 3 = 9$

10. If $xy = 4$, $z - y = 3$, and $2z = 10$, what is the value of $x + y + z$?

Answer: 9
Solve for z first. Then solve for y, and finally solve for x.
$2z = 10 \rightarrow z = 5$
$5 - y = 3 \rightarrow y = 2$
$x(2) = 4 \rightarrow x = 2$
$x + y + z = 9$

11. If $2a + 3b = 2b$, which of the following must equal $6a + 3b$? Ⓝ

   a) 0
   b) 1
   c) b
   d) $3b$

Answer: (A)
$2a + 3b = 2b$
$2a + b = 0$
$6a + 3b = 3(2a + b) = 0$

Hard

12. If $\frac{x + y}{x - y} = 4$ and $y \neq 0$, what is the value of $\frac{x}{y}$?

Answer: $\frac{5}{3}$
Cross multiply and then divide both sides by y.
$\frac{x + y}{x - y} = 4 \rightarrow x + y = 4(x - y)$
$\frac{x}{y} + 1 = 4(\frac{x}{y} - 1) = 4\frac{x}{y} + 4$
$\frac{x}{y} = \frac{5}{3}$

$$\sqrt{x + 2} = x - 1$$

13. For all values of x greater than 1, the equation above is equivalent to which of the following? Ⓝ

   a) $x = x^2$
   b) $x = x^2 - 1$
   c) $x = x^2 - 2x - 1$
   d) $x = x^2 - 2x + 1$

Answer: (C)
Square both sides of the equation.
$(\sqrt{x + 2})^2 = (x - 1)^2$
$x + 2 = x^2 - 2x + 1$
$x = x^2 - 2x - 1$

14. $\frac{1}{3}(6x^3 - 3x^2 + 3x + 9) = ax^3 + bx^2 + cx + d$, for all values of x, where a, b, c, and d are all constants, what is the value of $a + b + c + d$? Ⓝ

Answer: 5
Because the equation is true for all values of x, the two expressions have the same coefficients for corresponding terms.
$\frac{1}{3}(6x^3 - 3x^2 + 3x + 9) = 2x^3 - x^2 + x + 3 = ax^3 + bx^2 + cx + d$
$a = 2$, $b = -1$, $c = 1$, and $d = 3$
$a + b + c + d = 5$

15. A parallel circuit has two or more paths for current to flow through and has more than one resistor as shown below. In a house, there are many electrical appliances that connect in parallel so they would not affect each other when their switches are turned on or off.

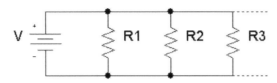

The total resistance, R_{Total}, in a parallel circuit can be calculated by the following formula:

$$\frac{1}{R_{Total}} = \frac{1}{R_1} + \frac{1}{R_2} + \frac{1}{R_3}$$

If three resistors are connected together in parallel and the resistors have values of 20 ohm, 30 ohm, and 60 ohm respectively, what is the total resistance of the circuit?

   a) 15 ohm
   b) 10 ohm
   c) 8 ohm
   d) 5 ohm

Answer: (B)

$\frac{1}{R_{total}} = \frac{1}{20} + \frac{1}{30} + \frac{1}{60} = \frac{1}{10}$

$R_{total} = 10\ ohm$

B. SOLVING A LINEAR EQUATION

CONCEPT OVERVIEWS

Slope of Two Points $= \dfrac{Rise}{Run} = \dfrac{y_2 - y_1}{x_2 - x_1}$

Slope-intercept Form: $y = mx + b$ where m is the slope and b is the y-intercept. A linear equation written as slope-intercept form has the properties illustrated by the following graph:

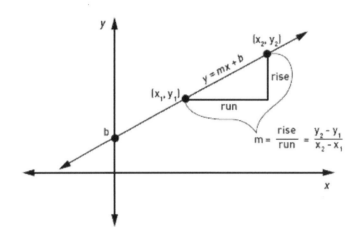

Point-slope Form: From the graph below, the equation of a line passing through the point (x_1, y_1) with the slope of m can be expressed as: $y - y_1 = m(x - x_1)$

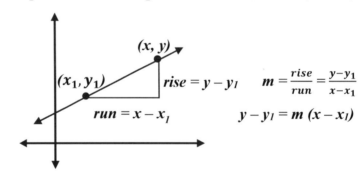

Standard Form: The standard form of a line is written as $ax + by = c$, where the slope of the line is $-\dfrac{a}{b}$.

Example: Find the slope of the line from the equation $4x - 2y + 2 = 0$.
Answer: Change the equation to any of the forms listed above.

        Convert to slope-intercept form: $2y = 4x + 2$ → $y = 2x + 1$
           $m = 2$ So, the slope is 2. (The graph slopes upward from left to right.)

        Convert to the standard form: $4x - 2y = -2$

The slope of a linear equation $ax + by + c = 0$ will be $-\frac{a}{b}$.

$$m = -\frac{a}{b} = -\frac{4}{-2} = 2$$

Two lines are perpendicular if their slopes are opposite reciprocals, i.e., the product of their slopes is –1.

Two different lines are parallel if their slopes are equal but they are not the same line.

Problem Solving Skills

Easy

1. What is the y-intercept of the linear equation
   $7y - x = -14$?
     a) –4
     b) –2
     c) 0
     d) 2

   Answer: (B)
   The y-intercept occurs when x = 0.
   $7y - 0 = -14$
   $y = -2$

2. What is the slope of a line that passes through the points
   $(1, -1)$ and $(-1, 5)$?
     a) –3
     b) –2
     c) 0
     d) 2

   Answer: (A)
   $Slope = \frac{Rise}{Run} = \frac{5-(-1)}{-1-1} = -3$

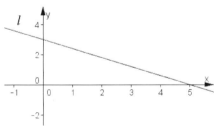

3. In the figure above, what is the slope of line *l*?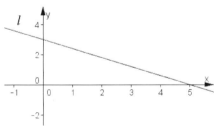
     a) $\frac{1}{4}$
     b) $\frac{1}{2}$
     c) $\frac{2}{5}$
     d) $-\frac{3}{5}$

   Answer: (D)
   $Slope = \frac{Rise}{Run} = \frac{0-3}{5-0} = -\frac{3}{5}$

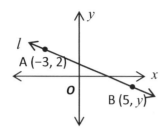

4. In the figure above, the slope of line l is $-\frac{1}{2}$. What is the value of y?

    a) $\frac{1}{2}$
    b) 1
    c) $-\frac{1}{2}$
    d) -2

Answer: (D)
$Slope = \dfrac{y-2}{5-(-3)} = -\dfrac{1}{2}$
$y - 2 = -4$
$y = -2$

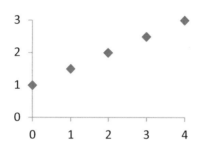

5. Which of the lines described by the following equations best fits those points above?

    a) $y = 0.5x - 1$
    b) $y = 0.5x + 1$
    c) $y = -0.5x - 1$
    d) $y = -0.5x + 1$

Answer: (B)
$Slope = \dfrac{Rise}{Run} = \dfrac{2-1}{2-0} = 0.5$
y-intercept = 1
$y = 0.5x + 1$

x	1	2	3	4
y	1	4	7	10

6. The table above represents a relationship between x and y. Which of the following linear equations describes the relationship?

    a) $y = 4x - 1$
    b) $y = 3x + 1$
    c) $y = 3x - 2$
    d) $y = -3x + 4$

Answer: (C)
The slope of the linear equation is
$\dfrac{4-1}{2-1} = 3.$
Point-slope-form: $y - 1 = 3(x - 1)$
$y = 3x - 2$

7. Which two lines are perpendicular to each other? 🚫

    a) $y = x - 1; x = 1$
    b) $y = x + 1; x = 1$
    c) $y = -1; x = 1$
    d) $x = -1; x = 1$

Answer: (C)
The value of the y coordinate is constant for a horizontal line.

8. The equation of line *l* is $x - 2y = 3$. Which of the following is an equation of the line that is perpendicular to line *l*?

   a) $y = x + 2$
   b) $y = -x + 2$
   c) $y = 2x - 1$
   d) $y = -2x + 1$

Answer: (D)
$x - 2y = 3$
$y = \frac{1}{2}x - 1.5$
Line l has a slope of $\frac{1}{2}$.
A line that is perpendicular to line l would have a slope of −2.

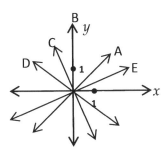

9. In the *xy*-coordinate system above, which of the following lines has a slope closest to 1?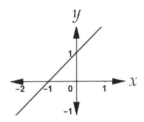

   a) A
   b) B
   c) C
   d) D

Answer: (A)
Line A has the slope closest to 1.

10. Which of the following is the graph of a linear function with a negative slope and a negative *y*-intercept?

   a)

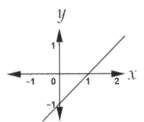

Answer: (D)
A line with a negative slope descends from left to right (d) has a negative slope and a negative y-intercept.

   b)

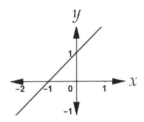

   c)

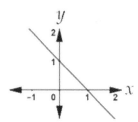

d)

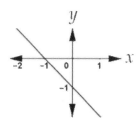

11. What is the y-intercept of the line that passes through the points $(1, 1)$ and $(5, 13)$?
    a) -2
    b) -1
    c) 1
    d) 2

Answer: (A)
$Slope = \frac{13-1}{5-1} = 3$
$y - 1 = 3(x - 1)$ *(point-slope form)*
$y = 3x - 2$
y-intercept $= -2$

12. In the xy-plane, the line $x - 2y = k$ passes through point $(4, -1)$. What is the value of k?
    a) 6
    b) 4
    c) 2
    d) -2

Answer: (A)
Plug in the values for x and y into the equation.
$4 - 2(-1) = k = 6$

Medium

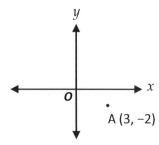

13. In the figure above, a line is to be drawn through point A so that it has a slope of 1. Through which of the following points must the line pass?
    a) $(-5, 1)$
    b) $(-4, 1)$
    c) $(1, 4)$
    d) $(1, -4)$

Answer: (D)
$Slope = 1 = \frac{y-(-2)}{x-3}$
$x - 3 = y + 2$
$y = x - 5$
Out of 5 answer choices, only
(1, −4) satisfies the equation
$y = x - 5.$

14. If a linear function passes through the points $(1, s)$, $(3, t)$ and $(5, 10)$, what is the value of $2t - s$?
    a) 2
    b) 8
    c) 10
    d) 12

Answer: (C)
The line segment connecting the first two points must have the same slope as the line segment connecting the last two points.
$$\frac{10-s}{5-1} = \frac{10-t}{5-3} \rightarrow \frac{10-s}{4} = \frac{10-t}{2}$$
$$40 - 4t = 20 - 2s \rightarrow 2t - s = 10$$

15. Which of the following could be the coordinates of point R in a coordinate plane, if points P(1, 1), Q(-1, 5), and R(x, y) lie on the same line?
    a) (0, 2)
    b) (2, -1)
    c) (0, -2)
    d) (2, 2)

Answer: (B)
Slope = $\frac{Rise}{Run} = \frac{5-1}{-1-1} = -2$
Point-slope-form: $y - 1 = -2(x - 1)$
The point $(2, -1)$ satisfies the above equation.

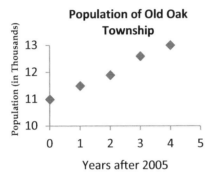

Population of Old Oak Township

16. The graph above shows the population of Old Oak Township since 2005. If y represents the population, in thousands, and x represents the number of years after 2005, which of the following equations best describes the data shown?
    a) $y = x + 11$
    b) $y = 2x + 11$
    c) $y = 2x - 11$
    d) $y = \frac{1}{2}x + 11$

Answer: (D)
Find the slope and y-intercept from the graph.
Slope = $\frac{1}{2}$
y-intercept = 11
$y = \frac{1}{2}x + 11$

17. What is the product of the slopes of all four sides of a rectangle if all four sides' slopes are not equal to zero?

    a) -2
    b) -1
    c) 0
    d) 1

Answer: (D)
The product of the slopes of two perpendicular lines is -1.
The product of the slopes of all four sides of rectangle is $-1 \times (-1) = 1$.

18. Joe goes on a business trip that includes 3 different types of transportation: bike, bus, and airplane, in that order. If all three transportations take roughly the same amount of time, which of the following could be the graph of the distance traveled by the three transportations? 🚫

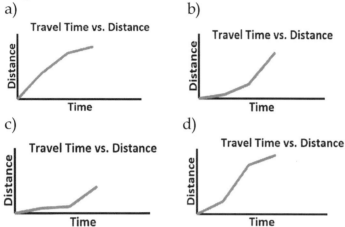

a)

Travel Time vs. Distance

Distance | Time

b)

Travel Time vs. Distance

Distance | Time

c)

Travel Time vs. Distance

Distance | Time

d)

Travel Time vs. Distance

Distance | Time

Answer: (B)
The higher the speed of the vehicle, the steeper (greater) the slope of the graph. Since bikes are slower than buses which are slower than planes, the graph must have three segments of increasing slope.

Hard

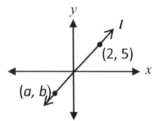

19. In the figure above, line l passes through the origin. What is the value of $\frac{b}{a}$? 🚫
   a) 1
   b) 1.5
   c) 2
   d) 2.5

Answer: (D)
$$\frac{b-0}{a-0} = \frac{5-0}{2-0}$$
$$\frac{b}{a} = \frac{5}{2} = 2.5$$

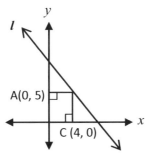

20. In the figure above, if line *l* has a slope of –2, what is the *x*-intercept of *l*?
    a) 6
    b) 6.5
    c) 7
    d) 13

Answer: (B)
Line l intersects the x-axis at (x, 0) and has a slope of −2.
$$\frac{0-5}{x-4} = -2$$
$$-2x + 8 = -5$$
$$x = \frac{13}{2} = 6.5$$

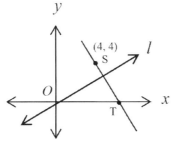

21. In the figure above, line *l* intersects ST between S and T and also passes through the origin. Which of the following could be line *l*'s slope?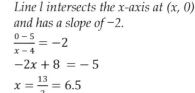
    a) −2
    b) −1
    c) $\frac{1}{2}$
    d) $\frac{3}{2}$

Answer: (C)
OT has a slope of 0 and OS has a slope of 1 so the slope of line l should be between 0 and 1.

22. In the *xy*-plane, line *l* passes through the origin and is perpendicular to the line $2x - y = b$, where *b* is a constant. If the two lines intersect at the point $(2a, a + 1)$, what is the value of *b*?
    a) − 1
    b) $-\frac{5}{2}$
    c) 0
    d) $\frac{1}{2}$

Answer: (B)
The slope of line $2x - y = b$ is 2. Line l is perpendicular, so it have a slope of $-\frac{1}{2}$. We also know that it passes through the origin.
$$y = -\frac{1}{2}x$$
$$a + 1 = -\frac{1}{2}(2a)$$
$$2a = -1, \quad a = -\frac{1}{2}$$
Therefore, point $(-1, \frac{1}{2})$ passes through $2x - y = b$
$$-2 - \frac{1}{2} = -\frac{5}{2} = b$$

C. SOLVING A SYSTEM OF EQUATIONS

CONCEPT OVERVIEWS

There must be at least one equation given in order to solve for one variable. In the same vein, at least two equations must be given to solve two variables, at least three equations for three variables, and so on. **In order to solve a system of equations, there must be at least the same number of equations given as the variables being solved for.** In the real world, tools such as matrices or computer algorithms are necessary to solve complicated system of equations. On the SAT, however, it is sufficient to use the following two methods:

- **Substitution**

    Example: Solve the following system of equations by substitution:

    $$x - y = 1 \qquad \text{(1)}$$
    $$2x + 3y = 7 \qquad \text{(2)}$$

    Solution: $x = y + 1$, from the first equation

    $2(y+1) + 3y = 7$, because they are equivalent, substitute x with $y + 1$ into the second equation

    $2y + 2 + 3y = 7$
    $5y = 5$
    $y = 1$
    $x = y + 1$
    $\quad = 1 + 1$
    $\quad = 2$
    $x = 2$ and $y = 1$

- **Elimination**

    Example: Solve the following system of equations by elimination:

    $$3x - y = 3 \quad ---(1)$$
    $$x + 2y = 15 \quad ---(2)$$

    Solution: In order to eliminate y, multiply equation (1) by 2.

    $2(3x - y) = 3 \times 2$ ---(3), add equations (2) and (3).
    $2(3x - y) + (x + 2y) = 3 \times 2 + 15$
    $6x - 2y + x + 2y = 21$, cancel out $-2y$ and $2y$.
    $7x = 21$
    $x = 3$, plug in the value for x into equation (1).
    $3 \times 3 - y = 3$
    $y = 6$
    $x = 3$ and $y = 6$

Problem Solving Skills

Easy

1. $y = x + 1$ and $x + 2y = 8$, what is the value of x? 🚫
   a) 1
   b) 2
   c) 3
   d) −2

Answer: (B)
Use the substitution method.
$y = x + 1$
$x + 2(x + 1) = 8$
$3x + 2 = 8$
$x = 2$

2. What is the value of x if $x + 2y = 6$ and $x + y = 5$? 🚫
   a) 2
   b) 3
   c) 4
   d) 5

Answer: (C)
Substitute y with 5 − x.
$x + 2(5 − x) = 6$
$x = 4$

3. If $3a − b = 3$ and $a + 2b = 15$, then $a + b$?
   a) −2
   b) −4
   c) 9
   d) 5

Answer: (C)
It is easier to use the method of elimination for this question.
$3a − b = 3$ (1)
$6a − 2b = 6$ (1a)
$a + 2b = 15$ (2)
Add (1a) and (2) to eliminate b.
$(1) + (2) → 7a = 21 → a = 3$
$3 × 3 − b = 3 → b = 6$
$a + b = 9$

4. There are 25 high school seniors who are taking the total of 112 AP classes this year. Some of them take 4 APs and the others take 5. How many seniors are taking 5 APs?
   a) 11
   b) 12
   c) 13
   d) 14

Answer: (B)
Let x be the number of students taking 5 APs and y be the number of students taking 4 APs.
$x + y = 25$
$y = 25 − x$
$5x + 4y = 112$ (substitution rule)
$5x + 4(25 − x) = 112$
$x + 100 = 112$
$x = 12$

5. At the school cafeteria, there are 30 tables and each table can seat either 2 or 4 students. If there are a total 80 students in one of the lunch sections, how many tables must seat exactly 4 students in this lunch section?
   a) 9
   b) 10
   c) 11
   d) 12

Answer: (B)
Let x be the number of tables that seat 4 students and y be the number of tables that seat 2 students.
$x + y = 30$
$y = 30 − x$
$4x + 2y = 80$ (substitution rule)
$4x + 2(30 − x) = 80$
$2x + 60 = 80 → x = 10$

6. Six erasers cost as much as 3 pencils. If Matt bought one eraser and one pencil for $1.50, how much does one pencil cost in dollars?
   a) 0.25
   b) 0.50
   c) 0.75
   d) 1.00

Answer: (D)
Let the price of one eraser be x and the price of one pencil be y.
Price of 6 Erasers = Price of 3 Pencils
$6x = 3y \rightarrow x = \frac{1}{2}y$
Price of 1Eraser = $\frac{1}{2}$ Price of 1 Pencil
$x + y = 1.50$
$\frac{1}{2}y + y = 1.50 \rightarrow y = 1.0$
The price of one pencil is $1.00.

Medium

7. There is $180 of cash in John's pocket. John only has 10 and 20 dollar bills. If John has a total of 13 bills, how many 20 dollar bills are in his pocket?

Answer: 5
Let x be the number of $20 bills and y be the number of $10 bills.
$x + y = 13 \rightarrow y = 13 - x$
$20x + 10y = 180$
$20x + 10(13 - x) = 180$
$130 + 10x = 180 \rightarrow x = 5$

$$3x - 4y = 8$$
$$5x + 3y = 23$$

8. Based on the above system of 2-equations, which of the following values will $(x + y)$ equal?
   a) 10
   b) 8
   c) 7
   d) 5

Answer: (D)
Use the method of elimination.
$(3x - 4y = 8) \times 5 \rightarrow$
$15x - 20y = 40$ (1)
$(5x + 3y = 23) \times (-3) \rightarrow$
$-15x - 9y = -69$ (2)
Add the equations (1) and (2)
$-29y = -29 \rightarrow y = 1$
$3x - 4 \times 1 = 8 \rightarrow x = 4$
$x + y = 5$

Hard

9. If $\frac{x}{w} = 28$ and $5yw = 3$, then $xy =$?

Answer: $\frac{84}{5}$
$\frac{x}{w} \times 5yw = 5xy = 28 \times 3 = 84$
$xy = \frac{84}{5}$

10. If $3x - z = 2y$ and $3x + 5y - z = 28$, what is the value of y?
    a) 3
    b) 4
    c) 5
    d) 6

Answer: (B)
Try to eliminate x and z.
$3x - z = 2y$ (1)
$3x + 5y - z = 28$ (2)
$(1) - (2) \rightarrow -5y = 2y - 28$
$28 = 7y \rightarrow y = 4$

D. Solving an Inequality

Concept Overviews

Definition of an Inequality: When comparing two real numbers, one number is greater than, less than, or equal to the other number.
 - $a > b$ means a is greater than b.
 - $a < b$ means a is less than b.
 - $a \geq b$ means a is greater than or equal to b.
 - $a \leq b$ means a is less than or equal to b.

To solve inequalities, follow rules that are similar to those applicable to equations. Isolate the variable that needs to be solved for on one side, move all other numbers or constants to the other side, and combine the like terms.

All the rules and techniques used in solving an equation apply to solving an inequality EXCEPT for multiplication and division by a **negative. When you multiply or divide both sides by a negative number, reverse the direction of the inequality**.

> *Example:* $4 > 3$, but if you multiply -1 on both sides, the inequality becomes $-4 < -3$.

The inequality is not preserved when both sides are multiplied by zero.

Absolute Value Inequality
The absolute value of a number is the distance from that number to the zero-mark on the number line. The absolute value of any number is always nonnegative.
 - If $|x - a| \leq b$, all values of x are between $a - b$ and $a + b$, inclusive, on the number line:
$$a - b \leq x \leq a + b$$

> *Example:* $|x - 1| \leq 3$
> $$-3 \leq x - 1 \leq 3$$
> $$1 - 3 \leq x \leq 1 + 3$$
> $$-2 \leq x \leq 4$$

 - If $|x - a| \geq b$, all values of x are either less than or equal to $a - b$ or larger than or equal to $a + b$ on the number line: $x \geq a + b$ or $x \leq a - b$.

> *Example:* $|x - 1| \geq 3$
> $$3 \leq x - 1 \text{ or } x - 1 \leq -3$$
> $$1 + 3 \leq x \text{ or } x \leq 1 - 3$$
> $$x \geq 4 \text{ or } x \leq -2$$

Problem Solving Skills

Easy

1. What is the smallest positive integer value of x for which $2x - 7 > 0$? Ⓝ

   Answer: 4
   If $2x - 7 > 0$, then $2x > 7$.
   $x > 3.5$
   So the smallest positive integer is 4.

2. Given that $4x + 3 < 12$, which of the following cannot be the value of x?
   a) 3
   b) 2
   c) 1
   d) 0

   Answer: (A)
   $4x + 3 < 12$
   $4x < 12 - 3$
   $4x < 9 \rightarrow x < 2.25$

3. What is the least value of integer x such that the value of $2x - 1$ is greater than 9? Ⓝ
   a) 7
   b) 6
   c) 5
   d) 4

   Answer: (B)
   $2x - 1 > 9$
   $2x > 10$
   $x > 5$
   The least value of integer is 6.

4. Alex has less money than Bob and Bob has less money than Chris. If a, b, and c represent the amounts of money that Alex, Bob, and Chris have, respectively, which of the following is true? Ⓝ
   a) $a < b < c$
   b) $c < b < a$
   c) $b < a < c$
   d) $a < c < b$

   Answer: (A)
   "Alex has less money than Bob"
   $\rightarrow a < b$
   "Bob has less money than Chris"
   $\rightarrow b < c$
   $a < b < c$

5. There are 15 boxes of apples in the storage room. Each box has at least 21 apples, and at most 28 apples. Which of the following could be the total number of apples in the storage room?
   a) 200
   b) 250
   c) 300
   d) 350

   Answer: (D)
   Set up the inequality for the number of apples and then multiply the inequality by 15.
   $(21 < x < 28) \times 15$
   $315 < 15x < 420$

6. If 3 less than x is a negative number and if 1 less than x is a positive number, which of the following could be the value of x?

    a) 3
    b) 2
    c) 1
    d) 0

Answer: (B)
"3 less than x is a negative" →
$x - 3 < 0$
$x < 3$
"1 less than x is a positive" →
$x - 1 > 0$
$x > 1$
Combine them together: $1 < x < 3$

7. Which of the following conditions would make $2x - y < 0$? Ⓝ

    a) $2x = y$
    b) $x > 0$
    c) $y > 0$
    d) $2x < y$

Answer: (D)
If $2x - y < 0$, then $2x < y$.

8. If $x - 1 > 2$ and $x + 2 < 7$, which of the following could be a value for x? Ⓝ

    a) 1
    b) 2
    c) 3
    d) 4

Answer: (D)
Solve the inequalities.
$x - 1 > 2 \rightarrow x > 3$
$x + 2 < 7 \rightarrow x < 5$
Combine them together.
$3 < x < 5$

9. If $|5 - 2x| < 3$, which of the following is a possible value of x? Ⓝ

    a) 3
    b) 4
    c) 5
    d) 6

Answer: (A)
If $|5 - 2x| < 3$, then $-3 < 5 - 2x < 3$.
$-3 - 5 < -2x < 3 - 5$
$-8 < -2x < -2$
$8 > 2x > 2 \rightarrow 4 > x > 1$

Medium

10. If $0 < xy$ and $y < 0$, which of the following statements must be true? Ⓝ

    I. $x < 0$
    II. $x < y$
    III. $x > 0$

    a) I only
    b) III only
    c) I and II
    d) II and III

Answer: (A)
$xy > 0 \rightarrow$ both x and y must have the same sign. (Both are positive or both are negative.)
$y < 0$ and $x < 0$

11. If $a + 3b < a$, which of the following must be true?
    a) $a > 0$
    b) $a = 0$
    c) $a < 0$
    d) $b < 0$

Answer: (D)
Subtract a from both sides.
$a + 3b < a$
$a + 3b - a < a - a$
$3b < 0 \rightarrow b < 0$

12. If $5 \le x \le 7$ and $-3 \le y \le 1$, which of the following gives the set of all possible values of xy?
    a) $-15 \le xy \le 7$
    b) $0 \le xy \le 7$
    c) $-21 \le xy \le 5$
    d) $-21 \le xy \le 7$

Answer: (D)
Try out different combinations of x and y.
$-21 \le xy \le 7$

13. If $0 > x > y$, which of the following is less than $\frac{x}{y}$?
    a) 1
    b) 2
    c) xy
    d) $\frac{x}{2y}$

Answer: (D)
If $0 > x > y$, then $\frac{y}{x} > 1 > \frac{x}{y} > 0$.

Hard

14. If $|x| < 1$, which of the following is the greatest?
    a) 2
    b) $1 - x$
    c) $1 + x$
    d) $2x$

Answer: (A)
$|x| < 1 \rightarrow -1 < x < 1 \rightarrow$
$-1 < -x < 1$; therefore,
b). $0 < 1 - x < 2$
c). $0 < 1 + x < 2$
d). $-2 < 2x < 2$
So among those answer choices the number 2 is the greatest value.
Shortcuts: Plug x = 0.5 into each answer choice and compare the results. This method works better when you try different values to verify your answer.

15. If x is an integer and $2x + 1$ is the median of three different integers $2x + 1$, $x - 1$, and $3x - 1$, which of the following could be a possible value of x?
    a) -1
    b) 0
    c) 1
    d) 3

Answer: (D)
If $x - 1 < 2x + 1 < 3x - 1$, then
$x - 1 < 2x + 1 \rightarrow -2 < x$ and
$2x + 1 < 3x - 1 \rightarrow 2 < x$.
Therefore, $2 < x$
If $3x - 1 < 2x + 1 < x - 1$, then
$3x - 1 < 2x + 1 \rightarrow x < 2$ and
$2x + 1 < x - 1 \rightarrow x < -2$
Therefore, $x < -2$
In conclusion, $2 < x$ or $x < -2$
Only answer (d) is correct.

16. The scores of a math class midterm are between 75 and 93. Which of the following inequalities can be used to determine the range of a student's midterm score, represented by h in this class? 🚫

    a) $|h - 75| < 18$
    b) $|h - 93| < 18$
    c) $|h - 84| < 18$
    d) $|h - 84| < 9$

Answer: (D)
Find the mid-value of 75 and 93.
$\frac{75 + 93}{2} = 84$
$84 - 75 = 9$
$93 - 84 = 9$
$|h - 84| < 9$

Questions 17 − 18 refer to the following information:
   Jenny has a summer job at an ice cream shop. She needs to order a few boxes of small cups and a few boxes of large cups. The storage room can hold up to 30 boxes. Each box of small cups costs \$20 and each box of large cups costs \$30. A maximum of \$720 is budgeted for cups.

17. If x represents the number of boxes of small cups and y represents the number of boxes of large cups that Jenny can order, which of the following systems of equations represents the number of each she could order?

    a) $\begin{cases} x \geq 0 \\ y \geq 0 \\ x + y \leq 30 \\ 20x + 30y \leq 720 \end{cases}$

    b) $\begin{cases} x \geq 0 \\ y \geq 0 \\ x + y < 30 \\ 20x + 30y < 720 \end{cases}$

    c) $\begin{cases} x \geq 0 \\ y \geq 0 \\ x + y > 30 \\ 20x + 30y > 720 \end{cases}$

    d) $\begin{cases} x \geq 0 \\ y \geq 0 \\ x + y \geq 30 \\ 20x + 30y \leq 720 \end{cases}$

Answer: (A)
The number of boxes must be greater or equal than zero. The storage room can hold up to 30 boxes and the maximum of \$720 can be spent; therefore, the answer is a).
$\begin{cases} x \geq 0 \\ y \geq 0 \\ x + y \leq 30 \\ 20x + 30y \leq 720 \end{cases}$

18. Which of the following graphs represents the number of boxes of each type of cup she could order?

a)

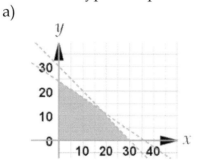

b)

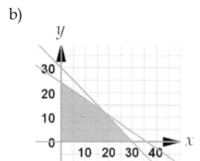

c)

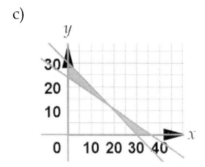

d)

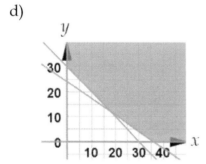

Answer: (B)
Only answer b) depicts the correct system of equations of the previous question.

$$\begin{cases} x \geq 0 \\ y \geq 0 \\ x + y \leq 30 \\ 20x + 30y \leq 720 \end{cases}$$

III. WORD PROBLEMS

CONCEPT OVERVIEWS

Translating from English to Algebraic Expressions

Keywords in the problem can help translating the words into algebraic expressions. For instance, the word "increase" indicates addition and "less" indicates subtraction. "2 times" refers to multiplying a number or variable by two, and "is" indicates equality in an equation.

If the question mentions finding "a number" without specifying the value of the number, assign a variable for that number and then solve for the value of the variable.

The following table lists the most common phrases and their translations.

Operations	Keywords	Sample Phrases	Algebraic Expressions
Addition	plus sum added to more than increased by	three plus a number the sum of a number and 3 three added to a number three more than a number a number increased by 3	$x + 3$
Subtraction	difference minus subtracted from less than decreased by reduced by deducted from	the difference of a number and three a number minus 3 three subtracted from a number three less than a number a number decreased by three a number reduced by three three deducted from a number	$x - 3$
Multiplication	of multiply times twice product of multiplied by	30% of 50 is 15. multiplying 3 by a number four times a number twice a number the product of a number and three a number multiplied by five	$0.3 \times 50 = 15$ $3x$ $4x$ $2x$ $3x$ $5x$
Division	divided by quotient of	a number divided by 3 the quotient of a number and 3	$\frac{x}{3}$
Equal	equal is is equal to	Three multiplied by a number equals 4. Half of 20 is 10. The sum of 5 and 4 is equal to 9.	$3x = 4$ $\frac{1}{2} \times 20 = 10$ $5 + 4 = 9$

Examples: Translate each of the following into an algebraic expression.

1. Three more than four times a number: $4x + 3$
2. Five times the sum of a number and two: $5(x + 2)$
3. Eleven subtracted from the product of two and a number: $2x - 11$
4. The quotient of two less than a number and twice the number: $\frac{(x - 2)}{2x}$
5. The sum of a number and its reciprocal is equal to three: $x + \frac{1}{x} = 3$
6. Six times the difference of a number and two is equal to twice the number: $6(x - 2) = 2x$
7. The product of a number and five is increased by the number: $5x + x$
8. Eight less than five times a number divided by twice the number: $\frac{(5x - 8)}{2x}$
9. The product of two numbers, if one number is three less than twice the other number: $x(2x - 3)$
10. If nine times a number is reduced by five, the result is three less than the number: $9x - 5 = x - 3$
11. The sum of three consecutive odd integers is 51: $x + (x + 2) + (x + 4) = 51$
12. The sum of three consecutive even integers is 36: $x + (x + 2) + (x + 4) = 36$
13. The product of the sum and difference of two numbers is equal to 15: $(x + y)(x - y) = 15$

Problem Solving Skills

Easy

1. During a lunch in the school cafeteria, if Kristin paid $3.50 for her lunch from her pocket and borrowed $1.50 from a friend, how much did she spend for this lunch?

   Answer: 5
   If she spent x money, then
   $3.5 - x = -1.5$.
   $3.5 - x = -1.5 \rightarrow x = 5$

2. The value of $5n - 7$ is how much greater than the value of $5n - 8$? Ⓝ

   a) 15
   b) 1
   c) $10n + 1$
   d) $5n - 1$

   Answer: (B)
   Find the difference between the two expressions.
   $(5n - 7) - (5n - 8) = 1$

3. A smartphone costs $30 less than four times the cost of a basic cell phone. If the smartphone and the basic phone together cost $570, how much more does the smartphone cost than the basic phone?

   a) $216
   b) $330
   c) $415
   d) $450

   Answer: (B)
   Let the price of a basic phone be x, then the price of a smartphone is $4x - 30$. Solve the equation $x + (4x - 30) = 570$, and get $x = 120$. Therefore, a basic phone costs $120 while a smartphone costs $4 \times 120 - 30 = \$450$.
   $450 - 120 = 330$

4. Triangles A, B, and C are different in size. Triangle A's area is twice the area of triangle B, and triangle C's area is four times the area of triangle A. What is the area of triangle C, in square inches, if the area of triangle B is 10 square inches?

    a) 20
    b) 40
    c) 60
    d) 80

Answer: (D)
A = 2B,
C = 4A
If B = 10, then
A = 20, and C = 4 × 20 = 80.

5. The local route from Maya's house to her college is 4 miles longer than the expressway. When she drives by the local route and returns by the expressway, the round trip is 30 miles. How many miles does Maya have to drive if she goes to school through the expressway?

    a) 13
    b) 15
    c) 17
    d) 19

Answer: (A)
Let the express way be x miles between Maya's house and her college. The local route would be x + 4 miles, which means that the round trip would be x + (x + 4) = 30.
x = 13

Subtract 5 from y
Divide this difference by 5
Multiply this quotient by 5

6. After completing the operations described above, which of the following is showing the result? Ⓝ

    a) $\frac{y-5}{5}$

    b) $\frac{y}{5}$

    c) $\frac{y+5}{5}$

    d) $y - 5$

Answer: (D)
Since division and multiplication are the inverse functions to each other, the last two operations will cancel each other. Hence, it will only need to perform the first operation: subtract 5 from y.

7. Which of the following is an equation you would use to find x if it is given that 10 more than the product of x and 5 is 30? Ⓝ

    a) $5(x - 10) = 30$
    b) $5x - 10 = 30$
    c) $5(x + 10) = 30$
    d) $5x + 10 = 30$

Answer: (D)
10 more than the product of x and 5 → 10 + 5x
5x + 10 = 30

8. If 10 percent of 40 percent of a positive number is equal to 20 percent of y percent of the same positive number, find the value of y.
    a) 10
    b) 15
    c) 20
    d) 35

Answer: (C)
$$\frac{10}{100} \times \frac{40}{100} \times A = \frac{20}{100} \times \frac{y}{100} \times A$$
$$\frac{10 \times 40}{100 \times 100} = \frac{20y}{100 \times 100}$$
Therefore, $10 \times 40 = 20y$
$y = 20.$

9. After 20 customers entered a deli store and 4 customers left, there were 3 times as many customers as there were at the beginning. How many customers were in that deli store at the very beginning? Ⓝ
    a) 6
    b) 7
    c) 8
    d) 12

Answer: (C)
Let x be the original number of customers, then $x + 20 - 4 = 3x$.
$x = 8$

10. The sum of $5x$ and 3 is equal to the difference of $2x$ and 3. Which of the following represents the above statement? Ⓝ
    a) $5x + 3 = 2x - 3$
    b) $5(x + 3) = 2(x - 3)$
    c) $5x - 3 = 2x + 3$
    d) $5x - 3 = 2x - 3$

Answer: (A)
Convert words into algebraic expressions.
$5x + 3 = 2x - 3$

Medium

11. How old was William 5 years ago if a years ago he was b years old (given that $a > 5$ and $b > 5$)? Ⓝ
    a) $a + b$
    b) $a + b + 5$
    c) $b - a - 5$
    d) $a + b - 5$

Answer: (D)
Let x be the current age.
$x - a = b \rightarrow x = a + b$
Current Age $= a + b$
William's Age 5 Years Ago $= a + b - 5$

12. If 14% of x is equal to 7% of y, which of the following is equivalent to y?
    a) 200% of x
    b) 20% of x
    c) 2% of x
    d) 98% of x

Answer: (A)
$$\frac{14}{100}x = \frac{7}{100}y$$
$$y = \frac{14}{100} \times \frac{100}{7}x$$
$y = 2x = 200\%x$

13. Which of the following represents the statement "When the square of the sum of x and y is added to the sum of the squares of x and $2y$, the result is 5 less than z"? Ⓝ

    a) $x^2 + y^2 + (x + 2y)^2 = z - 5$

    b) $(x + y)^2 + x^2 + 2y^2 = z - 5$

    c) $(x + y)^2 + (x + 2y)^2 = z - 5$

    d) $(x + y)^2 + x^2 + (2y)^2 = z - 5$

Answer: (D)
The square of the sum of x and y
$\rightarrow (x + y)^2$
The sum of the squares of x and
$2y \rightarrow x^2 + (2y)^2$
$(x + y)^2 + x^2 + (2y)^2 = z - 5$

14. The rate for a long distance call is $1.00 for the first minute and $.75 for each additional minute. Which of the following represents the cost, in dollars, of a phone call made for n minutes? Ⓝ

    a) $1.75n$

    b) $1.00 + n$

    c) $1.00 + 0.75(n - 1)$

    d) $1.00 + 1.75(n - 1)$

Answer: (C)
Each additional minute costs
$0.75.
For the n-minute phone call, the
total cost would be the first minute
($1.00) plus additional (n – 1)
minutes ($0.75(n – 1)), so the
total cost of n minute call is
1.00 + 0.75 (n – 1) dollars.

15. Bob needs two 60" pieces of duct tape to protect each window in his house during hurricane season. There are 12 windows in the house. Bob had an m-foot roll of duct tape when he started. If no tape was wasted, which of the following represents the number of feet of duct tape left after he finished taping all of his windows? Ⓝ

    a) $m - 240$

    b) $m - 120$

    c) $m - 60$

    d) $m - 20$

Answer: (B)
Every window needs 2 pieces of
tape and each piece of tape is 60
inches long, so 60 × 2 = 120
inches needed for each window.
Twelve windows, in total, would
need 12 × 120 inches of tape.
12 × 120 inches = 120 feet
(m – 120) feet left after the use.

Hard

16. The sum of x and the square of y is equal to the square root of the difference between x and y. Which of the following mathematic expressions represents the statement above? Ⓝ
    a) $x + y^2 = (\sqrt{x} - y)^2$
    b) $x + \sqrt{y} = \sqrt{x - y}$
    c) $(x + y)^2 = \sqrt{x} - \sqrt{y}$
    d) $x + y^2 = \sqrt{x - y}$

    Answer: (D)
    Sum of x and the square of y →
    $x + y^2$
    Square root of the difference between x and y → $\sqrt{x - y}$
    $x + y^2 = \sqrt{x - y}$

17. Mrs. Matt provides some markers to her Arts class. If each student takes 3 markers, there will be 2 markers left. If 6 students take 4 markers each and the rest of students take 1 marker each, there will be no markers left. How many students are in Mrs. Matt's Arts class?

    Answer: 8
    Let x be the number of students in Mrs. Matt's Arts class.
    $3x + 2 = 6 \times 4 + (x - 6) \times 1$
    $x = 8$

18. Find the product of 10 and the sum of m and 10. Then, find one-tenth of the difference between that product and 10. In terms of m, what is the final result? Ⓝ
    a) $m - 1$
    b) $m - 10$
    c) $m + 9$
    d) $m + 10$

    Answer: (C)
    $\dfrac{10(m + 10) - 10}{10}$
    $= \dfrac{10(m + 10 - 1)}{10}$
    $= m + 9$

19. The fee of a car rental includes:
    i. a basic rental fee
    ii. an additional charge for every 20 miles
    If the fee to rent a car and drive 60 miles is $210 and the fee to rent a car and drive 160 miles is $260, how much does it cost to rent a car and drive 250 miles?

    Answer: 305
    If the basic fee is $x and every 20 miles is charged $y, then
    $x + 3y = 210$ (1)
    $x + 8y = 260$ (2)
    Subtract (1) from (2).
    $5y = 260 - 210 = 50$
    $y = 10 \rightarrow x = 180$
    The rental to travel 250 miles:
    $x + \dfrac{250}{20}y = 180 + \dfrac{250}{20} \times 10 = \$305$

Chapter 2   Problem Solving and Data Analysis

I.   UNIONS AND INTERSECTIONS OF SETS

CONCEPT OVERVIEWS

Union and Intersection
The **Union** of two sets, denoted by $A \cup B$, is the set of elements which are in **either** set. It is similar to the "OR" logic among the sets.

Example: Let set $A = \{1, 2, 3\}$ and set $B = \{3, 4, 5\}$, the union of sets A and B is the set of elements that are included in ***A* or *B***, i.e. $A \cup B = \{1, 2, 3, 4, 5\}$.

The **Intersection** of two sets, denoted by $A \cap B$, is the set of elements which are in **both** sets. It is similar to the "AND" logic among the sets.

Example: The intersection of set A and set B, as the example above, is the set of elements that are included in A and B, i.e. $A \cap B = \{3\}$.

Venn Diagram

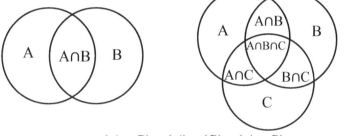

$$\{A \cup B\} = \{A\} + \{B\} - \{A \cap B\}$$
$$\{A \cup B \cup C\} = \{A\} + \{B\} + \{C\} - \{A \cap B\} - \{B \cap C\} - \{C \cap A\} + \{A \cap B \cap C\}$$

Example: In a class of 50 students, 18 students take chemistry, 26 students take biology, and 2 students take both chemistry and biology.

    a) How many students in the class are enrolled in either chemistry or biology?

      Solution: *{Enrolled in either chemistry or biology} = {Enrolled in chemistry} + {Enrolled in biology} – {Enrolled in both chemistry and biology}*
      = 18 + 26 – 2 = 42

    b) How many students in the class are **not** enrolled in either chemistry or biology?

      Solution: *{**Not** enrolled in either chemistry or biology} = Total Students – {Enrolled in either chemistry or biology} = 50 – 42 = 8*

Problem Solving Skills

Easy

Set X = {21, 22, 23}
Set Y = {22, 23, 24, 25, 26}

1. Sets X and Y are shown above. How many numbers are in the intersection of set X and set Y?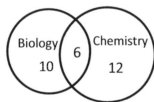
   a) Two
   b) Three
   c) Four
   d) Seven

Answer: (A)
Only 22 and 23 are both in set X and set Y.

2. Set A contains all odd positive numbers less than 10 and set B contains all prime numbers less than 20. What is the difference between the number of elements in the union of the two sets and the number of elements in their intersection?

Answer: 7
Union of two sets:
{1, 2, 3, 5, 7, 9, 11, 13, 17, 19}
Intersect of two sets: { 3, 5, 7 }

10 – 3 = 7

3. If A is the set of positive integers, B is the set of odd integers, and C is the set of integers multiple of 3, which of the following will be in all three sets?
   a) 24
   b) 18
   c) 15
   d) –21

Answer: (C)
The only odd positive integer that is also a multiple of 3 is 15.

4. The Venn diagram above shows the distribution of 28 students in a class who took biology, chemistry, or both. If there are total 30 students in this class, what percent of the students did not take either chemistry or biology?
   a) 5%
   b) 6.7%
   c) 9%
   d) 10%

Answer: (B)
30 – (10 + 12 + 6) = 2
$\frac{2}{30} = 0.067 = 6.7\%$

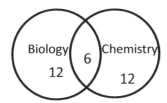

5. The Venn diagram above shows the distribution of 30 students in a class who took biology, chemistry, or both. If there are total 30 students in this class, what percent of the students studied chemistry?
    a) 30%
    b) 40%
    c) 50%
    d) 60%

Answer: (D)
Among the total 30 students, there were (6 + 12) students studied chemistry.

$\frac{18}{30} = 0.6 = 60\%$

Medium

6. What is the intersection of X and Y if X is the set of positive multiples of 3 and Y is the set of positive multiples of 4?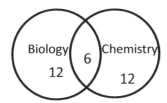
    a) the set of all positive integers
    b) the set of all positive real numbers
    c) the set of positive multiples of 12
    d) the set of positive multiples of 4

Answer: (C)
The common multiples of 3 and 4 will be the multiples of 12.

7. Set A contains all odd positive numbers less than 10 and set B contains all prime numbers less than 20. What is the difference between the number of elements in the union of the two sets and the number of elements in their intersection?

Answer: 7
Union of two sets:
{1, 2, 3, 5, 7, 9, 11, 13, 17, 19}
Intersect of two sets: { 3, 5, 7 }

10 – 3 = 7

8. If set A = {1, 3, 7, 10, 15} and set B consists of all the odd positive integers less than or equal to 13, how many elements are in the union of the two sets?
    a) 0
    b) 3
    c) 8
    d) 9

Answer: (D)
A ∪ B = A + B – (A ∩ B)
A = {1, 3, 7, 10, 15}
B= {1, 3, 5, 7, 9, 11, 13}
A ∩ B = { 1, 3, 7}
Number of Elements in (A ∪ B) =
5 + 7 – 3 = 9

Hard

9. For an end of the year party, Mrs. Scott ordered 40 slices of pizza for her class. Among those slices of pizza, 16 were topped with mushroom and 14 were topped with chicken. If 15 slices contained neither mushroom nor chicken, how many slices of pizza must be topped with both mushroom and chicken? Ⓝ
    a) 3
    b) 5
    c) 7
    d) 9

Answer: (B)
Use Venn diagram:
Mushroom ∪ Chicken = Total −
(No Mushroom ∩ No Chicken)
= Mushroom + Chicken −
(Mushroom ∩ Chicken)

Mushroom ∪ Chicken = 40 − 15 =
16 + 14 − (Mushroom ∩ Chicken)
25 = 30 − (Mushroom ∩ Chicken)
Mushroom ∩ Chicken = 5

10. Set X has x elements and set Y has y elements. If they have exactly w elements in common, how many elements are in set X or set Y but not in both set X and Y? Ⓝ
    a) $x + y$
    b) $x + y - w$
    c) $x + y - 2w$
    d) $x + y + 2w$

Answer: (C)
There are $(x - w)$ members belong to X only and $(y - w)$ members belong to Y only.

$(x - w) + (y - w) = x + y - 2w$

II. RATIOS, PROPORTIONS, AND RATES

CONCEPT OVERVIEWS

Setting up a Ratio
- A **ratio** is a comparison between two numbers or two measures with the same unit.
- Ratios can be expressed as a fraction. For example, $1:2$ can be written as $\frac{1}{2}$.
- Ratios can be reduced like a fraction. For example, $6:9$ can be reduced to $2:3$.

Setting up a Proportion
- A **proportion** is an equation relating two fractions or ratios.
- The phrase "a to b is equal to c to d" can be converted into an equation using ratios ($a:b=c:d$) or fractions ($\frac{a}{b}=\frac{c}{d}$), both of which can be solved by cross-multiplication.

Example 1: The proportion of x in $\frac{2}{3}$ is equal to $\frac{1}{3}$. What is x?

Answer: $\dfrac{x}{\frac{2}{3}}=\dfrac{1}{3}$ (apply cross-multiplication)

$$3x=\frac{2}{3}$$
$$x=\frac{2}{9}$$

Example 2: What proportion of $\frac{2}{3}$ is $\frac{1}{3}$?

Answer: $x\times\dfrac{2}{3}=\dfrac{1}{3}$

$$x=\frac{3}{2}\times\frac{1}{3}=\frac{1}{2}$$

Two variables are **directly proportional** if an increase in one is directly correlated with an increase in another. For example, in the following

$$\frac{x_1}{y_1}=\textbf{coefficient of proportionality}$$

- x_1 and y_1 are directly proportional, and their ratio is called the coefficient of proportionality. If we do not change the coefficient of proportionality, then if we increase or decrease x_1, we increase or decrease y_1 respectively by the same factor.

Two variables are **inversely proportional** if an increase in one is directly correlated with a decrease in another. For example, in the following

$$x_2 \times y_2 = \text{coefficient of proportionality (inverse)}$$

- x_2 and y_2 are inversely proportional. This can also be written as

$$x_2 = \frac{k}{y_2}$$

where k is the coefficient of inverse proportionality.

Solve a Proportion

To solve a problem involving ratios, you can often write as a proportion and solve it by **cross_multiplication**. For example, what proportion to10 is equal to the proportion of 3 out of 5? This problem can be written as $x : 10 = 3 : 5$. Changing the ratios to a fraction gives you $\frac{x}{10} = \frac{3}{5}$. Applying cross-multiplication gives you $5x = 30$. Solving for x gives you $x = 6$.

To solve conversions between units or scales, you can use ratios. Write the conversion's ratios so that you can cross out the unwanted unit.

Example: How many feet is 18 inches?

Answer:

$$\frac{1\ foot}{12\ inches} = \frac{x\ feet}{18\ inches}$$

$$\frac{18\ \cancel{inches}}{12\ \cancel{inches}} = \frac{x\ \cancel{feet}}{1\ \cancel{foot}}$$

$x = 1.5$ (18 inches × 1 foot/12 inches = 1.5 feet)

Rate and Work

A **rate** is a ratio that compares two different kinds of numbers, such as miles per hour or dollars per pound.

Rate Formula: $Rate = \frac{Distance}{Time}$

Example 1: Bob walks up and down a hill to get to school. He walks at 3 miles per hour up a hill and 4 miles per hour down a hill. The hill is 1 mile upwards and 1 mile downwards. What is his average rate?

Hint: If you get a question about the average rate traveled over several trips at different rates, you need to find the total distance and divide by the total time. Most people will think that they can average the two rates, 3.5 in this case – this does not work because you spend less time walking downhill and so you spend more than 50% of the time walking the slower rate.

Solution: The total distance traveled is obviously 2 miles (1 mile up and 1 mile down). The total time spent traveling is

$$1 \text{ mile} \times \frac{1 \text{ hour}}{3 \text{ miles}} + 1 \text{ mile} \times \frac{1 \text{ hour}}{4 \text{ miles}} = \frac{7}{12} \text{ hours}$$

If we traveled 2 miles in $\frac{7}{12}$ hours, then we have traveled an average rate of

$$\frac{2 \text{ miles}}{\frac{7}{12} \text{ hours}} = \frac{24}{7} \text{ miles per hour} = 3.43 \text{ miles per hour}$$

(Applying rate formula: $Rate = \frac{Distance}{Time}$)

So the average rate is **less** than the arithmetic average between the two rates (3.43 < 3.5). This is because we spend more time traveling the slower rate.

Example 2: A plane travels from New York to San Francisco at 500 miles per hour. However, there is a headwind (a wind blowing against the direction of motion) of 100 miles per hour. When the plane flies back from San Francisco to New York, the same wind is now a tailwind (a wind blowing in the direction of motion) of 100 miles per hour. Each trip is 3000 miles. What speed does the plane actually travel at for both trips? What is the combined rate of travel for the entire trip?

Hint: If there are currents or winds involved, add the speed of the current or wind when it is moving along the direction of motion and subtract the speed of the current or wind when it is moving against the direction of motion.

Answer: The speed of the plane flying from New York to San Francisco is

500 mph – 100 mph = 400 mph

The speed of the plane flying from San Francisco to New York is

500 mph + 100 mph = 600 mph

Using the technique we used in the previous example to calculate the average rate. First, we find the total distance traveled, which is 3000 × 2 = 6000 miles. Then, we find the time traveled:

$$3000 \text{ miles} \times \frac{1 \text{ hour}}{400 \text{ miles}} + 3000 \text{ miles} \times \frac{1 \text{ hour}}{600 \text{ miles}} = 12.5 \text{ hours}$$

So the average rate is

$\frac{6000 \text{ miles}}{12.5 \text{ hours}} = 480 \text{ mph}$ (Applying rate formula: $Rate = \frac{Distance}{Time}$)

Total Time Worked $= \frac{1}{\textbf{Rate of Work}}$. If there is more than one person working, then the total rate is equal to the sum of each person's rate.

Example 1: It took Joe 5 hours to paint a house. What is his rate of painting?

Answer: Rate of painting $= \frac{x\ house}{1\ hour} = \frac{1\ house}{5\ hours}$, applying cross multiplication to find x.

$x = \frac{1}{5}$ houses per hour

Example 2: Once again, Joe takes 5 hours to paint a house. How much of a house can he paint in 1 hour?

Hint: Set up a fractional equation and then cross multiply.

Answer: $\frac{5\ hours}{1\ house} = \frac{1\ hour}{x\ houses}$, applying cross multiplication to find x.

$x = \frac{1}{5}$ houses per hour.

Example 3: Joe's friend Bob joins him in painting a house. Bob takes 3 hours to paint a house. What is their total rate of painting?

Hint: If there is more than one person painting, then the total rate is equal to the sum of each person's rate.

Answer: We calculate the total rate by adding two persons' rates:

Joe: $\frac{1}{5}$ houses per hour

Bob: $\frac{1}{3}$ houses per hour

Total rate: $\frac{1}{5} + \frac{1}{3} = \frac{8}{15}$ houses per hour

If some objects must be counted as whole numbers, then their total should be the multiple of the sum of the ratios. For example, if the ratio is 1: 2: 3 for different colors of marbles in the bag, then the total number of marbles in the bag must be a multiple of (1 + 2 + 3).

Example: The ratio of boys to girls in Ms. Johnson's class is 5 to 6. Which of the following CANNOT be the number of students in her class?
 a) 11
 b) 22
 c) 33
 d) 45

Answer: Since the ratio of boys to girls is 5 : 6, the total number of students must be a multiple of 11, (5 + 6). Only choice (d) is not the multiple of 11. Answer is (d).

Problem Solving Skills

Easy

1. How many pounds of flour are needed to make 15 rolls of bread if 20 pounds of flour are needed to make 100 rolls of bread?
    a) 3
    b) 4
    c) 5
    d) 3.5

Answer: (A)
20 pounds : 100 rolls = x : 15 rolls
$$\frac{20\,pounds}{100\,rolls} = \frac{x\,pounds}{15\,rolls}$$
Cross multiply: 100x = 20 × 15
x = 3 pounds

2. A certain graph chart shows ♥ = 500 viewers in a particular TV show. Approximately how many viewers are represented by the symbols ♥♥♥♥?
    a) 1,000
    b) 2,000
    c) 3,500
    d) 4,500

Answer: (B)
4♥ = 4 × 500 = 2,000 viewers

3. John takes 8 minutes to bike 3 miles. At this rate, how many minutes will it take him to bike 4.5 miles?

Answer: 12
8 minutes : 3 miles = x minutes : 4.5 miles
x = 12

4. If 60 pounds of force can stretch a spring 5 inches, how many inches will the spring be stretched by a force of 84 pounds? Assume the force needed to stretch a spring varies directly with its stretch distance.
    a) 10
    b) 9
    c) 7
    d) 6

Answer: (C)
$$\frac{60\,pounds}{5\,inches} = \frac{84\,pounds}{X\,inches}$$
x = 7 inches

5. How many toy parts can a machine make in 10 minutes if this machine can make 36 toy parts in 1 hour?
    a) Two
    b) Three
    c) Five
    d) Six

Answer: (D)
36 parts : 60 minutes = x parts : 10 minutes
60x = 36 × 10 = 360
x = 6

6. For a certain type of heater, the increase in gas bills is directly proportional to the temperature setting (in Fahrenheit). If the gas bills increased by $20 when the temperature setting is increased by 4 degrees Fahrenheit, by how much will expenses increase when the temperature setting is increased by 10 degrees Fahrenheit?

    a) $35
    b) $40
    c) $50
    d) $60

Answer: (C)
$$\$20 : 4°\,F = \$x : 10°\,F$$
$$4x = 200$$
$$x = \$50$$

7. On a map, $\frac{1}{3}$ of an inch represents 18 miles. If a river is 45 miles long, what is its length, in inches, on the map?

    a) $\frac{5}{6}$
    b) $\frac{1}{2}$
    c) $\frac{1}{3}$
    d) 1

Answer: (A)
$$\frac{1}{3}\ inches : 18\ miles$$
$$= x\ inches : 45\ miles$$
$$\frac{\frac{1}{3}\,inches}{18\ miles} = \frac{x\ inches}{45\ miles}$$
$$x = \frac{15}{18} = \frac{5}{6}\ inches$$

8. If y is inversely proportional to x and y is equal to 12 when x is equal to 8, what is the value of y when $x = 24$?

    a) $\frac{1}{6}$
    b) $\frac{1}{4}$
    c) 4
    d) 2

Answer: (C)
$$8 \times 12 = y \times 24$$
$$y = 4$$

9. If y is directly proportional to x and y is equal to 40 when x is equal to 6, what is the value of y when $x = 9$?

    a) 60
    b) 55
    c) 50
    d) 45

Answer: (A)
$$\frac{40}{6} = \frac{y}{9}$$
$$y = 60$$

Medium

10. In a mixture of flour and sugar, the ratio of flour to sugar is 5 to 3 when measured by cups. How many cups of sugar will be used for 4 cups of this mixture?

Answer: 1.5
$$\frac{Sugar}{Total} = \frac{3}{5+3} = \frac{x}{4}$$
$$8x = 12$$
$$x = 1.5\ cups$$

11. Sam drove from home at an average speed of 50 miles per hour to her working place and then returned along the same route at an average speed of 40 miles per hour. If the entire trip took her 2.25 hours, what is the entire distance, in miles, for the round trip?

Answer: 100
Let one trip have x miles.
Time = 2.25 = $t_1 + t_2 = \frac{x}{50} + \frac{x}{40}$
2.25 = $x(\frac{1}{50} + \frac{1}{40})$
x = 50
Total Distance = 2 × 50 = 100

12. To make fruit punch, grapefruit juice, orange juice, and lemonade are mixed in with a ratio of 5:3:2 by volume, respectively. In order to make 5 liters of this drink, how much orange juice, in liters, is needed?
    a) 1
    b) 1.5
    c) 2
    d) 2.5

Answer: (B)
Every 10 liters, (2 + 3 + 5), of drink, 3 liters of orange juice will be needed. So 5 liters of this drink, we need $\frac{3}{10}$ × 5 of orange juice.
Orange Juice = 0.3 × 5 = 1.5 liters

13. If $x \neq 0$ and x is inversely proportional to y, which of the following is directly proportional to $\frac{1}{x^3}$? 🚫
    a) $\frac{1}{y^3}$
    b) $-\frac{1}{y^3}$
    c) y^3
    d) y^2

Answer: (C)
If "x is inversely proportional to y", then xy = k.
Raise power of 3 on both sides:
$(xy)^3 = k^3$
$x^3y^3 = k^3 \rightarrow y^3 = k^3 (\frac{1}{x^3})$
So $\frac{1}{x^3}$ directly proportional to y^3

Questions 14 − 15 refer to the following information:

Planetary Data of Solar System

Planet	Distance from the Sun (billion meters)	Orbital Period (Earth years)
Mercury	57.9	0.241
Earth	149.6	1.0
Mars	227.9	1.88
Saturn	Z	29.5
Uranus	2,870	84.0
Planet X	20,000	Y

The chart above shows our Solar System's planetary data applied to the Kepler's Third Law, which states that the square of the period of any planet is proportional to the cube of its distance from the Sun. For any planets in the Solar System, the square of the orbital period divided by the cube of its distance from the Sun should be a constant.

14. If Saturn has the period of 29.5 Earth years, find its distance from the Sun, in billion meters? (Round your answer to the nearest whole number.)

Answer: 1428
Kepler's Third Law:
$$\frac{(Orbital\ Period)^2}{(Distance\ from\ the\ Sun)^3} = K$$
$$\frac{29.5^2}{(Distance\ from\ the\ Sun)^3} = \frac{1^2}{149.6^3}$$
Distance = 1428 billion meters

15. If Planet X is 20,000 billion meters away from the Sun, what is its orbital period, in Earth years? (Round your answer to the nearest whole number.)

Answer: 1546

$$\frac{(Orbital\ Period)^2}{20000^3} = \frac{1^2}{149.6^3}$$

Orbital Period =
1546 Earth years

Questions 16 – 17 refer to the following information:
The fluid dynamics continuity model states that the rate at which mass enters a system is equal to the rate at which mass leaves the system. The rate of mass at any cross section in a pipe is the product of the cross sectional area and the speed of the fluid.

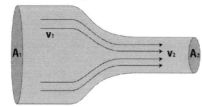

16. If water runs through a pipe with cross sectional area 0.4 m² at a speed of 6 m/s, calculate the speed of the water in the pipe when the pipe tapers off to a cross sectional area of 0.3 m².
    a) 8.0 m/s
    b) 7.5 m/s
    c) 7.0 m/s
    d) 5.5 m/s

Answer: (A)
$$A_1V_1 = A_2V_2$$
$$0.4 \times 6 = 0.3 \times V_2$$
$$V_2 = 8\ m/s$$

17. If water enters a certain type of garden hose with a diameter of 1.5 cm at a speed of 5 m/s, calculate the speed of water when it travels to the nozzle, which has diameter 0.7 cm.
    a) 30.66 m/s
    b) 22.96 m/s
    c) 17.23 m/s
    d) 14.21 m/s

Answer: (B)
$$A_1V_1 = A_2V_2$$
$$\pi\left(\frac{1.5}{2}\right)^2 \times 5 = \pi\left(\frac{0.7}{2}\right)^2 \times V_2$$
$$V_2 = 22.96\ m/s$$

Hard

18. Machine A makes 200 toys per hour. Machine B makes 300 toys per hour. If both machines begin running at the same time, how many minutes will it take the two machines to make a total of 1,000 toys?

Answer: 120
$$Total\ Time = \frac{Total\ Toys}{Total\ Rate}$$
Total Rate = 200 toys/hour + 300
Toys/Hour = 500 toys/hour
$$Total\ Time = \frac{1000\ toys}{500\ toys/hour}$$
= 2 hours = 120 minutes

19. Sean needs to finish reading his book in four days. He reads $\frac{1}{3}$ of the book on the first day, $\frac{1}{4}$ of the book on the second day, $\frac{1}{5}$ of the book on the third day. If he has 13 pages to finish on the fourth day, how many pages are there in the book?

Answer: 60
Find out the last portion of pages and set up ratio equation
The last portion of pages:
$$1 - \frac{1}{3} - \frac{1}{4} - \frac{1}{5} = \frac{13}{60} = \frac{13}{Total}$$
Total = 60

Questions 20 − 21 refer to the following information:

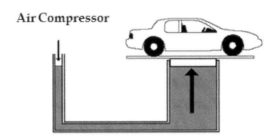

Air Compressor

The hydraulics system in the figure above uses liquids to create pressure and lift heavy objects. The pressure from one end of the hydraulics system (the air compressor) will always be equal to the pressure on the other end (the car). Pressure is defined as force divided by the cross sectional area:

$$Pressure = \frac{Force}{Area}$$

20. The cross sectional area of the cylinder underneath the car is 700 cm² and the cross sectional area of the cylinder at the end with the air compressor is 8 cm². If a car is lifted by a force of 2,800 kg, what force should be exerted by the air compressor?
    a) 32 kg
    b) 28 kg
    c) 24 kg
    d) 20 kg

Answer: (A)
$$\frac{Force_1}{Area_1} = \frac{Force_2}{Area_2}$$
$$\frac{2800}{700} = \frac{x}{8}$$
$$x = 32\ kg$$

21. In order to lift a car by a force of 2,800 kg, a 5 kg force is applied at the air compressor end. Find the ratio of the radii of the cylinder at the car end to the air compressor end.
    a) 27.3
    b) 25.5
    c) 23.7
    d) 15.3

Answer: (C)
$$\frac{Force_1}{Area_1} = \frac{Force_2}{Area_2}$$
$$\frac{2800}{\pi r_1^2} = \frac{5}{\pi r_2^2}$$
$$\frac{r_1}{r_2} = \sqrt{\left(\frac{2800}{5}\right)} = 23.7$$

III. Percentages

Concept Overviews

A percentage is a ratio of a part to a whole expressed as a fraction of 100. To calculate the percentage that a part represents in the whole, use the percent formula:

$$\text{Percentage} = \frac{Part}{Whole} \times 100\%$$

- Identify the part and the whole and then set up an equation using the percent formula.
- If you are performing **operations on percentages**, convert them into fractions first.

   Example: A baseball pitcher won 28 out of 35 games he pitched. How many percent of his games did he win?
   Answer: the percentage of winning = $\frac{28}{35} \times 100\% = 80\%$

Changing Decimals to Percentages
Multiply a decimal by 100 to get the equivalent percentage.

$$\text{Percentage} = \text{Decimal} \times 100\%$$

Example: 0.25 is equal to 0.25×100%, which is equal to 25%?

Changing Fractions to Percentages
Change a fraction into a decimal by dividing the denominator into numerator. Then convert the decimal into a percentage.

Example: Write $\frac{2}{5}$ as a percent.
Solution: $\frac{2}{5} = 0.4$ and $0.4 \times 100\% = 40\%$
   Therefore, $\frac{2}{5}$ is equal to 40%.

Changing Percentages to Decimals
Divide the percentage by 100 and get rid of the percent sign (%).

The easy way to divide a number by 100 is to move the decimal point two places to the left.

Example: Convert 35% to a decimal.
Solution: 35 (without the % sign) divided by 100 is equal to 0.35. The easy way to divide 35 by 100 is to move the decimal point two places to the left. 35.0 is equivalent to 0.35.

Changing Percentages to Fractions
Write the percent as a fraction out of 100 and reduce the fraction.
$$\text{Fraction} = \frac{The\ Percent\ (without\ the\ \%\ sign)}{100}$$

Example: Change 40% into a fraction.
Answer: Fraction $= \frac{40}{100} = \frac{2 \times 20}{5 \times 20} = \frac{2}{5}$

Percent Change (Percent Increase and Percent Decrease)
The percent change is defined as the percent of the initial value that was gained or lost.
$$\text{Percent Change} = \frac{Final\ Value - Initial\ Value}{Initial\ Value} \times 100\%$$

- Percent Change $> 0 \rightarrow$ Percent Increase
- Percent Change $< 0 \rightarrow$ Percent Decrease

Example: The population of a small town was 1200 in last year and became 1260 this year. What was its population percent change from last year to this year?

Answer: Percent Change $= \frac{This\ Year's\ Population - Last\ Year's\ Population}{Last\ Year's\ Population} \times 100\%$
$$= \frac{1260 - 1200}{1200} \times 100\% = 5\%$$

Keywords: When dealing with percent problems, the following keywords usually translate to the following actions:
- Percent in decimal form $\rightarrow$ divide by 100
- Decimal in percent form $\rightarrow$ multiply by 100
- 'is' $\rightarrow$ =
- 'of' $\rightarrow$ × *(multiplication)*
- 'what' or 'a number' $\rightarrow x$ (the value you are solving for)

Example 1: 5 is what percent of 20?
Answer: $5 = x \times 20$

$x = \frac{5}{20} = 0.25$
$0.25 \times 100\% = 25\%$
Changing 0.25 into a percent is equal to 25%.
Therefore, *5 is 25% of 20.*

Example 2: What is 15% of 60?
Answer: $x = \frac{12}{100} \times 60 = 9$

Example 3: 20% of what number is 16?
Answer: $\frac{20}{100} \times x = 16, \quad x = 80$

Example 4: What percent of 20 is 5?

Answer: $\frac{x}{100} \times 20 = 5$

$x = \frac{5 \times 100}{20} = 25\%$

Example 5: If 40 percent of 20 percent of a number is 20, what is the number?

Answer: Changing 40% into decimal form gives you 0.4. Changing 20% into decimal form gives you 0.2.

$0.4 \times 0.2 \times x = 20$

$x = \frac{20}{0.4 \times 0.2} = 250$

Discount: You might be asked a question that gives you two of the following: discount rate of an item, the original price of the item, and/or the total amount of money saved from purchasing the item at a discount, and asked to find the third term. To do this, you should use the discount formula:

Total Discount = Original Price × Discount Rate

Or if you are solving for or given the sale price of the item, you can either subtract the discount from the original price to get the sale price:

Original Price – Original Price × Discount Rate = Sale Price

Or multiply the original price by (1 – Discount Rate):

Sale Price = Original Price × (1 – Discount Rate)

Example 1: In a department store, a $50 T-shirt is marked "20% off." What is the sale price of the T-shirt?

Answer: Converting 20% to a decimal gives you 0.2.

Total Discount = $50×0.2 = $10

Sale Price of the T−shirt = $50 − $10 =$40

Example 2: An object that regularly sells for $125 is marked down to $100. What is the discount percentage?

Answer: Total Discount = $125 − $100 = $25

$25 = $125 × Discount Rate

Discount Rate = $\frac{25}{125}$ = 0.2

Changing 0.2 to percent gives you 20%.

The discount rate is equal to 20%.

Simple Interest

When you put money in a bank, you usually earn something called interest. This is money the bank pays you for leaving money (principal) with them. Simple interest can be calculated with the simple interest formula:

Total Interest Earned = Interest Rate × Principal × Time

When you are using the interest formula, be careful of units and make sure your time units match with your interest rate units!

Example: A bank is offering its customers 3% simple interest rate annually on savings accounts. If a customer deposits $2,500 in the account, without cashing out, how much money will be in his saving account after 4 years?

Answer: Changing 3% to decimal gives you 0.03.
Total Interest Earned = $0.03 \times \$2,500 \times 4 = \$300$
Money in Account = $\$2,500 + \$300 = \$2,800$
After 4 years, his saving account will have $2,800.

Compound Interest

Compound interest is the interest added to the principal of a deposit so that the interest earned also earns interest continuously. A formula for calculating annual compound interest is as follows:

$$A = P\left(1 + \frac{r}{100}\right)^t$$

A is the amount of money, in dollars, generated after *t* years by a principal amount *P* in a bank account that pays an annual interest rate of *r*%, compounded annually.

Example: How much would you need to deposit in your bank account today with an annual interest rate of 3% compounded annually in order to get $10,000 in your back account after 10 years? (Round your answer to the nearest dollar and ignore the dollar sign when gridding your response.)

Answer: $10000 = P\left(1 + \frac{3}{100}\right)^{10}$
$10000 = P \times (1.3439)$
$P = \$7,441$

Problem Solving Skills

Easy

1. If 70 percent of *x* is 28, then what is 30 percent of *x*?

    Answer: 12
    $\frac{70}{100} \times x = 28$
    x = 40
    40 × 0.3 = 12 (Note: 30% = 0.3)

2. If 60 percent of 30 percent of a number is 36.54, what is the number?

    Answer: 203
    This can be translated into 0.6 ×
    0.3 × A = 36.54.
    $A = \frac{36.54}{0.6 \times 0.3} = 203$

3. 50 percent of 210 is the same as 35 percent of what number?

a) 340
b) 300
c) 350
d) 275

Answer: (B)
This sentence can be translated into: $\frac{50}{100} \times 210 = \frac{35}{100} \times A$
$A = \frac{50}{35} \times 210 = 300$

4. If John earns $3,000 a month and he saves $600 out of his salary, what percent of John's earnings is his monthly savings?

a) 15%
b) 20%
c) 25%
d) 30%

Answer: (B)
$Percent = \frac{Part}{Whole} \times 100$
$\frac{600}{3000} \times 100 = 20$

5. A printer that regularly sells for $150 is marked down to $100. What is the discount percentage?

a) 33%
b) 42%
c) 45%
d) 50%

Answer: (A)
Discount = $150 − $100 = $50
$50 = $150 × Discount Rate
Discount Rate = $\frac{50}{150} = 0.33$
Changing 0.33 to percent gives you 33%.

Auto Sales

6. According to the circle graph above, how many types of automobiles show less than 30 percent of the total sales?

a) 0
b) 1
c) 2
d) 3

Answer: (C)
30% is slightly more than $\frac{1}{4}$ *(25%) of the whole graph.*
From the graph above, two types of automobiles make up less than $\frac{1}{4}$ *of the whole graph.*

7. The percent increase from 6 to 15 is equal to the percent increase from 12 to what number?

a) 20
b) 22
c) 24
d) 30

Answer: (D)
$\frac{15-6}{6} = \frac{x-12}{12}$ *(cross multiply)*
$9 \times 12 = 6(x - 12)$
$18 = x - 12$
$x = (18 + 12) = 30$

8. Based on Mrs. Johnson's grading policies, if a student answers 90 to 100 percent of the questions correctly in a math test, she will receive a letter grade of A. If there are 60 questions on the final exam, what is the minimum number of questions the student would need to answer correctly to receive a grade of A?

    a) 34
    b) 38
    c) 42
    d) 54

Answer: (D)

$$90\% = \frac{Correct\ Answers}{Total\ Questions}$$

$$\frac{x}{60} = \frac{90}{100} \ (cross\ multiply)$$

$$x = \frac{90 \times 60}{100} = 54$$

9. The price of a pair of shoes was first increased by 10 percent and then decreased by 25 percent. The final price was what percent of the original price?

    a) 80%
    b) 82.5%
    c) 85%
    d) 87.5%

Answer: (B)
Let the original price be 100, then the final price is 100 × (1 + 0.1) × (1 − 0.25) = 82.5.

10. A bank is offering its customers 2% simple interest rate annually on savings accounts. If a customer deposits $1,500 in the account, without cashing out, how much money will be in his saving account after 5 years?

Answer: 1650
Changing 2% to decimal gives you 0.02.
Total Interest Earned =
0.02×$1,500× 5 =$150
Money in Account = $1,500 + $150 = $1,650
After 5 years, his saving account will have $1,650.

Medium

11. $\frac{1}{5}$ of 100 is equal to what percent of 400?

    a) 5 %
    b) 10 %
    c) 15 %
    d) 20 %

Answer: (A)

$$\frac{1}{5}\ of\ 100\ \rightarrow\ \frac{1}{5} \times 100 = 20$$

$$20 = \frac{x}{100} \times 400$$

$$20 = 4x\ \rightarrow\ x = 5$$

Therefore, $\frac{1}{5} \times 100 = 20$ is equal to 400 × 5% = 20

12. In a certain year at Lion High School, exactly 68 out of the 400 students are taking AP Chemistry. What percent of students are NOT taking AP Chemistry that year?

    a) 15
    b) 17
    c) 50
    d) 83

Answer: (D)
Percentage of people taking AP Chemistry: $\frac{68}{400} \times 100 = 17\%$
Percentage NOT taking AP Chemistry: 100% − 17% = 83%

13. A family spent $350 on utilities in January. Due to the weather, they spent 20% more in February. How much did they spend on utilities in February?

Answer: 420
"20% more of 350" →350 × (1 + 0.2) = 420
x = 420

Questions 14 – 15 refer to the following information:
According to research, 90 percent of 20 to 36 month-old children in the United States need to have received measles vaccination in order to achieve herd immunity. In 2013, California did not meet the vaccination goal and Colorado, Ohio, and West Virginia had 86 percent of 20 to 36 month-olds received the vaccination.

14. If 89 percent of 20 to 36 month-olds received the measles vaccination in California in 2013 and the total number of 20-36 month-olds in California in 2013 is 1.41 million, which of the following could be the number of 20-36 month-olds who have received the measles vaccination in California in 2013?
   a) 1.24 million
   b) 1.25 million
   c) 1.26 million
   d) 1.27 million

Answer: (B)
The measles vaccination percentage in California is 89%. The number of 20 to 36 month-olds who had received measles vaccination in California need to be 1.41 million × 0.89 = 1.2549 million.

15. If the total number of 20 to 36 month-olds in Ohio in 2013 is 0.235 million, how many of 20 to 36 month-olds in Colorado have received the measles vaccination in 2013?
   a) 224,600
   b) 205,100
   c) 202,100
   d) 145,300

Answer: (C)
0.235 million × 0.86 = 0.2021 million = 202,100

16. A car salesman's monthly pay consists of $1000 plus 2% of his sales. If he got paid $3,000 in a certain month, what was the dollar amount, in thousands, of his sales for that month?

Answer: 100
Let his car sales be $x, then
3000 = 1000 + 0.02 × x
3000 − 1000 = 0.02x
x = $100,000

Questions 17 – 18 refer to the following information:
The unemployment rate is officially defined as the percentage of unemployed individuals divided by all individuals currently willing to work. To count as unemployed, a person must be 16 or older and have not held a job during the week of the survey. According to the Bureau of Labor Statistics, below is a comparison of the seasonally adjusted unemployment rates for certain states for the months of August and September 2015.

State	Rate (August 2015)	Rate (September 2015)
Nebraska	2.8	2.9
Hawaii	3.5	3.4
Texas	4.1	4.2
Wisconsin	4.5	4.3
Connecticut	5.3	5.2
New Jersey	5.7	5.6
Oregon	6.1	6.2
Alaska	6.6	6.4

17. Among those states shown in the table above, how many states have their unemployment rate drop from August 2015 to September 2015?

    a) 5

    b) 4

    c) 3

    d) 2

Answer: (A)
5 states, Hawaii, Wisconsin, Connecticut, New Jersey, and Alaska, have unemployment rate drop among those states shown above.

18. If about 251,400 residents of New Jersey were unemployed in September 2015, approximately how many New Jersey residents were willing to work in September 2015?

    a) 44,900

    b) 1,407,800

    c) 3,251,600

    d) 4,489,200

Answer: (D)
Let the number of residents who were willing to work be x.

$$\frac{251,400}{x} = 5.6\%$$

$$5.6x = 25,140,000$$

$$x = 4,489,286 \approx 4,489,200$$

Hard

Questions 19 − 20 refer to the following information:
Percent error is useful for determining the precision of a calculation. Percent error close to zero means the calculation is very close to the target value. The formula to measure percent error is:

$$Percent\ Error = \frac{Measured\ Data - Actual\ Data}{Actual\ Data} \times 100\%$$

19. The density of water at 4°C is known to be 1.00 g/mL. If Anny experimentally found the density of water be 0.9975 g/mL, what would be her percent error?
    a) 1.25%
    b) −1.25%
    c) 0.25%
    d) −0.25%

Answer: (D)
$Percent\ Error = \frac{0.9975-1}{1} \times$ 100%
$= -0.25\%$

20. Frank got his lab report back with "8.0% error" written in red on it. If he had examined the boiling point of an unknown liquid to be 92 °C, what could be the actual boiling point for his unknown liquid?
    a) 90.5 °C
    b) 85.2 °C
    c) 80.3 °C
    d) 75.1 °C

Answer: (B)
$8\% = \frac{92-x}{x} \times 100\%$
$9200 = 108x$
$x = 85.2\ °C$

IV. AVERAGES

CONCEPT OVERVIEWS

Average
The average of a set of values is equal to the sum of all values in that set divided by the number of values.

$$Average = \frac{Sum\ of\ Terms}{Number\ of\ Terms} \quad \text{(the average formula)}$$

The key to solving arithmetic average problems is using the average formula.

Example: John has the following scores on his math tests this semester: 80, 85, 89, and 90. What is his average score on his math tests that semester?

Answer: John's Average $= \frac{80 + 85 + 89 + 90}{4} = 86$

The average score of all of John's math tests is 86.

Sum of All Values in the Set
If you are given an average and asked to find the sum of all values in the set, multiply the average by the number of terms in the set.

$$Sum\ of\ Terms = Average \times Number\ of\ Terms$$

Number of Terms in the Set
On the other hand, if you are given an average and a sum and asked to find the number of terms in the set, divide the sum by the average to get the number of terms.

$$Number\ of\ Terms = \frac{Sum\ of\ Terms}{Average}$$

Example: The average score of a math quiz in a class is 81 and the sum of the scores is 1215. How many students are in this class?

Answer: Number of Students $= \frac{1215}{81} = 15$

Finding the Missing Number
If you know the average of a set, the number of items in that set, and the sum of all but one of the values, then you can find the value in that set missing from the sum by subtracting the sum from the average times the number of items.

Example: There were 4 tests in Joe's Algebra class. So far he received the following scores on his tests: 83, 93, and 87. What score does he need on the last test in order to get an average score of 90 and above?

Hint: The current sum (with one score missing) is 83 + 93 + 87 = 263. He wants an average of 90 or above.

Answer: 90 × 4 − 263 = 360 − 263 = 97.

Joe needs to get at least an 87 to get an average of 90 or above.

Mean, Median, and Mode

- **Mean:** The usual arithmetic average of a set.

    Example: The mean of the set {2, 6, 4, 5, 3} is $\frac{2+6+4+5+3}{5} = 4$.

- **Median:** The middle element (or average of two middle elements) when a set is sorted from least to greatest. If the set has an odd number of elements, the median is the middle element. If the set has an even number of elements, the median is the average of the two middle elements.

    Example 1: What is the median of the set {3, 11, 6, 5, 4, 7, 12, 3, 10}?
    Hint: Sort the numbers in order first: {3, 3, 4, 5, 6, 7, 10, 11, 12}
    Answer: There are 9 numbers in the set, so the median is the middle element in the sorted set. The median is 6.

    Example 2: What is the median of the set {3, 11, 6, 5, 4, 7, 12, 3, 10, 12}?
    Hint: Sort the numbers in order: {3, 3, 4, 5, 6, 7, 10, 11, 12, 12}
    Answer: There are 10 numbers in the set, so the median number is the average of the two middle numbers, 6 and 7. The median is 6.5.

- **Mode:** The value(s) that appear most often in the set.

    Example: What is the mode of the set {7, 13, 18, 24, 9, 3, 18}?
    Hint: Sort the numbers in order: {3, 7, 9, 13, 18, 18, 24}
    Answer: The number which occurs most often is 18. Therefore, the mode is 18.

Standard deviation is a measure of the spread of a set of data.
$$\sigma = \sqrt{\frac{1}{N}\sum_{i=1}^{N}(x_i - \bar{x})^2}$$
where σ is the standard deviation, N is the total number of data points, the x_is are the values of the N points, and $\bar{x}$ is the mean of all the x_is.

Example: Calculate the standard deviation of the following five data points:
Data: 85, 70, 78, 65, 90

Answer: $\bar{x} = \frac{85+70+78+65+90}{5} = 77.6$

$\sigma = \sqrt{\frac{1}{5}[(85 - 77.6)^2 + (70 - 77.6)^2 + (78 - 77.6)^2 + (65 - 77.6)^2 + (90 - 77.6)^2]}$

$= 9.22$

Problem Solving Skills

Easy

1. The average (arithmetic mean) of 5, 14, and x is 15. What is the value of x?
   - a) 25
   - b) 26
   - c) 27
   - d) 28

   Answer: (B)
   The average of these three numbers is 15, so the sum will be $3 \times 15 = 45$.
   $5 + 14 + x = 45$
   $x = 45 - 19 = 26$

2. If the average (arithmetic mean) of 2, X, and Y is 3, what is the value of X + Y? Ⓝ
   - a) 4
   - b) 5
   - c) 7
   - d) 8

   Answer: (C)
   $X + Y + 2 = 3 \times 3 = 9$
   $X + Y = 7$

3. Mary has the following scores on 7 quizzes in Algebra class: 84, 79, 83, 87, 81, 94, and 87. What was the median score of all of her Algebra quizzes? Ⓝ
   - a) 81
   - b) 84
   - c) 85
   - d) 86

   Answer: (B)
   Sort the scores in order.
   79, 81, 83, 84, 87, 87, 94
   The median is 84.

4. If the sum of 4 numbers is between 61 and 63, then the average (arithmetic mean) of the 4 numbers could be which of the following?
   - a) 15
   - b) 15.2
   - c) 15.5
   - d) 16

   Answer: (C)
   $\frac{61}{4} < Average < \frac{63}{4}$
   $15.25\ Average < 15.75$

5. Which of the following could be the sum of 8 numbers if the average of these 8 numbers is greater than 9 and less than 10?
   - a) 85
   - b) 83
   - c) 82
   - d) 79

   Answer: (D)
   Sum = Number of Elements × Average
   $9 \times 8 < Sum < 10 \times 8$
   $72 < Sum < 80$

6. When the average (arithmetic mean) of a list of grades is multiplied by the number of students, the result is n.

   What does n represent? Ⓝ
   a) the number of the grades
   b) the average of the grades
   c) the sum of the grades
   d) the range of the list of the grades

Answer: (C)
This is the definition of "sum."

7. Let A represents the average of all winter monthly heating bills for John's family. What is the result of

   multiplying A by the number of months in winter? Ⓝ
   a) The average of all heating expenses for John's family in the year.
   b) The highest monthly heating bill for John's family that winter.
   c) The sum of the eating expenses for the whole year for John's family.
   d) The sum of the heating expenses in winter for John's family.

Answer: (D)
Multiplying the average by the number of elements (months) in the set gives you the sum of all the elements.

8. The median of a set of 13 consecutive integers is 35. What is the greatest of these 13 integers?
   a) 37
   b) 38
   c) 40
   d) 41

Answer: (D)
The median is the 7th number of 13 consecutive integers. That means there are 6 integers less than the median and 6 integers greater than the median. The greatest integer is the 6th consecutive integer after 35.
35 + 6 = 41

9. If the average of $3a$, $4a$, and $5a$ is equal to 8, what is a equal to?

Answer: 2
The average of 3a, 4a and 5a is equal to 4a.
4a= 8 → a = 2

10. The average score of John's 5 math tests is 75. If the teacher decides not to count his lowest score, which is 55, what will be John's new average score?
    a) 78
    b) 79
    c) 80
    d) 81

Answer: (C)
John's original average is 75 for 5 tests.
5 × 75 = 375 (sum of 5 tests)
375 − 55 = 320 (sum of 4 tests)
$\frac{320}{4}$ = 80 (average of 4 tests)

Medium

11. On a certain test, the highest possible score is 100 and the lowest is 0. If the average score of 5 students is 82, what is the lowest possible score of the fifth student?
    a) 0
    b) 5
    c) 7
    d) 10

Answer: (D)
The lowest possible score is equal to the lowest score a student can get if each of other four students got the highest possible score (otherwise we can always increase another student's score and decrease the lowest score). Thus, each of other four students must get 100.
Total Score = 5 × 82 = 410
Lowest Score = 410 − 400 = 10

Math Midterm	
Scores	Number of Students
100	1
95	3
90	5
85	8
80	3

12. The scores of the math midterm for every student in Sam's class are shown in the table above. Sam, who was the only student absent, will take the test next week. If Sam receives a score of 95 on the test, what will be the median score for the test? 🚫
    a) 75
    b) 82.5
    c) 85
    d) 87.5

Answer: (C)
For an odd set, the median is the score in the middle when scores listed in order.
If we include Sam, the median will be the 11th highest score which is 85.

13. On an Algebra final exam, class A has an average score of 90 with 10 students. Class B has an average score of 85 with 20 students. When the scores of class A and B are combined, what is the average score of class A and B?
    a) 82
    b) 82.5
    c) 83
    d) 86.7

Answer: (D)
*This is **not** the average of the averages since the classes have different number of students! The final average is the sum of all students' scores divided by the total number of students.*
We know that the sum of all the students' scores in one class is just the average multiplied by the number of students.
$$Average = \frac{10 \times 90 + 20 \times 85}{10 + 20} = 86.67$$

14. If the average (arithmetic mean) of x, y, and z is k, which of the following is the average of w, x, y and z? Ⓝ

    a) $\dfrac{k+w}{2}$

    b) $\dfrac{2k+w}{3}$

    c) $\dfrac{3k+w}{3}$

    d) $\dfrac{3k+w}{4}$

Answer: (D)
$k = \dfrac{x+y+z}{3}$
$x + y + z = 3k$
Average: $\dfrac{x+y+z+w}{4} = \dfrac{3k+w}{4}$

15. On a biology test with total of 100 points, a class of 21 students had an average of 93. If 5 of the students had a perfect score, what was the average score for the remaining students?

    a) 89

    b) 90

    c) 91

    d) 91.5

Answer: (C)
Once again, the average gives a way to calculate the total score of all the students. Deduct from that sum the sum of the test scores that were perfect and divide by the remaining number of students.
Average: $\dfrac{Sum}{21} = 93$
Sum of all scores: $21 \times 93 = 1953$
Deduct 5 perfect scores:
$1953 - 500 = 1453$
New Average $= \dfrac{1453}{21-5} = 90.8 \sim 91$

Hard

16. We start out with a set of 7 numbers. We subtract 3 from 3 of these numbers. If the average (arithmetic mean) of these seven numbers was 11 originally, what is the new average?

    a) 7.5

    b) 8

    c) 8.5

    d) 9.7

Answer: (D)
Average: $\dfrac{Sum\ of\ Terms}{Number\ of\ Terms}$
$\dfrac{7 \times 11 - 3 \times 3}{7} = 9.7$

17. If the average (arithmetic mean) of a and b is m, which of the following is the average of a, b, and c? Ⓝ

    a) $\dfrac{2m+c}{3}$

    b) $\dfrac{m+c}{2}$

    c) $\dfrac{2m+c}{2}$

    d) $\dfrac{m+2c}{3}$

Answer: (A)
The average of a, b, and c is equal to the sum of a, b, and c divided by 3.
$a + b = 2m$
$a + b + c = 2m + c$
Average: $\dfrac{2m+c}{3}$

18. Class A has X students and class B has Y students. The average of the test scores of class A is 80, and the average of the test scores of class B is 90. When the scores of class A and B are combined, the average score is 88. What is the ratio of X to Y?

    a) $\frac{1}{2}$

    b) $\frac{1}{3}$

    c) $\frac{1}{4}$

    d) $\frac{2}{3}$

Answer: (C)

We want to find $\frac{X}{Y}$.

Average: $\frac{Sum\ of\ Terms}{Number\ of\ Terms}$

$\frac{80X + 90Y}{X + Y} = 88$ *(cross multiply)*

$80X + 90Y = 88 \times (X + Y)$

$80X + 90Y = 88X + 88Y$

$2Y = 8X$

$\frac{X}{Y} = \frac{2}{8} = \frac{1}{4}$

19. N students have an average of K scores on a math test. Another 3 students were absent and received zeroes on the test. What is the average score of this math test in terms of N and K, taking into accounts all of the students? 🚫

    a) $\frac{NK}{3}$

    b) $\frac{NK}{K+3}$

    c) $\frac{NK}{N+3}$

    d) $\frac{N-3}{K}$

Answer: (C)

$Average = \frac{Total\ Score}{Number\ of\ Students}$

$Average = \frac{K \times N}{N + 3}$

V. DATA ANALYSIS

CONCEPT OVERVIEWS

Reading and Interpreting Graphs, Charts, and Tables

SAT data analysis questions use graphs, charts, and tables to organize information.

Bar graphs use horizontal or vertical bars to represent data.

Example: The bar graph below shows the number of students taking honors and AP classes. For math classes, there are 20 students taking math honors and 15 students taking AP math.

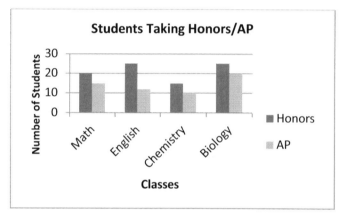

Pictographs use pictures to represent data. There is usually a scale provided that gives you an idea of what each picture represents.

Example: The pictograph below shows the car sales data from 1971 to 2010. The scale clearly states that each car represents 2 million cars. In the pictograph, we can see that the years 2001-2010 are drawn with four cars, which represents a total of 8 million cars sold. In the years 1981-1990, the pictograph shows $2\frac{1}{2}$ cars sold, which represents 5 million cars.

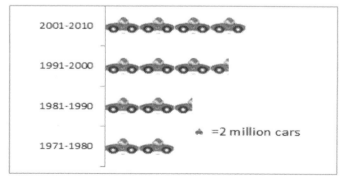

Car Sales from 1971 to 2010

Pie graphs use a circle (or pie) to display data. Pie graphs can be used to determine the proportion of an item out of a whole as well as ratios of different items to each other.

Example: The pie graph below shows Ellen's family's monthly expenses and the proportion of each expense out of all of their expenditures.

As we can see from the graph, food takes up about $\frac{1}{4}$ of all expenditures, and utilities take up about $\frac{1}{5}$ of all expenditures. The ratio of food expenditures to taxes is about 1:1.

Monthly Expenses

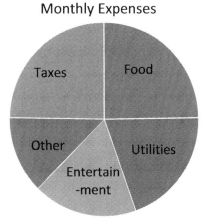

Sometimes you are asked to the value of a sector given the total value. You can figure out the proportion of the sector in the pie and solve for the missing value:

$$\text{Proportion of Sector in Pie} = \frac{Value\ of\ the\ Sector}{Total\ Value}$$

Example: If the Ellen's family's total expenses are $6000 per month, approximately how much do they pay in taxes per month?

Solution: Taxes take up around $\frac{1}{4}$ of the total pie.

$$\frac{1}{4} = \frac{Taxes}{6000}$$

$$Taxes = \$1500$$

Tables represent data in rows and columns. Tables are simple to understand. The top entry of a column usually explains the contents of that column. Elements are corresponded to all the other elements in the same row.

Example: The table below shows the number of students taking AP classes in school. The entry that contains a '1' under 'Number of APs' corresponds to the entry that contains a '6' under 'Number of Students.' In other words, there are 6 students taking 1 AP class.

Students Taking AP Classes	
Number of Aps	Number of Students
1	6
2	4
3	5
4	4

Line graphs record a change in data. Usually this change is graphed over time. Time is usually graphed on the *x*-axis.

Example: The line graph below records car sales (in millions) over four years.

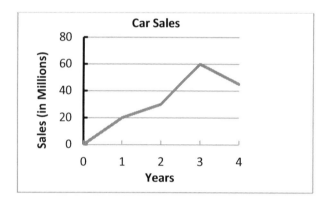

Scatterplots are similar to line graphs, but show the individual data points instead of connecting them with a line. Like line graphs, scatterplots show trends in the data.

Example: The scatterplot below shows the wolf population in a safari every 5 years.

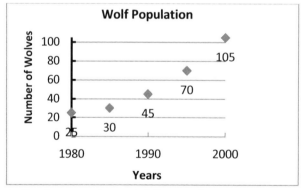

Tips to solve data analysis questions with graphs:
- Always look through the question first to check what the question is asking.
- Read the titles and axes to see what the graph is trying to show.
- Collect information from the graph as needed.
- Perform operations on the data you collected.

Problem Solving Skills

Easy

1. From the graph below, John sold how many more cars in year 3 than the sum of cars sold in years 1 and 2?

    Answer: (A)
    Year 1 + Year 2 = 20 + 30 = 50 cars
    Year 3 = 60 cars
    60 − 50 = 10 cars

    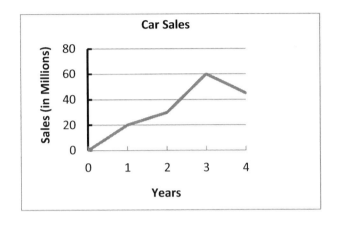

    a) 10
    b) 15
    c) 20
    d) 25

2. According to the graph below, how many students are taking honors classes altogether?

    Answer: (C)
    Total = (20 + 25 + 15 + 25) = 85

    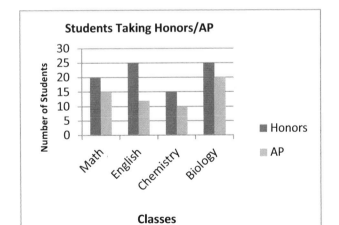

    a) 75
    b) 80
    c) 85
    d) 90

3. Of the following, which is the closest approximation of the cost per ticket when one purchases a book of 6?

Bus Ticket Price	
Number of Bus Tickets	Price
1	7.5
Book of 6	40
Book of 12	75

   a) $6.67
   b) $6.75
   c) $6.83
   d) $6.90

Answer: (A)
$\frac{\$40}{6\ Tickets} = \$6.67\ per\ ticket$

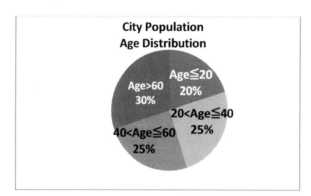

4. Town A has a population of 25,000 and the chart above shows their age distribution. How many people are 40 years or younger?
   a) 5,000
   b) 8,000
   c) 10,000
   d) 11,250

Answer: (D)
The number of population 40 years or younger:
$(25\% + 20\%) \times 25,000$
$= 45\% \times 25,000 = 0.45 \times 25,000$
$= 11,250$

5. What is the percent increase of sales from the third to the fourth year in the chart below?

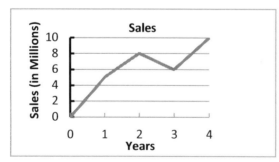

   a) 40%
   b) 55%
   c) 65%
   d) 67%

Answer: (D)
Percent increase =
$\frac{4^{th}\ Year\ Sales - 3^{rd}\ Year\ Sales}{3^{rd}\ Year\ Sales}$
$\times 100\%$
From the graph, sales in the 3rd year is 6 million and sales in the 4th year is 10 million.
Percent Increase = $\frac{10-6}{6} \times$
$100\% = 67\%$

6. According to the graph below, how many employees have salary less than or equal to $40,000?

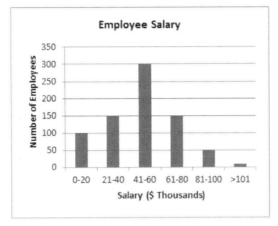

a) 100
b) 150
c) 250
d) 300

Monthly Expenses

7. The pie graph above shows Ellen's family's monthly expenses and the proportion of each expense out of all of their expenditures. If the family's total expenses are $3,000 per month, approximately how much do they pay on taxes per month?

a) $500
b) $600
c) $700
d) $750

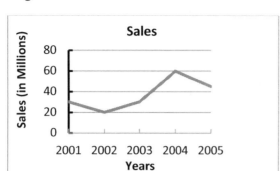

8.   Which of the following is closest to the decrease in sales in millions between 2004 and 2005 according to the graph above?
     a) 10
     b) 12
     c) 15
     d) 20

Answer: (C)
2004 Sales = 60 million units
2005 Sales = 45 million units
60 − 45 = 15 million units

Questions 9 − 10 refer to the chart below:

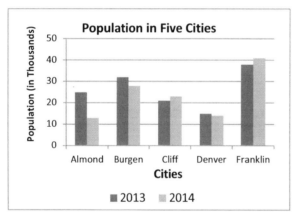

9.   Which of the following cities had a population in 2014 that was approximately 50% less than its population in 2013?
     a) Almond
     b) Burgen
     c) Cliff
     d) Denver

Answer: (A)
Almond's population in 2014 is around double its population in 2013.

10. The total population in all five cities increased by approximately what percent from 2013 to 2014?
     a) 10%
     b) 9%
     c) −10%
     d) −9%

Answer: (D)
Total Population in 2013 = 25 + 32 + 21 + 15 + 37 = 130 thousand.
Total Population in 2014 = 13 + 28 + 22 + 14 + 41 = 118 thousand. $\frac{118 - 130}{130} \times 100\%$
= −9.2% ~ −9%

Medium

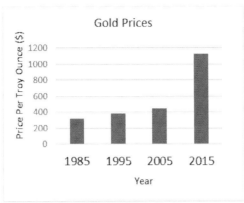

Annual Average Gold Price from 1985 to 2015
(U.S. dollars per troy ounce)

11. The figure above shows the change of the annual average gold price between 1985 and 2015, in U.S. dollars per troy ounce. A troy ounce is a traditional unit of gold weight. In 1985, a troy ounce of gold had an annual average price of around $317. Based on the information shown, which of the following conclusions is valid?

   a) A troy ounce of gold cost more in 1995 than in 2005.
   b) The price more than doubled between 2005 and 2015.
   c) The percent increase from 1985 to 2015 is more than 300%.
   d) The overall average gold price between 1985 and 2015 is around US $555.

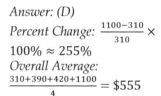

Answer: (D)

Percent Change: $\frac{1100-310}{310} \times 100\% \approx 255\%$

Overall Average:
$\frac{310+390+420+1100}{4} = \$555$

Questions 12 − 13 refer to the following information:

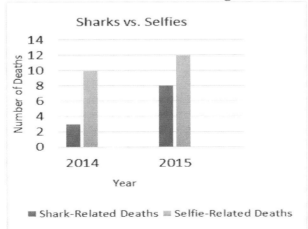

News outlet *Reuters* reports that taking a selfie is actually a dangerous endeavor, and that many people have been injured or died while taking a selfie. The figure above shows that more people around the world have died by taking selfies than by shark attacks in the years of 2014 and 2015. There have been twelve recorded selfie deaths in 2015 compared to eight people dying from shark attacks. The most common selfie-related deaths have been due to falling or being hit by a moving vehicle.

12. What is the percent change of total deaths of selfie-related and shark-related from 2014 to 2015?
    a) 54%
    b) 72%
    c) 100%
    d) 233%

Answer: (A)
Total deaths of 2014: 10 +3 = 13
Total deaths of 2015: 12 + 8 = 20
Percent Increase $= \frac{20-13}{13} \times$
100% = 54%

13. What is the difference between the percent changes of shark-related deaths and selfie-related deaths from 2014 to 2015?
    a) 20%
    b) 147%
    c) 167%
    d) 187%

Answer: (B)
Percent change of selfie-related deaths: $\frac{12-10}{10} \times 100\% = 20\%$
Percent change of shark-related deaths: $\frac{8-3}{3} \times 100\% = 167\%$
Difference: $167\% - 20\% =$
147%

14. The table below, describing number of students who passed or failed the Algebra I final exam, is partially filled in. Based on the information in the table, how many females have failed?

Algebra I Final Exam Results			
	Pass	Fail	Total
Male	125		
Female			145
Total	230		305

Answer: 40
The Number of Students Passing = the Number of Males Passing + the Number of Females Passing
230 = 125 + the Number of Females Passing
The Number of Females Passing = 105
Total Number of Females = Number of Females Passing + Number of Females Failing
The Number of Females Failing = 145 − 105 = 40

Age Distributions

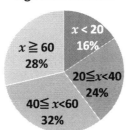

15. If there are 4,180 residents ranging in age from 40 to 59 in Green Village County according to the graph above, approximately how many residents are under the age of 20?

    a) 2,000
    b) 2,100
    c) 2,200
    d) 2,300

Answer: (B)
This is a proportion problem.
Percent of residents 40 to 59 years old: 32%.
Percent of residents under 20: 16%
32% : 4180 = 16% : x
x = 2090

Hard

Number of Hours of TV Watched

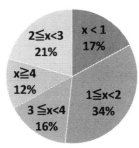

16. The graph above shows breakdown of the average number of hours of TV watched per day. 1,000 people were surveyed, and all but 120 people surveyed responded to the question. If x is the number of hours spent, about how many respondents watch TV for more than 3 hours a day?

    a) 200
    b) 220
    c) 250
    d) 280

Answer: (C)
Watching TV for more than 3 hours a day includes those who answered with $3 \leq x < 4$ and $4 \leq x$, which make up around 28% (12% + 16%) of those who answered.
Total Respondents = 1000 − 120 = 880 people
880 × 28% = 246 ~ 250 people

17. The number of books that have been checked out of the town public library in a particular week was recorded in the table below. If the median number of books checked out for the whole week was 93, which of the following could have been the number of books checked out on Saturday and Sunday, respectively, of the same week?

Answer: (D)
If the median number of books checked out for the whole week was 93, the number of books checked out on both Saturday and Sunday should be more than 93.

Town Library Checkout Records	
Day of the Week	Number of Books Checked Out
Monday	87
Tuesday	91
Wednesday	92
Thursday	93
Friday	96

a) 88 and 92
b) 89 and91
c) 90 and 97
d) 94 and 97

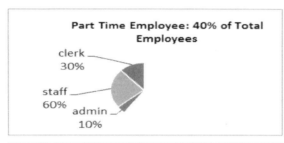

18. According to the graphs above, the total number of full-time employees is how many more than the total number of part time employees at Oak Town High School?
    a) 20
    b) 40
    c) 50
    d) 60

Answer: (B)
Number of Full Time Employees = 15 + 45 + 60 = 120
Full time employees comprise of 60% of the total.
0.6 × Number of Employees = 120
Number of Employees = 200
Part Time Employees = 200 × 0.4 = 80
Full Time Employees – Part Time Employees = 120 – 80 = 40

19. Which of the following CANNOT affect the value of the median in a set of nonzero unique numbers with more than two elements? 🚫

    a) Increase each number by 5
    b) Double each number
    c) Increase the smallest number only
    d) Decrease the smallest number only

Answer: (D)
The median of an odd-numbered set is the number in the middle when all numbers in the set have been sorted in numerical order. In an even-numbered set, it is the average of the two middle elements.
We can change the median by:
i. Changing the value of the median
ii. Changing order of numbers so that we have a new median
Choices (a) and (b) change all values so the median will be changed. Choice (c) could result in a new median if the number changed becomes the new median. Choice (d) reduces the element that is already the smallest, and we know that there are more than 2 elements, so the median does not get changed.

VI. COUNTING AND PROBABILITY

A. COUNTING RULES

CONCEPT OVERVIEWS

Multiplication Principle of Counting
If an event A happens in *p* possible ways and an event B happens independently in *q* possible ways, and then the total number of possible ways that event A **AND** B happen is *p* × *q* ways.

Example: Suppose that there are 5 different main course items and 6 different side dishes. How many different orders can a customer buy one main course and one side dish?
Hint: Because the customer is ordering a main course AND a side dish, use the Multiplication Principle.
Answer: 5 × 6 = 30

Addition Principle of Counting
If an event A happens in *p* possible ways and an event B happens in *q* different ways, and then the total number of possible ways that either event A **OR** event B happens is *p* + *q* ways.

Example: Suppose that there are 4 seafood main dishes and 6 chicken main dishes. How many different ways can a customer choose a main dish?
Hint: Because the customer can choose a seafood dish OR a chicken dish, use the Addition Principle.
Answer: 4 + 6 = 10

Venn Diagram: $n\{A \text{ or } B\} = n\{A\} + n\{B\} - n\{A \text{ and } B\}$

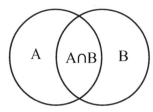

n!: The **factorial** of a whole number *n* is the product of all the positive integers less than or equal to *n*.

$$n! = n \times (n - 1) \times (n - 2) \times ... \times 2 \times 1.$$

Example: $5! = 5 \times 4 \times 3 \times 2 \times 1 = 120$

- ***0!*** is defined to be equal to 1.

$$0! = 1$$

Permutations: A permutation is a selection of objects from a set where the order of selection matters. For example, a selection of *apple, pear, apple* is different from a selection of *pear, apple, apple*.

The number of ways to select *M* objects from *N* objects, ($N \geq M$), where the order of the objects chosen is important is

$$P^N_M = \frac{N!}{(N-M)!}$$

Example: Mary, Sam, Eric, and Lucy are running for student council positions, president, secretary and treasurer. In how many ways can these positions be filled?

Answer: This is to select 3 positions from 4 candidates and order is important. For instance, Mary being elected as president is different from being elected as secretary. Therefore, this is a permutation question.
The answer is P^4_3 which is equal to $\frac{4!}{1!} = 4 \times 3 \times 2 \times 1 = 24$.

Combinations: In combinations, the order of selection does not matter. For example, a selection of *apple, pear, apple* is the same as a selection of *pear, apple, apple*.

The number of ways to select *m* objects from *n* objects ($n \geq m$), where order does not matter, is:

$$C^n_m = \frac{n!}{m! \times (n-m)!}$$

Example: Joe has four marbles with different colors in his pocket and he randomly pulls out three at one time. How many different color arrangements of marbles are possible?

Answer: Pulling out three out of 4 marbles from Joe's pocket means that order is not important and therefore makes this a combination.
The answer is C^4_3 which is equal to $\frac{4!}{3! \times 1!} = 4$.

The number of ways to arrange *n* distinct objects in order is *n!*.

Example: In how many ways can five different books be placed on the book shelf?

Answer: The number of ways to arrange five books in order is *5!*.
$5! = 5 \times 4 \times 3 \times 2 \times 1 = 120$

Problem Solving Skills

Easy

1. For a salad dish, each customer can choose from 5 types of vegetables and 4 types of dressings. How many distinct salad dishes containing one type of vegetable and one dressing are there? Ⓝ
    a) 20
    b) 16
    c) 14
    d) 8

Answer: (A)
For one vegetable AND one dressing, use the Multiplication Principle.
5 × 4 = 20

2. A restaurant offers a choice of one side dish when a main course is ordered. Customers can choose from a list of 5 different main courses and 6 different side dishes. How many different combinations are there of one main course and one side dish? Ⓝ
    a) 11
    b) 16
    c) 20
    d) 30

Answer: (D)
Because the customer is ordering a main course AND a side dish, use the Multiplication Principle.
Total number of choices: 5 × 6 = 30

3. There are four points A, B, C, and D on line *l*, and another four points W, X, Y, and Z on a different line parallel to line *l*. How many distinct lines can be drawn that include exactly two of these 8 points?

Answer: 16
Each of the four points on line l can be connected to each of the four points on the parallel line.
4 × 4 = 16

4. The figure above shows an indoor parking lot with the rectangular arrows indicating the different entrances and exits. What is the total number of distinct ways that a driver can enter and exit the parking lot? Ⓝ
    a) 9
    b) 5
    c) 4
    d) 20

Answer: (D)
Because cars entering the parking lot will also exit, so use the Multiplication Principle.
Total number of ways: 5 × 4 = 20

5. How many combinations of three dishes can be prepared if you have the recipes for 10 dishes?

Answer: 120
This is combination. The number of ways to select m objects from n objects ($n \geq m$), where order does not matter: ($C_m^n = \frac{n!}{m!(n-m)!}$)
To choose 3 from 10: $C_3^{10} = 120$

6. If there are 7 points in a plane, no three of which are collinear, how many distinct lines can be formed by connecting two of these points?
   a) 18
   b) 20
   c) 21
   d) 22

Answer: (C)
This is combination. The number of ways to select m objects from n objects ($n \geq m$), where order does not matter: $C_m^n = \frac{n!}{m!(n-m)!}$
To choose any two points among the 7 points: $C_2^7 = 21$

7. As a part of a vacation package, a travel agent offers 3 choices for the destination, 7 choices for the hotels and 2 choices for car rental companies. How many distinct vacation packages are there with a destination, hotel, and car rental company?
   a) 52
   b) 42
   c) 21
   d) 12

Answer: (B)
We want to find all distinct packages, so we want to solve for the total number of combinations. The total number of combinations of one hotel AND one car rental can be found by using the Multiplication Principle.
$3 \times 7 \times 2 = 42$

8. How many different positive four-digit integers can be formed if the digits 1, 2, 3, and 4 are each used exactly once? 🚫
   a) 10
   b) 12
   c) 14
   d) 24

Answer: (D)
$4 \times 3 \times 2 \times 1 = 24$

Medium

9. How many different positive 2-digit integers are there such that the tens digit is less than 5 and the units digit is even?
   a) 20
   b) 16
   c) 14
   d) 12

Answer: (A)
There are 4 choices for the tens digit and 5 choices for the units digit.
$4 \times 5 = 20$

10. There are 5 red, 5 green, 5 blue, and 5 yellow letters, each of which is inside one of twenty identical,

Answer: (C)

unmarked envelopes. What is the least number of envelopes that must be selected in order to have at least 3 letters of same color?

If 2 letters for each color have been picked, then the next pick has to make at least one color triple.
$2 \times 4 + 1 = 9$

a) 4
b) 8
c) 9
d) 12

11. The above design is to be painted using a different color for the face, the eyes (both of which have to be the same color), the nose, and the mouth. If 6 different colors are available, how many different designs are possible?

Answer: (C)
6 colors can be used to paint face, then 5 of the remaining colors can be used for the eyes, and 4 choices remain for the nose. There are 3 color left for the mouth. It doesn't matter in what order you paint the face, the number of color choices will always be 6, 5, 4, and 3 for the first, second, third, and fourth parts.
$6 \times 5 \times 4 \times 3 = 360$

a) 120
b) 240
c) 360
d) 720

12. There are four different games: Monopole, Good, Words with Ends, and Turner. Each of four friends wants to play a different game. How many different arrangements of who wants to play what are possible?

Answer: 24
The number of ways to arrange n distinct objects in order is n!.
$4! = 4 \times 3 \times 2 \times 1 = 24$

13. What is the total number of distinct line segments that must be drawn in the interior of the heptagon, as shown above, to connect all pairs of the vertices?

Answer: (C)
Each of the 7 vertices has to be connected to each of its 4 non-adjacent vertices, but this double counts the number of line segments needed because each line segment connects two vertices.
$(7 \times 4) \div 2 = 14$

a) 7
b) 8
c) 14
d) 28

Hard

14. A school choir consists of one row of singers, half of which are boys and the other half girls. Which of the following must be true?
    a) The first person and the last person have different genders.
    b) There are two girls next to each other.
    c) If there are two adjacent boys, there are also two adjacent girls.
    d) If the last two are girls, there are at least two adjacent boys.

Answer: (D)
There are no rules about how to arrange boys and girls, so (a) and (b) are incorrect.
If there is one girl at each end, then two boys must be adjacent. Therefore, (c) is wrong.
If the last two seated are girls, then two boys must be adjacent. (d) is correct.

15. 10 players participate in a tennis tournament. A game involves two players and each player plays three games with each of the other nine players. How many games will be played in total at this tournament?
    a) 90
    b) 120
    c) 132
    d) 135

Answer: (D)
This is combination. The number of ways to select m objects from n objects ($n \geq m$), where order does not matter: $C_m^n = \dfrac{n!}{m!(n-m)!}$
Choose any 2 players from 10 players to play a match.
$C_2^{10} = 45$
Each match has 3 games.
$3 \times 45 = 135$ games

B. PROBABILITY FORMULA

CONCEPT OVERVIEWS

Probability of an Event
Probability problems are very similar to counting problems. The **probability** of an event occurring is equal to the ratio of successful events to the total possible events.

$$\text{Probability of an Event} = \frac{Number\ of\ Successful\ Events}{Total\ Number\ of\ Possible\ Events}$$

Example: What is the probability of rolling a number less than 4 when you roll one dice?

Solution: Probability of Rolling a Number $< 4 = \frac{Rolling\ 1,2,or\ 3}{6} = \frac{3}{6} = \frac{1}{2}$

Sometimes probability problems take place over a multi-dimensional sample space. In these problems, use familiar geometric concepts to find the **geometric probability** of an event.

$$\text{Geometric Probability} = \frac{Size\ of\ Target\ Space}{Size\ of\ Sample\ Space}$$

where size could refer to the length, area, or volume of the space.

Example: The diagram below shows 2 concentric circles, with radii 1 and 3 respectively. What is the probability that a randomly selected point in the diagram will fall in the shaded region?

Solution: The shaded region is the target; therefore, the probability of falling in the shaded region is:

$$\frac{Size\ of\ the\ Target}{Total\ Size} = \frac{Size\ of\ Small\ Circle}{Size\ of\ Big\ Circle} = \frac{\pi(1)^2}{\pi(3)^2} = \frac{1}{9}$$

Problem Solving Skills

Easy

1. For every 20 cars sold by a dealer, 8 of them were red. What is the probability that a car sold that is selected at random would be red?
    a) $\frac{1}{5}$
    b) $\frac{2}{5}$
    c) $\frac{1}{3}$
    d) $\frac{2}{3}$

Answer: (B)
Probability =
$$\frac{Number\ of\ Successful\ Events}{Total\ Number\ of\ Possible\ Events}$$

$$\frac{8}{20} = \frac{2}{5}$$

2. There are 10 red boxes, 15 blue boxes, and 20 white boxes. If a blue marble is randomly placed into one of these boxes, what is the probability that it will be placed in a box that is the same color as it?
    a) $\frac{1}{4}$
    b) $\frac{2}{3}$
    c) $\frac{1}{3}$
    d) $\frac{1}{2}$

Answer: (C)
Probability =
$$\frac{Number\ of\ Successful\ Events}{Total\ Number\ of\ Possible\ Events}$$

$$\frac{15}{15 + 10 + 20} = \frac{1}{3}$$

3. A bag contains 15 tennis balls, 6 of which are yellow, 4 pink, and the rest blue. If one ball is randomly chosen from the bag, what is the probability that the ball is blue?
    a) $\frac{1}{2}$
    b) $\frac{1}{3}$
    c) $\frac{1}{4}$
    d) $\frac{3}{5}$

Answer: (B)
The number of blue balls:
$15 - 6 - 4 = 5$
Probability $= \frac{5}{15} = \frac{1}{3}$

4. In a high school pep rally, a student is to be chosen at random. The probability of choosing a freshman is $\frac{1}{8}$. Which of the following cannot be the total number of students in the pep rally?
    a) 20
    b) 24
    c) 32
    d) 80

Answer: (A)
The total number of students must be a multiple of 8. Note that the number of students must be a whole number.
Only (a) is not a multiple of 8.

5. At an intersection, a complete cycle of the traffic light takes 60 seconds. Within each cycle, the green light lasts for 30 seconds and the yellow light 10 seconds. If a driver arrives at the intersection at a random time, what is the probability that the light is red? 🚫

  a) $\frac{3}{4}$
  b) $\frac{2}{3}$
  c) $\frac{1}{3}$
  d) $\frac{1}{2}$

Answer: (C)
The red light takes 20 seconds.
60 – 30 – 10 = 20
Probability of Red Light = $\frac{20}{60} = \frac{1}{3}$

6. The center of a circle is the origin of a rectangular coordinate plane. If (−4, 0), (0, 4), and (4, 0) are three points on the circumference of the circle, what is the probability that a randomly picked point inside the circle would fall inside the triangle formed by those three points?

  a) $\frac{1}{2}$
  b) $\frac{1}{3}$
  c) $\frac{1}{\pi}$
  d) $\frac{2}{\pi}$

Answer: (C)
Radius of the Circle = 4
Area of the Circle = $\pi (4)^2 = 16\pi$
Area of the Triangle = $\frac{1}{2} \times 4 \times 8 = 16$
Probability = $\frac{16}{16\pi} = \frac{1}{\pi}$

7. Bella has 5 blue pens, 6 black pens, and 5 red pens in her pencil case. She takes out a pen at random and puts it aside because the pen is not blue. She then takes out a second pen randomly from her pencil case. What is the probability that the second pen will be a blue pen? 🚫

  a) $\frac{1}{4}$
  b) $\frac{1}{2}$
  c) $\frac{2}{3}$
  d) $\frac{1}{3}$

Answer: (D)
After first taking, there are 5 blue pens and a total of 15 pens left in her pencil case.
Probability to get a blue pen:
$\frac{5}{15} = \frac{1}{3}$

Medium

8. A bag contains red, blue, and green marbles. The probability of pulling out a red marble randomly is $\frac{1}{4}$ and the probability of pulling out a blue marble randomly is $\frac{1}{5}$. Which of the following could be the total number of marbles in the bag?

    a) 10
    b) 12
    c) 18
    d) 20

Answer: (D)
The total number of marbles should be a common multiple of 4 and 5.
The LCM of 4 and 5 is 20, so the total number of marbles has to be a multiple of 20.

9. The figure below shows a top view of a container with a square-shaped opening and which is divided into 5 smaller compartments. The side of the overall square is double the length of the side of the center square and the areas of compartments A, B, C, and D are all equal. If a baseball is thrown into the box at random, what is the probability that the baseball is found in compartment A?

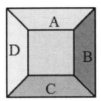

    a) $\frac{1}{4}$
    b) $\frac{2}{15}$
    c) $\frac{3}{16}$
    d) $\frac{1}{8}$

Answer: (C)
Find the ratio of the total area to the area of A.
If the total area is 1, the small square area in the middle will be $\frac{1}{4}$.

Area of A = $\frac{1-\frac{1}{4}}{4} = \frac{3}{16}$

Probability = $\frac{3}{16}$

10. A box contains red, blue and green pens. If one pen is chosen at random, the probability that a red pen will be chosen is two times the probability for a blue pen and three times the probability for a green pen. If there are 12 red pens in the box, how many pens are in the box?

    a) 20
    b) 22
    c) 24
    d) 28

Answer: (B)
Red : Blue : Green = $1 : \frac{1}{2} : \frac{1}{3}$
= 12 : 6 : 4
Total number of pens:
12 + 6 + 4 = 22

11. Linda's purse contains 4 quarters, 5 dimes, 2 nickels, and 4 pennies. If she takes out one coin at random, what is the probability that the coin is worth less than 10 cents?

Answer: $\frac{2}{5}$ or .4
If the coin is worth less than 10 cents, then the coin must be either a penny or a nickel.
Probability $= \frac{2+4}{4+5+2+4} = \frac{2}{5}$

12. Kat has some coins in her purse. Of the coins, 6 are pennies. If she randomly picks one of the coins from her purse, the probability of picking a penny is $\frac{1}{3}$. How many coins are in her purse? Ⓝ

Answer: 18
$\frac{6}{Total\ Coins} = \frac{1}{3}$
Total Coins = 18

Hard

13. 36 marbles, all of which are red, blue, or green, are placed in a bag. If a marble is picked from the bag at random, the probability of getting a red marble is $\frac{1}{4}$ and the probability of getting a blue marble is $\frac{1}{3}$. How many green marbles are in the bag?
    a) 15
    b) 12
    c) 8
    d) 5

Answer: (A)
The probability of getting green marbles: $1 - \frac{1}{4} - \frac{1}{3} = \frac{5}{12}$
$\frac{5}{12} = \frac{x}{36}$
$x = 15$

14. On a certain farm, every fifth tomato picked is rotten, and every fourth tomato picked is green. If a famer randomly picks a tomato from the farm, what is the probability that the tomato will be both green and rotten? Ⓝ
    a) $\frac{1}{8}$
    b) $\frac{1}{10}$
    c) $\frac{1}{15}$
    d) $\frac{1}{20}$

Answer: (D)
For every multiple of the LCM of 4 and 5, there will be a tomato that is both green and rotten. LCM of 4 and 5 is 20.
Probability $= \frac{1}{20}$

15. If a number is picked randomly from a set of numbers consisting of j positive numbers and k negative numbers, the probability of getting a positive number is $\frac{3}{8}$. What is the value of $\frac{j}{k}$?

Answer: $\frac{3}{5}$
The probability of picking a positive number is $\frac{3}{8}$ so the probability of picking a negative number is $\frac{5}{8}$.
$\frac{j}{k} = \frac{\frac{3}{8}}{\frac{5}{8}} = \frac{3}{5}$

VII.   LOGIC AND PATTERN

A.   SEQUENCE PATTERN

CONCEPT OVERVIEWS

Sequence and Pattern
A **sequence** is a group of objects, almost always numbers, which are in a certain order. The order can be defined by some rules, such as the following:
- **Arithmetic Sequence**: An arithmetic sequence is constructed by adding the same number to each term to get the next term. This number is called the **common difference.** If the common difference is 1, one possible sequence would be 1, 2, 3, 4... If the common difference is 3, one possible sequence would be 1, 4, 7, 10, 13....

To find the nth term in an arithmetic sequence:

$$a_n = a_1 + (n - 1) \times d$$

Where a_n is the nth term, a_1 is the first term, and d is the common difference in the sequence.

To find the sum of first n^{th} term in an arithmetic sequence:

$$S_n = \frac{n}{2} \times (a_1 + a_n)$$

Where a_n is the nth term and a_1 is the first term in the sequence.

- **Geometric Sequence**: A geometric sequence is constructed by multiplying the same number each time to get the next term. This number is called the **common ratio**. If the common ratio is 2, one possible sequence would be 2, 4, 8, 16, 32... If the common ratio is 10, one possible sequence would be 5, 50, 500, 5000....

To find the nth term in a geometric sequence:

$$a_n = a_1 \times r^{n-1}$$

Where a_n is the nth term, a_1 is the first term, and r is the common ratio in the sequence.

To find the sum of first n^{th} term in a geometric sequence:

$$S_n = \frac{a_1(r^n - 1)}{r - 1}$$

Where a_1 is the first term, and r is the common ratio in the sequence. $r \neq 1$.

To find a missing number in a sequence, figure out the rules or the pattern for the sequence and then apply the rules to find the missing number. Carefully examine at least 3 of its consecutive numbers to figure out a pattern and use additional data to verify this pattern.

In a sequence, if a pattern repeats itself every m consecutive terms, the nth term of the sequence is the same as the pth term, where p is the remainder of n divided by m. The remainder indicates the position within each cycle of the pattern and thus the value of the term.

Example: A sequence like 2, 3, 5, 7, 2, 3, 5, 7, 2, 3, 5...... repeats every 4 terms. In order to find the 2013rd term, you can find the remainder of 2013 ÷ 4 which is 1. Therefore, the number of the 2013rd term is same as the 1st term in this sequence which is 2. If the remainder is 0 that term would be equal to the last term of the cycle. Therefore, the 2012nd term of the above sequence is 7, which is the last term of the cycle of 2, 3, 5, 7.

Problem Solving Skills

Easy

1. In the sequence 1, 3, 9, x, 81, ... what is the value of x? 🚫

   a) 12
   b) 18
   c) 27
   d) 36

Answer: (C)
Examine the first few terms to figure out the pattern.
This is a geometric sequence constructed by multiplying the common ratio 3 each time to get the next term.
$9 \times 3 = 27$
$x = 27$

2. The first term of a sequence of numbers is −1. If each term after is the product of −3 and the preceding term, what is the 5th term of the sequence?

   a) 27
   b) −27
   c) −81
   d) 81

Answer: (C)
−1, 3, −9, 27, −81

k, 2k, 4k...

3. In the sequence above, k is the leading term and each successive term is 2 times the preceding term. If the sum of the first 6 terms is 315, what is the value of k?

Answer: 5
$k + 2k + 4k + 8k + 16k + 32k =$
$63k = 315$
$k = 5$

4. A student folded many paper planes of different colors in the following order: red, orange, yellow, green, blue, indigo and purple. If he finished 46 paper planes, and started with red, what color was the last paper plane?
    a) Yellow
    b) Green
    c) Blue
    d) Red

Answer: (B)
The student used 7 colors in total. Divide the number of planes he made by 7 and use the remainder to find the color of the last plane.

$46 \div 7 = 6$ with remainder 4
The color for the 4th plane is green.

5. In a sequence of numbers, the leading term is 3. Each successive term is formed by adding 2 to its preceding term and then multiplying the result by 2. What is the fifth term in the sequence?

Answer: 108
$((((((3 + 2) \times 2) + 2) \times 2) + 2) \times 2) = 108$

7, 23, 71, 215, ...

6. The leading term in the sequence above is 7, and each successive term is formed by multiplying the preceding term by x and then adding y. What is the value of y?
    a) 1
    b) 2
    c) 3
    d) 4

Answer: (B)
Use trial and error. Plug in each of the values from the answer choices.
$7 \times 3 + 2 = 23$
$23 \times 3 + 2 = 71$
$71 \times 3 + 2 = 215$
$y = 2$

1, 5, 17, t, 161, ...

7. In the sequence above, what is the value of t?
    a) 34
    b) 51
    c) 53
    d) 68

Answer: (C)
Examine the first few terms to figure out the pattern.
This is a sequence constructed by multiplying the previous term by 3 and then adding 2 to the product each time to get the next term.
$1 \times 3 + 2 = 5; 5 \times 3 + 2 = 17;$
$17 \times 3 + 2 = 53; t = 53$

$$-3, -2, -1, 0, 3, 2, 1, 0, -3, -2, -1, 0$$

8. The first twelve terms of a sequence are shown above. What is the sum of the first 95 terms?

Answer: 0
Observe that every 8 terms sum to 0.
95 ÷ 8 has a remainder 7, so the total sum of the sequence is equal to the sum of the first 7 terms.
−3 + (−2) + (−1) + 0 + 3 + 2 + 1 = 0

$$486, 162, \ldots$$

9. In the sequence above, each term after the 1st term is $\frac{1}{3}$ of the term preceding it. What is the 5th term of this sequence?

Answer: 6
The Fifth Term = $486 \times (\frac{1}{3})^4 = 6$

10. A sequence with first value of 5 is constructed by adding 7 to the term immediately preceding it. Which term in this sequence is equal to 5 + 54 × 7?
    a) The 56th term
    b) The 55th term
    c) The 54th term
    d) The 53rd term

Answer: (B)
The Value of Nth Term = 5 + (N − 1) × 7
5 + (N − 1) × 7 = 5 + 54 × 7
N − 1 = 54
N = 55

11. Find the sum of the first 20 terms of the arithmetical sequence 2, 5, 8, 11, …?
    a) 700
    b) 610
    c) 525
    d). 480

Answer: (B)
To find the sum of first n^{th} term in an arithmetic sequence, first find the 20th term:
$a_{20} = a_1 + (n − 1)d = 2 + 19 \times 3 = 59$
Then find the sum:
$S_{20} = \frac{n}{2}(a_1 + a_{20}) = \frac{20}{2} \times (2 + 59) = 610$

12. Find the sum of the first 10 terms of the geometric sequence 2, 4, 8, 16, …?
    a) 920
    b) 1024
    c) 1280
    d) 2046

Answer: (D)
To find the sum of first n^{th} term in a geometric sequence, first find the common ratio $r = \frac{4}{2} = \frac{8}{4} = 2$.
Now find the sum: $S_n = \frac{a_1(r^n - 1)}{r - 1}$
$S_{10} = \frac{2(2^{10} - 1)}{2 - 1} = 2046$

Medium

13. A total of 729 students participate in a school pep rally event. If every 30 minutes, $\frac{2}{3}$ of the students leave, after 2 hours, how many students will be still staying at the pep rally?

Answer: 9
Every 30 minutes, $\frac{1}{3}$ of the students still stay.
$729 \times \frac{1}{3}$; $729 \times (\frac{1}{3})^2$; $729 \times (\frac{1}{3})^3$
After two hours, the number of students staying:
$729 \times (\frac{1}{3})^4 = 9$

2, 7, 14, 15, 26, 29, 32, 37, 41

14. Based on the sequence of numbers above, a second sequence is generated by increasing each odd-valued term by 5 and decreasing each even-valued term by 3. What is the difference between the total sum of the elements in the original sequence and the total sum of the second sequence?
    a) 4
    b) 6
    c) 10
    d) 13

Answer: (D)
There are 5 odd-valued terms and 4 even-valued terms in this sequence.
$5 \times 5 - 4 \times 3 = 13$

7, −7, −1, ...

15. The sequence above starts with 7. Each even-numbered term is found by multiplying the previous term by −1, and each odd-numbered term is found by adding 6 to the previous term. What is the 101st term of the sequence?
    a) −7
    b) 7
    c) 1
    d) −1

Answer: (B)
Sometimes list out more items to find out the pattern.
7, −7, −1, 1, 7, −7, ...
The numbers repeat every 4 terms.
$101 \div 4 = 25$ and remainder is 1, so the value of 101th term is the same as the value of 1st term, which is 7.

0.202002000200002. . .

16. The decimal number above consists of only 2s and 0s. The first 2 is followed by one 0, the second 2 is followed by two 0s, and the third 2 is followed by three 0s. If such a pattern goes on, how many 0s are between the 105th 2 and the 108th 2?

Answer: 318
Following the pattern, find the number of 0s between the 105th 2 and the 108th 2.
$105 + 106 + 107 = 318$ zeroes

16, 10, 13, ...

17. In the sequence above, the first term is 16 and the second term is 10. Starting with the third term, each term is found by averaging the two terms before it. What is the value of the first non-integer term found in the sequence?

Answer: $\frac{23}{2}$
List out several more terms until you hit a non-integer.
16, 10, 13, $\frac{23}{2}$

Hard

2, 2, 4, 4, 4, 4, 6, 6, 6, 6, 6, 6, ...

18. The sequence above is made up of a list of positive even numbers. Each even number n appears in the sequence n times. On which term in the sequence does the number 10 first appear?

Answer: 21
The number 2 appears twice, the number 4 appears four times, and so on. The number of terms up to integer 8 appears $2 + 4 + 6 + 8 = 20$ times. The number 10 first appears in the sequence right after the last 8. $20 + 1 = 21$

19. In a sequence of numbers, each term after the first term is 2 greater than $\frac{1}{3}$ of the preceding term. If a_o is the first term and $a_o \neq 0$, which of the following represents the ratio of the first term to the second term? 🚫

a) $\frac{3a_0}{a_0 + 8}$

b) $\frac{3a_0}{a_0 + 6}$

c) $\frac{2a_0}{a_0 + 6}$

d) $\frac{a_0 + 2}{3a_0}$

Answer: (B)
1st Term = a_o,
2nd Term = $2 + \frac{1}{3} \times a_o$
Ratio = $\frac{a_0}{2 + \frac{1}{3}a_0} = \frac{3a_0}{a_0 + 6}$

B. SYMBOL FUNCTIONS

CONCEPT OVERVIEWS

Sometimes the SAT test will use strange symbols that define an invented operation.

To solve these kinds of questions, follow the formula defined in the problem and substitute any given values into the expressions given.

Problem Solving Skills

Easy

1. For all positive integer a and b, let $a \blacklozenge b$ to be defined *as* $\frac{a+b}{a-b}$. What is the value of $7 \blacklozenge 3$?

   Answer: 2.5
   Replace a with 7 and b with 3.

   $7 \blacklozenge 3 = \frac{7+3}{7-3} = 2.5$

2. For positive integers a, b, and c, let $(a \, \Omega \, b \, \Omega \, c)$ to be defined by $(a \, \Omega \, b \, \Omega \, c) = a^b - 2ac + c$. What is the value of $(2 \, \Omega \, 3 \, \Omega \, 4) = ?$
   - a) 2
   - b) 4
   - c) −4
   - d) −2

   Answer: (C)
   $(2 \, \Omega \, 3 \, \Omega \, 4) = 2^3 - 2 \times 2 \times 4 + 4 = -4$

3. If $x \clubsuit y$ is defined by the expression $x(x + y) + y(x - y)$, what is the value of $3 \clubsuit 2 = ?$
   - a) 52
   - b) 48
   - c) 20
   - d) 17

   Answer: (D)
   Substitute x with 3 and y with 2 into the given formula.
   $3 \clubsuit 2 = 3(3 + 2) + 2(3 - 2) = 17$

4. If $\heartsuit x \heartsuit$ is defined by $\heartsuit x \heartsuit = 3x - x \div 3$, then $\heartsuit 9 \heartsuit = ?$
   - a) 30
   - b) 27
   - c) 24
   - d) 6

   Answer: (C)
   Substitute x with 9.
   $\heartsuit 9 \heartsuit = 3 \times 9 - 9 \div 3 = 27 - 3 = 24$

5. For all numbers j and k, Let \$ be defined by $j\$k = j - k + 3$. What is the value of $(3\$6)\$2$?

   Answer: (B)
   Find the 3\$6 first.
   $3\$6 = 3 - 6 + 3 = 0$

a) 0
b) 1
c) 2
d) 3

0$2 = 0 − 2 + 3 = 1

Medium

6. Let $*m$ be defined as $*m = m^2 + 4$ for all values of m. If $*x = 2x^2$, which of the following could be the value of x?

   a) −2
   b) 1
   c) $\sqrt{2}$
   d) $-\sqrt{2}$

   Answer: (A)
   $*x = x^2 + 4$, $x^2 + 4 = 2x^2$
   $x^2 = 4$
   $x = \pm 2$

7. If M is a positive integer, let $*M*$ be defined as a set of all factors of M. Each of the elements in the three sets $*6*$, $*12*$, and $*15*$ can also be found in which of the following sets?

   a) $*6*$
   b) $*60*$
   c) $*72*$
   d) $*90*$

   Answer: (B)
   Looking for all the factors of 6, 12 and 15, all of which are also the factors of 60.

8. For all positive integer a, let ♥a be defined as the product of all even factors of a^2. For example, ♥6= 36 × 18 × 12 × 6 × 4 × 2. What is the value of ♥4?

   Answer: 1024
   ♥4 = 16 × 8 × 4 × 2 = 1024

9. For all numbers p and q, let $p@q$ be defined by $p@q = (p + 2)^2 \times (q − 1)^2$, what is the value of 7@5?

   a) 1,381
   b) 1,296
   c) 743
   d) 527

   Answer: (B)
   Replace p with 7 and q with 5.
   $7@5 = (7 + 2)^2 \times (5 − 1)^2 = 1296$

Hard

10. For all positive integers j and k, let $j \triangle k$ be defined as the sum of the quotient and remainder when j is divided by k. What is the result after the operation of $26\triangle3$?

Answer: 10
26 divided by 3 has a quotient 8 and a reminder 2.
$8 + 2 = 10$

11. Let <I, J> be defined as any integer greater than I but less than J, such as <−2, 4> = { −1, 0, 1, 2, 3}. Which of the following has the same elements as the intersection of <−1, 6> and <2, 8>? 🚫

    a) <−1, 3>
    b) <−3, 2>
    c) <1, 8>
    d) <2, 6>

Answer: (D)
Intersection of <−1, 6> and <2, 8>
= {0, 1, 2, 3, 4, 5} ∩ {3, 4, 5, 6, 7}
= {3, 4, 5}
The intersection has three elements.
(d) has 3 same elements {3, 4, 5}.

12. Let $\langle x \rangle$ is defined as $\langle x \rangle = x^2 + x$ for all values of x. If $\langle k \rangle = \langle k + 2 \rangle$, what is the value of k^2?

Answer: $\frac{9}{4}$
Set $\langle k \rangle = k^2 + k$ equal to $\langle x + 2 \rangle = (x + 2)^2 + x + 2$.
$k^2 + k = (k + 2)^2 + (k + 2)$
$k^2 + k = k^2 + 4k + 4 + k + 2$
$-6 = 4k \rightarrow k = -\frac{3}{2} \rightarrow k^2 = \frac{9}{4}$

C. LOGIC

CONCEPT OVERVIEWS

The statement "If *A*, then *B*" does not imply the statement "if *B*, then *A*".

Example 1: If it is snowing, then it is cold outside. However, we cannot conclude that if it is cold outside, then it is snowing.

Example 2: If a geometry shape is a square, then it is a rectangle. However we cannot say if a geometry shape is a rectangle, then it is a square.

"If A is true, then B is true" implies that **"If B is false, and then A is false"**.

Example 1: If it is snowing, then it is cold outside. We can conclude that if it is not cold outside, it must not be snowing.

Example 2: If he misses the bus then he will be late. If we know that he was not late, then we can conclude that he did not miss the bus.

Example 3: If a number is divisible by 4, then it is divisible by 2. This implies that if a number is not divisible by 2, then it is not divisible by 4.

If we know the following two statements **"If A is true, then B is true"** and **"If B is true, then C is true"**, we can conclude the following: **"If A is true, then C is true."**

Example: If John receives a grade C and above in math final exam, then he will pass math class. If he passes math class, then he can graduate from high school. This implies that if John receives a grade C and above in math final exam, then he will graduate.

One strategy to test whether a statement is true is to try special cases that may disprove the statement.

Example: Mitchell just had a cup of drink from a store that sells only soda and tea. Which of the following statements must be true?
    a) The cup of drink is tea.
    b) The cup of drink is not a coke.
    c) The cup of drink is not green tea.
    d) The cup of drink is not decaf coffee.

Solution: a) Mitchell may have had a cup of soda.   False
    b) Coke is a type of soda, and is thus a possible drink. False
    c) Green tea is a type of tea, and is thus a possible drink.   False
    d) The store did not sell coffee, so this is TRUE.
    Answer is (d).

A good problem-solving strategy is to list out all of the logical statements and check whether each choice fits the statements.

1	2	3	4

Example 1: The graph above shows four labeled colored boxes which are placed in a row. Each box is painted a different color. There is a red box next to a blue box. The green box is next to a red box and a yellow box. Which of the labeled boxes could be painted red?

    a) 1 only

    b) 2 only

    c) 3 only

    d) 2 or 3

Solution:

    According to the descriptions in the problem the red box is next to the blue box and the green box and the green box is next to the yellow box. In order from left to right, only the two configurations YGRB and BRGY can satisfy those conditions.

    Answer is (d).

Example 2: Eric sometimes reads historical fiction novels in the library. Betsy never reads mystery novels in the library.

If the two statements above are true, which of the following statements must also be true?

    I. Eric never reads mystery novels.

    II. Betsy sometimes reads historical fiction novels.

    III. Eric and Betsy never read mystery novels in the library together.

    a) I only

    b) II only

    c) III only

    d) I and III

Solution:

    Check each statement whether it is true.

    I. Eric never reads mystery novels. This is not always true because we only know Eric sometimes reads historical fiction novels.

    II. Betsy sometimes reads historical fiction novels. We are not sure about that either.

    III. Eric and Betsy never read mystery novels in the library together. This is true because we know Betsy never reads mystery novels Therefore, they never read mystery novels in the library together.

    Answer is (c).

Example 3: Some integers in set X are odd.

If the statement above is true, which of the following must also be true?

 a) If an integer is odd, it is in set X.
 b) If an integer is even, it is in set X.
 c) All integers in set X are odd.
 d) Not all integers in set X are even.

Solution:

 a) This is not necessarily true. We know that some integers that are odd are in set X, but not all odd integers.
 b) This is not necessarily true. We do not have any information about even integers.
 c) This is not necessarily true.
 d) This is true. We know some integers in set X are odd, which means that not all integers in set X are even.
 Answer is (d).

Problem Solving Skills

Easy

1. At the Essex High School, some students on the math team are also on the bowling team and none of the students on the bowling team are on the tennis team.

   Which of the following statements must be true? 🚫
    a) None of the students on the math team are also on the tennis team.
    b) More students on the math team than are on the bowling team.
    c) More students are on the bowling team than on the math team.
    d) Some of the students on the math team are not on the tennis team.

   Answer: (D)
   The students on both math and bowling teams will not be on tennis team.

    All integers in set X are negative.

2. If the statement above is true, which of the following must also be true? 🚫
    a) If an integer is negative, it is in set X.
    b) If an integer is positive, it is in set X.
    c) All integers in set X are positive.
    d) Not all integers in set X are positive.

   Answer: (D)
   If X only contains negative integers, then there are no positive integers in set X.

3. In a game, an integer is randomly picked. If the integer picked is smaller than 0, the square of that integer is shown. If the integer picked is greater than 0, the integer itself is shown. If the integer shown is 16, which of the following could have been the integer picked? Ⓝ

        I. 16

        II. –4

        III. 4

    a) I only

    b) II only

    c) III only

    d) I and II only

Answer: (D)
If 16 was picked, then 16 would have been shown. If −4 was picked, then (−4)(−4) = 16 would also have been shown. If 4 was picked, then 4 would have been shown. So only 4 could not have been picked.

4. At Old Town High School, some members of the math club are on the tennis team and no members of the tennis team are freshmen. Which of the following must also be true? Ⓝ

    a) No members of the math club are freshmen.

    b) Some members of the math club are freshmen.

    c) Some members of the math club are not freshmen.

    d) More tenth graders are on the tennis team than are on the math club.

Answer: (C)
Some students on math club also on tennis team in which there are no freshmen.

Medium

5. Helen threw a fair six sided dice 5 times. Each throw showed a different number according to the rules: Ⓝ

    The first roll was greater than 5.

    The second roll was less than 3.

    The third roll was 4.

    The fourth roll was the same as the first roll.

    The fifth roll was an even number.

Which of the following must be true?

    a) Helen could have rolled a 6 more than three times.

    b) Helen could have rolled a 5 only one time.

    c) Helen rolled more even numbers than odd numbers.

    d) Helen rolled 3 at least once.

Answer: (C)
List of results: 6, less than 3, 4, 6, even.
Only (c) could meet all the conditions.

Marble 1 is red.
Marble 2 has the same color as marble 3.
Marble 3 is blue.
Marble 4 has the same color as marble 6.
Marble 5 is not orange.
Marble 6 is orange.
Marble 7 is not the same color as marble 1.

6. If a bag contains 20 marbles that are red, orange, or blue, and the 7 marbles chosen follow the rules above, which of the following must be true? Ⓝ
    a) Only one red marble is drawn.
    b) At most two red marbles are drawn.
    c) Two red marbles are drawn.
    d) At least three blue marbles are drawn.

Answer: (B)
Marble 1 is red, and marble 5 could be either red or blue. Therefore, at most two red marbles are drawn.

Hard

7. In a certain card game, there are three types of card worth 2 points, 5 points, or 9 points. How many different combinations of these cards are possible in order to get a total of 19 points? Ⓝ
    a) One
    b) Two
    c) Three
    d) Four

Answer: (D)
There are 4 different combinations as below:
22222225, 222229, 22555, and 559

Chapter 3   Passport to Advanced Math

I.   FACTORS AND MULTIPLES

CONCEPT OVERVIEWS

Prime Number: An integer number greater than 1 that has only two positive divisors: 1 and itself.
  -   Prime numbers up to 50: 2, 3, 5, 7, 11, 13, 17, 19, 23, 29, 31, 37, 41, 43, 47

Prime Factorization: The prime factorization of an integer x is to find all the prime numbers that multiply together equal to x.

Example: 36 is equal to $2 \times 2 \times 3 \times 3$.

GCF (Greatest Common Factor) of Two Integers: the largest integer that divides exactly into both integers.

Example: GCF of 24 and 30 is 6.

Two numbers are relatively prime if their GCF is 1.

Example: 6 and 35 are relative prime with GCF 1.
          25 and 35 are not relative prime with their GCF equal to 5.

LCM (Least Common Multiple) of Two Integers: the smallest integer that is divisible by both integers. For example, LCM of 24 and 30 is 120.

We can use ladder method to figure out GCF and LCM of two integers.

GCF of 24 and 30 is $2 \times 3 = 6$ (numbers on the side)
LCM of 24 and 30 is $2 \times 3 \times 4 \times 5 = 120$ (all the numbers on the side and bottom)

Euclid's Algorithm: The GCF of two numbers does not change when you replace either number with the difference between the two numbers (the larger number minus the smaller number).

Example: The GCF of 168 and 189 is equal to the GCF of 168 and 21, (189 − 168), which is 21.
Total Number of Factors

To find the total number of unique factors of any integer, write that integer as the product of powers of the prime numbers in its **prime factorization**. For example, if an integer can be written as $x^a y^b z^c$ where x, y, z are prime numbers and a, b, c are positive integers, then the total number of unique factors it has is $(a + 1) \times (b + 1) \times (c + 1)$.

Example: How many unique factors does the number 24 have?
Solution: Since 24 is equal to $2 \times 3 \times 4$, it has a total of $(1 + 1) \times (1 + 1) \times (1 + 1)$ = 8 factors. If you list them out, they are 1, 2, 3, 4, 6, 8, 12, and 24.

Example: How many unique factors does the number 1800 have?
Solution: The number 1800 has a total 36 factors because 1800 is equal to $2^3 \times 3^2 \times 5^2$ and $(3 + 1) \times (2 + 1) \times (2 + 1) = 36$.

Problem Solving Skills

Easy

1. What is the least common multiple of 12, 16, and 28?
    a) 4
    b) 84
    c) 168
    d) 336

Answer: (D)
The least common multiple is the smallest multiple of all three numbers.
Find the multiples of 28, then find the smallest one that is divisible by 12 and 16.

2. What is the greatest common factor of 75, 125, 225?
    a) 5
    b) 9
    c) 25
    d) 35

Answer: (C)
The easiest strategy is to divide each of the numbers by each answer choice. 5, 9, and 25 are factors of all the numbers. 25 is the highest common factor of 75, 125, and 225.

3. Which of the following must be a factor of x if x is a multiple of both 9 and 12?
    a) 8
    b) 24
    c) 27
    d) 36

Answer: (D)
The LCM of 12 and 9 is 36.

4. If each cubical block has edges of length 6 inches, what is the number of such blocks needed to fill a rectangular box with inside dimensions of 30 inches by 36 inches by 42 inches?

Answer: 210
Calculate how many for each side and multiply them together.
$\frac{30}{6} \times \frac{36}{6} \times \frac{42}{6} = 5 \times 6 \times 7 = 210$

5. A supermarket has brand A juice smoothie on sale every 7 days and has brand B juice smoothie on sale every 4 days. Within a year (365 days), how many times does this supermarket have both brands of juice smoothie on sale on the same day?
    a) 9
    b) 12
    c) 13
    d) 24

Answer: (C)
The LCM of 7 and 4 is 28.
Every 28 days, A and B will be on sale on the same day.
$\frac{365}{28} = 13.035$

6. If x is the greatest prime factor of 34 and y is the greatest prime factor of 49, what is the value of $x - y$?
    a) 8
    b) 9
    c) 10
    d) 15

Answer: (C)
The greatest prime factor of 34 is 17 and the greatest prime factor of 49 is 7.
$x - y = 17 - 7 = 10$

7. Two numbers are relatively prime if their GCF is 1. Which of the following pairs of numbers are relatively prime?
    a) 22, 33
    b) 17, 34
    c) 35, 49
    d) 21, 64

Answer: (D)
a) GCF = 11
b) GCF = 17
c) GCF = 7
d) GCF = 1

Medium

8. In a toy factory production line, every 10th toy has their electronic parts checked and every 5th toy will have their safety features checked. In the first 150 toys, what is the probability that a toy will have both its electronic parts and safety features checked?

Answer: $\frac{1}{10}$
The LCM of 10 and 5 is 10.
The every 10th toy will have both of their electronic parts and safety features checked.
There are 15 such toys (150 divided by 10).
$\frac{15}{150} = \frac{1}{10}$

9. If x, y, and z are all integers greater than 1 and $xy = 14$ and $yz = 21$, which of the following must be true?
    a) $z > x > y$
    b) $y > z > x$
    c) $y > x > z$
    d) $x > z > y$

Answer: (B)
The only common factor of 14 and 21 other than 1 is 7, so $y = 7$.
$y = 7$
$x = \frac{14}{7} = 2$
$z = \frac{21}{7} = 3$

10. If x, y and z are three different prime numbers greater than 2 and $m = x \times y \times z$, how many positive factors, including 1 and m itself, does m have? Ⓢ
    a) 9
    b) 8
    c) 6
    d) 4

Answer: (B)
$m = x \times y \times z = x^1 \times y^1 \times z^1$
The total number of factors including 1 and m is $(1 + 1) \times (1 + 1) \times (1 + 1) = 8$.

11. If the area of a rectangle is 77 and its length and width are integers, which of the following could be the perimeter of the rectangle?
    a) 36
    b) 37
    c) 38
    d) 39

Answer: (A)
The length and width of the rectangle must be factors of 77. There are only two ways to factor 77 into 7×11 and 1×77.
$77 = 7 \times 11$
Perimeter $= 2 (7 + 11) = 36$ (a)
$77 = 1 \times 77$
Perimeter $= 2(1 + 77) = 156$ (not among the options)

Hard

12. How many positive factors does the number 24 have?
    a) 4
    b) 5
    c) 7
    d) 8

Answer: (D)
$24 = 2^3 \times 3^1$
Number of positive factors:
$(3 + 1) \times (1 + 1) = 8$

13. What is the greatest common factor of 225, 270, and 540?
    a) 145
    b) 120
    c) 90
    d) 45

Answer: (D)
Use prime factorization to rewrite 225, 270, and 540 as follows.
$225 = 1 \times 3^2 \times 5^2$
$270 = 1 \times 2 \times 3^3 \times 5$
$540 = 1 \times 2^2 \times 3^3 \times 5$
Therefore, the GCF of three numbers is $1 \times 3^2 \times 5 = 45$.

II. Operations on Fractions

Concept Overviews

A Fraction is a number of the form $\frac{a}{b}$ where a and b are integers and b is not a zero. A fraction can be expressed as a terminating or repeating decimal.

- When you multiply the top and bottom of a fraction by the same amount, it doesn't change its value, such as $\frac{2}{5} = \frac{2 \times 3}{5 \times 3} = \frac{6}{15}$.

- To add two fractions with different denominators, you must first convert both fractions to a **common denominator**, a common multiple of the two denominators. Then convert both fractions to equivalent fractions with the common denominator. Finally, add the numerators and keep the common denominator.

   Example: Add the two fractions $\frac{2}{3}$ and $\frac{-2}{5}$.
   Solution: Find the common denominator of 3 and 5. Use the common Denominator 15:
   $$\frac{2}{3} + \left(\frac{-2}{5}\right) = \left(\frac{2}{3}\right)\left(\frac{5}{5}\right) + \left(\frac{-2}{5}\right)\left(\frac{3}{3}\right) = \frac{10 - 6}{15} = \frac{4}{15}$$

- To multiply two fractions, the resulting numerator is the product of the two numerators and the resulting denominator is the product of the two denominators.

   Example: $\frac{2}{5}\left(\frac{-3}{7}\right) = \frac{2 \times (-3)}{5 \times 7} = \frac{-6}{35} - \frac{6}{35}$

- To divide one fraction by another, first **invert** the second fraction (find it's **reciprocal**), then multiply the first fraction by the inverted fraction.

   Example: $\frac{3}{5} \div \frac{6}{7} = \frac{3}{5} \times \frac{7}{6} = \frac{3 \times 7}{5 \times 6} = \frac{21}{30} = \frac{7}{10}$

- To simplify a fraction: Find the greatest common factor of the numerator and denominator and divide both numerator and denominator by the GCF.

   Example: $\frac{15}{20} = \frac{3 \times 5}{4 \times 5} = \frac{3}{4}$

- **Cross multiplying** is a way to solve an equation that involves a variable as part of two equal fractions.

   Example: If $\frac{9}{x} = \frac{3}{5}$, what is the value of x?
   Solution: Applying cross multiplying: $x \times 3 = 9 \times 5$
   $$x = \frac{45}{3} = 15$$

Problem Solving Skills

Easy

1. An hour-long workshop included 10 minutes of self-studies. What fraction of the hour-long workshop were self-studies?

   Answer: $\frac{1}{6}$

   $\frac{10}{60} = \frac{1}{6}$

2. If a movie is 120 minutes long, what fraction of the movie has been completed 20 minutes after it begins? 🚫

   a) $\frac{1}{5}$
   b) $\frac{1}{6}$
   c) $\frac{1}{4}$
   d) $\frac{1}{3}$

   Answer: (B)

   $\frac{20}{120} = \frac{1}{6}$

3. Which of the following numbers is between 1 and 2?

   a) $\frac{8}{9}$
   b) $\frac{7}{3}$
   c) $\frac{10}{4}$
   d) $\frac{11}{9}$

   Answer: (D)

   $1 < \frac{11}{9} < 2$

4. In a poll, 25 people supported the current city mayor, 14 people were against him, and 6 people had no opinion. What fraction of those polled supported the city mayor?

   Answer: $\frac{5}{9}$

   $\frac{Part}{Whole} = \frac{25}{25 + 14 + 6} = \frac{25}{45} = \frac{5}{9}$

5. Every Monday through Friday after school, John spends 1.5 hours playing tennis with his school team and 1.5 hours practicing violin for the school orchestra. What fraction of the total number of hours in these five days did he spend on his after school activities?

   a) $\frac{1}{5}$
   b) $\frac{1}{6}$
   c) $\frac{1}{8}$
   d) $\frac{1}{9}$

   Answer: (C)

   $\frac{Part}{Whole} = \frac{1.5 + 1.5}{24} = \frac{3}{24} = \frac{1}{8}$

6. If $\frac{20}{x} = \frac{y}{14}$, what is the value of xy?
   a) 300
   b) 280
   c) 200
   d) 210

Answer: (B)
Cross multiply: 20 × 14 = xy =
280

7. If $\frac{6}{q} = \frac{3}{7}$, what is the value of q?
   a) 10
   b) 11
   c) 12
   d) 14

Answer: (D)
Cross multiply.
6 × 7 = 3 × q → q = 14

Medium

8. An integer is divided by 3 more than itself. If the fraction is equal to $\frac{5}{6}$, what is the value of this integer?
   a) 12
   b) 15
   c) 18
   d) 20

Answer: (B)
$\frac{x}{x+3} = \frac{5}{6}$
6x = 5(x + 3)   (Cross multiply)
x = 15

9. Sean needs to finish reading his book in four days. He read $\frac{1}{3}$ of the book on the first day, $\frac{1}{4}$ of the book on the second day, $\frac{1}{5}$ of the book on the third day. If he has 13 pages to finish on the fourth day, how many pages are there in the book?
   a) 40
   b) 42
   c) 50
   d) 60

Answer: (D)
Find out the last portion of pages.
The last portion of pages: $1 - \frac{1}{3}$
$-\frac{1}{4} - \frac{1}{5} = \frac{13}{60} = \frac{13}{Total}$,
Total Number of Pages = 60

10. If $x = -\frac{1}{2}$, what is the value of $\frac{1}{x} - \frac{1}{x+1}$? 🚫
    a) 2
    b) –2
    c) 4
    d) –4

Answer: (D)
$\frac{1}{-\frac{1}{2}} - \frac{1}{-\frac{1}{2}+1} = -2 - 2 = -4$

Hard

11. Monday morning, Johnson starts out with a certain amount of money that he plans to spend throughout the week. Every morning after that, he spends exactly $\frac{1}{2}$ the amount he has left. 6 days later, on Sunday morning, he finds that he has $5 left. How many dollars did Johnson originally have in Monday morning?

    a) 320
    b) 300
    c) 280
    d) 260

    Answer: (A)
    Let's say Johnson has $x on Monday. On Sunday, he will have:$(\frac{1}{2} \times \frac{1}{2} \times \frac{1}{2} \times \frac{1}{2} \times \frac{1}{2})x$ dollars left.
    $\frac{x}{2^6} = 5$
    $x = 5 \times 2^6 = 320$ *dollars*

12. One-fourth of a bottle originally contains grape juice. It is then filled to the top with a fruit juice mix with equal amounts of orange, grape, and apple juices. What fraction of the final mixture is grape juice?

    a) $\frac{2}{3}$
    b) $\frac{1}{2}$
    c) $\frac{1}{3}$
    d) $\frac{1}{4}$

    Answer: (B)
    $\frac{1}{4}$ *of the bottle is originally grape juice. Then $\frac{3}{4}$ of the bottle is filled with a mixture that is $\frac{1}{3}$ grape juice. The fraction that is grape juice is equal to:*
    $$\frac{Amount\ of\ Grape\ Juice}{Amount\ of\ All\ Juice} = \frac{\frac{1}{4} + \frac{3}{4}(\frac{1}{3})}{1} = \frac{1}{2}$$

III. Algebraic Factoring

Concept Overviews

Factoring out Common Factors

A **common factor** is a non-negative number other than 1 (or an expression) that can divide into every term. For instance, the common factors of $2x^5, 4x^4, 6x^2, 2x$ are $2, x,$ and $2x$.

Example: Factor $2x^2 + 14x$.
Solution: Take out the common factors $2x$.
$$2x^2 + 14x = 2x(x + 7)$$

Example: Factor $3x^2y + 9xy^2 + 6xy$.
Solution: Take out the common factors $3xy$.
$$3x^2y + 9xy^2 + 6xy = 3xy(x + 3y + 2)$$

Factoring by Grouping

Sometimes not all the terms in an expression have a common factor but we can still do some factoring. One strategy of factoring is to factor "in pairs". To factor "in pairs," split the expression into two pairs of terms, and then factor the pairs separately.

Example: Factor $12x^2 + 3x + 4xy + y$.
Solution: First, group in pairs.
$$(12x^2 + 3x) + (4xy + y)$$
Then, factor out the common factor from each pair.
$$(12x^2 + 3x) + (4xy + y) = 3x(4x + 1) + y(4x + 1) = (4x + 1)(3x + y)$$

Factoring by the Difference of Two Squares

An expression which has one square subtracted by another square can be factored into the sum of the two variables multiplied by the difference of the two variables.

$$x^2 - y^2 = (x + y)(x - y)$$

Example: Factor $x^2 - 1$.
Solution: $x^2 - 1 = x^2 - 1^2 = (x + 1)(x - 1)$.

Factoring Trinomials

To factor $x^2 + bx + c$ where b and c are integers:
First, by using FOIL we know that $(x + m)(x + n) = x^2 + (m + n)x + mn$.
Therefore, by using backwards logic, in order to factorize $x^2 + bx + c$, numbers m and n must be found to satisfy the equations $m + n = b$ and $mn = c$.

To factor $ax^2 + bx + c$ where a, b and c are integers and $a \neq 1$:

a) Set $ax^2 + bx + c$ equal to $a(x + \frac{d_1}{a})(x + \frac{d_2}{a})$ where d_1 and d_2 are two numbers whose product is $a \times c$ and whose sum is b.

b) Factor a into two numbers, a_1 and a_2, so that $a_1 \times \frac{d_1}{a}$ and $a_2 \times \frac{d_2}{a}$ are two integers.

Example: Factor $4x^2 - 4x - 3$.

Solution: First, find two numbers whose product is –12 and sum is –4. The two numbers are –6 and 2.

$$4x^2 - 4x - 3 = 4(x + \frac{2}{4})(x - \frac{6}{4}) \rightarrow \text{Simplify into } 4(x + \frac{1}{2})(x - \frac{3}{2}).$$

$$4\left(x + \frac{1}{2}\right)\left(x - \frac{3}{2}\right) = \left(2x + 2 \times \frac{1}{2}\right)\left(2x - 2 \times \frac{3}{2}\right) = (2x + 1)(2x - 3)$$

Perfect Square of Trinomial

A **trinomial** is an expression with three unlike terms such as $x^2 + 2x + 3$. **Perfect square formulas** are two of the most important formulas in algebra that are worth remembering:

$$x^2 + 2xy + y^2 = (x + y)^2$$
$$x^2 - 2xy + y^2 = (x - y)^2$$

A quadratic equation can be solved with by creating a perfect square using the perfect square formula. A perfect square has the form $a^2 + 2ab + b^2$ where a and b can be any algebraic expression or integer.

Example: Solve for x if $x^2 - 2x - 2 = 0$.

Solution: $x^2 - 2x - 2 = 0$

$\quad\quad\quad x^2 - 2x = 2$ add 1 to both sides to make a perfect square on the left

$\quad\quad\quad x^2 - 2x + 1 = 2 + 1$

$\quad\quad\quad (x - 1)^2 = 3$ take the square root on both sides

$\quad\quad\quad x - 1 = \pm\sqrt{3}$

$\quad\quad\quad x = 1 \pm \sqrt{3}$

Problem Solving Skills

Easy

1. If $c = 5$, which of the following is the equivalent to $cx^2 + cx + c$?
   a) $(5x^3 + 5)$
   b) $5(x + 1)^2$
   c) $(x^2 + 1)$
   d) $5(x^2 + x + 1)$

   Answer: (D)
   Replace c with the value 5.
   $5x^2 + 5x + 5 = 5(x^2 + x + 1)$

2. Which of the following is a factor of $x^2 + x - 20$?
   a) $x + 4$
   b) $x - 5$
   c) $x - 4$
   d) $x + 6$

   Answer: (C)
   $x^2 + x - 20 = (x + 5)(x - 4) = 0$

3. If $xy = 5$ and $x - y = 3$, then $x^2y - xy^2 =$?
   a) 3
   b) 5
   c) 10
   d) 15

   Answer: (D)
   Factor out the common factors.
   $x^2y - xy^2 = xy(x - y) = 5 \times 3 = 15$

4. If $x^2 - y^2 = 15$, and $x - y = 3$, what is the value of $x + y$?
   a) 1
   b) 3
   c) 5
   d) 10

   Answer: (C)
   $x^2 - y^2 = (x - y)(x + y)$
   $3(x + y) = 15$
   $x + y = 5$

5. Which of the following is the greatest common factor of $15x^3y^5$ and $27x^2y^4z$?
   a) $3xyz$
   b) $3x^2y^3$
   c) $3x^2y^4$
   d) $5x^2y^3$

   Answer: (C)
   Find the GCF of 15 and 27, which is 3. Find the GCF of two like variables, always take the smallest power.
   Therefore, the answer is $3x^2y^4$.

6. Which of the following is a factor of $2x^2 + 5x - 12$?
   a) $2x - 3$
   b) $2x - 4$
   c) $x - 4$
   d) $x - 6$

   Answer (a)
   First, find two numbers whose product is –24 and sum is 5. These two numbers are –3 and 8.
   $2x^2 + 5x - 12 = 2(x + \frac{8}{2})(x - \frac{3}{2})$
   $\rightarrow 2(x + 4)(x - \frac{3}{2})$
   $= (x + 4)\left(2x - 2 \times \frac{3}{2}\right)$
   $= (x + 4)(2x - 3)$

Medium

7. If x and y are positive integers and $x^2 - y^2 = 5$, what is the value of x?
   a) 1
   b) 2
   c) 3
   d) 4

   Answer: (C)
   $x^2 - y^2 = (x - y)(x + y) = 5$
   $5 = 1 \times 5$
   $x - y = 1$
   $x + y = 5$
   $2x = 6$
   $x = 3$

8. If $x^2 + y^2 = 128$ and $xy = 36$, find the value of $(x - y)^2 =$?
   a) 56
   b) 92
   c) 108
   d) 200

   Answer: (A)
   $(x - y)^2 = x^2 + y^2 - 2xy$
   $128 - 2 \times 36 = 56$

9. If $x^2 - y^2 = 55$ and $x + y = 11$, find the value of y.
   a) 1
   b) 3
   c) 5
   d) 7

   Answer: (B)
   $x^2 - y^2 = (x - y)(x + y)$
   $55 = (x - y) \times 11$
   $x - y = 5$
   $x + y = 11$
   $y = 3$

10. Which of the following is the expression $x^2 + 3xy + 5x^3 + 15x^2y$ in fully factored form?
    a) $xy(1 + 5x)(x + 3)$
    b) $(x + 5x^2)(x + 3y)$
    c) $x(1 + 5x)(x + 3y)$
    d) $(1 + 5x)(x + 3y)$

    Answer: (C)
    $x^2 + 3xy + 5x^3 + 15x^2y$
    $= x(x + 3y) + 5x^2(x + 3y)$
    $= (x + 5x^2)(x + 3y)$
    $= x(1 + 5x)(x + 3y)$

Hard

11. Which of the following could be the factor of $4x^4 - 5x^2 + 1$?
    a) $x^2 + 1$
    b) $4x - 1$
    c) $4x^2 + 1$
    d) $2x - 1$

    Answer: (D)
    $4x^4 - 5x^2 + 1$
    $= (x^2 - 1)(4x^2 - 1)$
    $= (x + 1)(x - 1)(2x + 1)(2x - 1)$

12. If $2x + 1 = y$, then $6x + 4 =$?
    a) $y + 3$
    b) $3y + 3$
    c) $3y + 1$
    d) $2y + 3$

    Answer: (C)
    $6x + 4 = 3(2x + 1) + 1 = 3y + 1$

13.   Solve for x if $x^2 - 4x - 1 = 0$.

    a) $x = \pm\sqrt{5}$

    b) $x = 2 \pm \sqrt{5}$

    c) $x = \pm\sqrt{3}$

    d) $x = 2 \pm \sqrt{3}$

Answer: (B)

$x^2 - 4x - 1 = 0$

$x^2 - 4x = 1$

Add 4 to both sides to make a perfect square on the left.

$x^2 - 4x + 4 = 1 + 4$

$(x - 2)^2 = 5$

Take the square root on both sides

$x - 2 = \pm\sqrt{5}$

$x = 2 \pm \sqrt{5}$

IV. FUNCTIONS

Concept Overviews

Functions

A function is a set of data that has a single output for each input. Functions describe the relationship between an input and its output.

Here are some of the common words associated with input and output:
- **Input:**
    - x-value
    - **independent variable**
    - **domain** – the possible value(s) of the function's input
    - For a real function, input values could be restricted because of the nature of the function itself. For instance, x cannot be equal to zero when $f(x) = \frac{1}{x}$ because $f(x)$ would become undefined. Apply the following rules when checking possible values of x:
      1) The denominator cannot be zero.
      2) Values inside a square root or an even radical must be nonnegative.

      Example 1: What value(s) of x are not possible for the function $f(x) = \frac{2}{x-3}$?
      Answer: Apply rule 1), the denominator cannot be zero; therefore, x cannot be 3.

      Example 2: What are the possible values of x when the function $f(x) = \sqrt{x+3}$?
      Answer: Apply rule 2), the values inside a square root must be nonnegative.
      $$x + 3 \geq 0$$
      $$x \geq -3$$
      x could be any number greater than or equal to -3.

- **Output:**
    - y-value
    - **dependent variable**
    - **range** – the possible value(s) that the function's output can take on

      Example: Determine the domain and range of the function $y = x^2$
      Answer: Domain: all real numbers
      Range: all numbers greater than or equal to 0

Graphs of Functions
- Every point (x, y) on the graph of $y = f(x)$ satisfies $y = f(x)$.
- **Vertical Line Test:** A test to determine whether the graph is a graph of a function. If any vertical line intersects the graph at more than one point, then the graph is not a graph of a function.

Domain: All possible inputs to a function (otherwise known as the independent variable or, frequently, the x variable).

For a real function,
- The value inside a square root must be greater or equal to zero.
- Denominators CANNOT be zero.

Range: All possible outputs of a function (otherwise known as the dependent variable or, frequently, $f(x)$ or y). Be careful of square root functions and absolute value functions.

Examples: Find the domain and range for each of the following functions:

    a) $f(x) = \frac{5}{x-3}$

       Domain: $\{x \mid -\infty < x < 3 \ \cup \ 3 < x < \infty\}$

       Range: all real numbers

    b) $f(x) = \sqrt{16 - x^2}$

       $16 - x^2 \geq 0$

       $x^2 - 16 \leq 0$

       $(x - 4)(x + 4) \leq 0$

       $-4 \leq x \leq 4$

       Domain: $\{x \mid -4 \leq x \leq 4\}$

       Range: $0 \leq f(x) \leq 4$

    c) $f(x) = \frac{\sqrt{x-5}}{x-12}$

       $x - 5 \geq 0$

       $x \geq 5$ and $x \neq 12$

       Domain: $\{x \mid 5 \leq x < 12 \ \cup \ 12 < x < \infty\}$

       Range: all real numbers

    d) $f(x) = 3|x - 4| - 2$

       Domain: all real numbers

       Range: $f(x) \geq -2$

Function Properties: For two functions f and g,

$$(f + g)(x) = f(x) + g(x)$$
$$(f - g)(x) = f(x) - g(x)$$
$$(f \cdot g)(x) = f(x) \times g(x)$$
$$\frac{f}{g}(x) = \frac{f(x)}{g(x)} \quad \text{where } g(x) \neq 0$$
$$(f \circ g)(x) = f(g(x))$$

Examples:

If $f(x) = x^2 - 4$ and $g(x) = x + 2$, evaluate the following:

    a. $(f + g)(x)$
        Solution: $(f + g)(x) = x^2 - 4 + x + 2 = x^2 + x - 2$

    b. $(f - g)(x)$
        Solution: $(f - g)(x) = x^2 - 4 - x - 2 = x^2 - x - 6$

    c. $(f \cdot g)(x)$
        Solution: $(f \cdot g)(x) = (x^2 - 4)(x + 2) = x^3 - 4x + 2x^2 - 8$
                                    $= x^3 + 2x^2 - 4x - 8$

    d. $\left(\dfrac{f}{g}\right)(x)$
        Solution: $\left(\dfrac{f}{g}\right)(x) = \dfrac{x^2-4}{x+2} = x - 2$

Composition of Functions
When the results of a function $g(x)$ are plugged into a function $f(x)$ to create a new function, the result is called the composition of $f(x)$ and $g(x)$. The notation used for the composition of functions is

$$(f \circ g)(x) = f(g(x))$$

Example: If $f(x) = x^2 - 4$ and $g(x) = x + 2$, evaluate $(f \circ g)(x)$.
Solution: $(f \circ g)(x) = f(g(x)) = (x + 2)^2 - 4 = x^2 + 4x + 4 - 4 = x^2 + 4x$

Graph Translations
A **translation** of a graph moves the graph horizontally or vertically. If $y = f(x)$ is a graph on a xy-coordinate system and c is a positive constant number, then

- $y = f(x) + c$ will shift the graph of $y = f(x)$ up c units.
- $y = f(x) - c$ will shift the graph of $y = f(x)$ down c units.
- $y = f(x - c)$ will shift the graph of $y = f(x)$ to the right c units.
- $y = f(x + c)$ will shift the graph of $y = f(x)$ to the left c units.

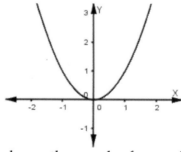

Example: If the figure above shows the graph of a quadratic function $f(x)$, then what would the graphs of $f(x + 1)$, $f(x - 1)$, $f(x) + 1$, and $f(x) - 1$ look like?
Answer: $f(x + 1)$ shows the graph shifted to the left 1 unit.

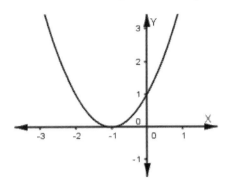

f(x − 1) shows the graph shifted to the right 1 unit.

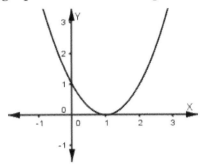

f(x) + 1 shows the graph shifted up 1 unit.

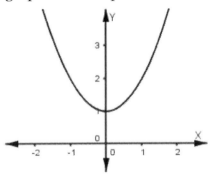

f(x) − 1 shows the graph shifted down 1 unit.

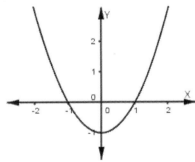

Graph Reflections
The **reflection** of a graph looks like a mirror image. The **line of reflection** (the **line of symmetry**) is line across which the graph is reflected. The part of the graph that intersects the line of reflection will stay the same.

If $y = f(x)$ is a graph on a *xy*-coordinate system, then:

- $y = -f(x)$ will show $y = f(x)$ reflected about the *x-axis*, that is, for every point (x, y) will be replaced with a new point at $(x, -y)$.
- $y = f(-x)$ will show $y = f(x)$ reflected about the *y-axis*, that is, for every point (x, y) will be replaced with a new point at $(-x, y)$.
- $y = -f(-x)$ will show $y = f(x)$ reflected about the origin, that is, every point (x, y) will be replaced with a new point at $(-x, -y)$.

If a graph is **symmetric** across a line *l*, then if you fold an image of the graph at line *l*, the two parts of the graph will match up perfectly.

Example 1: Sketch a graph that is symmetric about the *x*-axis.
Answer: If a graph is symmetric about the *x*-axis, then for a point (x, y), there will also be a point $(x, -y)$ on the graph.

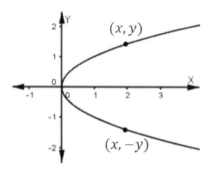

Example 2: Sketch a graph that is symmetric about the *y*-axis.
Answer: If a graph is symmetric about the *y*-axis, then for a point (x, y), there will also be a point $(-x, y)$ on the graph.

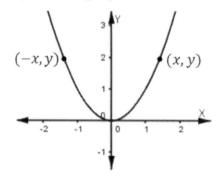

Example 3: Sketch a graph that is symmetric about the origin.
Answer: If a graph is reflected (symmetric) about the origin, then for a point of (x, y), there will also be a point $(-x, -y)$ on the graph.

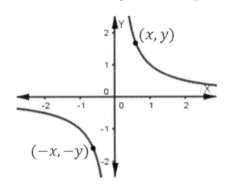

Problem Solving Skills

Easy

x	-1	3	j
$f(x)$	1	j	k

1. In the table above, if $f(x) = 3x + 4$, what is the value of k?

    a) 19
    b) 25
    c) 37
    d) 43

Answer: (D)
Plug x = 3 into the function.
y = 3 × 3 + 4 = 13 = j
When x = j = 13,
y = 3 × 13 + 4 = 43 = k

2. If $f(x) = \frac{x+3}{x}$ and $g(x) = x^2 - 10$, what is the difference between $f(x)$ and $g(x)$ when $x = 3$?

Answer: 3
Substitute 3 for x in both functions. The difference between f(3) and g(3) is f(3) – g(3).
$\frac{3+3}{3} - [(3)^2 - 10] = 2 - (-1) = 3$

3. If $f(x) = 2x - 1$ and $g(x) = \sqrt{x^2 - 8}$, what is the value of $f(g(3))$?

Answer: 1
$g(3) = \sqrt{3^2 - 8} = \sqrt{1} = 1$
$f(g(3)) = f(1) = 2(1) - 1 = 1$

4. The number of water lilies in a pond has doubled every four years since time $t = 0$. This relation is given by $y = (x) \times 2^{\frac{t}{4}}$, where t is in number of years, y is the number of water lilies in the pond at time t, and x is the original number of water lilies. If there were 600 water lilies in this pond 8 years after $t = 0$, then what was the original number of water lilies?

Answer: 150
Plug in t = 8 and y = 600 in the function.
600 = (x) × 2^(8/4) = x × 2² = 4x
x = 150

5. Which of the following is a graph of a function?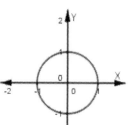

    a)

    b)

    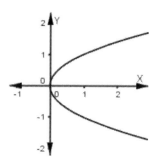

    c)

    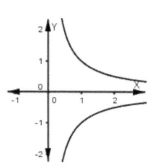

    d)

    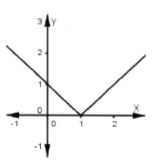

Answer: (D)
Apply Vertical Line Test.
A function has at most one
intersection with any vertical line.

6. The amount of money A, in dollars, earned from a school fundraiser by selling x cookies is given by $A(x) = 1.5x - 80$. How many cookies must the event sell in order to raise 220 dollars?

Answer: 200
Set A(x) equal to 220.
$1.5x - 80 = 220$
$x = 200$

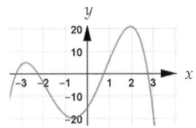

7. The figure above shows the graph of $y = f(x)$. For what value of x in this interval does the function f have its highest value between $x = -3$ to $x = 3$?
    a) –1
    b) 0
    c) 1
    d) 2

Answer: (D)
Maximum value is the value of y at the highest point, which occurs when x = 2.

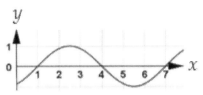

8. According to the graph above of the function f, what are the values of x where $f(x)$ is negative?
    a) $1 < x < 4$
    b) $0 < x < 1$ or $4 < x < 7$
    c) $x < 1$ or $x > 7$
    d) $1 < x < 4$ or $7 < x$

Answer: (B)
There are two regions which have negative values of f(x), which are 0 < x < 1 and 4 < x < 7.

9. If $g(x) = 5x - 10$, then at what value of x does the graph of $g(x)$ cross the x-axis?
    a) – 6
    b) –3
    c) 0
    d) 2

Answer: (D)
The value of x where g(x) crosses the x-axis is the value of x where g(x) is equal to 0.
0 = 5x – 10
x = 2

$$f(x) = \sqrt{x^2 - 1}$$

10. Which of the following values of x makes $f(x)$ undefined?
    a) −2
    b) 0
    c) 2
    d) 1

Answer: (B)
The value under the square root must be greater than or equal to zero.

11. The domain of the function $y = \frac{x-2}{(x-1)(x+3)}$ consists of all real numbers except?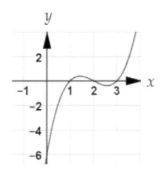
    a) $x \neq 1$
    b) $x \neq 2$
    c) $x \neq 1$, $x \neq 2$, and $x \neq -3$
    d) $x \neq 1$ and $x \neq -3$

Answer: (D)
This function is defined everywhere except when the denominator is equal to zero.

Medium

12. The graph of $y = f(x)$ is shown above. If $f(3) = a$, which of the following could be the value of $f(a)$?
    a) -2
    b) -4
    c) -6
    d) 2

Answer: (C)
As seen from the graph above, $f(3) = 0$, hence $a = 0$.
$f(a) = f(0) = -6$ (from graph above)

13. At what value(s) of x does the function $f(x) = x^2 - 9$ cross the x-axis?
    a) 0 only
    b) 3 only
    c) -3 only
    d) -3 and 3

Answer: (D)
"$f(x)$ crosses the x-axis" means $f(x) = 0$.
$x^2 - 9 = 0$, $x = \pm 3$

x	0	1	2	4
$f(x)$	-5	-3	-1	3

14. The table above shows input values as x and the output values of the linear function $f(x)$. Which of the following is the expression for $f(x)$?
    a) $f(x) = \frac{1}{2}x - 5$
    b) $f(x) = -\frac{1}{2}x - 5$
    c) $f(x) = 2x - 5$
    d) $f(x) = -2x - 5$

Answer: (C)
$f(x) - y_0 = m(x - x_0)$
m (the slope) $= \frac{-3 - (-5)}{1 - 0} = 2$
$f(x) + 5 = 2(x - 0)$
$f(x) = 2x - 5$

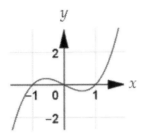

15. The figure above shows the graph of $y = f(x)$. If the function g is defined by $g(x) = f\left(\frac{x}{3}\right) - 2$, what is the value of $g(3)$?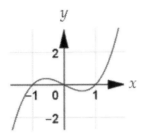
    a) −2
    b) −1
    c) 0
    d) 1

Answer: (A)
$g(3) = f(\frac{3}{3}) - 2 = f(1) - 2$
From the graph above, $f(1) = 0$
$g(3) = 0 - 2 = -2$

16. If $f(x) = x^2 - 1$ and $g(x) = \frac{1}{x}$, write the expression $f(g(x))$ in terms of x.
    a) $\frac{(1+x)(1-x)}{x^2}$
    b) $\frac{(1+x)}{x^2}$
    c) $\frac{(1-x)}{x^2}$
    d) $\frac{1}{x^2}$

Answer: (A)
$f(g(x)) = \left(\frac{1}{x}\right)^2 - 1$
$= \frac{1-x^2}{x^2}$
$= \frac{(1+x)(1-x)}{x^2}$

17. If $f(x) = x + 7$ and $f(g(2)) = 3$, which of the following functions could be $g(x)$?
    a) $x - 6$
    b) $x + 6$
    c) $3x - 1$
    d) $2x - 1$

Answer: (A)
$f(g(2)) = g(2) + 7 = 3$
$g(2) = -4$
Only (a) satisfies this condition.

18. The monthly cost of renting an apartment increases every year by 5%. John paid $600 per month this year on his rental. What is the monthly cost for John's rental n years from now?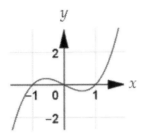
    a) 600×0.05^n
    b) $600 \times 1.05 \times n$
    c) 600×1.05^n
    d) $600^n \times 1.05$

Answer: (C)
Increasing every year by 5% is to multiply $(1 + \frac{5}{100})$ for each additional year.
$C(n) = (1.05)^n \times 600$
$= 600 \times (1.05)^n$

Hard

19. If $f\left(\frac{3x}{x-4}\right) = x^2 + x + 1$, what is the value of $f(5)$?
    a) 18
    b) 55
    c) 100
    d) 111

Answer: (D)
$\frac{3x}{x-4} = 5 \rightarrow x = 10$
$f\left(\frac{3x}{x-4}\right) = f(5) = x^2 + x + 1$
$= 100 + 10 + 1$
$= 111$

Questions 20 − 21 refer to the following information:
Boyle's law says that when all other factors are constant, the pressure of a gas decreases as the volume of that gas increases and vice versa. Therefore, the relationship of the pressure and volume of a gas, according to Boyle's law, is inversely proportional when the temperature remains unchanged.

20. According to Boyle's law, which of the following graphs represents the relationship between the pressure and volume of a gas if temperature is constant?

a)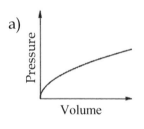

b)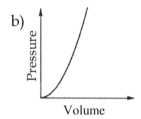

c)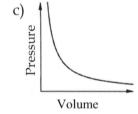

d)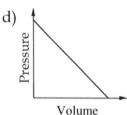

Answer: (C)
The relationship of the pressure and the volume of a gas is inversely proportional.
Graph c) represents the inversely proportional relationship: $PV = k$.

21. Assume that a gas has a volume of 20 liters and a pressure of 5 atmospheres initially. After some force is applied, the pressure becomes 8 atmospheres. According to Boyle's law, what is the final volume, in liters, of this gas? (Atmosphere (atm) is a unit of pressure.)
    a) 24.5
    b) 18.5
    c) 15.5
    d) 12.5

Answer: (D)
As the pressure increases, the volume of the gas decreases proportionately.
$P_1V_1 = P_2V_2$
$5 \times 20 = 8 \times V_2$
$V_2 = 12.5 \ liters$

Questions 22 − 23 refer to the following information:
A new machine in a manufacturing factory is depreciated approximately 10% for the first 5 years and 5% for the next 10 years. If this machine costs $10,000 brand new, the following equations are used to model its value for the first 15 years:

$$\begin{cases} V_t = \$10{,}000 \times r_1^t & \text{when } 0 < t \le 5 \\ V_t = V_5 \times r_2^{t-5} & \text{when } 5 < t \le 15 \end{cases}$$

V_t is the value of the machine at time t, the number of years after purchasing.

22. What is the value of $r_1 + r_2$?
    a) 1.55
    b) 1.76
    c) 1.85
    d) 1.98

Answer: (C)
The machine depreciates 10% each year for the first 5 years:
$V_t = 10{,}000 \times (1 - 0.1)^t$
$r_1 = 0.9$
The machine depreciates 5% each year for the next 10 years:
$V_t = V_5 \times (1 - 0.05)^{t-5}$
$r_2 = 0.95$
$r_1 + r_2 = 0.9 + 0.95 = 1.85$

23. After how many years will a brand new machine be worth less than $5,000?
    a) 9
    b) 8
    c) 7
    d) 6

Answer: (A)
After the first five years:
$V_5 = 10{,}000 \times (0.9)^5 = 5{,}904.9$
$5{,}904.9 \times (0.95)^{t-5} < 5{,}000$
$0.95^{t-5} < 0.85$
With calculator, the first whole number value of t that satisfies the above inequality is 9.
After 9 years, the value of the machine will be less than $5,000

24. Let the function g be defined by: $g(x) = 2x + 1$. If $\frac{1}{3}g(x^2) = 1$, what could be the value of x?
    a) 0
    b) 1
    c) 2
    d) 3

Answer: (B)
Replace x with x^2 and solve the equation.
$\frac{1}{3}g(x^2) = 1$
$g(x^2) = 3$
$2(x^2) + 1 = 3$
$x^2 = 1 \rightarrow x = \pm 1$

Questions 25 − 26 refer to the following information:
According to the combined ideal gas law, if the amount of gas stays constant, the relationship between pressure, volume, and temperature is as follows:

$$\frac{PV}{T} = constant$$

P is the pressure measured in atmospheres (atm), V is the volume measured in liters (L), and T is the temperature measured in Kelvin (K).

The relationship between Kelvin and Celsius is as follows:

$$K = 273 + °C$$

K is the temperature in Kelvin and °C is the temperature in Celsius.

The relationship between Celsius and Fahrenheit is as follows:

$$°C = (°F - 32) \times \frac{5}{9}$$

Where °C is the temperature in Celsius and °F is the temperature in Fahrenheit.

25. What will be the final volume, in liters, if the pressure of 6-liter sample of an ideal gas is changed from 1 atm to 3 atm and the temperature is changed from 273 K to 400 K? (Round your answer to the nearest tenth.)

Answer: 2.9
$\frac{PV}{T} = constant$
$\frac{P_1 V_1}{T_1} = constant = \frac{P_2 V_2}{T_2}$
$\frac{1 \times 6}{273} = \frac{3 \times V_2}{400} \rightarrow v_2 = 2.9 \ liters$

26. If the initial volume of a gas is 6 liters and the pressure of 1 atm, what will be the approximate new volume, in liters, when the temperature is changed from 32 °F to 212 °F and the pressure remains unchanged? (Round your answer to the nearest tenth.)

Answer: 8.2
$T_1 = (32 - 32) \times \frac{5}{9} = 0 \ °C = 273 + 0 = 273 \ K$
$T_2 = (212 - 32) \times \frac{5}{9} = 100 \ °C = 273 + 100 = 373 \ K$
$\frac{1 \times 6}{273} = \frac{1 \times V_2}{373}$
$V_2 = 8.2 \ liters$

27. Which of the following is the graph of $y = |-3x+3|$?

a)

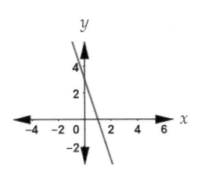

b)

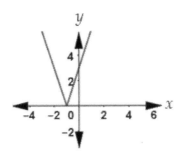

c)

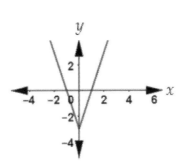

d)

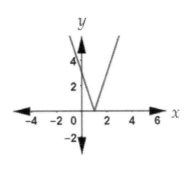

Answer: (D)
After taking the absolute value of (-3x + 3), any negative values on the graph will flip across the x-axis and become positive values. The graph of y = -3x + 3 is shown below:

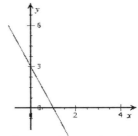

After flipping all negative values to positive values, the graph of y = |-3x + 3| will look like graph (d).

V. COMPLEX NUMBERS

Concept Overviews

A **complex number** is a number of the form $a + bi$, where a and b are real numbers and i is the imaginary unit.

$$i = \sqrt{-1}$$
$$i^2 = -1$$
$$i^3 = -i$$
$$i^4 = 1$$

When two complex numbers are equal, their real parts are equal and their imaginary parts are also equal. For example, if $a + bi = c + di$, it must be true that $a = c$ and $b = d$.

Example: $3x + yi = 2x + 2 + 3i$
$$3x = 2x + 2 \rightarrow x = 2$$
$$yi = 3i \rightarrow y = 3$$

The expressions $a + bi$ and $a - bi$ are called **complex conjugates**. Multiplying a complex number by its complex conjugate will give you a real number.
$$(a + bi) \times (a - bi) = a^2 + b^2$$

Example: $(3 + 4i) \times (3 - 4i) = 3^2 + 4^2 = 25$

Rationalizing the Complex Number

We can rationalize a fraction involving a complex number, such as $\dfrac{1}{1 + 2i}$, by making the denominator a real number. **Complex conjugates** are used to simplify the fraction when the denominator is a complex number.

Example: $\dfrac{1}{1+2i} = \dfrac{1}{1+2i} \times \dfrac{1-2i}{1-2i} = \dfrac{1(1-2i)}{1^2+2^2} = \dfrac{1-2i}{5} = \dfrac{1}{5} - \dfrac{2}{5}i$

Operations on Complex Numbers

Let $z_1 = a + bi$ and $z_2 = c + di$. Then,
$$z_1 + z_2 = (a + c) + (b + d)i$$
$$z_1 - z_2 = (a - c) + (b - d)i$$
$$z_1 \times z_2 = (a + bi) \times (c + di) = (ac - bd) + (ad + bc)i$$
$$\frac{z_1}{z_2} = \frac{a+bi}{c+di} = \frac{a+bi}{c+di} \times \frac{c-di}{c-di} = \frac{ac+bd}{c^2+d^2} + \frac{bc-ad}{c^2+d^2}i \quad \text{where } z_2 \neq 0$$

Example: If $z = 3 - 2i$, what is the value of z^2 ?

$$z^2 = (3 - 2i)(3 - 2i) = 3^2 - 2^2 - 6i - 6i = 5 - 12i$$

Example: Write $\frac{i}{2-i}$ as a standard form complex number.

$$\frac{i}{2-i} = \frac{i}{2-i} \times \frac{2+i}{2+i} = \frac{2i-1}{2^2-i^2} = \frac{2i-1}{4-(-1)} - \frac{1}{5} + \frac{2}{5}i$$

Example: Find $(1+i)^8$.

$$(1+i)^2 = 1 - 1 + 2i = 2i$$
$$(1+i)^8 = [(1+i)^2]^4 = (2i)^4 = 2^4 = 16$$

Powers of *i* have a repeating pattern:

$$i = i = \sqrt{-1} \rightarrow i^{4n+1} = i$$
$$i^2 = -1 \quad\quad \rightarrow i^{4n+2} = -1$$
$$i^3 = -i \quad\quad \rightarrow i^{4n+3} = -i$$
$$i^4 = 1 \quad\quad \rightarrow i^{4n} = 1$$

Example: $i^{2012} + i^{2013} + i^{2015} = ?$

$$i^{2012} = i^{4(503)} = 1$$
$$i^{2013} = i^{4(503)+1} = i$$
$$i^{2015} = i^{4(503)+3} = -i$$
$$i^{2012} + i^{2013} + i^{2015} = 1$$

Complex numbers can be represented as a two-dimensional complex plane where the **horizontal axis** is **real component** and the **vertical axis** is the **imaginary component**. In the following figure, the complex number *a + bi* can be identified with the *point (a, b)* in the complex plane.

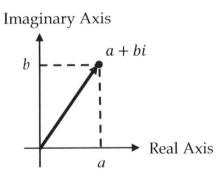

The Complex Plane

The magnitude of $a + bi$, denoted by $|a + bi|$, is equal to $\sqrt{a^2 + b^2}$.

Example: What is $|4 + 3i|$?

$$|4 + 3i| = \sqrt{4^2 + 3^2} = \sqrt{25} = 5$$

Problem Solving Skills

Easy

1. What is the value of $(2 - i)(2 + i)$? Ⓝ
   a) 5
   b) $4i$
   c) 3
   d) $2i$

   Answer: (A)
   $(2 - i)(2 + i) = 2^2 - (i)^2 = 4 - (-1) = 5$

2. What is the magnitude of $4 + 3i$?
   a) 4
   b) 5
   c) 6
   d) 7

   Answer: (B)
   $|4 + 3i| = \sqrt{4^2 + 3^2} = 5$

3. If $i = \sqrt{-1}$ and n is a positive integer, which of the following statements is FALSE? Ⓝ
   a) $i^{4n} = 1$
   b) $i^{4n+1} = -i$
   c) $i^{4n+2} = -1$
   d) $i^{n+4} = i^n$

   Answer: (B)
   If you don't remember the pattern, you can try plugging in n = 0 into each of the choices.
   $i = \sqrt{-1} \rightarrow i^{4n+1} = i$
   $i^2 = -1 \rightarrow i^{4n+2} = -1$
   $i^3 = -i \rightarrow i^{4n+3} = -i$
   $i^4 = 1 \rightarrow i^{4n} = 1$

4. $(3 - \sqrt{-4} + (5 - 2\sqrt{-9})) =$
   a) $8i$
   b) 8
   c) $8 - 8i$
   d) $8 + 8i$

   Answer: (C)
   $(3 - \sqrt{-4} + (5 - 2\sqrt{-9}))$
   $= 3 - 2\sqrt{-1} + 5 - 6\sqrt{-1}$
   $= 8 - 8i$

5. $(2 - 5i) - (5 + 2i) =$
   a) 0
   b) $10i$
   c) $3 + 7i$
   d) $-3 - 7i$

   Answer: (D)
   $(2 - 5i) - (5 + 2i)$
   $= (2 - 5) + (-5 - 2)i$
   $= -3 - 7i$

6. If $i^n = 1$, what could n be? Ⓝ
   a) 7
   b) 8
   c) 9
   d) 10

   Answer: (B)
   n must be a multiple of 4.

7. If $a - bi = i(3 - 7i)$, what is the value of $a + b$?

   Answer: 4
   $a - bi = i(3 - 7i) = 3i - 7i^2$
   $= 7 + 3i$
   $a = 7$ and $b = -3 \rightarrow a + b = 4$

8. $i^{24} + i^{25} + i^{26} + i^{27} =?$ Ⓝ
   a) 1
   b) i
   c) 0
   d) $-i$

Answer: (C)
$i = \sqrt{-1} \quad \rightarrow i^{4n+1} = i$
$i^2 = -1 \quad \rightarrow i^{4n+2} = -1$
$i^3 = -i \quad \rightarrow i^{4n+3} = -i$
$i^4 = 1 \quad \rightarrow i^{4n} = 1$
$i^{24} + i^{25} + i^{26} + i^{27}$
$= 1 + i - 1 - i = 0$

9. $(3 - 3i)^4 =?$
   a) 324
   b) -324
   c) $18i$
   d) $-18i$

Answer: (B)
$(3 - 3i)^2 = 9 - 2 \times 3 \times 3i + (3i)^2$
$= -18i$
$(3 - 3i)^4 = [(3 - 3i)^2]^2$
$= (-18i)^2 = -324$

10. Which of the following is the fraction $\frac{1}{2-i}$ equivalent to?
    a) $-2i$
    b) $2 + i$
    c) $\frac{2-i}{3}$
    d) $\frac{2+i}{5}$

Answer: (D)
Rationalize the denominator.
$\frac{1}{2-i} \times \frac{2+i}{2+i} = \frac{2+i}{4-i^2} = \frac{2+i}{5}$

11. If $a - bi = \frac{2+i}{1-i}$ which of the following is true?
    a) $a = 1, b = 3$
    b) $a = -\frac{1}{2}, b = -\frac{3}{2}$
    c) $a = \frac{3}{2}, b = \frac{1}{2}$
    d) $a = \frac{1}{2}, b = -\frac{3}{2}$

Answer: (D)
Rationalize the denominator.
$\frac{2+i}{1-i} \times \frac{1+i}{1+i} = \frac{1+3i}{1+1} = \frac{1}{2} + \frac{3}{2}i$
$a - bi = \frac{1}{2} + \frac{3}{2}i$
$a = \frac{1}{2} \quad and \quad b = -\frac{3}{2}$

12. If $a + bi = \frac{2+i}{1+i}$, what is the value of $a + b$?
    a) $3i$
    b) $\frac{1}{2}$
    c) 1
    d) $\frac{3}{2}$

Answer: (C)
Rationalize the denominator.
$\frac{2+i}{1+i} = \frac{(2+i)(1-i)}{(1+i)(1-i)} = \frac{3-i}{2} = \frac{3}{2} - \frac{1}{2}i =$
$a + bi$
$a = \frac{3}{2} \quad and \quad b = -\frac{1}{2}$
$a + b = \frac{3}{2} + \left(-\frac{1}{2}\right) = 1$

Medium

13. Which of the following is the equivalent of $\frac{3-2i}{4+3i}$?
    a) $\frac{12-4i}{7}$
    b) $\frac{6+17i}{25}$
    c) $\frac{6-10i}{7}$
    d) $\frac{6-17i}{25}$

Answer: (D)
Rationalize the denominator.
$\frac{3-2i}{4+3i} \times \frac{4-3i}{4-3i} = \frac{(3-2i)(4-3i)}{16+9} =$
$\frac{6-17i}{25}$

14. In $a + bi$ form, the reciprocal of $2 + 5i$ is

    a) $\frac{2}{29} - \frac{5}{29}i$

    b) $\frac{-2}{21} + \frac{5}{21}i$

    c) $\frac{1}{29} + \frac{5}{29}i$

    d) $\frac{2}{21} - \frac{5}{21}i$

Answer: (A)

The reciprocal of $(2 + 5i)$ is $\frac{1}{2+5i}$.

Rationalize the denominator.

$\frac{1}{2+5i} \times \frac{2-5i}{2-5i} = \frac{2-5i}{4+25} = \frac{2-5i}{29}$

15. What is the value of $|4 - 3i|$?

    a) 5

    b) $5\sqrt{2}$

    c) $2\sqrt{5}$

    d) $4 - 3i$

Answer: (A)

$|4 - 3i| = \sqrt{4^2 + 3^2} = \sqrt{25} = 5$

16. $i^{2016} + i^{2017} + i^{2018} = ?$

    a) -1

    b) 1

    c) $-i$

    d) i

Answer: (D)

$i^{2016} = i^{4(508)} = 1$

$i^{2017} = i^{4(508)+1} = i$

$i^{2018} = i^{4(508)+2} = -1$

$i^{2016} + i^{2017} + i^{2018} = i$

Hard

17. If $3 - 2i$ is a root of $2x^2 + ax + b = 0$, then the value of b is

    a) 7.5

    b) -7.5

    c) 26

    d) It cannot be determined.

Answer: (C)

The product of the roots is $\frac{b}{2}$. The sum of the roots is $-\frac{b}{a}$.

$(3 - 2i)(3 + 2i) = 13 = \frac{b}{2}$

$b = 26$

18. If $f(x) = 4x^3 - 3x^2 + 2x - 3$, then $f(i) = ?$ 🚫

    a) 2

    b) -2

    c) $-2i$

    d) $2i$

Answer: (C)

$f(x) = 4x^3 - 3x^2 + 2x - 3$

$f(i) = 4i^3 - 3i^2 + 2i - 3$

$= -4i + 3 + 2i - 3$

$= -2i$

$$(1 - i)(3 + i) = a + bi$$

19. In the equation above, a and b are two real numbers. What is the value of $a + b$?

Answer: 2

$(1 - i)(3 + i) = 4 - 2i = a + bi$

$a = 4$ *and* $b = -2$

$a + b = 2$

VI. POLYNOMIALS

Concept Overviews

Factoring Polynomials

The **common factors** of two or more terms in a polynomial are nonnegative numbers (other than 1) or polynomials that can divide evenly into the original polynomial.

A polynomial can be factored using the Greatest Common Factor, such as the GCF for the terms $30x^2, 5x^2$, and $25x$ is $5x$; Therefore the polynomial $30x^3 + 5x^2 + 25x$ can be factored to $5x(6x^2 + x + 5)$.

One way to see if polynomials can be factored is to factor "in pairs." Split the expression into pairs of terms and try to factor the pairs separately.

Example: Factor $x^3 - 7x^2 - 2x + 14$.

Solution: Group into pairs:
$$x^3 - 7x^2 - 2x + 14 = (x^3 - 7x^2) - (2x - 14)$$
Take out the common factor from each pair:
$$x^3 - 7x^2 - 2x + 14 = (x^3 - 7x^2) - (2x - 14)$$
$$= x^2(x - 7) - 2(x - 7) = (x - 7)(x^2 - 2)$$

An expression in the form of the difference of two squares can always be factored as such:

$$x^2 - y^2 = (x + y)(x - y)$$

Example: Factor $x^4 - 16$.

Solution: $x^4 - 16 = [(x^2)^2 - 4^2] = (x^2 + 4)(x^2 - 4) = (x^2 + 4)(x + 2)(x - 2)$

To factor a trinomial, or a polynomial of the form $ax^2 + bx + c$, we split the cases up into two:

1. Where b and c are integers: First, by FOIL, we know that

    $$(x + m)(x + n) = x^2 + (m + n)x + mn$$

    Therefore, by backwards logic, in order to factor $x^2 + bx + c$, numbers m and n must be found such that $m + n = b$ and $mn = c$.

2. Where a, b, and c are integers and $a \neq 1$: Set $ax^2 + bx + c$ equal to $a(x + \frac{d_1}{a})(x + \frac{d_2}{a})$ where d_1 and d_2 are two numbers whose product is $a \times c$ and whose sum is b. Factor a into two numbers, a_1 and a_2, so that $a_1 \times \frac{d_1}{a}$ and $a_2 \times \frac{d_2}{a}$ are two integers.

    Example: Factor $4x^2 - 4x - 3$.

Solution: First, find two numbers whose product is –12 and sum is –4. The two numbers are –6 and 2.

$$4x^2 - 4x - 3 = 4\left(x + \frac{2}{4}\right)\left(x - \frac{6}{4}\right) = 4\left(x + \frac{1}{2}\right)\left(x - \frac{3}{2}\right)$$

$$4\left(x + \frac{1}{2}\right)\left(x - \frac{3}{2}\right) = \left(2x + 2 \times \frac{1}{2}\right)\left(2x - 2 \times \frac{3}{2}\right) = (2x + 1)(2x - 3)$$

A perfect square trinomial is the result of multiplying a binomial by itself. It would be worth remembering the following formulas:

$$x^2 + 2xy + y^2 = (x + y)^2$$
$$x^2 - 2xy + y^2 = (x - y)^2$$

Any Polynomial $P(x)$ can always be written into the following form:

$$P(x) = (x - r)Q(x) + P(r)$$

Where $Q(x)$ is the quotient, $(x - r)$ is the divisor, and $P(r)$ is the remainder.

Example: If $P(x) = x^{10} + 3x^5 - 2x + 4$ is divided by $(x - 1)(x + 1)$, what is the remainder?

Solution: We can solve this problem by using long division but it will be very tedious. If we rewrite the equation as

$$P(x) = (x + 1)(x - 1)Q(x) + a(x - 1) + b$$

then the problem will become easier to solve.

$x^{10} + 3x^5 - 2x + 4 = (x + 1)(x - 1)Q(x) + a(x - 1) + b$

If $x = 1$, then $1 + 3 - 2 + 4 = 0 + a \times 0 + b \rightarrow b = 6$

If $x = -1$, then $(-1)^{10} + 3(-1)^5 - 2(-1) + 4 = 0 + a(-1 - 1) + 6 \rightarrow a = 1$

So the remainder of $\frac{x^{10} + 3x^5 - 2x + 4}{(x+1)(x-1)}$ is $(x - 1) + 6 = x + 5$.

The **remainder theorem** states that if polynomial $P(x)$ is divided by $x - r$, the remainder will be $P(r)$.

Example: If $P(x) = x^{100} + 2$ is divided by $x + 1$, what is the remainder?

Solution: The remainder of $\frac{P(x)}{x+1}$ is $P(-1) = (-1)^{100} + 2 = 3$

The **factor theorem** states that if $x - r$ is a factor of $P(x)$, then $P(r) = 0$. Also, r is an x-intercept of $P(x)$.

Example: If $P(x) = x^7 + kx + 1$ has the factor $x + 1$, what is the value of k?

Solution: Since $P(x)$ has the factor $x + 1$, $P(-1) = 0$

$(-1)^7 + k(-1) + 1 = 0$

$k = 0$

Sums and Products of the Roots of Polynomials

If a real polynomial $P(x) = a_n x^n + a_{n-1} x^{n-1} + \cdots + a_1 x + a_0$ has n roots, then

$$P(x) = a_n x^n + a_{n-1} x^{n-1} + \cdots + a_1 x + a_0 = a_n (x - r_n)(x - r_{n-1}) \ldots (x - r_1)$$

Sum of all roots: $r_n + r_{n-1} + r_{n-2} \ldots + r_2 + r_1 = -\dfrac{a_{n-1}}{a_n}$

Product of all roots: $r_n \times r_{n-1} \times r_{n-2} \ldots \times r_2 \times r_1 = (-1)^n \dfrac{a_0}{a_n}$

Example: What is the sum and product of all roots of the following polynomial:
$$P(x) = x^8 + 7x^7 + 5x^3 - 3x + 1$$
Solution: Sum of all roots: $= \dfrac{-7}{1} = -7$

   Product of all roots: $(-1)^8 \dfrac{1}{1} = 1$

Example: If $f(x) = x^2 - 3x - 2$ has two roots at r_1 and r_2, what is the value of $\dfrac{1}{r_1} + \dfrac{1}{r_2}$?

Solution: $\dfrac{1}{r_1} + \dfrac{1}{r_2} = \dfrac{r_1 + r_2}{r_1 r_2}$

   Sum of all roots: $r_1 + r_2 = 3$

   Product of all roots: $r_1 r_2 = -2$

   $\dfrac{1}{r_1} + \dfrac{1}{r_2} = \dfrac{r_2 + r_1}{r_1 r_2} = -\dfrac{3}{2}$

Problem Solving Skills

Easy

1. Which of the following is the equivalent of $x^3 - 3x^2 - 2x + 6$?
   a) $(x^2 - 2) + (x - 3)$
   b) $(x^2 - 2) + (x + 3)$
   c) $(x^2 - 2)(x - 3)$
   d) $(x^2 - 2)(x + 3)$

   Answer: (C)
   Factor by Grouping.
   First, group in pairs.
   $x^3 - 3x^2 - 2x + 6 = (x^3 - 3x^2) - (2x - 6)$
   Then, factor out the common factor from each pair.
   $x^2(x - 3) - 2(x - 3)$
   $= (x^2 - 2)(x - 3)$

2. Which of the following is the fully factored form of $30x^3 + 5x^2 - 25x$?
   a) $(6x^2 + x - 5)$
   b) $5x(6x^2 + x - 5)$
   c) $5x(6x + 5)(x - 1)$
   d) $5x(6x - 5)(x + 1)$

   Answer: (D)
   $30x^3 + 5x^2 - 25x$
   $= 5x(6x^2 + x - 5)$
   $= 5x(6x - 5)(x + 1)$

3. Which of the following is the equivalent of $x^4 - 1$.
   a) $(x^2 + 1)(x + 1)(x - 1)$
   b) $(x^2 - 1)(x + 1)(x - 1)$
   c) $(x + 1)^2(x - 1)$
   d) $(x + 1)(x - 1)^2$

   Answer: (A)
   $x^4 - 1 = [(x^2)^2 - 1^2]$
   $= (x^2 + 1)(x^2 - 1)$
   $= (x^2 + 1)(x + 1)(x - 1)$

4. What is the remainder when $2x^4 - 3x^3 + 4x^2 - 5x + 6$ is divided by $x - 3$?
   a) 108
   b) 96
   c) 87
   d) 75

Answer: (A)
The remainder theorem states that if polynomial $P(x)$ is divided by $x - r$, its remainder is $P(r)$.
$P(3) = 2 \times 3^4 - 3 \times 3^3 + 4 \times 3^2 - 5(3) + 6 = 108$

5. If $(x + 1)$ is a factor of $3x^6 + kx^5 - 4x^3 + 1$, what is the value of k?
   a) 8
   b) 6
   c) 5
   d) 3

Answer: (A)
$P(-1) = 3 \times (-1)^6 + k \times (-1)^5 - 4 \times (-1)^3 + 1 = 0$
$k = 8$

6. If -2 and 4 are both zeros of the polynomial $f(x)$, then a factor of $f(x)$ could be
   a) $x - 2$
   b) $x^2 - 2x - 8$
   c) $x^2 - 2x + 8$
   d) $x + 4$

Answer: (B)
$f(x)$ should be divisible by $(x + 2)$, $(x - 4)$, and $(x^2 - 2x - 8)$.

7. If $3x + 6$ is a divisor of $3x^3 + 5x^2 - 4x + d$ with a remainder of 0, what is the value of d?
   a) 8
   b) 4
   c) -4
   d) -8

Answer: (C)
$3x + 6 = 0, \; x = -2$
$P(-2) = 3 \times (-2)^3 + 5 \times (-2)^2 - 4 \times (-2) + d = 0$
$d = -4$

8. Which of the following is the sum of the roots of $6x^3 + 4x^2 - 3x = 0$?
   a) $-\frac{1}{2}$
   b) $\frac{1}{2}$
   c) $-\frac{2}{3}$
   d) $\frac{2}{3}$

Answer: (C)
If a real polynomial $P(x) = a_n x^n + a_{n-1} x^{n-1} + \cdots a_0$ has n roots: Sum of all roots $= -\frac{a_{n-1}}{a_n}$
Product of all roots $= (-1)^n \frac{a_0}{a_n}$
Sum of the roots of $6x^3 + 4x^2 - 3x = 0$ is $-\frac{4}{6} = -\frac{2}{3}$.

9. What is the product of all roots of the polynomial:
   $$P(x) = 2x^6 + 4x^5 + 6x^3 - 2x + 4$$
   a) 1
   b) 2
   c) 3
   d) $\frac{1}{2}$

Answer: (B)
If a real polynomial $P(x) = a_n x^n + a_{n-1} x^{n-1} + \cdots a_0$ has n roots, then:
Sum of all roots $= -\frac{a_{n-1}}{a_n}$
Product of all roots $= (-1)^n \frac{a_0}{a_n}$
Product of all roots: $(-1)^8 \times \frac{4}{2} = 2$

Medium

10. If the $f(x) = x^5 + bx^4 + cx^3 + dx^2 + ex + k$, $f(-1) = 0$, and $f(3) = 0$, then $f(x)$ is divisible by
    a) $x - 1$
    b) $x + 3$
    c) $x^2 + 3x + 2$
    d) $x^2 - 2x - 3$

Answer: (D)
f(x) should be divisible by $(x + 1)$, $(x - 3)$, and $(x^2 - 2x - 3)$.

11. If the equation $x^3 - 9x^2 + px - q = 0$ has 3 equal roots, then
    a) each root = 2
    b) each root = -3
    c) $q = 27$
    d) $q = 3$

Answer: (C)
Let each root be r, then
$(x - r)^3 = x^3 - 3x^2r + 3xr^2 - r^3$
Therefore, $3r = 9$ (sum of roots = 9)
$r = 3, q = 27, and\ p = 27$

12. If $f(x) = x^2 - 2x - 3$ has two roots at r_1 and r_2, what is the value of $\frac{1}{r_1} + \frac{1}{r_2}$?
    a) $-\frac{2}{3}$
    b) $-\frac{3}{2}$
    c) $\frac{2}{3}$
    d) $\frac{3}{2}$

Answer: (A)
$\frac{1}{r_1} + \frac{1}{r_2} = \frac{r_1 + r_2}{r_1 r_2}$
Sum of all roots: $r_1 + r_2 = 2$
Product of all roots: $r_1 r_2 = -3$
$\frac{1}{r_1} + \frac{1}{r_2} = \frac{r_2 + r_1}{r_1 r_2} = -\frac{2}{3}$

Questions 13 – 14 refer to the following information: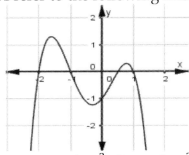

The function $f(x) = -x^4 - \frac{3}{2}x^3 + 2x^2 + \frac{3}{2}x - 1$ is graphed in the xy-plane above.

13. If c is a constant such that the equation $f(x) = c$ has four real solutions, which of the following could NOT be the value of c?
    a) 1
    b) 0
    c) $-\frac{1}{2}$
    d) -1

Answer: (A)

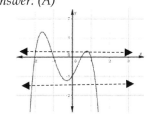

According to the graph above, there are four intersection points when the value of c is roughly between −1.3 and 0.3.

14. How many real solutions are there if $f(x) = x$?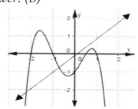
    a) 1
    b) 2
    c) 3
    d) 4

Answer: (B)

From the graph above, there are two intersection points between the line $f(x) = x$ and the graph of $f(x) = -x^4 - \frac{3}{2}x^3 + 2x^2 + \frac{3}{2}x - 1$.

Hard

15. The length of a rectangular piece of cardboard is 15 inches longer than its width. If a 5-inch square is cut from each corner of the cardboard, and the remaining piece is folded up to form a box, the volume of the box is 2,250 cubic inches. Find the sum of the length and the width, in inches, of the original cardboard.
    a) 65
    b) 62
    c) 54
    d) 46

Answer: (A)
If the width of the cardboard is x inches, the length of the carboard is $15 + x$ inches. After 5-inch square is cut from each corner and the cardboard is folded to form a box, the width will be $x - 10$, the length will be $x + 5$, and the height will be 5 inches.
$(x - 10)(x + 5)(5) = 2250$.
$x^2 - 5x - 500 = 0$
$(x + 20)(x - 25) = 0 \rightarrow x = 25$
$25 + (25 + 15) = 65$ inches

16. Which of the following is the equation of the polynomial with roots at 0 and $3 - \sqrt{2}$?
    a) $x^3 + 6x^2 - 9x = 0$
    b) $x^3 - 6x^2 - 7x = 0$
    c) $x^3 + 6x^2 + 7x = 0$
    d) $x^3 - 6x^2 + 7x = 0$

Answer: (D)
The equation should also have a root at $3 + \sqrt{2}$, because all of the answer choices have rational coefficients. Therefore, the polynomial is $x[x - (3 - \sqrt{2})][x - (3 + \sqrt{2})] = x\left[(x - 3)^2 - (\sqrt{2})^2\right] = (x^2 - 6x + 7) = x^3 - 6x^2 + 7x = 0$

VII.   QUADRATIC FUNCTIONS AND EQUATIONS

Concept Overviews

Quadratic functions are functions of the form $(x) = ax^2 + bx + c$, where $a \neq 0$.

Important Properties of Quadratic Functions

- The vertex of a quadratic function is located at coordinate $(\frac{-b}{2a}, \frac{-b^2+4ac}{4a})$.
- The axis of symmetric of $f(x)$ is $= -\frac{b}{2a}$.
- If $a > 0$, the quadratic function opens upwards and has a minimum value at the vertex.
- If $a < 0$, the quadratic function opens downwards and has a maximum value at the vertex.
- The domain of a quadratic function is $(-\infty, \infty)$.
- The range of a quadratic function is
    - $\left(\frac{-b^2+4ac}{4a}, \infty\right)$ when $a > 0$.
    - $\left(-\infty, \frac{-b^2+4ac}{4a}\right)$ when $a < 0$.

Quadratic Equations
A quadratic equation is an equation where the greatest exponent of the variable is 2. It can be converted into standard form, which is expressed as $ax^2 + bx + c = 0$, where a, b, and c are real number coefficients, $a \neq 0$, and x is the variable.

Zero-Product Rule: If the product of two or more terms is zero, at least one of the terms has to be zero. For instance, $(x - 1)(x - 2) = 0$, so either $(x - 1) = 0 \rightarrow x = 1$ or $(x - 2) = 0 \rightarrow x = 2$. Both 1 and 2 are the two roots of x.

Solving a Quadratic Equation Method 1: Factoring
$x^2 - 3x + 2 = 0$
$(x - 1)(x - 2) = 0$ *(trinomial factoring)*
$x = 1 \text{ or } 2$ *(zero-product rule)*

Solving a Quadratic Equation Method 2: Complete the Square
$x^2 + 4x - 5 = 0$
$x^2 + 4x = 5$
$x^2 + 4x + 2^2 = 5 + 2^2$ *(add 2^2 on both side to make left hand side a perfect square)*
$(x + 2)^2 = 9$
$x + 2 = \pm 3$
$x = -2 \pm 3$
$x = 1 \text{ or } -5$

Solving a Quadratic Equation Method 3: Quadratic Formula $x = \frac{-b \pm \sqrt{b^2 - 4ac}}{2a}$

$2x^2 - 7x + 3 = 0$

$$x = \frac{-(-7) \pm \sqrt{(-7)^2 - 4 \times (2) \times (3)}}{2 \times 2} = \frac{7 \pm \sqrt{49 - 24}}{4} = \frac{7 \pm 5}{4}$$

$x = 3 \ or \ \frac{1}{2}$

The Discriminant of Quadratic Equations: For a quadratic equation in standard form ($ax^2 + bx + c = 0$), the discriminant Δ is equal to $b^2 - 4ac$. The discriminant gives information about the roots.
- If $\Delta > 0$, then this quadratic equation has two real roots.
- If $\Delta = 0$, then this quadratic equation has one real double root (i.e., two roots have the same real value.)
- If $\Delta < 0$, then this quadratic equation has two complex roots with imaginary parts.

Important Properties of Quadratic Equations
- The sum of two roots of a quadratic equation written in the form $ax^2 + bx + c = 0$ is $\frac{-b}{a}$.
- The product of two roots of a quadratic equationwriiten in the form $ax^2 + bx + c = 0$ is $\frac{c}{a}$.
- If $a > 0$ and $\Delta < 0$, the graph will go upwards and no interception with x-axis, then $ax^2 + bx + c$ is always greater than 0.
- If $a < 0$ and $\Delta < 0$, the graph will go downwards and no interception with x-axis, then $ax^2 + bx + c$ is always less than 0.

Problem Solving Skills

Easy

1. What are the solutions of x for which $(x - 1)(x + 2) = 0$? Ⓝ
   a) –1
   b) –2
   c) 1 and –2
   d) –1 and 2

   Answer: (C)
   $(x - 1)(x + 2) = 0$
   $x - 1 = 0, \ x = 1 \ \ or$
   $x + 2 = 0, \ x = -2$

2. If $x^2 - 5x - 6 = 0$, what are the possible values of x?
   a) –1, 6
   b) 1, –6
   c) –1, –6
   d) 2, –3

   Answer: (A)
   Use trinomial factoring.
   $x^2 - 5x - 6 = (x - 6)(x + 1) = 0$
   $x = 6 \ \ or \ -1$

3. How many points does the graph of function, $f(x) = x^2 - 1$, cross the x-axis?

   a) 0
   b) 1
   c) 2
   d) 3

Answer: (C)
The graph of f(x) intersects the x-axis when f(x) = 0.
$0 = x^2 - 1$
$x = \pm 1$

4. If $x^2 - 64 = 0$, which of the following could be a value of x?

   a) −4
   b) −8
   c) 2
   d) 4

Answer: (B)
$x^2 - 64 = 0$
$x^2 = 64$
$x = \pm 8$

5. Which of the following is one of the values of x if $2x^2 + 3x - 1 = 0$?

   a) 0.8
   b) 0.48
   c) 1.78
   d) −1.78

Answer: (D)
Since the equation set to 0, we can solve this using quadratic formula,
$x = \frac{-b \pm \sqrt{b^2 - 4ac}}{2a}$
$a = 2, b = 3, c = -1$
$\frac{-3 \pm \sqrt{3^2 - 4ac}}{2a} = \frac{-3 \pm \sqrt{3^2 - 4(2)(-1)}}{2(2)}$
$= \frac{-3 \pm \sqrt{17}}{4} = -1.78 \text{ or } 0.28$

6. If $x^2 = 16$ and $2y^3 = -16$, which of the following could be true?

   I. $x = 4$
   II. $y = 2$
   III. $x + y = 2$
   a) I only
   b) II only
   c) I and III only
   d) I, II, and III

Answer: (C)
Solve for x first.
$x^2 = 16 \rightarrow x = \pm 4$
$2y^3 = -16$
$y^3 = -8 \rightarrow y = -2$
Only I and III are correct.

7. If $x(x - 4) = -4$, what is the value of $x^2 + 3x - 5$?
   a) 3
   b) 5
   c) 1
   d) 0

Answer: (B)
$x^2 - 4x + 4 = 0$
$(x - 2)^2 = 0$
$x = 2$
$x^2 + 3x - 5 = 2^2 + 3 \times 2 - 5 = 5$

8. The axis of symmetry for $f(x) = x^2 + 3x - 2$ is $x = ?$
   a) 3
   b) −1
   c) 1
   d) −1.5

Answer: (D)
The axis of symmetry is $= -\frac{b}{2a}$.
$x = -\frac{3}{2} = -1.5$

9. Equation $(x + 2)(x + a) = x^2 + 4x + b$ where a and b are constants. If the equation is true for all values of x, what is the value of b?

    a) 8
    b) 6
    c) 4
    d) 2

Answer: (C)
This is an identity equation question. The two expressions have the same coefficients for corresponding terms.
$(x + 2)(x + a) = x^2 + (2 + a)x + 2a$
By comparison: $2 + a = 4$ and $2a = b$
$a = 2$ and $b = 4$

10. Which of the following is one of the values of x if $x^2 - 2x - 2 = 0$?

    a) $1 - \sqrt{3}$
    b) $1 - \sqrt{2}$
    c) $\sqrt{3} - 1$
    d) $\sqrt{2} - 1$

Answer: (A)
Complete the square.
$x^2 - 2x - 2 = 0$
$x^2 - 2x = 2$ add 1 to both sides to make a perfect square on the left
$x^2 - 2x + 1 = 2 + 1$
$(x - 1)^2 = 3$ take the square root on both sides
$x - 1 = \pm\sqrt{3} \rightarrow x = 1 \pm \sqrt{3}$

11. At what points the graph of $y = x^2 + 2x - 8$ cuts the x-axis?

    a) $(-2, 0)$ and $(0, 0)$
    b) $(0, 0)$ and $(2, 0)$
    c) $(2, 0)$ and $(-4, 0)$
    d) $(4, 0)$ and $(2, 0)$

Answer: (C)

$x^2 + 2x - 8 = 0$
$(x - 2)(x + 4) = 0$
The graph intersects the x-axis at $(2, 0)$ and $(-4, 0)$.

Medium

12. If $x < 2$ and $a(x - 2)(x - 3) = 0$, what is the value of a?

    a) 3
    b) 2
    c) 1
    d) 0

Answer: (D)
Solve for x by zero-product rule.
$a(x - 2)(x - 3) = 0$
One of the terms a, (x − 2), and (x − 3) must be equal to zero.
Given that x < 2, only a can be equal to zero.

13. If $x - 2$ is a factor of $x^2 - kx - 8$, what is the value of k ?

    a) 1
    b) 4
    c) −3
    d) −2

Answer: (D)
$x^2 - kx - 8 = 0$
$(x - 2)(x + 4) = 0$
$x^2 + 2x - 8 = x^2 - kx - 8 = 0$
$-k = 2 \rightarrow k = -2$

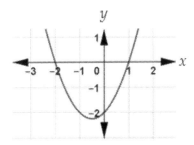

14. Which of the following equations best describes the curve in the figure above?
    a) $y = x^2 - 2$
    b) $y = x^2 + 2$
    c) $y = x^2 + x + 2$
    d) $y = x^2 + x - 2$

Answer: (D)
From the graph above, there are two roots, −2 and 1.
$y = (x + 2)(x − 1) = x^2 + x − 2$

15. What is the x value at the minimum point of the equation $f(x) = x^2 + 4x + 2$?
    a) 7.75
    b) 2.25
    c) 0
    d) −2

Answer: (D)
The vertex of a quadratic function is $(\frac{-b}{2a}, \frac{-b^2+4ac}{4a})$.
If $a > 0$, $f(x)$ opens upwards and has a minimum value at the vertex. If $a < 0$, $f(x)$ opens downwards and has a maximum value at the vertex.
The equation $f(x) = x^2 + 4x + 2$ has a minimum value of x equal to $\frac{-b}{2a} = \frac{-4}{2} = -2$.

16. A baseball is hit and flies into a field at a trajectory defined by the equation $d = -1.2t^2 + 100$, where t is the number of seconds after the impact and d is the horizontal distance from the home plate to the outfield fence. How many seconds have passed if the ball is 50 meters away from the outfield fence?

Answer: 6.45
$50 = -1.2t^2 + 100$
$t = 6.45$

17. If $h(x) = 6 + \frac{x^2}{4}$ and $h(2m) = 5m$, what is one possible value of m?

Answer: 2, 3
Substitute 2m for x solve for m.
$h(2m) = 6 + \frac{(2m)^2}{4} = 5m$
$6 + m^2 = 5m$
$m^2 - 5m + 6 = 0$
$(m - 2)(m - 3) = 0$
$m = 2, or 3$

18. If the function *f* is defined by $f(x) = ax^2 + bx + c$, where *a* < 0, *b* >0, and *c* > 0, which of the following could be the graph of $f(x)$? Ⓝ

a)

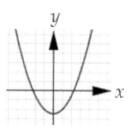

b)

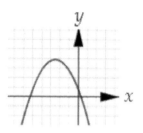

c)

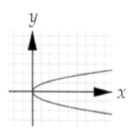

d)

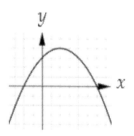

Answer: (D)
The leading coefficient of a quadratic function −1 means the curve goes downwards; the positive constant c means y-intercept is positive. The value of b is positive, so x-coordinate of the maximum point is positive. Only (d) meets all these conditions.

19. Which of the following could be a graph of the equation $y = ax^2 + bx + c$, where $b^2 - 4ac = 0$?

a)

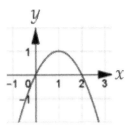

b)

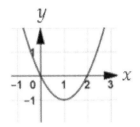

c)

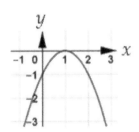

d)

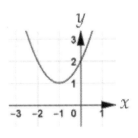

Hard

$$h(t) = -5t^2 + at + b$$

20. At time $t = 0$, a ball was thrown upward from the top of a building. Before the ball hit the ground, its height $h(t)$, in feet, at the time t seconds is given by the function above. a and b are constants. If the ball reached its maximum height of 125 feet at time $t = 3$, what could be the height of the building?

Answer: 80
The height of the building is equal to the height of the ball when t equals 0.
The maximum height occurs when
$t = \dfrac{-a}{2 \times (-5)} = 3$, *solve for a, a = 30*
$125 = -5(3)^2 + 30(3) + b$
$b = 80$
$h(0) = b = 80$ *feet*

21. In the xy-plane, the point $(-1, 2)$ is the minimum of the quadratic function $f(x) = x^2 + ax + b$. What is the value of $|a - 2b|$?

Answer: 4
The vextex of the quadratic function $f(x) = x^2 + ax + b$ is
$(-\frac{a}{2}, f(-\frac{a}{2}))$
$-\frac{a}{2} = -1 \to a = 2$
$2 = (-1)^2 + 2(-1) + b \to b = 3$
$|a - 2b| = |2 - 2 \times 3| = 4$

VIII. POWERS AND ROOTS

A. EXPONENT OPERATIONS

CONCEPT OVERVIEWS

Raising a number to the nth power is the product of multiplying n copies of that number. The number being raised to a power is denoted as the **base.** The **power** is also called the **exponent**, and is expressed as a small number written on the top right of the base number.

> *Example:* "y to the 4th power" may be written as y^4. The base number is y and the exponent is 4. This denotes 4 copies of y being multiplied together. $y^4 = y \times y \times y \times y$.

Multiplying and Dividing Numbers with Exponents
- **Same Base**: Keep the same base and add the exponents when multiplying. Keep the same base but subtract the exponents when dividing.

  Examples:
  $$x^4 \times x^3 = x^{4+3} = x^7 \qquad x^4 \div x^3 = x^{4-3} = x^1$$

- "$x^3 \times x^2$" denotes $(x \times x \times x)$ being multiplied by $(x \times x)$. There are 5 copies of x being multiplied together, which means that $x^3 \times x^2 = x \times x \times x \times x \times x = x^5$.

- Same exponent but different base: Keep the same exponent but combine the bases.

  Examples:
  $$x^3 \times y^3 = (x \times y)^3 \qquad x^3 \div y^3 = \left(\frac{x}{y}\right)^3$$

- "$\frac{x^5}{x^2}$" is equal to 5 copies of x divided by 2 copies of x. This is equal to only 3 copies of x multiplied together, which is also x^3.
  $$\frac{x^5}{x^2} = x^{5-2} = x^3$$

Raising One Power to Another (Raising an Exponent to Another Exponent): To raise an exponent to another exponent, multiply their exponents.

Example:
$$(x^4)^3 = x^{4\times3}$$

Basic Exponent Rules to Be Memorized

- $x^a x^b = x^{a+b}$
- $(x^a)^b = x^{ab}$
- $x^a y^a = (xy)^a$
- $\dfrac{x^a}{x^b} = x^{a-b}$
- $x^0 = \dfrac{x^a}{x^a} = x^{a-a} = 1$
- $x^{-a} = \dfrac{x^0}{x^a} = \dfrac{1}{x^a}$

Multiplying a Decimal Number by 10^n: If n is a positive integer, then this operation will move the decimal point n places to the right. If n is a negative integer, then this operation will move the decimal point $|n|$ places to the left.

Problem Solving Skills

Easy

1. If $2^{x+1} = 8$, then what is the value of x?
   a) 0
   b) 1
   c) 2
   d) 3

   Answer: (C)
   Change both sides of equation to the same base 2.
   $2^{(x+1)} = 2^3$
   $x + 1 = 3 \rightarrow x = 2$

2. Which of the following is equal to 0.00126691?
   a) 1.26691×10^{-3}
   b) 1.26691×10^{-2}
   c) 1.26691×10^{-1}
   d) 12.6691×10^{-2}

   Answer: (A)
   1.26691 multiplied by 10^{-3} will move its decimal point 3 places to the left.
   $1.26691 \times 10^{-3} = 0.00126691$

3. If $n > 0$, what is the value of $4^n + 4^n + 4^n + 4^n$?
   a) $4^{(n+4)}$
   b) $4^{(n+1)}$
   c) $4^{(4n+1)}$
   d) $4^{(4n+3)}$

   Answer: (B)
   $4^n + 4^n + 4^n + 4^n = 4 \times 4^n = 4^{(n+1)}$

4. If $xyz \neq 0$, then $\dfrac{x^2y^4z^8}{x^6y^4z^2} = ?$ 🚫

    a) xyz

    b) $\dfrac{z^3}{x^3}$

    c) $\dfrac{z^4}{x^3}$

    d) $\dfrac{z^6}{x^4}$

Answer: (D)
Apply exponent rules.

$\dfrac{x^2y^4z^8}{x^6y^4z^2} = \left(\dfrac{x^2}{x^6}\right)\left(\dfrac{y^4}{y^4}\right)\left(\dfrac{z^8}{z^2}\right) = \dfrac{z^6}{x^4}$

5. $(-2x^2y^6)^3 = ?$ 🚫

    a) $4x^5y^9$
    b) $-8x^6y^{18}$
    c) $4x^6y^{18}$
    d) $8x^6y^{18}$

Answer: (B)
Raise power for each term inside the parentheses and apply the $(x^a)^b$
$= x^{ab}$ rule.
$(-2x^2y^6)^3 = (-2)^3 (x^2)^3 (y^6)^3$
$= -8x^6 y^{18}$

6. If $a^x \cdot a^4 = a^{16}$ and $(a^3)^y = a^{12}$, what is the value of $x + y$?

    a) 17
    b) 16
    c) 15
    d) 13

Answer: (B)
$a^x \cdot a^4 = a^{(x+4)} = a^{16}$
$(a^3)\,^y = a^{3y} = a^{12}$
$x = 12$
$y = 4$
$x + y = 16$

7. If x, y and z are different positive integers and $2^x \times 2^y \times 2^z = 64$, then $x + y + z$? 🚫

    a) 12
    b) 3
    c) 4
    d) 6

Answer: (D)
$2^x \times 2^y \times 2^z = 2^{(x+y+z)} = 64 = 2^6$
$x + y + z = 6$

8. If x and y are positive integers and $5^2x + 5^2y = 100$, what is the value of $x + y$? 🚫

    a) 1
    b) 2
    c) 4
    d) 8

Answer: (C)
$5^2x + 5^2y = 25(x + y) = 100$
$x + y = 4$

9. Positive integers x, y, and z satisfy the equations $x^{-\frac{1}{2}} = \dfrac{1}{2}$ and $y^z = 8$, $z > y$, what is the value of $x + y + z$?

    a) 5
    b) 7
    c) 9
    d) 11

Answer: (C)
$x^{-\frac{1}{2}} = \dfrac{1}{2}$, $x = \left(\dfrac{1}{2}\right)^{-2} = 2^2 = 4$
$8 = 2^3 = y^z$
$y = 2$ and $z = 3$
$x + y + z = 2 + 3 + 4 = 9$

10. If x is a positive integer, then $(5 \times 10^{-x}) + (2 \times 10^{-x})$ must be equal to? 🚫

Answer: (D)
$(5 \times 10^{-x}) + (2 \times 10^{-x}) = 7 \times 10^{-x}$
$7 \times 10^{-x} = \dfrac{7}{10^x}$

a) $\dfrac{10}{10^x}$

b) $\dfrac{1}{10^x}$

c) $\dfrac{7}{10^{-x}}$

d) $\dfrac{7}{10^x}$

11. If m is a positive number, which of the following is equal to $m^3 \times m^{-3}$? Ⓝ

   a) 0
   b) 1
   c) m^{-6}
   d) m

Answer: (B)
Except the number 0, any numbers raised to the power of 0 is equal to 1.
$m^3 \times m^{-3} = m^0 = 1$

Medium

12. If $7 = m^x$, then $7m^2 = ?$ Ⓝ

   a) m^{2x}
   b) m^{7x}
   c) m^{x+2}
   d) m^{x+7}

Answer: (C)
$7m^2 = m^x \times m^2 = m^{(x+2)}$

13. If $81 = a^x$, where a and x are both positive integers and $x > a$, what is the value of x^a?

   a) 16
   b) 27
   c) 64
   d) 81

Answer: (C)
$a = 3$ and $x = 4$

$4^3 = 64$

14. If $3^{7x+6} = 27^{3x}$, what is the value of x? Ⓝ

   a) 1
   b) 2
   c) 3
   d) 4

Answer: (C)
When solving the equation, convert both sides to the same base.
$3^{7x+6} = 27^{3x} = [(3)^3]^{3x} = 3^{9x}$
$7x + 6 = 9x \rightarrow x = 3$

15. If $3^4 = x$, which of the following expressions is equal to 3^{10}? Ⓝ

   a) $3x^2$
   b) $9x^2$
   c) $27x^2$
   d) x

Answer: (B)
$3^{10} = 3^2 \times (3^4)^2 = 9x^2$

16. $10^{xy} = 1,000$, where x and y are positive integers and $x >$ y, what is one possible value of x? ⊗
    a) 3
    b) 4
    c) 5
    d) 7

Answer: (A)
Change both sides to the base 10.
$10^{xy} = 10^3 \rightarrow xy = 3$
Since both x and y are positive
integers, both x and y can only be
equal to 1 or 3.
$x > y \rightarrow x = 3$

Questions 17 − 18 refer to the following information:
Compound interest is the interest added to the principal of a deposit so that the interest earned also earns interest continuously. A formula for calculating annual compound interest is as follows:

$$A = P\left(1 + \frac{r}{100}\right)^t$$

A is the amount of money, in dollars, generated after t years by a principal amount P in a bank account that pays an annual interest rate of r%, compounded annually.

17. If Bill deposits $1,000 in his bank account today with an annual interest rate of 3% compounded annually, what will be the amount of money in his bank account after 5 years? (Round your answer to the nearest dollar and ignore the dollar sign when gridding your response.)

Answer: 1159
$A = 1,000(1 + 0.03)^5 = \$1,159$

18. What is the fewest whole number of years that he will have $2,000 or more in the bank?

Answer: 24
$1,000(1 + 0.03)^t \geq 2,000$
$1.03^t \geq 2$
With calculator, the first whole
number value of t that satisfies
above inequality is 24.
Therefore, the fewest number of
years required for him to accrue
$2,000 is 24.

Questions 19 – 20 refer to the following information:
In chemistry, a chemical reaction proceeds at a rate dependent on the concentration of its reactant. For reactant A, the rate of a reaction is defined as:

$$Rate = k\,[A]^n$$

k is a constant and [A] is the concentration of A. The order of reaction of a reactant A is the exponent n to which its concentration term in the rate equation is raised.

19. When n is equal to −1, it is called an order (−1) with espect to reactant A. Which of the following graphs depicts an order (−1) with respect to concentration A and reaction rate?

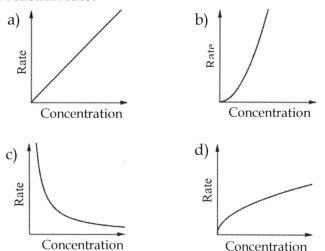

a) Rate vs Concentration   b) Rate vs Concentration

c) Rate vs Concentration   d) Rate vs Concentration

Answer: (C)
Rate = $k[A]^{-1}$
Rate × [A] = k
When n = −1, the rate of the reaction is inversely proportional to the concentration A.
Only graph c) represents the inversely proportional relationship.

20. If the graph below shows the reaction rate versus the concentration of reactant A, what is the most likely order of reactant A?

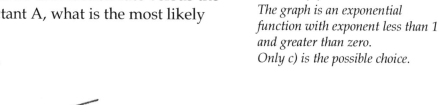

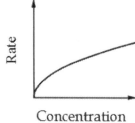

Rate vs Concentration

   a) 1st order
   b) 2nd order
   c) $\frac{1}{2}$ order
   d) 0th order

Answer: (C)
The graph is an exponential function with exponent less than 1 and greater than zero.
Only c) is the possible choice.

Hard

21. If x is a positive integer and $3^{2x} + 3^{(2x+1)} = y$, what is $3^{(2x+2)}$ in terms of y?

    a) $\frac{y-1}{3}$

    b) $4y$

    c) $9y$

    d) $\frac{9}{4}y$

Answer: (D)
$3^{2x} + 3^{(2x+1)} = 4 \times 3^{2x}$
$4 \times 3^{2x} = y$
$3^{2x} = \frac{y}{4}$
$3^{(2x+2)} = 9 \times 3^{2x} = 9 \times \frac{y}{4} = \frac{9y}{4}$

22. If K is a positive integer, find the least value of K for which 27K is a perfect cube?

    a) 1

    b) 3

    c) 8

    d) 9

Answer: (A)
$27K = 3^3 K$
Look for the least cube number which is 1.

B. ROOTS AND RADICAL OPERATIONS

CONCEPT OVERVIEWS

Taking the Square Root

Taking the **square root** of a number is the inverse operation of squaring the number. The square root of a number is a value that can be multiplied by itself to give the original number.

Examples:

$$\sqrt{y} \times \sqrt{y} = y \quad \text{and} \quad \sqrt{4} \times \sqrt{4} = 4$$

A **square root** of a variable represents the variable's exponent being divided by 2.
Examples:

$$\sqrt{x} = x^{\frac{1}{2}} \quad \text{and} \quad \sqrt{x^4} = x^{\frac{4}{2}} = x^2$$

Taking n^{th} Root of a Number

Taking n^{th} **"root" (or "radical")** of a number is the inverse operation of taking the nth power of the number. The nth root of a number is a value that can be multiplied n copies of that value to give the original number.

Examples:

$$\sqrt[3]{8} = 2 \text{ while } 2^3 = 8 \quad \text{and} \quad 3^4 = 81 \text{ while } \sqrt[4]{81} = 3$$

In general, $\sqrt[n]{x} = x^{\frac{1}{n}}$ and $\sqrt[n]{x^m} = x^{\frac{m}{n}}$.

Examples:

$$\sqrt[3]{8} = 8^{\frac{1}{3}} = \sqrt[3]{2^3} = 2^{\frac{3}{3}} = 2 \quad \text{and} \quad \sqrt[3]{5^2} = 5^{\frac{2}{3}}$$

Multiplying and Dividing Radicals

When multiplying or dividing two variables **with the same radical**, multiply or divide two variables and keep the original radical.

Examples:

$$\sqrt{x} \times \sqrt{y} = \sqrt{xy} \quad \text{and} \quad \frac{\sqrt{x}}{\sqrt{y}} = \sqrt{\frac{x}{y}}$$

When multiplying or dividing two radicals **with same variable**, add or subtract their exponents.

Examples:

$$\sqrt{x} \times \sqrt[3]{x} = x^{\frac{1}{2}} \times x^{\frac{1}{3}} = x^{\frac{1}{2}+\frac{1}{3}} = x^{\frac{5}{6}}$$

$$\frac{\sqrt{x}}{\sqrt[3]{x}} = \frac{x^{\frac{1}{2}}}{x^{\frac{1}{3}}} = x^{\frac{1}{2}-\frac{1}{3}} = x^{\frac{1}{6}} = \sqrt[6]{x}$$

Only numbers with the same radicals can be combined through multiplication or division. The product of two radicals is equal to the radical of the product. The quotient of two radicals is equal to the radical of the quotient.

Examples:

$$\sqrt{2} \times \sqrt{6} = \sqrt{2 \times 6} = \sqrt{12} \qquad\qquad \frac{\sqrt{6}}{\sqrt{2}} = \sqrt{\frac{6}{2}} = \sqrt{3}$$

Adding and Subtracting Radicals
Adding and Subtracting Radicals only apply when both the root and the base are the same (when the terms are like terms).

Example:
$$2\sqrt{3} + 3\sqrt{3} = 5\sqrt{3}$$

Consider $\sqrt{3}$ as a unit. 2 units plus 3 units of $\sqrt{3}$ is equal to 5 units of $\sqrt{3}$. Therefore simply add the coefficients of like terms.

Simplify a Square Root
To simplify a square root, factor out all perfect squares and place its square root outside.

Example:
$$\sqrt{18} = \sqrt{3^2 \times 2} = 3\sqrt{2}$$

Similar steps apply to different radicals. To simplify a cube root, factor out cubes (factors with an exponent of 3) and place its cube root (base) outside.

Example:
$$\sqrt[3]{54} = \sqrt[3]{3^3 \times 2} = 3\sqrt[3]{2}$$

Rationalize a Denominator with a Square Root: multiply the top and bottom of the fraction by the square root in the denominator to get a rational denominator.

Example 1:
$$\frac{\sqrt{12}}{\sqrt{2}} = \frac{\sqrt{12} \times \sqrt{2}}{\sqrt{2} \times \sqrt{2}} = \frac{\sqrt{24}}{2} = \frac{\sqrt{2^2 \times 6}}{2} = \frac{2\sqrt{6}}{2} = \sqrt{6}$$

Example 2: Rationalize a denominator with a square root by using the conjugate.

$$\frac{2 + \sqrt{2}}{1 - \sqrt{2}} = \frac{(2 + \sqrt{2})(1 + \sqrt{2})}{(1 - \sqrt{2})(1 + \sqrt{2})} = \frac{2 + 3\sqrt{2} + 2}{1^2 - (\sqrt{2})^2} = -4 - 3\sqrt{2}$$

Problem Solving Skills

Easy

1. If $4 + \sqrt{k} = 7$, then $k = ?$
   a) 3
   b) 6
   c) 9
   d) $\sqrt{3}$

Answer: (C)
If $4 + \sqrt{k} = 7$, then $\sqrt{k} = 3$.

Square both sides: $k = 9$

2. If $\sqrt{x} = 2$ then $x + 4 = ?$ 🚫
   a) 2
   b) 4
   c) 8
   d) 80

Answer: (C)
Square both sides of the radical equation.
$\sqrt{x} = 2$
$(\sqrt{x})^2 = 2^2$
$x = 4$
$x + 4 = 8$

3. If $\sqrt{2x} - 4 = 2$, then $x = ?$
   a) −9
   b) −18
   c) 27
   d) 18

Answer: (D)
$\sqrt{2x} - 4 = 2$
$\sqrt{2x} = 2 + 4 = 6$
$(\sqrt{2x})^2 = 6^2$
$2x = 36 \rightarrow x = 18$

4. If $x^{\frac{1}{3}} = 2$, what is the value of x?
   a) 2
   b) 4
   c) 6
   d) 8

Answer: (D)
$x^{\frac{1}{3}} = 2$
$x = 2^3 = 8$

5. If $\frac{\sqrt{x} + y}{\sqrt{x} + 5} = 1$, then $y = ?$ 🚫
   a) 1
   b) 3
   c) 5
   d) 8

Answer: (C)
$\sqrt{x} + y = \sqrt{x} + 5 \rightarrow y = 5$

Medium

6. If $x^{\frac{1}{4}} = \sqrt{3}$, then what is the value of x^2?
   a) 81
   b) 72
   c) 36
   d) 27

Answer: (A)
$(x^{\frac{1}{4}})^8 = x^2$
$(\sqrt{3})^8 = 81$

7. If $\frac{5\sqrt{3}}{\sqrt{5}} = 2x$, then what is the value of x?

   a) $\sqrt{\frac{15}{2}}$

   b) $\sqrt{15}$

   c) $\frac{\sqrt{15}}{2}$

   d) $5\sqrt{3}$

Answer: (C)
Rationalize a denominator with a square root.
$\frac{5\sqrt{3}}{\sqrt{5}} = \frac{5\sqrt{3}\times\sqrt{5}}{\sqrt{5}\times\sqrt{5}} = \frac{5\sqrt{3\times5}}{5} = \sqrt{15} = 2x$
$x = \frac{\sqrt{15}}{2}$

8. If $x^{\frac{3}{2}} = \frac{1}{27}$, then what does x equal?
   a) −9
   b) −3
   c) $\frac{1}{9}$
   d) $-\frac{1}{9}$

Answer: (C)
Tips:
$x^{\frac{3}{2}} = \frac{1}{27}$
$x = (\frac{1}{27})^{\frac{2}{3}}$
$\frac{1}{27} = 3^{-3}$
$x = (3^{-3})^{\frac{2}{3}} = 3^{-2} = \frac{1}{9}$

9. $\frac{5}{\sqrt{3}} + \frac{4}{\sqrt{2}} = ?$

   a) $\frac{15}{\sqrt{5}}$

   b) $\frac{9\sqrt{6}}{\sqrt{6}}$

   c) $\frac{5\sqrt{2}+4\sqrt{3}}{\sqrt{3}+\sqrt{2}}$

   d) $\frac{5\sqrt{3}+6\sqrt{2}}{3}$

Answer: (D)
$\frac{5}{\sqrt{3}} + \frac{4}{\sqrt{2}} = \frac{5\sqrt{2}}{\sqrt{3}\times\sqrt{2}} + \frac{4\sqrt{3}}{\sqrt{2}\times\sqrt{3}} =$
$\frac{5\sqrt{2}+4\sqrt{3}}{\sqrt{6}} = \frac{(5\sqrt{2}+4\sqrt{3})\times\sqrt{6}}{\sqrt{6}\times\sqrt{6}} =$
$\frac{5\sqrt{12}+4\sqrt{18}}{6} = \frac{10\sqrt{3}+12\sqrt{2}}{6} = \frac{5\sqrt{3}+6\sqrt{2}}{3}$

10. If x and y are positive integers and $(x^{\frac{1}{6}} y^{\frac{1}{6}})^3 = 8$, what is the value of xy? 🔋
    a) 8
    b) 32
    c) 64
    d) 128

Answer: (C)
$(x^{\frac{1}{6}} y^{\frac{1}{6}})^3 = (xy)^{\frac{1}{2}}$
$(xy)^{\frac{1}{2}} = 8$
$xy = 64$

Hard

11. If $12\sqrt{12} = x\sqrt{y}$ where x and y are positive integers and $x > y$, which of the following could be the value of xy?
    a) 32
    b) 48
    c) 72
    d) 102

Answer: (C)
$12\sqrt{12} = 12 \times 2\sqrt{3} = 24\sqrt{3}$
$x = 24$ and $y = 3$
$xy = 24 \times 3 = 72$

12. If $x^2 > 9$, which of the following must be true? 🚫
    a) $x > 3$
    b) $x < 3$
    c) $x < -3$
    d) $x > 3$ or $x < -3$

Answer: (D)
$x^2 > 9 \rightarrow x^2 - 9 > 0$
$(x - 3)(x + 3) > 0$
The terms $(x - 3)$ and $(x + 3)$ must be both positive or both negative for the term $(x - 3)(x + 3)$ to be greater than 0.
$x > 3$ or $x < -3$

13. If $2 \times 2^x + 2^x + 2^x = 2^5$, what is the value of x? 🚫
    a) 0
    b) 1
    c) 2
    d) 3

Answer: (D)
$2 \times 2^x = 2^x + 2^x$
$2^x + 2^x + 2^x + 2^x$
$= 4 \times 2^x = 2^5$
$2^{x+2} = 2^5$
$x = 3$

14. If $9^y = \dfrac{27^{y-1}}{27}$, what is $y =$? 🚫
    a) 6
    b) 5
    c) 3
    d) 1

Answer: (A)
Change both sides of equation to the same base.
$9^y = 3^{2y} = \dfrac{27^{y-1}}{27} = 27^{(y-2)} = $
$3^{3(y-2)} \rightarrow 3^{2y} = 3^{3(y-2)}$
$2y = 3y - 6 \rightarrow y = 6$

Chapter 4 Additional Topics in Math

I. Lines and Triangle

A. Parallel Lines and Their Transversals

Vertical Angles Are Congruent
In the figure below, ∠1 and ∠3 are vertical angles, and ∠2 and ∠4 are vertical angles. Thus, $m\angle 1 = m\angle 3$ and $m\angle 2 = m\angle 4$.

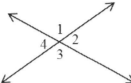

Lines
- Only one distinct line can pass through any two distinct points.
- Two different lines can intersect at most one point.
- If two lines intersect at right angles, they are **perpendicular**.

Parallel Lines and Their Transversals
- Two lines on the same plane that never intercept each other are **parallel** lines.
- If two distinct lines on the same plane are both perpendicular to another line, the two lines must be parallel.

If lines l and m are parallel and line n crosses both lines, line n is a **transversal** of lines l and m. Then the following holds:

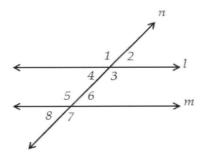

- **Corresponding angles** are congruent: pairs of corresponding angles include ∠1 and ∠5, ∠2 and ∠6, ∠4 and ∠8, and ∠3 and ∠7.
- **Alternate interior angles** are congruent: pairs of alternate interior angles include ∠3 and ∠5, and ∠4 and ∠6.
- **Consecutive interior angles** are supplementary: pairs of consecutive interior angles include ∠3 and ∠6, and ∠4 and ∠5.
- **Alternate exterior angles** are congruent: pairs of alternate exterior angles include ∠1 and ∠7, and ∠2 and ∠8.
- Pairs of **vertical angles** are always congruent, such as ∠1 and ∠3, and ∠6 and ∠8.

Example: From the graph below, if l_1 is parallel to l_2 and $x = 50$, what are the values of $a, b, c,$ and d?

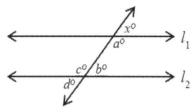

Answer: $b = 50$ (Corresponding angles x and b are congruent.)

$d = 50$ (Alternate exterior angles d and x are congruent.)

$a = 130$ (Consecutive interior angles a and b are supplementary.)

$c = 130$ (Alternate interior angles a and c are congruent.)

Problem Solving Skills

Easy

1. In the figure below, lines l_1 and l_2 are parallel. What is the value of $-y$?

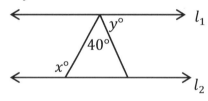

Answer: 40
$40 + y = x$
$x - y = 40$

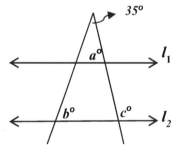

2. In the figure above, if $l_1 \parallel l_2$ and $c = 110$, what is the value of b, in degrees?
   a) 70
   b) 75
   c) 80
   d) 85

Answer: (B)
Corresponding angles are congruent.
$a = 180° - c = 70°$
$a + b + 35° = 180°$
$b = 75°$

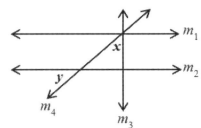

3. In the figure above, if m_1 is parallel to m_2 and m_3 is perpendicular to m_1, what is the sum of x and y, in degrees?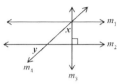
    a) 180°
    b) 120°
    c) 100°
    d) 90°

Answer: (D)

We are given that $m_1 \parallel m_2$, so if $m_1 \perp m_3$, then $m_2 \perp m_3$. x plus the vertical angle of y equals 90° since $m_2 \perp m_3$. Thus, x + y = 90°

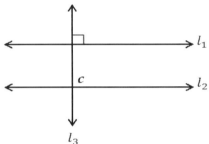

4. In the figure above, $l_1 \parallel l_2$ and $l_3 \perp l_1$. Which of the following must be true?
    a) c < 90°
    b) c > 90°
    c) c = 90°
    d) $l_1 \perp l_2$

Answer: (C)
∠C is the supplementary angle of a right angle.
c = 90°

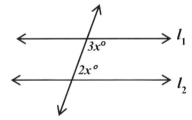

5. In the figure above $l_1 \parallel l_2$, what is the value of x?
    a) 36
    b) 40
    c) 45
    d) 54

Answer: (A)
Consecutive interior angles are supplementary.
2x + 3x = 180
x = 36

6. In the figure below, lines l_1 and l_2 are parallel. What is the value of y?

Answer: 150
x = 50

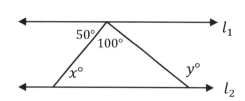

$$180 - 100 - 50 = 30$$
$$y = 180 - 30 = 150$$

Medium

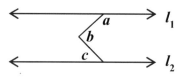

7. In the figure above, $l_1 \parallel l_2$, $a = 130°$, and $c = 40°$. What is the value of b?
    a) 50°
    b) 60°
    c) 70°
    d) 90°

Answer: (D)
Draw an auxiliary line extending to l_2:

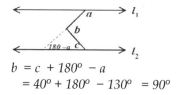

$b = c + 180° - a$
$\quad = 40° + 180° - 130° = 90°$

8. In the figure below, $l_1 \parallel l_2$ and $b = 2a + 6$. What is the value of a, in degrees?

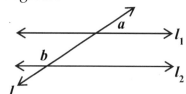

Note: Figure not drawn to scale.

Answer: 58
$a + b = 180°$
$2a + 6 + a = 180°$
$3a = 174$
$a = 58°$

9. In the figure below, $l_1 \parallel l_2$. What is the value of x?

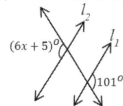

    a) 15
    b) 16
    c) 17
    d) 18

Answer: (B)
$6x + 5 = 101$
$x = 16$

Hard

10. In the figure below, $l_1 \parallel l_2$. Which of the following statements must be true?

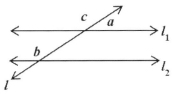

Note: Figure not drawn to scale.

  I. $a + c = 180°$
  II. $b + c = 180°$
  III. $a + b = 180°$

 a) I only
 b) I and II only
 c) I and III only
 d) I, II, and III

Answer: (C)
$a + c = 180°$
$c = 180°- a$
$a + b = 180°$
$a = 180° - b$
$c = 180° - (180° - b)$
$b = c$

11. In the figure below, $l_1 \parallel l_2$ and $a = b$. Which of the following statements must be true?

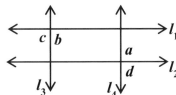

Note: Figure not drawn to scale.

  I. l_1 and l_2 are parallel
  II. l_3 and l_1 are perpendicular
  III. $c = d$

 a) I only
 b) I and II only
 c) III only
 d) I, II, and III

Answer: (C)
Two angles placed adjacently make a straight angle, these two angles are **supplementary angles**. *The sum of two supplementary angles is* $180°$.
$a + d = 180°$
$b + c = 180°$
If $a = b$ then $c = d$

B. INTERIOR ANGLES OF A TRIANGLE

CONCEPT OVERVIEWS

Sum of Interior Angles Theorem: The sum of the three interior angles of a triangle is 180°.

Example: Find the value of *x*.

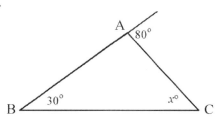

Answer: $80^o + \angle BAC = 180^o = 30 + x + \angle BAC$
$80^o = 30^o + x^o \rightarrow x = 50$

An **equilateral triangle** is a triangle with three equal sides and three equal interior angles measuring 60°.

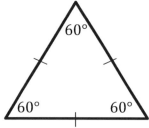

An **isosceles triangle** is a triangle with two equal sides and congruent corresponding base angles. If two sides of a triangle are equal in length, their opposite angles must be congruent as well.

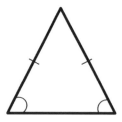

NOTE: The height of an isosceles triangle always bisects the triangle, creating two equal right triangles.

A **right triangle** is a triangle with a 90° angle. The two perpendicular sides are called legs and the side opposite the right angle is called the hypotenuse.

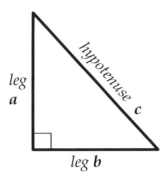

Pythagorean Theorem for right triangles: $a^2 + b^2 = c^2$

Special Right Triangles: Two special right triangles you need to get familiar with: 45°-45°-90° and 30°-60°-90° right triangles.

- The ratio of the sides of a 45-45-90 right triangle is $1 : 1 : \sqrt{2}$.
- The ratio of the sides of a 30-60-90 right triangles is $1 : \sqrt{3} : 2$.

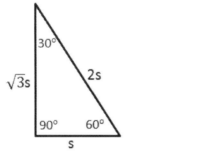

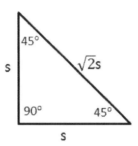

30-60-90 right triangle   45-45-90 right triangle

Example: Find the values of x and y.

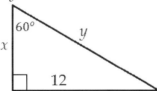

Answer: This is a 30-60-90 special right triangle. The ratio of sides is $1 : \sqrt{3} : 2$.

$$\frac{1}{x} = \frac{\sqrt{3}}{12} = \frac{2}{y}$$

Therefore, $x = 4\sqrt{3}$ and $y = 8\sqrt{3}$.

Problem Solving Skills

Easy

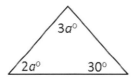

Note: Figure not drawn to scale.

1. Based on the figure above, what is the value of *a*?
   a) 25
   b) 30
   c) 35
   d) 40

Answer: (B)
Sum of Interior Angles = 180º
3a + 2a + 30 = 180
a = 30

2. In a triangle, one angle is double the size of another angle. If the measure of the third angle is 30 degrees, what is the measure of the largest angle in degrees?
   a) 70°
   b) 80°
   c) 90°
   d) 100°

Answer: (D)
Let x and 2x be two unknown angles.
30 + 2x + x = 180°
x = 50°
The largest angle is 2 × 50 = 100°.

3. In the figure below, if *a* = 3*c*, and *b* = 2*a*, what is the value of c? 🚫

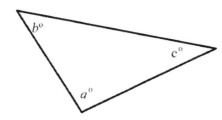

Note: Figure not drawn to scale.
   a) 18
   b) 20
   c) 28
   d) 34

Answer: (A)
a + b + c = 180
3c + 6c + c = 180
c = 18

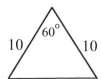

4. What is the length of the third side in the triangle above?

   a) 8
   b) 9
   c) 10
   d) 12

Answer: (C)
Isosceles triangle with base angles of 60° is an equilateral triangle.
The two angles at the base must be equal, so this triangle must be an equilateral triangle. This means that the third side has length 10.

5. In the figure below, ΔABC is an equilateral triangle. What is the value of $x + y$ in degrees?

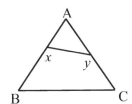

Answer: 240
The sum of the interior angles of a quadrilateral triangle is 360°.
$60° + 60° + x + y = 360°$
$x + y = 240°$

6. A 24-foot-long ladder is placed against a building to form a triangle with the sides of the building and ground. If the angle between ladder and ground is 60°, how far is the bottom of the ladder to the base of the building?

   a) 10
   b) $10\sqrt{3}$
   c) 12
   d) $12\sqrt{3}$

Answer: (C)
Since the building makes a 90° angle with the ground, the triangle must be a 30−60−90 special right triangle. The ladder itself is the hypotenuse and the bottom of the ladder to the base of the building is across from the 30° angle. Therefore, the distance between the bottom of the ladder and the base of the building is one half of the length of the ladder.

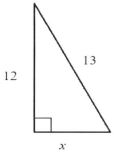

7. In the right triangle above, what is the value of x?

Answer: 5
Use the Pythagorean Theorem.
$x^2 + 12^2 = 13^2$
$x = 5$

8. A square and an equilateral triangle have equal perimeter. If the square has an area of 36 square feet, what is the length of one side of the triangle, in feet?
   a) 4
   b) 6
   c) 8
   d) 10

Answer: (C)
The length of a side of the square: $\sqrt{36}$ = 6. The perimeter of this square is 4 × 6 = 24. Let x be the length of one side of the triangle. The perimeter of the triangle is 3x.
3x = 24 → x = 8

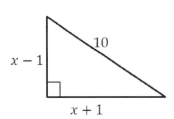

9. The figure above is a right triangle. If $x > 1$, what is the value of x?
   a) 6
   b) 7
   c) 8
   d) 9

Answer: (B)
Use the Pythagorean Theorem.
$(x-1)^2 + (x+1)^2 = 10^2$
$x^2 - 2x + 1 + x^2 + 2x + 1 = 100$
$2x^2 + 2 = 100$
$x^2 = 49$
$x = 7$

Medium

10. In the figure below shows ▲ABC and its exterior angle ∠DAC. What is the value of a?

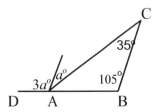

Answer: 35
3a + a = 35 + 105 = 140
4a = 140
a = 35

11. The three interior angle measures of a triangle have the ratio 3 : 4 : 5. What is the sum of the measures, in degrees, of the smallest and largest angles?
    a) 100°
    b) 110°
    c) 120°
    d) 140°

Answer: (C)
We can define the measures of the three angles to be 3x, 4x, and 5x.
$3x + 4x + 5x = 180°$
$x = 15°$
$3x + 5x = 8x = 8 × 15 = 120°$

12. The three angles of a triangle have measures $x°$, $2x°$, and $4y°$, where $x > 56$. If x and y are integers, what is one possible value of y?

Answer: 1 or 2
$x + 2x + 4y = 180$
$4y = 180 - 3x$
$4y < 180 - 3 \times 56$
$4y < 12 \rightarrow y < 3$
$y = 1, 2$

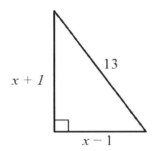

13. In the figure shown above, we assume that $x > 1$. What is the value of $2x^2 + 1$?
   a) 166
   b) 167
   c) 168
   d) 169

Answer: (C)
Use the Pythagorean Theorem.
$(x - 1)^2 + (x + 1)^2 = 13^2$
$x^2 - 2x + 1 + x^2 + 2x + 1 = 169$
$2x^2 + 1 = 168$

14. The lengths of the sides of a right triangle are consecutive even integers, and the length of the shortest side is x. Which of the following equations could be used to find x?
   a) $x^2 + (x + 1)^2 = (x + 2)^2$
   b) $x^2 + (x + 2)^2 = (x + 4)^2$
   c) $x + x + 2 = x + 4$
   d) $x^2 = (x + 2)(x + 4)$

Answer: (B)
Consecutive even integers can be written as x, $x + 2$, and $x + 4$. The longest side, $x + 4$, is the hypotenuse.
Apply the Pythagorean Theorem.
$x^2 + (x + 2)^2 = (x + 4)^2$

Hard

15. In the figure below, $\triangle ABC$ is an equilateral triangle with side of length 8. What is the radius of a circle that is inscribed inside of $\triangle ABC$?

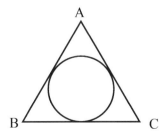

Answer: 2.30 or 2.31

The inner triangle is a 30-60-90 special right triangle. The ratio of its sides is $2 : \sqrt{3} : 1$
$\frac{r}{4} = \frac{1}{\sqrt{3}}$
$r = \frac{4}{\sqrt{3}} = \frac{4\sqrt{3}}{3} = 2.309$

16. In the figure below, ΔABC is an isosceles triangle where $m∠B = m∠C$ and **ΔDEF** is an equilateral triangle. If the measure of $∠ABC$ is 55° and the measure of $∠BDE$ is 75°, what is the measure of $∠DFA$?

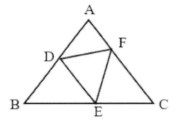

a) 40°
b) 55°
c) 60°
d) 65°

Answer: (D)
ΔDEF is an equilateral triangle, so m∠FDE = 60°.
m∠BDE + m∠FDE +
m∠FDA = 180°
180° − 75° − 60° =m∠FDA =
45°
m∠DFA + m∠FDA + m∠ A
= 180°
ΔABC is an isosceles Δ where
m∠B = m∠C.
m∠A = 180° − 2 × ∠B = 180°
− 2 × 55° = 70°
m∠DFA + 45° + 70° = 180°
m∠DFA = 65°

C. SIMILAR TRIANGLES

CONCEPT OVERVIEWS

When two triangles are similar, their corresponding angles are congruent and their corresponding sides are proportional.

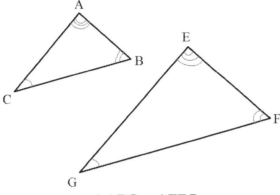

$$\Delta ABC \sim \Delta EFG$$
$$m\angle A = m\angle E, \, m\angle B = m\angle F, \, m\angle C = m\angle G$$
$$\frac{AB}{EF} = \frac{AC}{EG} = \frac{BC}{FG}$$

Similarity Theorems
- **SSS (Side-Side-Side) Similarity Theorem**: If the ratios of all three pairs of corresponding sides are equal, then the triangles are similar.
- **AA (Angle-Angle) Similarity Theorem**: If two angles of the first triangle are congruent to two angles of the second triangle, then the triangles are similar.
- **SAS (Side-Angle-Side) Similarity Theorem**: If the ratios of two pairs of corresponding sides are equal, and their included angles are congruent, then the triangles are similar.

Example: Find the length of $\overline{QS}$.

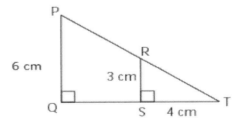

Answer: $\Delta RTS \sim \Delta PTQ$ by the AA (Angle-Angle) Similarity Theorem. Therefore,
$$\frac{TS}{TQ} = \frac{RS}{PQ} \rightarrow \frac{4}{TQ} = \frac{3}{6}$$
$$TQ = 8 \, ; QS = 8 - 4 = 4$$

Problem Solving Skills

Easy

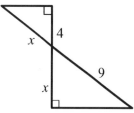

1. In the figure above, what is the value of x? 🚫
   a) 9
   b) 8
   c) 6
   d) $3\sqrt{5}$

Answer: (C)
The two triangles are similar by the AA Similarity Theorem.
$$\frac{x}{9} = \frac{4}{x}$$
$$x^2 = 36$$
$$x = 6$$

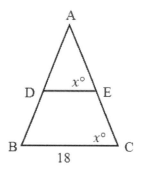

2. In the figure above, if $\overline{AD} = \overline{DB}$, what is the length of $\overline{DE}$? 🚫
   a) 6
   b) 9
   c) $9\sqrt{2}$
   d) 12

Answer: (B)
$\triangle ABC$ and $\triangle ADE$ are similar by the AA Similarity Thoerem.
$$\frac{AD}{AB} = \frac{1}{2} = \frac{DE}{BC}$$
$$\frac{1}{2} = \frac{DE}{18}$$
$$DE = 9$$

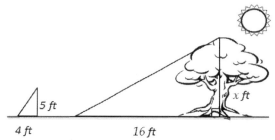

3. At a certain time of day, a tree casts a 16-foot shadow and a 5-foot stick casts a 4-foot shadow. What is the height, in feet, of the tree?

Answer: 20
The corresponding sides of two similar triangles are proportional.
$$\frac{5}{4} = \frac{x}{16} \rightarrow x = 20 \, ft$$

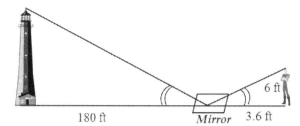

4. John places a mirror on the ground 180 feet from the base of a lighthouse. He walks backward until he can see the top of the lighthouse in the middle of the mirror. At that point, John's eyes are 6 feet above the ground and he is 3.6 feet from the mirror. Find the height, in feet, of the lighthouse.

Answer: 300
The two triangles are similar; therefore, their corresponding sides are proportional.
$$\frac{x}{180} = \frac{6}{3.6}$$
$x = 300\ feet$

Medium

5. In the figure below, points D is the mid-point of $\overline{AB}$ and point E is the mid-point of $\overline{AC}$. If AB = 10, AC = 12, and DE = 7, what is the perimeter of quadrilateral DBCE?

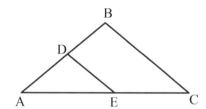

   a) 29
   b) 30
   c) 31
   d) 32

Answer: (D)
Point D is the mid-point of $\overline{AB}$ and point E is the mid-point of $\overline{AC}$, so $\frac{AD}{AB} = \frac{AE}{AC} = \frac{1}{2}$
Therefore, $\triangle ADE \sim \triangle ABC$ by SAS Similarity theorem
AB = 10
DB = 5
$\frac{1}{2} = \frac{DE}{BC}$
DE = 7
BC = 14
$EC = \frac{1}{2} AC = 6$
Perimeter of DBCE = 5 + 7 + 14 + 6 = 32

6. The figure below shows four squares with sides of length 4, 6, 9, and L. Line l_1 hits the upper left corner of each square. What is the value of L?

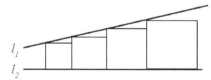

Answer: 13.5
There are 3 similar triangles between l_1 and the first 3 squares. Their heights have the same ratio as the ratio of the sides of the squares.
The first triangle has height 6 – 4 = 2. The second triangle has height 9 – 6 = 3. We will use y to denote the height of the third triangle.
4 : 6 : 9 = 2 : 3 : y
y = 4.5
L = Length of 3ʳᵈ Square + y = 9 + 4.5 = 13.5

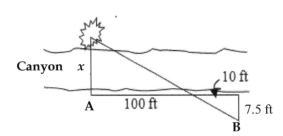

7. A bush fire is sighted on the other side of a canyon at points A and B as shown in the figure above. Find the width, in feet, of the canyon.

Answer: 75
The two triangles are similar; therefore, their corresponding sides are proportional.
$$\frac{x}{100} = \frac{7.5}{10} \rightarrow x = 75 \, feet$$

8. Jon walks 10 meters away from a wall outside his school building as shown in the figure below. At the point he stands, he notices that his shadow reaches to the same spot as the shadow of the school. If Jon is 1.6 meters tall and his shadow is 2.5 meters long, how high is the school building, in meters?

Answer: 8
Let the height of the school building be x.
The two triangles are similar; therefore, their corresponding sides are proportional.
$$\frac{2.5}{10 + 2.5} = \frac{1.6}{x}$$

$$x = 8 \, m$$

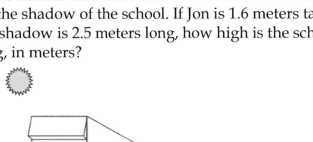

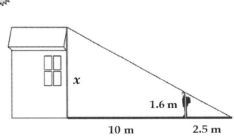

D. TRIANGLE INEQUALITY THEOREM

CONCEPT OVERVIEWS

The bigger side of a triangle is always opposite the bigger angle and the smaller side is always opposite the smaller angle.

Example: List the angles from largest to smallest based on the following triangle:

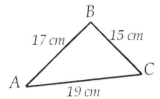

Answer: ∠B > ∠C > ∠A

Triangle Inequality Theorem: The length of one side of a triangle is always less than the sum of the lengths of the other two sides but greater than their difference.

Example: Which of the following could be the length of $\overline{YZ}$?

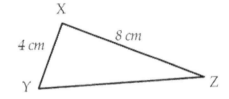

   a) 3
   b) 4
   c) 10
   d) 12

Answer: The difference of the lengths of any two sides of a triangle is less than the length of the third side in the triangle. The sum of the lengths of any two sides of a triangle is greater than the length of the third side of the triangle.
$8 - 4 < \overline{YZ} < 8 + 4$
$4 < \overline{YZ} < 12$
Only (c) satisfies these conditions.

Problem Solving Skills

Easy

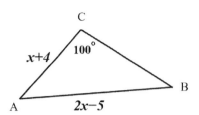

1. In ΔABC above, which of the following must be true?
    a) $x < 18$
    b) $x > 18$
    c) $x < 9$
    d) $x > 9$

    Answer: (D)
    ∠C is the biggest angle so that
    $\overline{AB}$ must be the longest side.
    $2x - 5 > x + 4$
    $x > 9$

2. If one triangle has two sides that have lengths of 3 and 8, which of the following CANNOT be the length of the third side of the triangle?
    a) 5
    b) 6
    c) 8
    d) 9

    Answer: (A)
    The length of the 3rd side should be smaller than the sum of the lengths of the other two sides and greater than their difference.
    $8 - 3 < x < 8 + 3$
    $5 < x < 11$

3. Which of the following cannot be the lengths of the three sides of a triangle?
    a) 6, 4, and 3
    b) 6, 3, and 5
    c) 6, 5, and 11
    d) 6, 6, and 10

    Answer: (C)
    Let the lengths of the two sides other than the side with length 6 be x and y, where x > y.
    $x - y < 6 < x + y$
    Only (c) violates above condition.

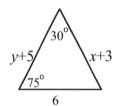

Note: Figure not drawn to scale.

4. In the triangle above, which of the following must be true?
    a) $x = y$
    b) $x = 6$
    c) $x < y$
    d) $x = y + 2$

    Answer: (D)
    The degree of the 3rd interior angle is 180° – 30° –75° = 75°.
    Since this triangle has two angles that are 75°, it is an isosceles triangle.
    $y + 5 = x + 3$
    $x = y + 2$

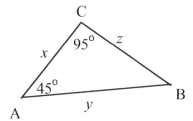

5. Which of the following must be true about x, y, and z in the figure above?
    a) $x < z < y$
    b) $z < x < y$
    c) $x < y < z$
    d) $z < y < x$

Answer: (A)
The bigger angle is always facing the bigger side.
$m\angle C > m\angle A > m\angle B$
$y > z > x$

6. An isosceles triangle has one side that has length 6. All of the following could be the lengths of the other two sides EXCEPT?
    a) 4, 4
    b) 6, 3
    c) 6, 10
    d) 6, 12

Answer: (D)
Case 1:length of three sides: 6, 6, x
$6 - 6 < x < 6 + 6$
$0 < x < 12$
Case 2 length of three sides: 6, x, x
$6 - x < x < 6 + x$
$x > 3$
(a), (b), and (c) all satisfy either case 1 or case 2.

7. In $\triangle ABC$ below, $\angle ACB$ is 91°. Which of the following segments has the longest length?

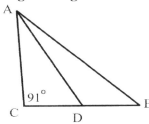

    a) Segment AD
    b) Segment AC
    c) Segment CB
    d) Segment AB

Answer: (D)
In a triangle, bigger angles will always face bigger sides. No angle in $\triangle ABC$ will have degree greater than 91, so the side facing $\angle ACB$ will be largest.
$\angle ADB > \angle ACD$ (by exterior angle theorem)
$AB > AD > AC$ and CD

Medium

8. What is one possible integer length of $\overline{AC}$ if $\angle A > \angle B > \angle C$?

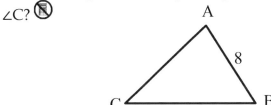

Answer: 9
The longest side of a triangle is opposite the largest angle.
Since $\angle A > \angle B > \angle C$,
$\overline{BC} > \overline{AC} > \overline{AB}$, and so
$10 > \overline{AC} > 8$. The only possible integer is 9.

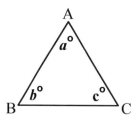

Note: Figure not drawn to scale.

9. The triangle above is isosceles and $a > b$. Which of the following must be FALSE?
   a) $AB = BC$
   b) $BC = AC$
   c) $AC = AB$
   d) $a = c$

Answer: (B)
If $a > b$, then $BC > AC$.

Hard

10. If the lengths of the sides of a certain triangle are x, y, and z, which of the following statements could be true?
    a) $x = y + z + 1$
    b) $x = y - z - 1$
    c) $x = 2y + z$
    d) $x = z + \frac{1}{2}y$

Answer: (D)
$y - z < x < y + z$
Only (d) meets the above conditions.

11. The lengths of two sides of a triangle are $(x + 1)$ and $(x + 3)$, where x is a positive number. Which of the following ranges includes all the possible values of the third side?
    a) $(0, x)$
    b) $(0, 2x)$
    c) $(2, 2x)$
    d) $(2, 2x + 4)$

Answer: (D)
$(x + 3) - (x + 1) < y < (x + 3) + (x + 1)$
$2 < y < 2x + 4$

II. POLYGONS AND CIRCLES

A. POLYGONS

CONCEPT OVERVIEWS

A **polygon** is a plane figure composed of three or more line segments that are connected at both ends.

The Properties of a Parallelogram
A **parallelogram** is a special type of quadrilateral where both pairs of opposite sides are parallel. Parallelograms have the following properties:
   1. Opposite sides are equal in length and parallel.

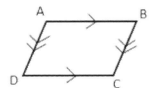

$$\overleftrightarrow{AB} \parallel \overleftrightarrow{DC} \text{ and } \overleftrightarrow{AD} \parallel \overleftrightarrow{BC}$$
$$\overline{AB} = \overline{DC} \text{ and } \overline{AD} = \overline{BC}$$

   2. Opposite angles are congruent.

   3. Consecutive angles are supplementary.

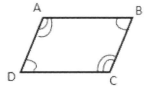

$$\angle A \cong \angle C \text{ and } \angle B \cong \angle D$$

$$m\angle A + m\angle B = 180^\circ \qquad m\angle A + m\angle D = 180^\circ$$
$$m\angle D + m\angle C = 180^\circ \qquad m\angle B + m\angle C = 180^\circ$$

   4. A diagonal of any parallelogram makes two congruent triangles.

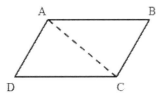

$$\triangle ABC \cong \triangle CDA$$

   5. The diagonals of any parallelogram bisect each other.

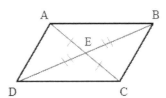

$$\overline{AE} = \overline{CE} \text{ and } \overline{DE} = \overline{BE}$$

Special Parallelograms
- A **rhombus** is a parallelogram with four equal sides. Rhombuses have the following properties in addition to the properties of parallelograms:
    - ○ Diagonals are perpendicular.

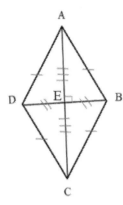

$\overline{AB} = \overline{CD}$ and $\overline{AD} = \overline{BC}$
$\overline{AC} \perp \overline{DB}$

- A **rectangle** is a parallelogram with four right angles. Rectangles have the following properties in addition to the properties of parallelograms:
    - ○ Diagonals are equal in length.

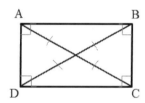

$\overline{AC} = \overline{BD}$

- A **square** is a regular quadrilateral with four equal sides and four right angles. Squares have all the properties of parallelograms, rhombuses, and rectangles, since they are a special case of all three.
    - ○ Diagonals are equal.
    - ○ Diagonals are perpendicular.

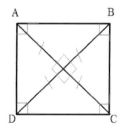

$\overline{AC} = \overline{BD}$ and $\overline{AC} \perp \overline{DB}$

Sum of Interior Angles of a Polygon
Since an n-sided polygon can be divided into (n – 2) triangles without overlapping and the sum of the interior angles of each triangle is 180°, the sum of the interior angles of a polygon is equal to **(n − 2) × 180°**

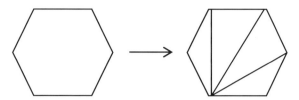

- A **regular polygon** is a polygon where all sides are equal in length and all angles have the same degree measure.

- Each interior angle of a regular polygon is $(\frac{(n-2) \times 180}{n})°$.

Sum of Exterior Angles of a Polygon

For an n-sided polygon, the sum of its exterior angles is equal to

$$n \times 180° - (n-2) \times 180° = 360°.$$

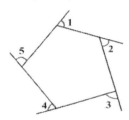

The 5 exterior angles of a pentagon sum to 360°.

Example: Find the measure of each interior angle of a regular heptagon as shown below and find the measure of x.

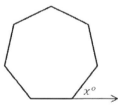

Answer: When $n = 7$, the measure of each interior angle is $\frac{(7-2) \times 180°}{7} = 128.6°$.

$x = 180 - 128.6 = 51.4$

Problem Solving Skills

Easy

1. If the perimeter of an equilateral triangle equals the perimeter of a square, what is the ratio of the length of a side of the square to the length of a side of the triangle?

    a) 1 : 1
    b) 2 : 3
    c) 3 : 4
    d) 4 : 3

Answer: (C)
Let the length of the side of the triangle be x and the length of the side of the square be y.
3x = 4y
y : x = 3 : 4

2. The perimeter of square X is 5 times the perimeter of square Y. If the area of square Y is 36, then what is the length of the side of square X?
    a) 18
    b) 24
    c) 28
    d) 30

Answer: (D)
Area of a Square = Side²
Side of X : Side of Y = 5 : 1
Area of X : Area of Y = 25 : 1
Area of X = 25 × 36 = 900
Side of X = √900 = 30

3. Point A is a vertex of a 10-sided polygon. When all possible diagonals are drawn from point A to any other vertex of the polygon, how many triangles are formed?

    a) 10
    b) 9
    c) 8
    d) 7

Answer: (C)
There are always (n – 2) non-overlapping triangles formed by drawing all the possible non-intersecting diagonals in an n-sided polygon.
10 – 2 = 8 triangles

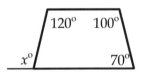

Note: Figure not drawn to scale.

4. What is the value of x in the figure above?
    a) 70
    b) 100
    c) 105
    d) 110

Answer: (D)
The sum of the interior angles of a quadrilateral is equal to 360°.
120 + 100 + 70 + (180 – x) = 360
x = 110

5. The figure shown below is composed of five straight line segments, what is the value of x?

Answer: 80

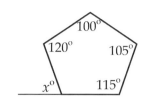

Note: Figure not drawn to scale.

The sum of all interior angles of a pentagon is (5 − 3) × 180 = 540°.
540 = 120 + 100 + 105 + 115 + (180 − x)
x = 80

6. The figure shown below is a regular octagon with center O. What is the value of *a*?

a) 90
b) 72.5
c) 70
d) 67.5

Answer: (D)

There are two congruent isosceles triangles shown above. The measure of a is one half of an interior angle.
The interior angle of a regular octagon is $\frac{(8-2) \times 180}{8}$ degrees.
$a = \frac{6 \times 180}{8} \times \frac{1}{2} = 67.5$

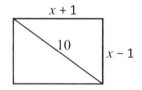

7. The figure above is a rectangle. What is the perimeter of the rectangle?
   a) 32
   b) 28
   c) 25
   d) 24

Answer: (B)
Use the Pythagorean Theorem to find x.
$(x - 1)^2 + (x + 1)^2 = 10^2$
$x^2 - 2x + 1 + x^2 + 2x + 1 = 100$
$2x^2 + 2 = 100$
$x^2 = 49 \rightarrow x = 7$
Perimeter = 2(7 + 1) + 2(7 − 1) = 28

8. In the figure below, a regular polygon is inscribed in a circle O. If O is the center of the circle, what is the value of *a*?

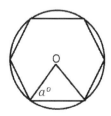

Answer: 60
The measurement of a is half of an interior angle of the regular polygon.
$a = \frac{1}{2} \times (\frac{6-2}{6} \times 180) = 60$

Medium

9. In quadrilateral ABCD, $m\angle A = m\angle B = 128°$, and $m\angle D$ is 10° less than 5 times of $m\angle C$. Find $m\angle D$.

Answer: 85
$A + B + C + D = 360°$
$128°+128°+ 5x –10°+ x = 360°$
$x = 19°$
$5x –10°= 85°$

10. In the figure below, what is the value of a?

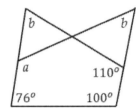

Answer: 110
Use the two quadrilaterals to set up an equation.
$b + 110 + 100 + 76$
$= b + a + 76 + 100$
$a = 110°$

11. The area of a rectangle is 2,400 square meters. If the length of one side of the rectangle is 80 meters, what is the perimeter of the rectangle, in meters?

Answer: 220
Area of a Rectangle = Length × Width
$2400 = 80x$
$x = 30$; Perimeter $= (30 + 80) × 2$
$= 220$ meters

12. In the figure below, what is the value of $a + b + c$?

Answer: 410
The sum of all interior angles is equal to $180 × (7 – 2)$.
$180 × (7 – 2) = 900 = a + b + c + 130 + 125 + 120 + 115$
$a + b + c = 410$

Note: Figure not drawn to scale.

Hard

13. If the perimeter of the figure below is 30, what is the sum of x and y?

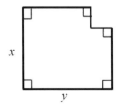

Answer: 15
The perimeter of the figure should be the same as the perimeter of the rectangle: $2(x + y) = 30$
$x + y = 15$

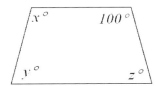

Note: Figure not drawn to scale.

14. In the quadrilateral above, if $x > 90$, which of the following is one possible value of $y + z$?
    a) 240
    b) 200
    c) 180
    d) 100

Answer: (D)
The sum of the interior angles of a quadrilateral is equal to 360°.
$360 = 100 + x + y + z$
$x + y + z = 260$
$x > 90 \rightarrow y + z < 170$
$x < 180 \rightarrow y + z > 80$
$80 < z + y < 170$

15. The figure below shows an arrangement of 14 squares, each with side length of x inches. The perimeter of the figure is P inches and the area of the figure is A square inches. If $7P = A$, what is the value of x?

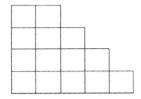

Answer: 9
Area of a Square = Side²
The perimeter P is equal to 18x and its area is equal to 14 × x².
$7P = A$
$7 \times 18x = 14x^2$
$x = 9$

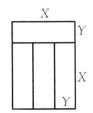

16. The unit above is composed of four congruent rectangular tiles which are each X inches long and Y inches wide. If this pattern unit will be used repeatedly to fully cover a square which has a side of 24Y inches, how many of rectangular tiles with dimension X×Y will be used?
    a) 192
    b) 144
    c) 122
    d) 96

Answer: (A)
X is equal to 3Y, so the unit is 3Y × 4Y.
The total number of units needed is $\frac{24}{3} \times \frac{24}{4} = 48$. The total number of rectangular tiles used is $48 \times 4 = 192$.

B. Circles

Concept Overviews

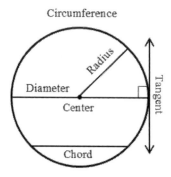

Segments of a Circle

The **radius** is a line segment that connects the center of a circle with any point on the circle. The lengths of all the radii of a circle are equal. A **chord** is a line segment that connects any two points on a circle. The **diameter** is a chord that passes through the center of the circle. The diameter is the longest chord in the circle and has length equal to twice the radius. A **tangent** line is a line that intersects the circle at exactly one point. A radius that touches the point of the tangent is perpendicular to the tangent line.

A radius that is perpendicular to a chord bisects the chord:

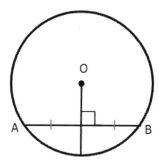

Arc Length and Circumference of the Circle

An **arc** is a curved segment of the circle. Connecting two endpoints of the arc to the center of the circle forms a **central angle**. An arc with a central angle less than 180° is called **minor arc** while an arc with a central angle greater than 180° is called **major arc**. A diameter divides its circle into two equal arcs of 180° known as **semicircles**.

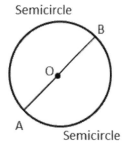

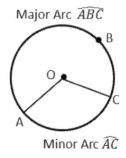

Circumference of a Circle

The **circumference** of a circle is equal to $2\pi r$, where r is the radius of the circle.

Example: Find the circumference of the circle below.

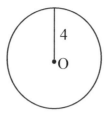

Answer: $r = 4$

$2\pi r = 2\pi \times 4 = 8\pi$

Length of an Arc

A whole circle has 360°. An arc with a central angle of θ is $\dfrac{\theta}{360}$ of a whole circle, so the

length of the arc is equal to : $\dfrac{\theta}{360} \times 2\pi r$

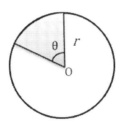

Example: Find the length of arc AB in the figure below.

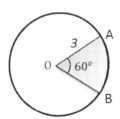

Answer: $r = 3$, so the length of arc $AB = \dfrac{\theta}{360} \times 2\pi r = \dfrac{60}{360} \times 2\pi (3) = \pi$.

Area of a Circle

The area of a circle is πr^2, where r is the radius of the circle.

Example: Find the area of the circle below.

Answer: $r = 5$

$\pi r^2 = \pi \times 5^2 = 25\pi$

Area of a Sector

A **sector** with a central angle of θ is $\dfrac{\theta}{360}$ of a whole circle, so the area of the sector is $\dfrac{\theta}{360}\pi r^2$.

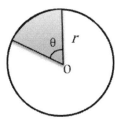

Example: Find the area of sector with the central angle 60° in the figure below.

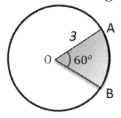

Answer: $\dfrac{\theta}{360}\pi r^2 = \dfrac{60}{360}\pi(3)^2 = \dfrac{3}{2}\pi$

Equations of Circles

A circle is the set of all points on a plane that are a fixed distance from a point, its center. The fixed distance is the radius of the circle. Any equation that can be written in the form of $(x - h)^2 + (y - k)^2 = r^2$ is a graph of the circle with radius r and center at point (h, k).

Example: Find the center and radius of the circle given by the equation
$$(x - 2)^2 + (y + 1)^2 = 4.$$
Answer: According to the standard equation of a circle, the center of this circle is $(2, -1)$ and the radius is 2.

Example: Find the center and radius of the circle given by the equation $x^2 + y^2 - 4x + 2y = 20$.
Answer: Rewrite the original equation into the standard equation of a circle:
$$x^2 + y^2 - 4x + 2y = 20$$
$$(x^2 - 4x + 2^2) + (y^2 + 2y + 1^2) = 20 + 2^2 + 1^2 = 25$$
$$(x - 2)^2 + (y + 1)^2 = 5^2$$
The center of the circle is $(2, -1)$ and the radius is 5.

Problem Solving Skills

Easy

1. The diameter of a semi-circle is 4. What is its perimeter?
   a) $2\pi + 2$
   b) $2\pi + 4$
   c) $2\pi + 6$
   d) $\pi + 2$

Answer: (B)
The perimeter of semicircle is the sum of half of the circumference of a circle plus the length of the diameter.
Perimeter $= \frac{1}{2}(2\pi\, r) + 2r$
$= \frac{1}{2} \times 2\pi \times 2 + 2 \times 2 = 2\pi + 4$

2. A chord of a circle is 2 inches away from the center of the circle at its closest point. If the circle has a 3-inch radius, what is the length of this chord, in inches?
   a) 1
   b) $\sqrt{5}$
   c) 2
   d) $2\sqrt{5}$

Answer: (D)

$x = \sqrt{3^2 - 2^2} = \sqrt{5}$
Length of Chord $= 2\sqrt{5}$ inches

3. Point O is the center of the circle in the figure below. If angle ∠PQO = 65°, what is the measure of the center angle ∠POQ in degrees?

Answer: 50
Triangle PQO is an isosceles triangle with base angles 65°.
$2 \times m\angle PQO + m\angle POQ = 180°$
$m\angle PQO = 65°$
$m\angle POQ = 180 - 2 \times 65 = 50°$

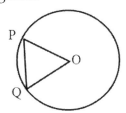

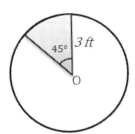

4. In the figure above, the circle has a center O and radius of 3 ft. What is the area of the shaded portion, in square feet?
   a) $\frac{3}{4}\pi$
   b) $\frac{9}{8}\pi$
   c) $\frac{11}{8}\pi$
   d) 1.5π

Answer: (B)
The area of the shaded portion is $\frac{45}{360}$ of the area of the whole circle.
Shaded Area $= \frac{45}{360} \times \pi \times 3^2 = \frac{9}{8}\pi$

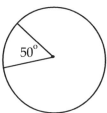

5. In the figure above, a piece with a 50° center angle has been cut out of an 18-ounce pie. How many ounces was the piece of pie that was cut out?

Answer: 2.5
Weight of Pie : 360° = Weight of Piece : 50°
$18 : 360° = x : 50°$
$\frac{18}{360} = \frac{x}{50} \rightarrow x = 2.5 \text{ ounces}$

6. In the figure below, points A and B lie on circle O. If $\angle AOB = y°$, what is the value of x in term of y?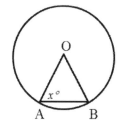

Answer: (D)
ΔOAB is an isosceles Δ.
$2 \times x + y = 180$
$x = \frac{1}{2}(180 - y) = 90 - \frac{1}{2}y$

a) y
b) $90 - y$
c) $180 - y$
d) $90 - \frac{1}{2}y$

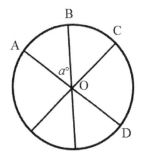

<u>Note</u>: Figure not drawn to scale.

7. In the figure above, O is the center of the circle, $\widehat{AB} = \widehat{BC}$, and $\widehat{AC} = \widehat{CD}$. What is the value of a, in degrees?

Answer: 45
$\widehat{AB}$ is half of $\widehat{AC}$ so it is $\frac{1}{4}$ of $\widehat{AD}$.
$a = \frac{1}{4} \times 180°$
$a = 45°$

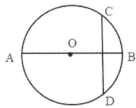

8. The figure above shows a circle with center O. Segments AB and CD are perpendicular and AB passes through point O. If the length of AB is 10 and length of CD is 8, what is the distance of O to line CD?

   a) 2
   b) 3
   c) 4
   d) 5

Answer: (B)

$$Distance = \sqrt{\overline{OC}^2 - \left(\frac{\overline{CD}}{2}\right)^2}$$
$$= \sqrt{5^2 - 4^2} = 3$$

9. In the circle below, hexagon ABCDEF is equilateral. What is the ratio of the length of arc ABCD to the length of arc AFE?

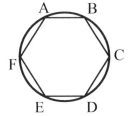

   a) 1 to 2
   b) 2 to 3
   c) 3 to 2
   d) 4 to 5

Answer: (C)
The arc ABCD is 3 times the arc AB and arc AFE is 2 times the arc AB (since the polygon is regular).
ABCD : AFE = 3 : 2

10. The area of circle A is 9 times the area of circle B. What is the ratio of the diameter of circle A to the diameter of circle B?

   a) 9 : 1
   b) 6 : 1
   c) 3 : 1
   d) 3 : 2

Answer: (C)
The ratio of the diameter of two circles is the square root of the ratio of their areas.
Ratio = $\sqrt{9} : \sqrt{1}$ = 3 : 1

11. What is the difference, in degrees, between an arc that is $\frac{3}{8}$ of a circle and an arc that is $\frac{1}{3}$ of a circle?

   a) 20°
   b) 18°
   c) 15°
   d) 12°

Answer: (C)
$\left(\frac{3}{8} - \frac{1}{3}\right) \times 360° = 15°$

12. Segment $\overline{AB}$ is the diameter of a circle with center O. Another point C lies on circle O. If AC = 6 and BC = 8, what is the area of circle O?

    a) 25π
    b) 50π
    c) 100π
    d) 200π

Answer: (A)
$\triangle ABC$ is a right triangle.
$AB^2 = AC^2 + BC^2$
$AB = \sqrt{6^2 + 8^2} = 10$
$Radius = \frac{1}{2}(10) = 5$
$Area = \pi \times 5^2 = 25\pi$

13. One circle has a radius of 3 and another circle has a radius of 2. What is the ratio of the area of the larger circle to the area of the smaller circle?

    a) $3:2$
    b) $9:4$
    c) $3:1$
    d) $4:1$

Answer: (B)
The ratio of the areas of two circles is equal to the square of the ratio of their radius.
$3^2 : 2^2 = 9 : 4$

Medium

14. In the figure below, rectangle ABOC is drawn in circle O. If OB = 3 and OC = 4, what is the area of the shaded region?

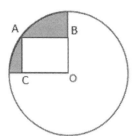

    a) $6\pi - 3$
    b) $\frac{25\pi}{4} - 12$
    c) $25\pi - 12$
    d) $\frac{25\pi}{4} - 3$

Answer: (B)
OA is the radius of the circle and the shaded area is the area of the quarter circle minus the area of the rectangle.
$Radius = \sqrt{OB^2 + OC^2} = \sqrt{3^2 + 4^2} = 5$
$Shaded\ Area = Area\ of\ \frac{1}{4}\ Circle -$
$Area\ of\ Rectangle =$
$\frac{1}{4}(\pi \times 5^2) - 4 \times 3$
$= \frac{1}{4} \times 25\pi - 12$
$= \frac{25\pi}{4} - 12$

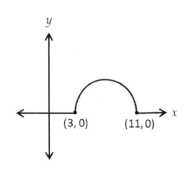

15. In the figure above, what is the sum of the x and y coordinates of the highest point on the above semicircle?

    a) 6

    b) 8

    c) 9

    d) 11

Answer: (D)
The highest point is at the middle of semicircle.

y-Coordinate = Radius = $\frac{11-3}{2} = 4$

x-Coordinate = $\frac{1}{2}(3 + 11) = 7$

x-Coordinate + y-Coordinate = 11

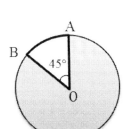

16. The circle above has an area of 16π. What is the perimeter of the shaded region?

    a) $8 - \frac{1}{3}\pi$

    b) $8 + 7\pi$

    c) $8 + \frac{2}{3}\pi$

    d) $8 + \frac{1}{3}\pi$

Answer: (B)
The perimeter of the shaded region is equal to the major arc length plus twice the radius.
Perimeter = Major Arc Length + 2 × Radius
To find the radius, we solve:
    $\pi r^2 = 16\pi \;\rightarrow\; r = 4$
Arc Length of Shaded Region =
$\frac{2 \times \pi r \times (360^{o} - 45^{o})}{360^{o}} = 7\pi$
Perimeter of Shaded Region =
$7\pi + 8$

17. In the figure below, the two circles are tangent at point P and OQ = 9. If the area of the circle with center O is four times the area of the circle with center Q, what is the length of OP?

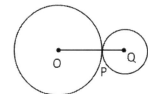

Answer: (C)
Since the area of circle O is four times the area of circle Q, the radius of circle O is $\sqrt{4}$ times of the radius of circle Q.
If PQ = r, OP = 2r, then r + 2r = 9.
r = 3 = PQ
OP = 9 – 3 = 6

a) 2
b) 4
c) 6
d) 8

18. In the figure above, O is the center of the two circles. If the bigger circle has a radius of 5 and the smaller circle has a radius of 4, what is the area of shaded region?

    a) 2π
    b) π
    c) $\frac{9}{8}\pi$
    d) $\frac{1}{2}\pi$

Answer: (C)
$Area = \frac{45}{360}(\pi \times 5^2 - \pi \times 4^2) = \frac{9}{8}\pi$

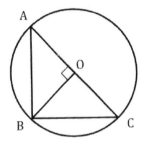

19. In the figure above, a circle O with diameter $\overline{AC}$ has an area of 16π. What is the length of segment $\overline{AB}$?

    a) 4
    b) 6
    c) $6\sqrt{2}$
    d) $4\sqrt{2}$

Answer: (D)
$\triangle OAB$ is a 45–45–90 special right triangle.
$Radius = OA = \sqrt{16} = 4 = OB$
$AB = \sqrt{OA^2 + OB^2} = 4\sqrt{2}$

Hard

20. Circle A has an area of 4π and circle B has an area of 9π. If the circles intersect at only one point, what is the sum of all possible distances from the center of circle A to the center of circle B?

Answer: 6
There are only two possible distances. The longer distance is the sum of the two radii and the shorter distance is the difference of the two radii.
Radius of Big Circle = 3
Radius of Small Circle = 2
$x = 3 - 2$ *or* $3 + 2$ → $x = 1$ *or* 5

$1 + 5 = 6$

21. In the diagram below, AB is tangent to circle O at point B. AB = 2AC and the radius has length 3. What is the length of $\overline{AO}$?

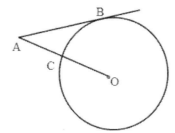

Answer: 5
ΔOAB is a right triangle with hypotenuse $\overline{OA}$, so use the Pythagorean Theorem.
$OB = OC = 3$
$AC = x \rightarrow AB = 2x$
$AO = 3 + x$
$(2x)^2 + 3^2 = (3 + x)^2$
$4x^2 + 9 = x^2 + 6x + 9$
$3x^2 = 6x \rightarrow x = 2$
$AO = 5$

22. In the figure below, circle O is tangent to a square at points A and B. If the area of ΔABC is 8, what is the area of the circle?

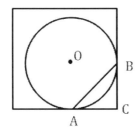

Answer: (D)
Since CB = CA, ΔABC is an isosceles right triangle.
Area of $\Delta ABC = \frac{1}{2} \times AC^2 = 8$
$AC = 4$
Since OB is a radius of the circle and it is equal to AC, the radius of the circle has length 4.
Area of Circle $= \pi \times 4^2 = 16\pi$

a) 4π
b) 6π
c) $6\sqrt{2}\pi$
d) 16π

III. AREAS AND VOLUMES

CONCEPT OVERVIEWS

Area of a Triangle

$$Area\ of\ a\ Triangle = \frac{Base \times Height}{2}$$

The **height** of a triangle is the perpendicular distance from the **base** to the opposite vertex.

Some different triangles with different bases and heights are shown below:

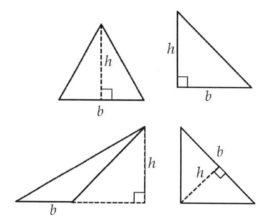

Area of an Equilateral Triangle $= \frac{\sqrt{3}}{4} s^2$, where s is the length of a side.

Example: Find the area of this triangle.

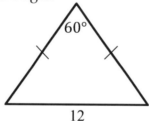

Solution: This is an equilateral triangle with equal side length of 12.
The easy way to solve this problem is to apply the formula for finding the area of an equilateral.

$$A = \frac{\sqrt{3}}{4}s^2 = \frac{\sqrt{3}}{4} \times 12^2 = 36\sqrt{3}$$

If the ratio of the corresponding sides of two similar triangles is $a : b$, then the ratio of their areas is $a^2 : b^2$.

Example: Find the area of triangle B if the triangles A and B are similar.

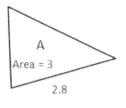
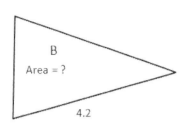

Solution: In two similar triangles, the ratio of their areas is equal to the square of the ratio of their sides.

Let the area of B be x.

Set up the proportion: $\left(\dfrac{2.8}{4.2}\right)^2 = \dfrac{3}{x} \rightarrow \dfrac{0.44}{1} = \dfrac{3}{x}$

Cross multiply: $0.44x = 3 \rightarrow x = 6.82$

Area of a Parallelogram: Base × Height
$$A = b \times h$$

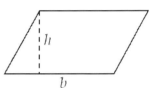

Area of a Rectangle: Length × Width
$$A = l \times w$$

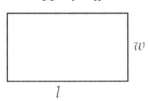

Area of a Square:
- Side × Side = (Side)^2
- $\dfrac{1}{2}$ × (Diagonal)^2

$$A = s^2 = \dfrac{1}{2}d^2$$

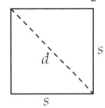

Area of a Rhombus: $\frac{1}{2}$ × Diagonal 1 × Diagonal 2

$$A = \frac{1}{2} \times d_1 \times d_2$$

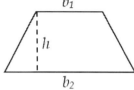

Area of a Trapezoid: $\frac{1}{2}$ × (Base 1 + Base 2) × Height

$$A = \frac{1}{2} \times (b_1 + b_2) \times h$$

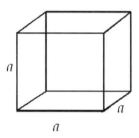

Volumes of 3-D Figures
Cubes
Surface area: $6a^2$
Volume: a^3

Rectangular Prisms
Surface area: $2(w \times h + l \times w + l \times h)$
Volume: $l \times w \times h$

Diagonal of a rectangular prism: $d = \sqrt{h^2 + l^2 + w^2}$

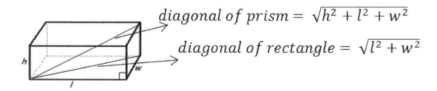

$$\text{diagonal of prism} = \sqrt{h^2 + l^2 + w^2}$$
$$\text{diagonal of rectangle} = \sqrt{l^2 + w^2}$$

Cylinders

Surface area: $2\pi r^2 + 2\pi rh$

Volume: $\pi r^2 h$

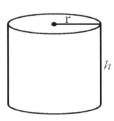

Cones

Volume: $\frac{1}{3}$ (Area of Base) × (Height) = $\frac{1}{3}\pi r^2 h$

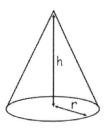

Pyramids

Volume: $\frac{1}{3}$ (Area of Base) × (Height) = $\frac{1}{3} l \times w \times h$

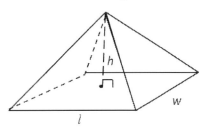

Problem Solving Skills

Easy

1. A rectangular storage room has a volume of 9,375 cubic feet. If its length is 75 feet and its height is 5 feet, what is the width of the room?

Answer: 25
Volume = Length × Height × Width
9375 = 75 × 5 × Width
Width = 25 feet

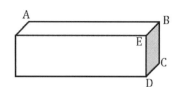

2. In the rectangular solid above, the area of BCDE is 10 and $\overline{AB}$ = 12. What is the volume of this solid?
   a) 120
   b) 180
   c) 240
   d) 90

Answer: (A)
Volume = Area of Base × Height =
10 × 12 = 120

3. A truck has a container with dimensions 40 × 12 × 8 feet. How many cubic boxes with side length of 2 feet can fit into the container?

Answer: 480
Total Number of Boxes =
$\frac{40}{2} \times \frac{12}{2} \times \frac{8}{2}$ = 480 boxes

4. A rectangular box is 24 inches long, 18 inches wide, and 12 inches high. What is the least number of cubic boxes that can be stored perfectly in this box?
   a) 12
   b) 18
   c) 24
   d) 36

Answer: (C)
Cubic boxes' length, width, and height have the same length, so the number of cubic boxes must be a common factor of 24, 18, and 12. To find the minimum number of boxes, we need to find the GCF (greatest common factor) of these three numbers.
The GCF of 24, 18 and 12 is 6, so there are $\frac{24}{6} \times \frac{18}{6} \times \frac{12}{6}$ cubic boxes.
$\frac{24}{6} \times \frac{18}{6} \times \frac{12}{6}$ = 24

5. The dimensions of the rectangular storage box shown on the above left are 2 feet by 2 feet by 1 foot. What is the maximum number of Lego blocks (shown on the right) that can fit inside the storage box if each Lego block has dimensions 4 inches by 4 inches by 1 inch?

Answer: 432

2 feet by 2 feet by 1 foot = 24 inches by 24 inches by 12 inches
$\frac{24}{4} \times \frac{24}{4} \times \frac{12}{1}$ = 432 Legos

Medium

6. The cube shown above has side length a. What is the length of its diagonal as drawn?
   a) a
   b) $2a$
   c) $\sqrt{2}a$
   d) $\sqrt{3}a$

Answer: (D)

Diagonal $= \sqrt{a^2 + a^2 + a^2} = \sqrt{3}a$

7. What is the volume of a cube if its total surface area is 96 square units?

Answer: 64
Let a be the length of one side of the cube.
Surface Area $= 6 \times a^2 = 96$
a = 4
Volume $= a^3 = 4^3 = 64$

Questions 8 − 9 refer to the following information:
   Density describes how compact or concentrated a material is. It is defined as the ratio between mass and volume, or mass per unit volume. The formula to calculate the density is:
$$Density = \frac{Mass}{Volume}$$

8. The kilobar of gold is 1,000 grams in mass. If the density of the gold bar is 19.3 grams per cm^3, what would be the volume of the kilobar, in cm^3? (Round your answer to the nearest tenth)

Answer: 51.8

$Density = \frac{Mass}{Volume}$

$19.3 = \frac{1000}{Volume}$

$Volume = \frac{1000}{19.3} = 51.8\ cm^3$

9. If a cylinder gold block has a diameter of 2 centimeters and height of 10 centimeters, what would be its mass, in grams? (Round your answer to the nearest whole number.)

Answer: 606
$Volume = \pi r^2 h = \pi \times 1^2 \times 10$
$Mass = 19.3 \times 10\pi = 606.3$

Hard

10. In the rectangular solid below, the total surface area is 40. Face A has an area 4 and face B has an area 8. What is the volume of the rectangular solid?

Answer: 16
Area of Face C $= \frac{1}{2} \times 40 -$ Area of Face A − Area of Face B = 20 − 4 − 8 = 8
Let the lengths of the three different sides be x, y, and z respectively, then the volume of the solid is x × y × z.
Area of Face A = x × y = 4
Area of Face B = y × z = 8
Area of Face C = x × z = 8
(xy) × (yz) × (zx) = 4 × 8 × 8
$(xyz)^2 = 256$
$xyz = \sqrt{4 \times 8 \times 8} = 16$

11. In the figure below, a circular cylinder has radius 3 and height 5. What is the volume of the smallest rectangular box that can store this circular cylinder inside?

a) 120
b) 150
c) 180
d) 200

Answer: (C)
The smallest rectangular box that can contain this cylinder should have both its width and length equal to the diameter of the cylinder, and its height equal to the height of the cylinder.
Volume of Rectangle =
$(2 \times r)^2 \times h$
$6^2 \times 5 = 180$

12. The right circular cylinder above has radius *r* and height *h*. Which of the following can represent the volume of the biggest rectangular box that is completely inscribed inside the cylinder?
    a) $r \times h$
    b) $2 \times r^2 \times h$
    c) $2 \times r^2 \times h^2$
    d) $\frac{(2r + h)^2}{2}$

Answer: (B)
The diagonal of the base of the rectangular box must be equal to diameter of the cylinder in order to be inscribed inside the cylinder.
The biggest rectangular box inside the cylinder must have a square of base.
Area of Base $= \frac{1}{2} \times Diagonal^2$
$= 2r^2$
Volume of Box $= 2r^2 \times h$

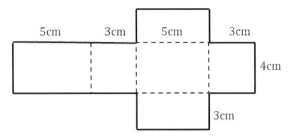

5cm   3cm   5cm   3cm

4cm

3cm

13. If the figure above is folded along the dashed lines, a rectangular box will be formed. What is the volume of the box in cubic centimeters?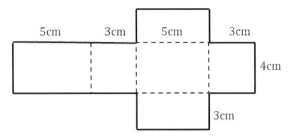

a) 45
b) 60
c) 72
d) 81

Answer: (B)
After folding, the height of the box will be 3 cm, the length will be 5 cm, and the width will be 4cm.
Volume = 3 cm × 4 cm × 5 cm = 60 cm³

IV. TRIGONOMETRIC FUNCTIONS

Concept Overviews

Right Triangle Trigonometry

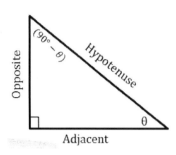

SOH CAH TOA

$$sin(\theta) = \frac{Opposite}{Hypotenuse} = cos(90° - \theta)$$

$$cos(\theta) = \frac{Adjacent}{Hypotenuse} = sin(90° - \theta)$$

$$tan(\theta) = \frac{Opposite}{Adjacent} = cot(90° - \theta)$$

Pythagorean Theorem: $Hypotenuse^2 = Adjacent^2 + Opposite^2$

Example: If $0 < \theta < 90°$ and $sin(\theta) = \frac{3}{5}$, what are the values of $cos(\theta)$ and $tan(\theta)$?

Solution: If $sin(\theta) = \frac{3}{5}$, we can represent $sin(\theta)$ as the following triangle:

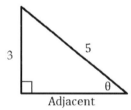

According to the Pythagorean Theorem, the length of the adjacent side is $\sqrt{5^2 - 3^2} = 4$. Therefore, $cos(\theta) = \frac{4}{5}$ and $tan(\theta) = \frac{3}{4}$

Example: What is the height of the tree according to the following figure?

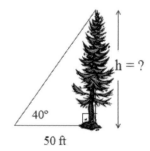

Solution: $tan(40°) = \frac{h}{50}$

$h = 50 \times tan(40°) = 50 \times 0.8391 = 41.95$ ft.

A unit circle is a circle with a radius of 1 centered at the origin on the coordinate plane as shown in the figure below.

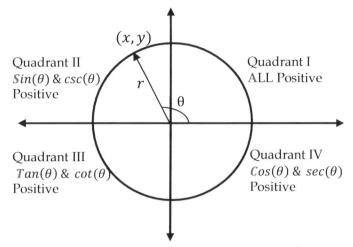

Use the mnemonic "All Students Take Calculus!"

$$sin(\theta) = \frac{y}{r} \qquad cos(\theta) = \frac{x}{r} \qquad tan(\theta) = \frac{y}{x}$$
$$csc(\theta) = \frac{r}{y} \qquad sec(\theta) = \frac{r}{x} \qquad cot(\theta) = \frac{x}{y}$$

There are two **special right triangles** that you need to remember:

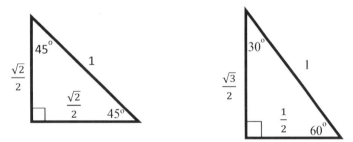

Some important angles, 0°, 30°, 45°, 60°, and 90°, and their sine, cosine, and tangent values are summarized below:

θ	$sin(\theta)$	$cos(\theta)$	$tan(\theta)$
0°	0	1	0
30°	$\frac{1}{2}$	$\frac{\sqrt{3}}{2}$	$\frac{\sqrt{3}}{3}$
45°	$\frac{\sqrt{2}}{2}$	$\frac{\sqrt{2}}{2}$	1
60°	$\frac{\sqrt{3}}{2}$	$\frac{1}{2}$	$\sqrt{3}$
90°	1	0	undefined

A **cofunction** is a trigonometric function whose value for the complement of a given angle is equal to the value of a trigonometric function of the angle itself. Pairs of cofunctions are sine and cosine, tangent and cotangent, and secant and cosecant.

$$sin(\theta) = cos(90° - \theta) \qquad cos(\theta) = sin(90° - \theta)$$
$$tan(\theta) = cot(90° - \theta) \qquad cot(\theta) = tan(90° - \theta)$$
$$sec(\theta) = csc(90° - \theta) \qquad csc(\theta) = sec(90° - \theta)$$

Example: One angle measures x, where $sin(x) = \frac{2}{3}$. What is $cos(90° - x)$?

Solution: $cos(90° - x) = sin(x) = \frac{2}{3}$

Radians and **degrees** are two units for measuring angles. A full circle has a total angle of 360 degrees or 2π radians.

The formulas to convert between degrees and radians are:
$$\text{Degrees} = \frac{180}{\pi} \times \text{Radians}$$
$$\text{Radians} = \frac{\pi}{180} \times \text{Degrees}$$

Example: What is the angle $225°$ in radians?

Solution: $\text{Radians} = \frac{\pi}{180} \times 225 = \frac{5}{4}\pi$

Example: Convert 2.36 radians to degrees.

Solution: $\text{Degrees} = \frac{180}{\pi} \times 2.36 = 135°$

Problem Solving Skills

Easy

1. If $0 < \theta < 90°$ and $cos(\theta) = \frac{5}{13}$, what is the value of $sin(\theta)$?   *Answer: (A)*

    a) $\frac{12}{13}$

    b) $\frac{5}{13}$

    c) $\frac{4}{5}$

    d) $\frac{5}{12}$

$$12 \quad \diagup \quad 13$$
$$\theta$$
$$5$$
$$sin(\theta) = \frac{12}{13}$$

2. A seven feet long ladder leans against a wall and makes an angle of 60° with the ground. How high up the wall does the ladder reach?

a) $\frac{2\sqrt{3}}{7}$

b) $\frac{7\sqrt{3}}{2}$

c) $\frac{\sqrt{3}}{14}$

d) $7\sqrt{3}$

Answer: (B)

$sin(60°) = \frac{Height}{7} = \frac{\sqrt{3}}{2}$

$Height = 7 \times \frac{\sqrt{3}}{2} = \frac{7\sqrt{3}}{2}$

3. In the triangle above, the sine of $b°$ is 0.8. What is the cosine of $a°$?

a) 0.8

b) 0.6

c) 0.4

d) 0.2

Answer: (A)
Use the value of $sin(b°)$ and the Pythagorean Theorem to find the ratio of lengths of sides of the right

triangle.
$cos(a°) = sin(90° - a°) = 0.8$
Or $cos(a°) = \frac{8}{10} = 0.8$

4. If $sin(\frac{\pi}{2} - x) = 0.35$, what is $cos\,x$?

a) 0.35

b) 0.43

c) 0.45

d) 0.53

Answer: (A)
Cofuntion: The value of a trigonometric function of an angle is equal to the value of the cofunction of the complement of that angle.
$sin(\theta) = cos(90° - \theta)$
$cos(\theta) = sin(90° - \theta)$

5. If $a + b = 90°$, which of the following must be true?

a) $cos(a) = cos(b)$

b) $sin(a) = sin(b)$

c) $sin(a) = cos(b)$

d) $sin(a) = -cos(b)$

Answer: (C)
Cofuntion: The value of a trigonometric function of an angle is equal to the value of the cofunction of the complement of that angle.
$sin(\theta) = cos(90° - \theta)$
$cos(\theta) = sin(90° - \theta)$

6. 45° is equivalent to an angle measure of
   a) $\frac{1}{4}$ radians
   b) $\frac{\pi}{4}$ radians
   c) $\frac{\pi}{3}$ radians
   d) $\frac{\pi}{2}$ radians

Answer: (B)
$$Radians = \frac{\pi}{180} \times 45 = \frac{\pi}{4}$$

7. How many degrees are in 1.65 radians?
   a) 94.54
   b) 78.56
   c) 10.88
   d) 0.029

Answer: (A)
$$Degrees = \frac{180}{\pi} \times 1.65 = 94.54$$

8. Which of the following trigonometric functions is (are) positive in the third Quadrant? 🔲
   a) $sin(x)$
   b) $cos(x)$
   c) $tan(x)$
   d) All of the above

Answer: (C)
Use the mnemonic "All Students Take Calculus!!"

9. Which of the following cofunctions is (are) true?
   a) $sin(90° - x) = cos(x)$
   b) $cos(90° - x) = sin(x)$
   c) $tan(90° - x) = cot(x)$
   d) All of the above

Answer: (D)
Cofuntion: The value of a trigonometric function of an angle is equal to the value of the cofunction of the complement of that angle.

10. A shaft, pivoted at one end, spins through $\frac{4\pi}{3}$ radians. If the shaft is 15 centimeters long, what is the distance (in cm) that the shaft travels?
    a) 5π
    b) 10π
    c) 15π
    d) 20π

Answer: (D)
Find the length of the arc.
$$l = r\theta = 15 \times \frac{4\pi}{3} = 20\pi$$

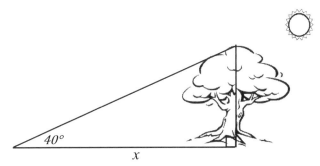

11. When the Sun is 40° above the horizon, how long is the shadow cast by a tree which is 55 feet tall? (Round your answer to the nearest tenth.)

Answer: 65.5

$$tan\,(40°) = \frac{55}{x}$$

$$x = \frac{55}{tan(40°)} = \frac{55}{0.8391} = 65.5$$

12. If an angle θ measured counter-clockwise from the positive x-axis terminates in the third Quadrant, which of the following is true?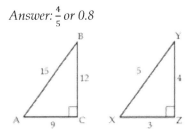
    a) Both of $sin(\theta)$ and $cos(\theta)$ are negative.
    b) Both of $sin(\theta)$ and $cos(\theta)$ are positive.
    c) $sin(\theta)$ is negative and $cos(\theta)$ is positive.
    d) $sin(\theta)$ is positive and $cos(\theta)$ is negative.

Answer: (A)
Use the mnemonic "All Students Take Calculus!!"

Medium

13. In triangle ABC, the measure of ∠C is 90°, AB = 15, and BC = 12. Triangle XYZ is similar to triangle ABC, where vertices $X, Y,$ and Z correspond to vertices $A, B,$ and C, respectively. If each side of triangle XYZ is $\frac{1}{3}$ the length of the corresponding side of triangle ABC, what is the value of $sin(X)$?

Answer: $\frac{4}{5}$ or 0.8

$$sin(X) = \frac{YZ}{XY} = \frac{4}{5}$$

Note: Figures not drawn to scale.

14. The angles shown above are acute, and $sin(x^o) = cos(y^o)$. If $x = 3k - 11$ and $y = 2k - 9$, what is the value of k?

    a) 12
    b) 22
    c) 23.5
    d) 27.5

Answer: (B)
$(3k - 11) + (2k - 9) = 90$
$k = 22$

15. A ramp is 60 meters long and set at a 25° angle of inclination. If you walk up to the top of the ramp, how high off the ground will you be?

    a) 25.357 meters
    b) 26.561 meters
    c) 27.91 meters
    d) 28.13 meters

Answer: (A)

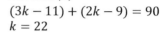

$sin(25°) = \frac{x}{60}$
$x = sin(25°) \times 60$
$x = 25.357$

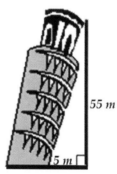

16. If the Leaning Tower of Pisa is 55 meters tall and the top edge of the tower leans 5 meters out from the bottom edge, what is *sine* of the angle created between the ground and the tower?

    a) 1
    b) 0.091
    c) 0.993
    d) 0.996

Answer: (D)
Use the Pythogoream Theorm to find the hypotenuse.
$Hypotenuse = \sqrt{55^2 + 5^2} = 55.23\ m$
$sin(\theta) = \frac{55}{55.23} = 0.996$

Chapter 5 Ten SAT Math Practice Tests

SAT Math Practice Test No. 1

SECTION 3

Math Test — NO Calculator   25 MINUTES, 20 QUESTIONS

Directions:
For questions 1-15, solve each problem, choose the best answer from the choices provided, and fill in the corresponding circle on your answer sheet. **For questions 16-20,** solve the problem and enter your answer in the grid on the answer sheet. Please refer to the directions before question 16 on how to enter your answers in the grid. You may use any available space in your test booklet for scratch work.

Notes:
1. **No calculator** is allowed for this section. All numbers used are real numbers.
2. Figures that accompany problems in this test are intended to provide information useful in solving the problems. They are drawn as accurately as possible EXCEPT when it is stated in a specific problem that the figure is not drawn to scale. All figures lie in a plane unless otherwise indicated.
3. Unless otherwise specified, the domain of any function $f(x)$ assumed to be the set of all real numbers x for which $f(x)$ is a real number.

References:

$A = \pi r^2$ $A = lw$ $A = \frac{1}{2}bh$ $V = lwh$ $V = \pi r^2 h$ $c^2 = a^2 + b^2$ **Special Right Triangles**
$C = 2\pi r$

The number of degrees of arc in a circle is 360; the number of radians of arc in a circle is 2π.
The sum of the degree measures of the angles in a triangle is 180.

---

1. What is the solution of $9n + 20 = -16$?
   - a) -4
   - b) $-\frac{20}{9}$
   - c) $\frac{4}{9}$
   - d) 4

2. If $\sqrt{k+3} - 6 = 0$, k is a constant. What is the value of k?
   - a) 1
   - b) 3
   - c) 9
   - d) 33

3. What are the solutions of the quadratic equation $2x^2 - 4x - 6 = 0$?
   - a) $x = -1$ or $x = -3$
   - b) $x = -1$ or $x = 3$
   - c) $x = 1$ or $x = -3$
   - d) $x = 1$ or $x = 3$

4. If $\frac{3\sqrt{x} + y}{\sqrt{x} + 1} = 3$ then $y = ?$
   - a) 1
   - b) 3
   - c) 5
   - d) 8

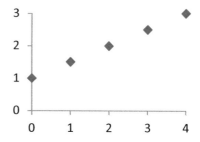

5. Which of the lines described by the following equations best fits those points above?
   a) $y = 0.5x - 1$
   b) $y = 0.5x + 1$
   c) $y = -0.5x - 1$
   d) $y = -0.5x + 1$

$$\frac{4}{x-2} + \frac{2}{x} = \frac{8}{x^2 - 2x}$$

6. What value of x satisfies the equation above?
   a) 0
   b) 2
   c) 14
   d) No value of x satisfies the equation.

7. If $x + y = 13$ and $x - y = 3$, what is the value of $x^2 - y^2$?
   a) 10
   b) 16
   c) 39
   d) 169

$$2ax - 15 = 3(x + 5) + 5(x - 1)$$

8. In the equation above, a is a constant. If no value of x satisfies the equation, what is the value of ?
   a) 1
   b) 2
   c) 3
   d) 4

9. Let A represents the average of all winter monthly heating bills for John's family. What is the result of multiplying A by the number of months in winter?
   a) The average of all heating expenses for John's family in the year.
   b) The highest monthly heating bill for John's family that winter.
   c) The sum of the eating expenses for the whole year for John's family.
   d) The sum of the heating expenses in winter for John's family.

10. When the average (arithmetic mean) of a list of grades is multiplied by the number of students, the result is n. What does n represent?
    a) the number of the grades
    b) the average of the grades
    c) the sum of the grades
    d) the range of the list of the grades

11. The pressure exerted on an object under water increases by 1 atmosphere every 33 feet below the surface of the water. At sea level, the pressure is 1 atmosphere. Which equation gives the total pressure p, in atmospheres, exerted on an underwater object at a depth of f feet below sea level?
    a) $p = \frac{f}{33}$
    b) $p = 33f$
    c) $p = 33f + 1$
    d) $p = \frac{f}{33} + 1$

12. If $\sqrt{x} = 2$ then $x + 4 = ?$
    a) 2
    b) 4
    c) 8
    d) 80

13. The equation $p = 15 + 0.5d$ approximates the pressure p, in pounds per square inch, exerted on a diver at a depth of d feet (ft) below the surface of the water. What is the increase in depth that is necessary to increase the pressure by 1 pound per square inch?
    a) $\frac{1}{0.5}$ ft
    b) $\frac{1}{15}$ ft
    c) 0.5 ft
    d) 15 ft

14. If $x^{\frac{1}{4}} = \sqrt{3}$, then what is the value of x^2?
    a) 81
    b) 72
    c) 36
    d) 27

15. What is the set of all solutions to the equation $\sqrt{x + 2} = -x$
    a) $\{-1, 2\}$
    b) $\{-1\}$

c) {2}

d) There are no solutions to the given equation.

Directions:

For questions 16-20, solve the problem and enter your answer in the grid, as described below, on the answer sheet.

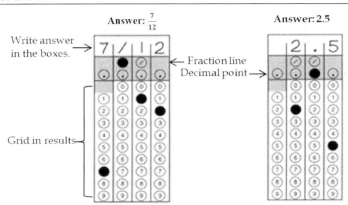

Answer: $\frac{7}{12}$

Write answer in the boxes.

Fraction line
Decimal point

Grid in results

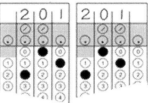

Answer: 2.5

Answer: 201
Either position is correct.

Note: You may start your answers in any column, space permitting. Columns not needed should be left blank.

- Mark no more than one circle in any column.
- Because the answer sheet will be machine-scored. **You will receive credit only if the circles are filled in correctly.**
- Although not required, it is suggested that you write your answer in the boxes at the top of the columns to help you fill in the circles accurately.
- Some problems may have more than one correct answer. In such case, grid only one answer.
- No question has a negative answer.
- **Mixed numbers** such as $3\frac{1}{2}$ must be

gridded as 3.5 or $\frac{7}{2}$. (If [3|1/2] is gridded, it will be interpreted as $\frac{31}{2}$, not $3\frac{1}{2}$.)

- **Decimal Answer:** If you obtain a decimal answer with more digits than the grid can accommodate, it may be either rounded or truncated, but it must fill the entire grid. The acceptable ways to grid $\frac{2}{3}$ are:

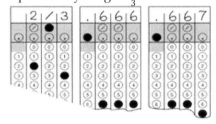

---

16. If $a + bi = \frac{2+i}{1+i}$, what is the value of $a + b$?

17. What is the positive solution of x for which $(x - 1)(x + 2) = 0$?

18. In the complex number system, what is the value of the expression $6i^4 - 5i^2 + 4$?
    (Note: $i = \sqrt{-1}$)

19. An angle measure of 270 degrees was written in radians as $x\pi$. What is the value of ?

20. When twice a number is reduced by 25, the result is 225. What is the number?

SECTION 4

Math Test — Calculator   **55 MINUTES, 38 QUESTIONS**

Directions:

For questions 1-30, solve each problem, choose the best answer from the choices provided, and fill in the corresponding circle on your answer sheet. **For questions 31-38,** solve the problem and enter your answer in the grid on the answer sheet. Please refer to the directions before question 31 on how to enter your answers in the grid. You may use any available space in your test booklet for scratch work.

Notes:

1. Acceptable calculators are allowed for this section. All numbers used are real numbers.
2. Figures that accompany problems in this test are intended to provide information useful in solving the problems. They are drawn as accurately as possible EXCEPT when it is stated in a specific problem that the figure is not drawn to scale. All figures lie in a plane unless otherwise indicated.
3. Unless otherwise specified, the domain of any function $f(x)$ assumed to be the set of all real numbers x for which $f(x)$ is a real number.

References:

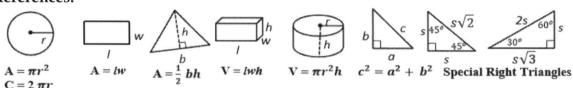

$A = \pi r^2$ $A = lw$ $A = \frac{1}{2} bh$ $V = lwh$ $V = \pi r^2 h$ $c^2 = a^2 + b^2$ **Special Right Triangles**
$C = 2\pi r$

The number of degrees of arc in a circle is 360; the number of radians of arc in a circle is 2π.
The sum of the degree measures of the angles in a triangle is 180.

---

1. Triangles A, B, and C are different in size. Triangle A's area is twice the area of triangle B, and triangle C's area is three times the area of triangle A. What is the area of triangle C, in square inches, if the area of triangle B is 10 square inches?
   a) 20
   b) 40
   c) 60
   d) 80

2. Equation $(x + 3)(x + a) = x^2 + 4x + b$ where a and b are constants. If the equation is true for all values of x, what is the value of b?
   a) 8
   b) 6
   c) 4
   d) 3

3. N students have an average of K scores on a math test. Another 3 students were absent and received zeroes on the test. What is the average score of this math test in terms of N and K, taking into accounts all of the students?
   a) $\frac{NK}{3}$
   b) $\frac{NK}{K+3}$
   c) $\frac{NK}{N+3}$
   d) $\frac{N-3}{K}$

4. An isosceles right triangle has a hypotenuse with a length of $6\sqrt{2}$. What is the area of this triangle?
   a) 12
   b) 15
   c) 18
   d) $12\sqrt{3}$

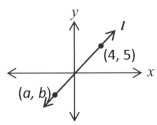

5. In the figure above, line l passes through the origin. What is the value of $\frac{b}{a}$?
   a) 1
   b) 1.25
   c) 1.33
   d) 1.5

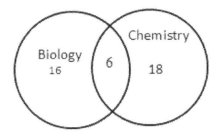

6. The Venn diagram above shows the distribution of 40 students at a school who took biology, chemistry, or both. What percent of the students studied chemistry?
   a) 30%
   b) 45%
   c) 50%
   d) 60%

Questions 7 - 8 refer to the following information:

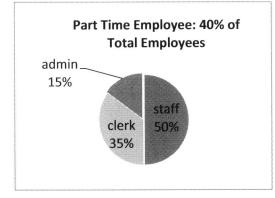

7. According to the graphs above, the total number of full-time employees is how many more than the total number of part-time employees at Oak Town High School?
   a) 20
   b) 40
   c) 50
   d) 60

8. According to the graphs above, how many part-time staff members are at Oak Town High School?
   a) 60
   b) 50
   c) 40
   d) 30

9. How many positive three-digit integers have the hundreds digit equal to the multiple of 3 and the units digit (ones digit) is an even digit?
   a) 150
   b) 160
   c) 162
   d) 180

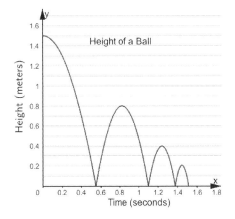

10. A ball was dropped from a height of 1.5 meters and hit the ground several times. The graph above represents the height h, in meters, of the ball t seconds after it was dropped. Of the following, which best approximates the maximum height, in meters, of the ball between the second and third time it hit the ground?
a) 0.2
b) 0.4
c) 0.8
d) 1.5

11. Which of the following is the graph of $y = |-3x+3|$?
a)
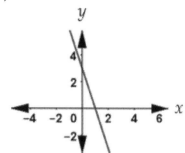

b)
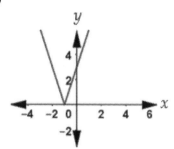

c)
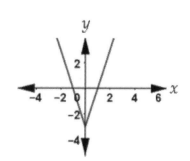

d)

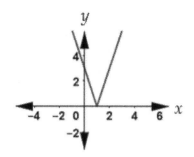

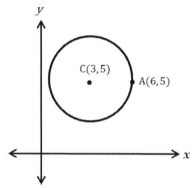

12. In the figure above, what is the circumference of the circle with center C?
a) 4π
b) 5π
c) 6π
d) 7π

$$h(t) = -16t^2 + 320t + h_o$$

13. At time $t = 0$, a rocket was launched from a height of h_o feet above the ground. Until the rocket hit the ground, its height, in feet, after t seconds was given by the function h above. For which of the following values of t did the rocket have the same height as it did when $t = 5$.
a) 10
b) 15
c) 18

d) 20

14. The center of a circle is the origin of a rectangular coordinate plane. If (−5, 0), (0, 5), and (5, 0) are three points on the circumference of the circle, what is the probability that a randomly picked point inside the circle would fall inside the triangle formed by those three points?

a) $\frac{1}{2}$

b) $\frac{1}{3}$

c) $\frac{1}{\pi}$

d) $\frac{2}{\pi}$

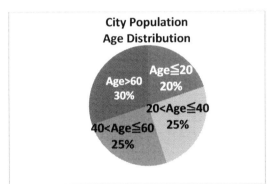

15. Town A has a population of 25,000 and the chart above shows their age distribution. How many people are 40 years or younger?

a) 5,000

b) 8,000

c) 10,000

d) 11,250

$$(4x + 4)(ax - 1) - x^2 + 4$$

16. In the expression above, a is a constant. If the expression is equivalent to bx, where b is a constant, what is the value of b ?

a) −5

b) −3

c) 0

d) 12

17. A data set consists of the values 230, 300, 410, 450, 700, and 20,160. If the outlier is removed, what will happen to the value of the mean of the data set?

a) The mean will remain the same.

b) The mean will decrease.

c) The mean will increase.

d) There is not enough information to determine how the mean will change.

$$1, 5, 17, t, 161, ...$$

18. In the sequence above, what is the value of t?

a) 34

b) 51

c) 53

d) 68

Questions 19 and 20 refer to the following Information.

$$d = 2,565 - 500t$$

An airplane flies directly from a city in Pennsylvania to a city in Ecuador. The equation above estimates the distance, d, in miles, from the city in Ecuador of the airplane t hours after taking off from the city in Pennsylvania.

19. Which of the following is the best interpretation of the number 2,565 in this equation?

a) The speed, in miles per hour, of the airplane

b) The distance, in miles, the airplane travels in one hour

c) The distance, in miles, the airplane travels between the two cities

d) The time, in minutes, it takes the airplane to reach the city in Ecuador

20. According to the equation, approximately how many hours will it

take the airplane to travel between the two cities?

a) 6.2
b) 5.8
c) 5.3
d) 5.1

21. The graph of the exponential function h in the xy-plane, where $y = h(x)$, has a y-intercept of d, where d is a positive constant. Which of the following could define the function h?

a) $h(x) = -3(d)^x$
b) $h(x) = 3(x)d$
c) $h(x) = d(-x)^3$
d) $h(x) = d(3)^x$

22. If an angle θ measured counter-clockwise from the positive x-axis terminates in the third Quadrant, which of the following is true?

a) Both of $sin(\theta)$ and $cos(\theta)$ are negative.
b) Both of $sin(\theta)$ and $cos(\theta)$ are positive.
c) $sin(\theta)$ is negative and $cos(\theta)$ is positive.
d) $sin(\theta)$ is positive and $cos(\theta)$ is negative.

23. If $x > y > 0.1$, which of the following is less than $\frac{x}{y}$?

a) $\frac{x+0.1}{y+0.1}$
b) $\frac{2x}{2y}$
c) $\frac{x-0.1}{y-0.1}$
d) $(\frac{x}{y})^2$

24. In a sequence of numbers, each term after the first term is 4 greater than $\frac{1}{4}$ of the preceding term. If a_o is the first term and a_o

$\neq 0$, which of the following represents the ratio of the third term to the second term?

a) $\frac{a_0+16}{4}$
b) $\frac{a_0+6}{4a_0}$
c) $\frac{a_0+4}{4a_0}$
d) $\frac{a_0+80}{4a_0+64}$

25. Alice bought two pairs of shoes at the same price from a store with "buy one pair get second pair 50% off "sale. The total amount she paid was p dollars, including the 7 percent sales tax and the discounted price. Which of the following represents the original price of each pair in terms of p?

a) $\frac{P}{2 \times 1.07}$
b) $\frac{P \times 1.07}{2}$
c) $\frac{P}{1.5 \times 1.07}$
d) $\frac{P}{1.07}$

26. If $x = -\frac{1}{2}$, what is the value of $\frac{1}{x} - \frac{1}{x+1}$?

a) 2
b) –2
c) 4
d) –4

27. The cost of a long-distance call using phone company A is $1.00 for the first three minutes and $.10 for each additional minute. The same call using the phone company B is charged flat rate at $0.15 per minute for any amount of time. For a call that lasts t minutes, the cost using company A is the same as the cost using the company B, what is the value of t?

a) 15
b) 14
c) 12
d) 10

28. If the positive integer n is divided by 7, the remainder is 2. What is the remainder when $4n$ is divided by 7?

    a) 1
    b) 2
    c) 3
    d) 4

30. A poster has an area of 436 square inches. The length x, in inches, of the poster is 6 inches longer than the width of the poster. Which of the following equations can be solved to determine the length, in inches, of the poster?

    a) $x^2 - 436 = 6$
    b) $x^2 + 6x = 436$
    c) $x^2 + 6 = 436$
    d) $x^2 - 6x = 436$

29. If -2 and 4 are both zeros of the polynomial $f(x)$, then a factor of $f(x)$ could be

    a) $x - 2$
    b) $x^2 - 2x - 8$
    c) $x^2 - 2x + 8$
    d) $x + 4$

Directions:

For questions 31-38, solve the problem and enter your answer in the grid, as described below, on the answer sheet.

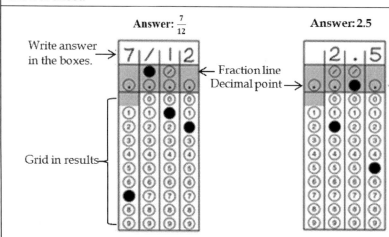

- Mark no more than one circle in any column.
- Because the answer sheet will be machine-scored. **You will receive credit only if the circles are filled in correctly.**
- Although not required, it is suggested that you write your answer in the boxes at the top of the columns to help you fill in the circles accurately.
- Some problems may have more than one correct answer. In such case, grid only one answer.
- No question has a negative answer.
- **Mixed numbers** such as $3\frac{1}{2}$ must be

gridded as 3.5 or $\frac{7}{2}$. (If ▨ is gridded, it will be interpreted as $\frac{31}{2}$, not $3\frac{1}{2}$.)

- **Decimal Answer:** If you obtain a decimal answer with more digits than the grid can accommodate, it may be either rounded or truncated, but it must fill the entire grid. The acceptable ways to grid $\frac{2}{3}$ are:

Note: You may start your answers in any column, space permitting. Columns not needed should be left blank.

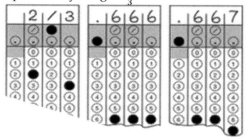

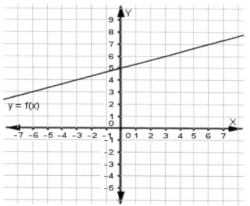

31. The graph of the linear function f is shown in the xy-coordinate plane above. If the slope of the graph g is 6 times the slope of the graph of f, and the graph of g passes through the point $(0, -3)$, what is the value of $g(10)$?

32. A doctor prescribes a medication for an 88-pound child. In each dose, the child is to be given 10 milligrams of the medication for every kilogram of the child's body weight. The medication is to be given to the child 2 times per day for 5 days. How much medication, in milligrams, should be provided for the entire 5-day treatment plan? (1 kilogram = 2.2 pounds)

33. Seven different surveys of the daily commuting time, in minutes, of Chicago-based employees yielded the values 30, 15, 42, 32, 55, 22, 40. Seven different surveys of the daily commuting time, in minutes, of San Francisco-based employees yielded the values 44, 31, 20, 32, 46, x, 39. If these two data sets have the same mean, what is the value of x?

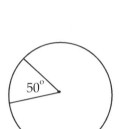

34. In the figure above, a piece with a 50° center angle has been cut out of an 18-ounce pie. How many ounces was the piece of pie that was cut out?

35. George took a nonstop flight from Dallas to Los Angeles, a total flight distance of 1,233 miles. The plane flew at a speed of 460 miles per hour for the first 75 minutes of the flight and at a speed of 439 miles per hour for the remainder of the flight. To the nearest minute, for how many minutes did the plane fly at a speed of 439 miles per hour?

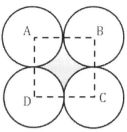

36. The figure above consists of four congruent, tangent circles with radius 2. What is the area of the shaded region? (Round your answer to the nearest hundredth)

Questions 37 and 38 refer to the following information.

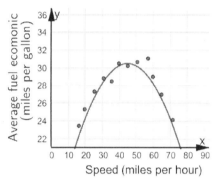

The scatterplot above shows the average fuel economy for a certain class of car driven at 12 different. The graph of a quadratic model for the data is also shown.

37. For what fraction of the 12 speeds does the model overestimate the average fuel economy?

38. The quadratic model predicts the average fuel economy to be 26 miles per gallon for how many different speeds?

SAT MATH PRACTICE TEST No. 1 ANSWER KEYS

Section 3

1. (A)	2. (D)	3. (B)	4. (B)	5. (B)	6. (D)	7. (C)	8. (D)	9. (D)	10. (C)
11. (D)	12. (C)	13. (A)	14. (A)	15. (B)	16. 1	17. 1	18. 15	19. 1.5	20. 125

Section 4

1. (C)	2. (D)	3. (C)	4. (C)	5. (B)	6. (D)	7. (B)	8. (C)	9. (A)	10. (B)
11. (D)	12. (C)	13. (B)	14. (C)	15. (D)	16. (B)	17. (B)	18. (C)	19. (C)	20. (D)
21. (D)	22. (A)	23. (A)	24. (D)	25. (C)	26. (D)	27. (B)	28. (A)	29. (B)	30. (D)
31. 17	32. 4000	33. 22	34. 2.5	35. 90	36. 3.43	37. $\frac{1}{6}$	38. 2		

Section 3

1. Answer: (A)
$$9n + 20 = -16$$
$$9n = -36$$
$$n = -4$$

2. Answer: (D)
$$\sqrt{k+3} - 6 = 0$$
$$k + 3 = 36$$
$$k = 33$$

3. Answer: (B)
$$2x^2 - 4x - 6 = 0$$
$$2(x^2 - 2x - 3) = 0$$
$$2(x - 3)(x + 1) = 0$$
$$x = -1 \text{ or } x = -3$$

4. Answer: (B)
$$3\sqrt{x} + y = 3\sqrt{x} + 3$$
$$y = 3$$

5. Answer: (B)
$$Slope = \frac{Rise}{Run} = \frac{2-1}{2-0} = 0.5$$
y-intercept = 1
$$y = 0.5x + 1$$

6. Answer: (D)
$$\frac{4}{x-2} + \frac{2}{x} = \frac{4x+2(x-2)}{x^2-2x} = \frac{6x-4}{x^2-2x}$$
$$\frac{6x-4}{x^2-2x} = \frac{8}{x^2-2x}$$
$$6x - 4 = 8$$
$$6x = 12$$
$x = 2$ but $x = 2$ can't be a solution because it makes the denominator of $\frac{4}{x-2}$ equal to zero.

7. Answer: (C)
$$x^2 - y^2 = (x + y)(x - y) =$$
$$(13)(3) = 39$$

8. Answer: (D)
$$2ax - 15 = 3(x + 5) + 5(x - 1)$$
$$2ax - 15 = 8x + 10$$
If $a = 4$, then the equation has no solution because $-15 \neq 10$. The answer is d).

9. Answer: (D)
Multiplying the average by the number of elements (months) in the set gives you the sum of all the elements.

10. Answer: (C)
This is the definition of "sum."

11. Answer: (D)
A linear equation:
"Pressure increases by 1 atmosphere every 33 feet below" → Slope $= \frac{1}{33}$
The pressure at water surface is 1atm → y-intercept is 1
$$p = \frac{1}{33}f + 1$$

12. Answer: (C)
Square both sides of the radical equation.
$$\sqrt{x} = 2$$
$$\left(\sqrt{x}\right)^2 = 2^2$$
$$x = 4$$
$$x + 4 = 8$$

13. *Answer: (A)*
This is a linear model.
Slope = 0.5
For every foot, the pressure increases 0.5 pound per square inch. For every pound per square inch, it needs $\frac{1}{0.5}$ feet.
The answer is a).

14. *Answer: (A)*
$(x^{\frac{1}{4}})^8 = x^2$
$(\sqrt{3})^8 = 81$

15. *Answer: (B)*
$\sqrt{x+2} \geq 0$
$\sqrt{x+2} = -x \geq 0 \rightarrow x \leq 0$
$x = -1$
$\sqrt{-1+2} = -(-1) \rightarrow 1 = 1$

16. *Answer: 1*
Rationalize the denominator.
$\frac{2+i}{1+i} = \frac{(2+i)(1-i)}{(1+i)(1-i)} = \frac{3-i}{2} = \frac{3}{2} - \frac{1}{2}i = a + bi$
$a = \frac{3}{2}$ and $b = -\frac{1}{2}$
$a + b = \frac{3}{2} + \left(-\frac{1}{2}\right) = 1$

17. *Answer: 1*
$(x-1)(x+2) = 0$
$x - 1 = 0, \ x = 1 \ or$
$x + 2 = 0, \ x = -2$

18. *Answer: 15*
$6i^4 - 5i^2 + 4 =$
$6(1) - 5(-1) + 4 = 15$

19. *Answer: 1.5*
$\frac{270}{x\pi} = \frac{180}{\pi}$
$x = 1.5$

20. *Answer: 125*
$2a - 25 = 225 \rightarrow a = 125$

Section 4

1. *Answer: (C)*
$A = 2B,$
$C = 3A$
If B = 10, then
$A = 20, C = 3 \times 20 = 60.$

2. *Answer: (D)*
This is an identity equation question. The two expressions have the same coefficients for corresponding terms.
$(x+3)(x+a) = x^2 + (3+a)x + 3a$
By comparison, $3 + a = 4$ and $3a = b$
$a = 1$ and $b = 3$

3. *Answer: (C)*
$Average = \frac{Total\ Score}{Number\ of\ Students}$
$Average = \frac{K \times N}{N + 3}$

4. *Answer: (C)*
An isosceles right triangle is a 45−45−90 triangle.
Length of Leg $= 6\sqrt{2} \times \frac{\sqrt{2}}{2} = 6$
Area of Triangle $= \frac{1}{2} \times 6 \times 6 = 18$

5. *Answer: (B)*
$\frac{b-0}{a-0} = \frac{5-0}{4-0}$
$\frac{b}{a} = \frac{5}{4} = 1.25$

6. *Answer: (D)*
Among the total 40 students, there were (18 + 6) students studied chemistry.
$\frac{24}{40} = 0.6 = 60\%$

7. *Answer: (B)*
Number of Full Time Employees = 25 + 45 + 50 = 120 employees.
Full time employees comprise of 60% of the total.
0.6 × Number of Employees = 120.
Number of Employees = 200.
Part Time Employees = 200 × 0.4 = 80.
Full Time Employees − Part Time Employees
= 120 − 80 = 40 employees

8. *Answer: (C)*
Number of Part time staff = number of Part Time Employees × 0.5 = 80 × 0.5 = 40.

9. *Answer: (A)*
The hundreds has 3 choices (3, 6, 9) and the units digit has 5 choices (2, 4, 6, 8, 0). There are 10 possible values of tens digit (0 − 9).
Total = 3 × 5 × 10 = 150

10. *Answer: (B)*
    The time between the second and third time it hit the ground is about 1.3 seconds. Its max height is 0.4 meters.

11. *Answer: (D)*
    After taking the absolute value of (-3x + 3), any negative values on the graph will flip across the x-axis and become positive values.
    The graph of y = -3x + 3 is shown below:

    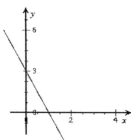

    After flipping all negative values to positive values, the graph of y = |-3x + 3| will look like graph (d).

12. *Answer: (C)*
    Radius = $\overline{CA}$ = $\sqrt{(6-3)^2 + (5-5)^2}$ = 3
    Circumference = 2 πr = 6π

13. *Answer: (B)*
    h(5) = −16(5)² + 320(5) + h_o = −16t² + 320t + h_o
    divided by 16
    −25 + 100 = −t² + 20t
    t² − 20t + 75 = 0
    (t − 5) (t − 15) = 0
    t = 5 or 15

14. *Answer: (C)*
    Radius of the Circle = 5
    Area of the Circle = π (5)² = 25π
    Area of the Triangle = $\frac{1}{2}$ × 5 × 10 = 25
    Probability = $\frac{25}{25\pi}$ = $\frac{1}{\pi}$

15. *Answer: (D)*
    The number of population 40 years or younger:
    (25% + 20%) × 25,000
    = 45% × 25,000 = 0.45 × 25,000 = 11,250

16. *Answer: (B)*
    (4x + 4)(ax − 1) − x² + 4 = 4ax² − 4x + 4ax − 4 − x² + 4 = x²(4a − 1) + x(4a − 4) = bx
    (4a − 1)x² = 0 → a = $\frac{1}{4}$
    x(4a − 4) = −3x = bx
    b = −3

17. *Answer: (B)*
    The outlier 20,160, the biggest number in this data set, will be removed; therefore, the mean will decrease.

18. *Answer: (C)*
    Examine the first few terms to figure out the pattern. This is a sequence constructed by multiplying the previous term by 3 and then adding 2 to the product each time to get the next term.
    1 × 3 + 2 = 5; 5 × 3 + 2 = 17;
    17× 3 + 2 = 53; t = 53

19. *Answer: (C)*
    When t = 0 → d = 2656
    It is the distance between two cities.

20. *Answer: (D)*
    The plane arrives when d = 0.
    0 = 2565 − 500t → t = 5.1

21. *Answer: (D)*
    The y-intercept, d, is the initial value of this exponential function, while x = 0.
    Among the choices, h(x) = d(3)^x is the only exponential function with y-intercept, d, a positive constant.

22. *Answer: (A)*
    Use the mnemonic "$\underline{A}$ll $\underline{S}$tudents $\underline{T}$ake $\underline{C}$alculus!!"

23. *Answer: (A)*
    x > y > 0.1
    Plug in x = 2, and y = 1
    Only answer (a), $\frac{2.1}{1.1}$, less than 2.

24. *Answer: (D)*
    1st Term = a_0
    2nd Term = 4 + $\frac{1}{4}$ × a_0
    3rd Term = 4 + $\frac{1}{4}$ (4 + $\frac{1}{4}$ a_0)
    *   = 5 + $\frac{1}{16}$ a_0*
    Ratio = $\frac{5 + \frac{1}{16}a_0}{4 + \frac{1}{4}a_0}$ = $\frac{a_0 + 80}{4a_0 + 64}$

25. *Answer: (C)*
    The Money Paid = P
    If the original price of each pair is x, then
    (x + 0.5x) × (1 + 0.07) = P
    1.5 x = $\frac{P}{1.07}$ → x = $\frac{P}{1.5 \times 1.07}$

26. *Answer: (D)*

$$\frac{1}{-\frac{1}{2}} - \frac{1}{-\frac{1}{2}+1} = -2 - 2 = -4$$

27. *Answer: (B)*

$$1 + (t - 3) \times 0.1 = 0.15t \ \rightarrow \ t = 14$$

28. *Answer: (A)*

If the remainder of n divided by 7 is 2, then n can be represented as:

$n = 7 \times q + 2$

$4n = 4 \times 7 \times q + 8$

The remainder of 4n divided by 7 is equal to the remainder of 8 divided by 7 which is 1.

Or simply pick an easy number, such as 9 for n, then

$4n = 4 \times 9 = 36.$

36 divided by 7 will have a remainder 1.

29. *Answer: (B)*

f(x) should be divisible by $(x + 2)$, $(x - 4)$, and $(x^2 - 2x - 8)$.

30. *Answer: (D)*

Width $= x - 6$

$(x)(x - 6) = 436$

$x^2 - 6x = 436$

31. *Answer: 17*

The graph of f passes through the points (0, 5) and (3, 6)

Slope of f $= \frac{6-5}{3-0} = \frac{1}{3}$

$y - 5 = \frac{1}{3}x$

$y = f(x) = \frac{1}{3}x + 5$

$g(x) = \frac{6}{3}x - 3 = 2x - 3$

$g(10) = 20 - 3 = 17$

32. *Answer: 4000*

$$10 \times \frac{88}{2.2} \times 2 \times 5 = 4000 \ mg$$

33. *Answer: 22*

If these two data sets have the same mean,

$$\frac{30+15+42+32+55+22+40}{7} = \frac{46+31+20+32+46+x+39}{7}$$

$x = 22$

34. *Answer: 2.5*

Weight of Pie : 360º = Weight of Piece : 50º

$18 : 360º = x : 50º$

$$\frac{18}{360} = \frac{x}{50} \ \rightarrow \ x = 2.5 \ ounces$$

35. *Answer: 90*

$$Time = \frac{Distance}{Speed}$$

$$\frac{1233 - 460 \times \frac{75}{60}}{439} \times 60 = 90$$

36. *Answer: 3.43*

Area of Shaded Region = Area of Square – 4 × Area of a Quarter-Circle

$4^2 - \pi \times 2^2 = 16 - 4\pi = 3.43$

37. *Answer: $\frac{1}{6}$*

There are only 2 points whose actual values are less than their estimated values.

Fraction $= \frac{2}{12} = \frac{1}{6}$

38. *Answer: 2*

There are 2 speeds that have 26 miles per gallon fuel economy.

SAT Math Practice Test No. 2

SECTION 3

Math Test — NO Calculator   25 MINUTES, 20 QUESTIONS

Directions:

For questions 1-15, solve each problem, choose the best answer from the choices provided, and fill in the corresponding circle on your answer sheet. **For questions 16-20**, solve the problem and enter your answer in the grid on the answer sheet. Please refer to the directions before question 16 on how to enter your answers in the grid. You may use any available space in your test booklet for scratch work.

Notes:

1. **No calculator** is allowed for this section. All numbers used are real numbers.
2. Figures that accompany problems in this test are intended to provide information useful in solving the problems. They are drawn as accurately as possible EXCEPT when it is stated in a specific problem that the figure is not drawn to scale. All figures lie in a plane unless otherwise indicated.
3. Unless otherwise specified, the domain of any function $f(x)$ assumed to be the set of all real numbers x for which $f(x)$ is a real number.

References:

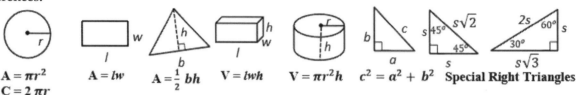

$A = \pi r^2$ $A = lw$ $A = \frac{1}{2}bh$ $V = lwh$ $V = \pi r^2 h$ $c^2 = a^2 + b^2$ **Special Right Triangles**
$C = 2\pi r$

The number of degrees of arc in a circle is 360; the number of radians of arc in a circle is 2π.
The sum of the degree measures of the angles in a triangle is 180.

1. Larry spent a total of $200 to lease snowboard equipment at Winter Mountain during his vacation. Each day of his vacation, he purchased a lift ticket for $44. If Larry purchased t lift tickets, how much money, in dollars, did Larry spend during his vacation at Winter Mountain on snowboard equipment and lift tickets?
    a) $44t$
    b) $44t - 200$
    c) $200 + 44t$
    d) $200 - 44t$

2. For the function f above, what is the value of (1) ?
    a) $\frac{2}{3}$
    b) $\frac{2}{5}$
    c) 1
    d) 2

3. Which of the following equations represents the line in the xy-plane that passes through $(0, 4)$ and has a slope of -2 ?
    a) $y = -2x$
    b) $y = -2x + 4$
    c) $y = 2x - 4$
    d) $y = 2x + 4$

$$f(x) = \frac{x+3}{2}$$

4. If $3a - 2b = 5$ and $a + 2b = 23$, then $a + b$?
    a) -5
    b) 5

c) 10
d) 15

5. Which of the following represents the graph of the function $f(x) = |-2x + 3|$ in the xy-plane?

    a)

    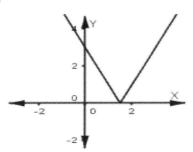

    b)

    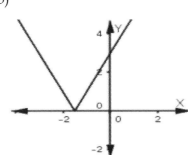

    c)

    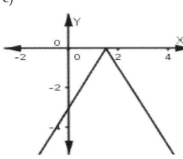

    d)

    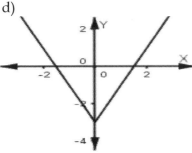

6. If $(3x + 6)(1 - x) = 0$, what are all the possible values of x?
    a) 1 only
    b) −2 only
    c) 0 only
    d) 1 and −2 only

7. A school choir consists of one row of singers, half of which are boys and the other half girls. Which of the following must be true?
    a) The first person and the last person have different genders.
    b) There are two girls next to each other.
    c) If the last two are girls, there are at least two adjacent boys.
    d) If there are two adjacent boys, there are also two adjacent girls.

$$2ax - 15 = 3(x + 5) + 5(x - 1)$$

8. In the equation above, a is a constant. If no value of x satisfies the equation, what is the value of ?
    a) 1
    b) 2
    c) 3
    d) 4

9. Which of the following is an equation of the line that is perpendicular to the y-axis and passes through the point $(2, 1)$?
    a) $y = 1$
    b) $y = -1$
    c) $y = x$
    d) $y = -x$

10. If $x = 2y^2 + 3y + 4$ and $z = -y + 1$, what is x in terms of z?
    a) $2z^2 - 7z - 9$
    b) $2z^2 - 7z + 7$
    c) $2z^2 + 7z + 9$
    d) $2z^2 - 7z + 9$

11. a, b, x, and y are positive numbers. If $x^{-2/3} = a^{-2}$ and $y^{2/3} = b^4$, what is $(xy)^{-1/3}$ in terms of a and b?
    a) ab
    b) $a^{-1}b^{-2}$
    c) a^2b^2

d) $a^{-2}b^{-2}$

d) 3.5

12. If A is the set of positive integers, B is the set of odd integers, and C is the set of integers multiple of 3, which of the following will be in all three sets?
    a) 24
    b) 18
    c) 15
    d) –21

13. How many pounds of flour are needed to make 15 rolls of bread if 20 pounds of flour are needed to make 100 rolls of bread?
    a) 3
    b) 4
    c) 5

14. If $x = 1$, what is $2y(6 - 5x)$ in terms of y?
    a) $2y - 10$
    b) $2y$
    c) $12y - 10$
    d) $12y$

15. Which of the following expressions is equivalent to $(4x^3)^{\frac{2}{3}}$?
    a) $2x^3\sqrt[3]{2}$
    b) $x^3\sqrt[3]{16}$
    c) $2x^2\sqrt[3]{2}$
    d) $2x^2\sqrt[3]{4}$

Directions:

For questions 16-20, solve the problem and enter your answer in the grid, as described below, on the answer sheet.

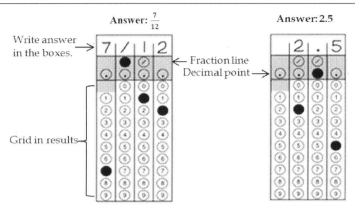

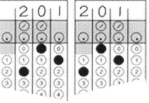

- Mark no more than one circle in any column.
- Because the answer sheet will be machine-scored. **You will receive credit only if the circles are filled in correctly.**
- Although not required, it is suggested that you write your answer in the boxes at the top of the columns to help you fill in the circles accurately.
- Some problems may have more than one correct answer. In such case, grid only one answer.
- No question has a negative answer.
- **Mixed numbers** such as $3\frac{1}{2}$ must be

gridded as 3.5 or $\frac{7}{2}$. (If [grid image] is gridded, it will be interpreted as $\frac{31}{2}$, not $3\frac{1}{2}$.)

- **Decimal Answer:** If you obtain a decimal answer with more digits than the grid can accommodate, it may be either rounded or truncated, but it must fill the entire grid. The acceptable ways to grid $\frac{2}{3}$ are:

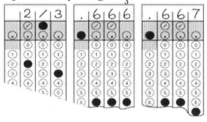

16. In the figure above, four line segments intercept at a point. How many degrees is x?

17. A car salesman's monthly pay consists of $1000 plus 2% of his sales. If he got paid $3,000 in a certain month, what was the dollar amount, in thousands, of his sales for that month?

18. If a certain kind of bird can fly at 2 feet per second, how many feet can it fly in an hour?

19. Kat has some coins in her purse. Of the coins, 5 are pennies. If she randomly picks one of the coins from her purse, the probability of picking a penny is $\frac{1}{4}$. How many coins are in her purse?

20. If the average of $3a$, $4a$, and $5a$ is equal to 8, what is a equal to?

SECTION 4

Math Test — Calculator   55 MINUTES, 38 QUESTIONS

Directions:

For questions 1-30, solve each problem, choose the best answer from the choices provided, and fill in the corresponding circle on your answer sheet. **For questions 31-38**, solve the problem and enter your answer in the grid on the answer sheet. Please refer to the directions before question 31 on how to enter your answers in the grid. You may use any available space in your test booklet for scratch work.

Notes:

1. Acceptable calculators are allowed for this section. All numbers used are real numbers.
2. Figures that accompany problems in this test are intended to provide information useful in solving the problems. They are drawn as accurately as possible EXCEPT when it is stated in a specific problem that the figure is not drawn to scale. All figures lie in a plane unless otherwise indicated.
3. Unless otherwise specified, the domain of any function $f(x)$ assumed to be the set of all real numbers x for which $f(x)$ is a real number.

References:

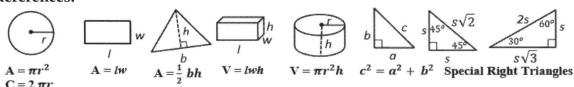

$A = \pi r^2$ $A = lw$ $A = \frac{1}{2}bh$ $V = lwh$ $V = \pi r^2 h$ $c^2 = a^2 + b^2$ **Special Right Triangles**
$C = 2\pi r$

The number of degrees of arc in a circle is 360; the number of radians of arc in a circle is 2π.
The sum of the degree measures of the angles in a triangle is 180.

1. Mrs. Anderson currently has 550 followers on an online professional networking site. Her goal is to have at least 1,000 followers. If she wants to meet this goal in 25 weeks, what is the minimum number of followers per week, on average, she should add?
    a) 18
    b) 19
    c) 21
    d) 22

2. When $3x$ is added to 28 and the sum is divided by 6 subtracted from x, the result equals 5. What is the value of x?
    a) 12
    b) 18
    c) 24
    d) 29

3. What is the product of the slopes of all four sides of a rectangle if all four sides' slopes are not equal to zero?
    a) –2
    b) –1

    c) 0
    d) 1

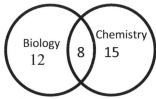

4. The Venn diagram above shows the distribution of 35 students at a school who took biology, chemistry, or both. What percent of the students who take both chemistry and biology?
    a) 15%
    b) 20%
    c) 23%
    d) 25%

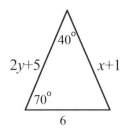

5. In the triangle above, which of the following must be true?
   a) $x = y$
   b) $x = 5$
   c) $x < y$
   d) $x = 2y + 4$

6. A development company is advertising that the mean area of the apartments in a new complex is 1,500 square feet. The complex consists of 10 buildings with a total of 1,000 apartments. A sample of 100 apartments will be selected from the complex to test the company's statement about the mean apartment area. Which of the following is an unbiased sampling method?
   a) Select the first 100 apartments built.
   b) Select the first 100 apartments that are occupied.
   c) Select at random 5 top-floor apartments from each of the buildings.
   d) Select at random 100 apartments from all the apartments in the 10 buildings.

Questions 7 – 8 refer to the following information:

In chemistry, a chemical reaction proceeds at a rate dependent on the concentration of its reactant. For reactant A, the rate of a reaction is defined as:

$$Rate = k\,[A]^n$$

k is a constant and $[A]$ is the concentration of A. The order of reaction of a reactant A is the exponent n to which its concentration term in the rate equation is raised.

7. When n is equal to 2, A is called a 2nd order reactant. Which of the following graphs depicts a 2nd order of reactant with respect to concentration and reaction rate?

a) 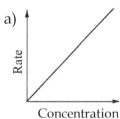   b)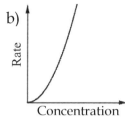

c) 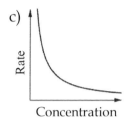   d)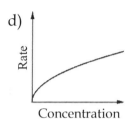

8. If the graph below shows the reaction rate versus the concentration of reactant A, what is the most likely order of reactant A?

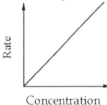

   a) 1st order
   b) 2nd order
   c) 3rd order
   d) 0th order

Zoos

Animal Types	Phila-delphia	National	Phoenix	Total
Amphi-bians	8	20	4	32
Birds	25	71	57	153
Fish	12	39	3	54
Mam-mals	71	84	50	205
Reptiles	20	50	19	89
Total	136	264	113	533

9. The table above shows the number of animals in three different zoos, categorized by type. If an animal is to be selected at random from the Philadelphia zoo for observation, what is the probability that the animal will be an amphibian?
   a) $\frac{8}{253}$
   b) $\frac{8}{136}$
   c) $\frac{32}{553}$
   d) $\frac{8}{32}$

10. The average score of John's 5 math tests is 75. If the teacher decides not to count his lowest score, which is 55, what will be John's new average score?
   a) 78
   b) 79
   c) 80
   d) 81

11. If $f(x) = x^2 + x^{3/2}$, what is the value of $f(3) =$?
   a) $3 \times (1 + 3\sqrt{3})$
   b) $(1 + 3\sqrt{3})$
   c) $3 \times (1 + 3\sqrt{3})$
   d) $3 \times (3 + \sqrt{3})$

12. The diameter of a sphere is 6 inches. What is the volume of the sphere? Use the formula $V = \frac{4}{3}\pi r^3$.
   a) 328π
   b) 72π
   c) 36π
   d) 24π

13. Megan began a one-way 10-mile bicycle trip by riding very slowly for 5 miles. She rested for 30 minutes and then rode quickly

for the rest of the trip. Which of the following graphs could correctly represents the trip?

a)
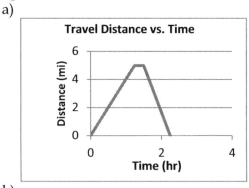

b)
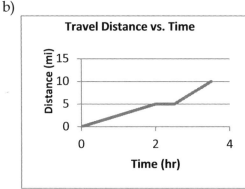

c)
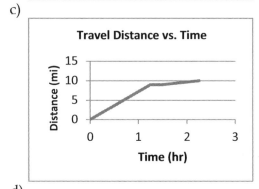

d)
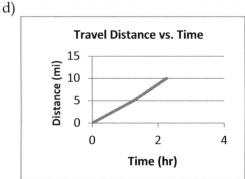

14. Segment $\overline{AB}$ is the diameter of a circle with center O. Another point C lies on circle O.

If AC = 5 and BC = 12, what is the area of circle O?

a) $\frac{169}{2}\pi$

b) $\frac{169}{4}\pi$

c) 100π

d) 50π

15. What would be the least amount of money needed to purchase exactly 21 tickets according the table below?

Bus Ticket Price	
Number of Bus Tickets	Price
1	7.5
Book of 6	40
Book of 12	75

a) $155

b) $142.5

c) $137.5

d) $135

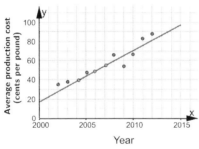

Year

16. The scatterplot above shows the average production cost, in cents per pound, of coffee in Ecuador for the years from 2002 to 2012. A line of best fit is also drawn. Which of the following is closest to the difference, in cents per pound, between the actual average production cost in 2012 and the average production cost in 2012 predicted by the given line of best fit?

a) 4

b) 8

c) 16

d) 50

17. Bella has 5 blue pens, 6 black pens, and 5 red pens in her pencil case. She takes out a pen at random and puts it aside because the pen is not blue. She then takes out a second pen randomly from her pencil case. What is the probability that the second pen will be a blue pen?

a) $\frac{1}{4}$

b) $\frac{1}{2}$

c) $\frac{2}{3}$

d) $\frac{1}{3}$

Questions 18-20 refer to the following information.

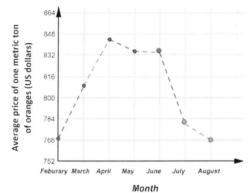

Month

The line graph above shows the average price of one metric ton of oranges, in dollars, for each of seven months in 2018.

18. Between which two consecutive months shown did the average price of one metric ton of oranges decrease the most?

a) March to April

b) May to June

c) June to July

d) July to August

19. Which of the following is closest to the mean price, in dollars, of the seven recorded prices of one metric ton of oranges?

a) 835

b) 806

c) 782

d) 769

20. In 2018, the average price of one metric ton of oranges decreased by 2.36% from January (not shown) to February. Which of

the following is closest to the price of one metric ton of oranges in January 2018?
- a) 710
- b) 772
- c) 786
- d) 829

21. After 8 new customers entered the grocery store and 2 customers left the store, there were three times as many customers in the store as there were before. How many customers were originally in the grocery store?
- a) 1
- b) 2
- c) 3
- d) 4

22. If $sin(x - \frac{\pi}{2}) = 0.2$, what is $\cos x$?
- a) 0.8
- b) 0.98
- c) −0.2
- d) 0.2

23. If $x > y > 0.1$, which of the following is less than $\frac{x}{y}$?
- a) $\frac{x+0.1}{y+0.1}$
- b) $\frac{2x}{2y}$
- c) $\frac{x-0.1}{y-0.1}$
- d) $(\frac{x}{y})^2$

16, 10, 13, ...

24. In the sequence above, the first term is 16 and the second term is 10. Starting with the third term, each term is found by averaging the two terms before it. What is the value of the first non-integer term found in the sequence?

25. What is the area of the trapezoid below if $h = 8$?

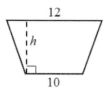

$$(3x + 4a) + 2(ax - 3) = 7x + 2$$

26. In the equation above, a is a constant. If the equation holds true for all value of x. What is the value of a?
- a) 6
- b) 4
- c) 2
- d) 0

27. From the graphs below, how many more graduates went on to a four-year college in 2013 than in 2012?

2012 Graduates Plans
total number of graduates: 400

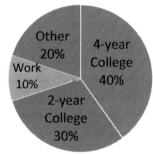

2013 Graduates Plans:
Total Number of Graduates: 420

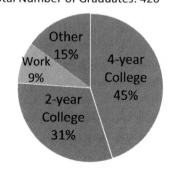

- a) 29
- b) 32
- c) 33
- d) 35

28. The width of Mitchell's room is 3 feet less than its length. If the area of his room is 180

square feet, what is the width of his room in feet?

    a) 9

    b) 12

    c) 14

    d) 15

29. If $7 = m^x$, then $7m^2$=?

    a) m^{2x}

    b) m^{7x}

    c) m^{x+2}

    d) m^{x+7}

30. If the $f(x) = x^5 + bx^4 + cx^3 + dx^2 + ex +$

k, $f(-1) = 0$, and $f(3) = 0$, then $f(x)$ is divisible by

    a)$x - 1$

    b)$x + 3$

    c) $x^2 + 3x + 2$

    d) $x^2 - 2x - 3$

Directions:

For questions 31-38, solve the problem and enter your answer in the grid, as described below, on the answer sheet.

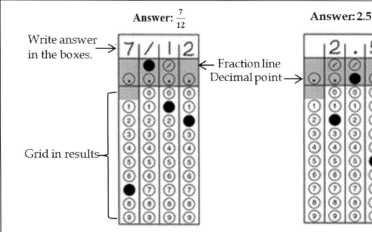

Answer: $\frac{7}{12}$

Write answer in the boxes.

← Fraction line

Decimal point →

Grid in results

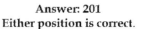

Answer: 2.5

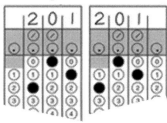

Answer: 201

Either position is correct.

- Mark no more than one circle in any column.
- Because the answer sheet will be machine-scored. **You will receive credit only if the circles are filled in correctly.**
- Although not required, it is suggested that you write your answer in the boxes at the top of the columns to help you fill in the circles accurately.
- Some problems may have more than one correct answer. In such case, grid only one answer.
- No question has a negative answer.
- **Mixed numbers** such as $3\frac{1}{2}$ must be

Note: You may start your answers in any column, space permitting. Columns not needed should be left blank.

gridded as 3.5 or $\frac{7}{2}$. (If [3 1/2] is gridded, it will be interpreted as $\frac{31}{2}$, not $3\frac{1}{2}$.)

- **Decimal Answer:** If you obtain a decimal answer with more digits than the grid can accommodate, it may be either rounded or truncated, but it must fill the entire grid. The acceptable ways to grid $\frac{2}{3}$ are:

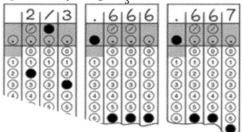

31. Find the radius of the circle given by the equation $x^2 + y^2 - 4x + 2y = 20$.

32. In quadrilateral ABCD, $m\angle A = m\angle B = 128°$, and $m\angle D$ is 10° less than 5 times of $m\angle C$. Find $m\angle D$.

33. The three angles of a triangle have measures $x°$, $2x°$, and $4y°$, where $x > 56$. If x and y are integers, what is one possible value of y?

34. Monday morning, Jason starts out with a certain amount of money that he plans to spend throughout the week. Every morning after that, he spends exactly $\frac{1}{3}$ the amount he has left. 6 days later, on Sunday morning, he finds that he has $64 left. How many dollars did Jason originally have on Monday morning?

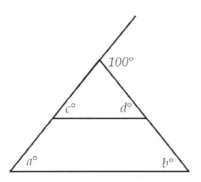

35. In the figure above, what is the value of $2a + 2b - c - d$?

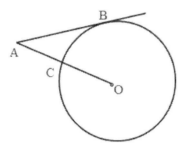

36. In the diagram above, AB is tangent to circle O at point B. AB = 2AC and the radius has length 3. What is the length of $\overline{AO}$?

Questions 37 and 38 refer to the following information:

Planetary Data of Solar System

Planet	Distance from the Sun (billions meters)	Orbital Period (Earth years)
Mercury	57.9	0.241
Earth	149.6	1.0
Mars	227.9	1.88
Saturn	1,427	29.5
Uranus	2,870	84.0
Neptune	Y	165
Planet X	30,000	X

The chart above shows our Solar System's planetary data applied to the Kepler's Third Law, which states that the square of the period of any planet is proportional to the cube of its distance from the Sun. For any planets in the Solar System, the square of the orbital period divided by the cube of its distance from the Sun should be a constant.

37. If Neptune has a period of 165 Earth years, find its distance from the Sun, in billions of meters? (Round your answer to the nearest whole number.)

38. If Planet X is 30,000 billion meters away from the Sun, what is its orbital period, in Earth years? (Round your answer to the nearest whole number.)

SAT MATH PRACTICE TEST No. 2 ANSWER KEYS

Section 3

1. (C)	2. (D)	3. (B)	4. (D)	5. (A)	6. (D)	7. (C)	8. (D)	9. (A)	10. (D)
11. (B)	12. (C)	13. (A)	14. (B)	15. (C)	16. 40	17. 100	18. 7200	19. 20	20. 2

Section 4

1. (A)	2. (D)	3. (D)	4. (C)	5. (D)	6. (D)	7. (B)	8. (A)	9. (B)	10. (c)
11. (D)	12. (C)	13. (B)	14. (B)	15. (C)	16. (B)	17. (D)	18. (C)	19. (B)	20. (C)
21. (C)	22. (C)	23. (A)	24. $\frac{23}{2}$	25. 88	26. (C)	27. (A)	28. (B)	29. (C)	30. (D)
31. 5	32. 85	33. 1 or 2	34. 729	35. 100	36. 5	37. 4500	38. 2840		

Section 3

1. Answer: (C)
   This is a linear model.
   $y = 44t + 200$

2. Answer: (D)
   $f(1) = \frac{1+3}{2} = 2$

3. Answer: (B)
   Slope is -2 and y-intercept is 4.
   $y = mx + b$
   $m = -2$
   $4 = (0)(-2) + b \rightarrow b = 4$
   Therefore, $y = -2x + 4$

4. Answer: (D)
   It is easier to use the method of elimination for this question.
   $3a - 2b = 5$ (1)
   $a + 2b = 23$ (2)
   Add equations (1) and (2) to eliminate b.
   $(1) + (2) \rightarrow 4a = 28$
   $a = 7$
   $3 \times 7 - 2b = 5 \rightarrow b = 8$
   $a + b = 15$

5. Answer: (A)
   $f(x)$ should have its vertex at $\left(\frac{3}{2}, 0\right)$ and all positive.
   The answer is (a).

6. Answer: (D)
   Solve for x by zero-product rule.
   $(3x + 6)(1 - x) = 0$
   $3x + 6 = 0$ or $1 - x = 0$
   $x = 1$ or -2

7. Answer: (C)
   There are no rules about how to arrange boys and girls, so (a) and (b) are incorrect.
   If there is one girl at each end, then two boys must be adjacent. Therefore, (d) is wrong.
   If the last two seated are girls, then two boys must be adjacent. (c) is correct.

8. Answer: (D)
   $2ax - 15 = 3(x + 5) + 5(x - 1)$
   $2ax - 15 = 8x + 10$
   If $a = 4$, then the equation has no solution because $-15 \neq 10$. The answer is d).

9. Answer: (A)
   The line perpendicular to the y-axis is a horizontal line. The value of the y coordinate is constant for a horizontal line.
   $y = 1$

10. Answer: (D)
    Plug in $y = 1 - z$ to the first equation and then apply FOIL method and the distributive law.
    $x = 2(1 - z)^2 + 3(1 - z) + 4$
    $x = 2z^2 - 7z + 9$

11. Answer: (B)
    $x^{-\frac{2}{3}} = a^{-2}$
    $x = (a^{-2})^{(-3/2)} = a^3$
    $y^{\frac{2}{3}} = b^4, \quad y = (b^4)^{(3/2)} = b^6$
    $(xy)^{-\frac{1}{3}} = (a^3 b^6)^{(-\frac{1}{3})} = a^{-1} b^{-2}$

12. Answer: (C)
    The only odd positive integer that is also a multiple of 3 is 15.

13. Answer: (A)

20 pounds : 100 rolls = x : 15 rolls

$$\frac{20\ pounds}{100\ rolls} = \frac{x\ pounds}{15\ rolls}$$

Cross multiply: $100x = 20 \times 15$

$x = 3$ pounds

14. Answer: (B)

Replace x with 1 in the equation.

$2y(6 - 5 \times 1) = 2y$

15. Answer: (C)

$(4x^3)^{\frac{2}{3}} = (2^2)^{\frac{2}{3}} \left(x^{\frac{9}{2}} \right)$ should be $(x^3)^{\left(\frac{2}{3}\right)}$ should be (x^3)

$= 2^{\frac{4}{3}} x^2 = 2\sqrt[3]{2}x^2$

16. Answer: 40

$360^o = 2x + 3x + 2x + 2x$

$360^o = 9x \quad \rightarrow x = 40^o$

17. Answer: 100

Let his car sales be $x, then

$3000 = 1000 + 0.02 \times x$

$3000 - 1000 = 0.02x$

$x = \$100,000$

18. Answer: 7200

Distance = Time × Speed

One Hour = 60×60 Seconds

Total Feet = $2 \times 60 \times 60 = 7,200$ ft.

19. Answer: 20

$$\frac{5}{Total\ Coins} = \frac{1}{4}$$

Total Coins = 20

20. Answer: 2

The average of 3a, 4a and 5a is equal to 4a.

$4a = 8 \rightarrow a = 2$

Section 4

1. Answer: (A)

The number of followers added each week is C: $25C \geq (1000 - 550)$

$C \geq 18$

2. Answer: (D)

$$\frac{3x + 28}{x - 6} = 5$$

$3x + 28 = 5(x - 6)$

$3x + 28 = 5x - 30$

$58 = 2x \rightarrow x = 29$

3. Answer: (D)

The product of the slopes of two perpendicular lines is −1.

The product of the slopes of all four sides of rectangle is $-1 \times (-1) = 1$.

4. Answer: (C)

$$\frac{8}{35} = 0.23 = 23\%$$

5. Answer: (D)

The degree of the 3rd interior angle is $180^o - 40^o - 70^o = 70^o$.

Since this triangle has two angles that are 70°, it is an isosceles triangle.

$2y + 5 = x + 1$

$x = 2y + 4$

6. Answer: (D)

It needs to select samples randomly in order to be unbiased.

7. Answer: (B)

When n = 2, the graph will be a parabola curve.

8. Answer: (A)

A linear line represents a 1st order reaction.

9. Answer: (B)

$$p = \frac{Amphibian\ In\ philadelphia}{Total\ in\ Philadelphia}$$

$$= \frac{8}{136}$$

10. Answer: (C)

John's original average is 75 for 5 tests.

$5 \times 75 = 375$ (sum of 5 tests)

$375 - 55 = 320$ (sum of 4 tests)

$\frac{320}{4} = 80$ (average of 4 tests)

11. Answer: (D)

The value of f(3) is calculated by replacing x with 3 in the function.

$3^2 + 3^{3/2} = 9 + 3\sqrt{3} = 3(3 + \sqrt{3})$

12. Answer: (C)

$$V = \frac{4}{3}\pi r^3 = \frac{4}{3}\pi \left(\frac{6}{2}\right)^3 = \frac{4}{3}\pi(3^3) = 36\pi$$

13. Answer: (B)

Slower speeds have smaller (flatter) slopes. Resting speeds have horizontal slope. Higher speeds have bigger (steeper) slopes.

14. Answer: (B)
ΔABC is a right triangle.
$AB^2 = AC^2 + BC^2$
$AB = \sqrt{5^2 + 12^2} = 13$
Radius $= \frac{1}{2}(13) = 6.5$
Area $= \pi \times 6.5^2 = 42.25\pi = \frac{169}{4}\pi$

15. Answer: (C)
The lowest price for 21 tickets is to purchase 1 book of 12, 1 book of 6 and 3 single tickets.
$75 + $40 + $7.5 \times 3 = 137.5

16. Answer: (B)
Based on the graph, the difference is $89 - 81 = 8$.

17. Answer: (D)
After first taking, there are 5 blue pens and a total of 15 pens left in her pencil case.
Probability to get a blue pen: $\frac{5}{15} = \frac{1}{3}$

18. Answer: (C)
Based on the graph, the two consecutive months that the average price of one metric ton of oranges decreases the most is between June to July.

19. Answer: (B)
$\frac{768+808+844+835+835+768+782}{7} = 805.7$

20. Answer: (C)
$x(1 - 0.0236) = 768$
$x = 786.56$

21. Answer: (C)
Let x be the number of customers before the changes. After adding 8 new customers and subtracting 2 customers who left, the number of customers equals three times as many as x.
$x + 8 - 2 = 3x$
$x = 3$

22. Answer: (C)
$cos(x) = sin\left(\frac{\pi}{2} - x\right)$
$= -sin\left(x - \frac{\pi}{2}\right) = -0.2$

23. Answer: (A)
$x > y > 0.1$
Plug in $x = 2$, and $y = 1$
Only answer (a), $\frac{2.1}{1.1}$, less than 2.

24. Answer: $\frac{23}{2}$
List out several more terms until you hit a non-integer.
$16, 10, 13, \frac{23}{2}$

25. Answer: 88
Area of a Trapezoid $= \frac{1}{2} \times$ (Base 1 + Base 2) $\times$ Height
$= \frac{1}{2}(10 + 12) \times 8 = 88$

26. Answer: (C)
Just plug in any value of x:
When $x = 0$, $4a - 6 = 2 \rightarrow a = 2$

27. Answer: (A)
In 2013, the total number of graduates going to 4-year college is $420 \times 0.45 = 189$.
In 2012, the total number of students heading to 4-year college is $400 \times 0.4 = 160$.
$189 - 160 = 29$

28. Answer: (B)
Let the length be x, then the width is $x - 3$.
$x(x - 3) = 180$
$x^2 - 3x = 180 \rightarrow x = 15$
$15 - 3 = 12$
The width of the room is 12 and the length is 15.

29. Answer: (C)
$7m^2 = m^x \times m^2 = m^{(x+2)}$

30. Answer: (D)
$f(x)$ should be divisible by $(x + 1)$, $(x - 3)$, and $(x^2 - 2x - 3)$.

31. Answer: 5
Rewitte to the standard equation for a circle:
$x^2 - 4x + 4 + y^2 + 2y + 1 = 20 + 5$
$(x - 2)^2 + (y + 1)^2 = 5^2$
The center of the circle is $(2, -1)$ and the radius is 5.

32. Answer: 85
$A + B + C + D = 360°$
$128° + 128° + 5x - 10° + x = 360°$
$x = 19°$
$5x - 10° = 85°$

33. Answer: 1 or 2
$x + 2x + 4y = 180$
$4y = 180 - 3x$
$4y < 180 - 3 \times 56$
$4y < 12 \rightarrow y < 3 \rightarrow y = 1, 2$

34. *Answer: 729*
Jason spends $\frac{1}{3}$ of his money each day, so he has $\frac{2}{3}$ of his money left next morning.
Let Jason have x on Monday. On Sunday, he will have:$(\frac{2}{3} \times \frac{2}{3} \times \frac{2}{3} \times \frac{2}{3} \times \frac{2}{3} \times \frac{2}{3})x$ dollars left.
$\frac{2^6 x}{3^6} = 64$
$x = 3^6 = 729$ *dollars*

35. *Answer: 100*
$100 = c + d = a + b$
$2(a + b) - c - d = 200 - 100 = 100$

36. *Answer: 5*
ΔOAB *is a right triangle with hypotenuse* $\overline{OA}$*, so use the Pythagorean Theorem.*
$OB = OC = 3$
$AC = x \quad AB = 2x \quad AO = 3 + x$
$(2x)^2 + 3^2 = (3 + x)^2$
$4x^2 + 9 = x^2 + 6x + 9 \quad 3x^2 = 6x \rightarrow x = 2 \quad$ *so* $AO = 5$

37. *Answer: 4500*
Kepler's Third Law states:
$\frac{(Orbital\ Period)^2}{(Distance\ from\ the\ Sun)^3} = constant$
$\frac{165^2}{(Distance\ from\ the\ Sun)^3} = \frac{1^2}{149.6^3}$
Distance = 4500 billion meters

38. *Answer: 2840*
$\frac{(Orbital\ Period)^2}{30000^3} = \frac{1^2}{149.6^3}$
Orbital Period = 2840 Earth years

SAT Math Practice Test No. 3

SECTION 3

Math Test — NO Calculator   25 MINUTES, 20 QUESTIONS

Directions:
For questions 1-15, solve each problem, choose the best answer from the choices provided, and fill in the corresponding circle on your answer sheet. **For questions 16-20,** solve the problem and enter your answer in the grid on the answer sheet. Please refer to the directions before question 16 on how to enter your answers in the grid. You may use any available space in your test booklet for scratch work.

Notes:
1. **No calculator** is allowed for this section. All numbers used are real numbers.
2. Figures that accompany problems in this test are intended to provide information useful in solving the problems. They are drawn as accurately as possible EXCEPT when it is stated in a specific problem that the figure is not drawn to scale. All figures lie in a plane unless otherwise indicated.
3. Unless otherwise specified, the domain of any function $f(x)$ assumed to be the set of all real numbers x for which $f(x)$ is a real number.

References:

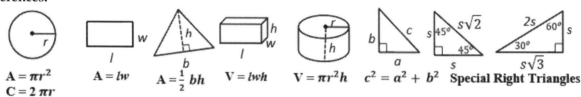

$A = \pi r^2$ $A = lw$ $A = \frac{1}{2}bh$ $V = lwh$ $V = \pi r^2 h$ $c^2 = a^2 + b^2$ **Special Right Triangles**
$C = 2\pi r$

The number of degrees of arc in a circle is 360; the number of radians of arc in a circle is 2π.
The sum of the degree measures of the angles in a triangle is 180.

---

1. If $3x - 1 = 3$, then $12x - 4 = ?$
    a) 6
    b) 8
    c) 12
    d) 16

2. If $3^{1-2x} = 243$, what is the value of x?
    a) −1
    b) −2
    c) 1
    d) 2

3. Find the product of 10 and the sum of m and 10. Then, find one-tenth of the difference between that product and 10. In terms of m, what is the final result?
    a) $m - 1$
    b) $m - 10$
    c) $m + 9$
    d) $m + 10$

4. In the figure below, $l_1 \parallel l_2$. Which of the following statements must be true?

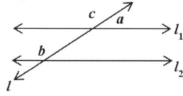

Note: Figure not drawn to scale.
    I. $a + c = 180°$
    II. $b + c = 180°$
    III. $a + b = 180°$

    a) I only
    b) I and II only
    c) I and III only
    d) I, II, and III

5. The equation of line l is $x - 2y = 3$. Which of the following is an equation of the line that is perpendicular to line l?
   a) $y = x + 2$
   b) $y = -x + 2$
   c) $y = 2x - 1$
   d) $y = -2x + 1$

6. What is the value of x if $x + 2y = 6$ and $x + y = 5$?
   a) 2
   b) 3
   c) 4
   d) 5

7. If x is 7 more than y, and y is 5 less than z. What is x when $z = 5$?
   a) -9
   b) -5
   c) 7
   d) 9

8. In the xy-plane, line l passes through the origin and is perpendicular to the line $2x - y = b$, where b is a constant. If the two lines intersect at the point $(2a, a + 1)$, what is the value of b?
   a) -1
   b) $-\frac{5}{2}$
   c) 0
   d) $\frac{1}{2}$

$$Q = \sqrt{\frac{3dk}{h}}$$

9. The formula above is used to estimate the ideal quantity, Q, of items a store manager needs to order, given the demand quantity, d, the setup cost per order, k, and the storage cost per item, h. Which of the following correctly expresses the storage cost per item in terms of the other variables?
   a) $h = \sqrt{\frac{3dk}{Q}}$
   b) $h = \frac{\sqrt{3dk}}{Q}$
   c) $h = \frac{3dk}{Q^2}$

d) $h = \frac{Q^2}{3dk}$

$$(ax + 3)(5x^2 - bx + 4)$$
$$= 20x^3 - 9x^2 - 2x + 12$$

10. The equation above is true for all x, where a and b are constants. What is the value of ab?
   a) 18
   b) 20
   c) 24
   d) 40

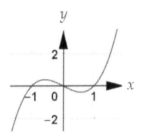

11. The figure above shows the graph of $y = f(x)$. If the function g is defined by $g(x) = f\left(\frac{x}{3}\right) - 2$, what is the value of $g(3)$?
   a) -2
   b) -1
   c) 0
   d) 1

12. If $3x + 1 = a$, then $6x + 1$?
   a) $a + 3$
   b) $a - 3$
   c) $2a - 1$
   d) $2a + 1$

13. The ratio of 1.5 to 1 is equal to which of the following ratios?
   a) 1 to 2
   b) 2 to 1
   c) 3 to 1
   d) 3 to 2

14. Let $*m$ be defined as $*m = m^2 + 4$ for all values of m. If $*x = 3x^2$, which of the following could be the value of x?

a) −2
b) 1
c) 2
d) −$\sqrt{2}$

15. If the average (arithmetic mean) of a, b and c is m, which of the following is the average of a, b, c and d?

a) $\dfrac{2m+d}{3}$

b) $\dfrac{m+d}{2}$

c) $\dfrac{3m+d}{4}$

d) $\dfrac{m+2d}{2}$

Directions:

For questions 16-20, solve the problem and enter your answer in the grid, as described below, on the answer sheet.

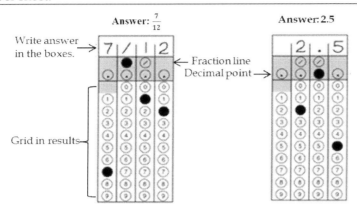

Answer: $\frac{7}{12}$

Write answer in the boxes.

← Fraction line
Decimal point →

Grid in results

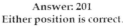

Answer: 2.5

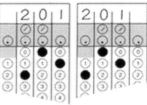

Answer: 201
Either position is correct.

Note: You may start your answers in any column, space permitting. Columns not needed should be left blank.

- Mark no more than one circle in any column.
- Because the answer sheet will be machine-scored. **You will receive credit only if the circles are filled in correctly.**
- Although not required, it is suggested that you write your answer in the boxes at the top of the columns to help you fill in the circles accurately.
- Some problems may have more than one correct answer. In such case, grid only one answer.
- No question has a negative answer.
- **Mixed numbers** such as $3\frac{1}{2}$ must be

gridded as 3.5 or $\frac{7}{2}$. (If [3 1/2] is gridded, it will be interpreted as $\frac{31}{2}$, not $3\frac{1}{2}$.)

- **Decimal Answer:** If you obtain a decimal answer with more digits than the grid can accommodate, it may be either rounded or truncated, but it must fill the entire grid. The acceptable ways to grid $\frac{2}{3}$ are:

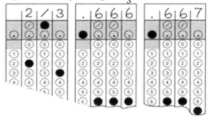

16. If $a + bi = \frac{2+i}{1+i}$, what is the value of $a + b$?

17. A circle with center at coordinates $(4, 3)$ touches the x-axis at only one point. What is the radius of the circle?

18. A bag contains only red, white, and blue marbles. If randomly choosing a blue marble is three times as likely as randomly choosing a white marble, and randomly choosing a red marble is twice as likely as randomly choosing a blue marble, then what is the smallest possible number of marbles in the bag?

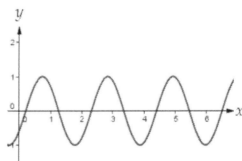

19. According to the graph shown above, how many distinct positive values of x are there on the graph when $y = 0.5$?

20. In the figure below, what is the value of x
    if $x : y = 3 : 1$?

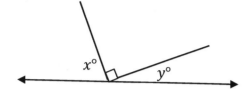

SECTION 4
Math Test — Calculator   55 MINUTES, 38 QUESTIONS

Directions:
For questions **1-30**, solve each problem, choose the best answer from the choices provided, and fill in the corresponding circle on your answer sheet. For questions **31-38**, solve the problem and enter your answer in the grid on the answer sheet. Please refer to the directions before question 31 on how to enter your answers in the grid. You may use any available space in your test booklet for scratch work.

Notes:
1. Acceptable calculators are allowed for this section. All numbers used are real numbers.
2. Figures that accompany problems in this test are intended to provide information useful in solving the problems. They are drawn as accurately as possible EXCEPT when it is stated in a specific problem that the figure is not drawn to scale. All figures lie in a plane unless otherwise indicated.
3. Unless otherwise specified, the domain of any function $f(x)$ assumed to be the set of all real numbers x for which $f(x)$ is a real number.

References:

$A = \pi r^2$ $A = lw$ $A = \frac{1}{2}bh$ $V = lwh$ $V = \pi r^2 h$ $c^2 = a^2 + b^2$ **Special Right Triangles**
$C = 2\pi r$

The number of degrees of arc in a circle is 360; the number of radians of arc in a circle is 2π.
The sum of the degree measures of the angles in a triangle is 180.

1. If $3(x + 5) = 18$, then what is the value of x?
   a) 1
   b) 3
   c) 6
   d) 9

2. The number of people who rode a certain bus each day of a week is shown in the table below.

Day	Number of Riders
Monday	612
Tuesday	798
Wednesday	655
Thursday	773
Friday	808
Saturday	480
Sunday	229

Which of the following is true based on these data?
   a) The bus had the most riders on Tuesday.
   b) Each day from Tuesday through Sunday, the number of riders on the bus was greater than the previous day.
   c) Each day from Tuesday through Sunday, the number of riders on the bus was less than the previous day.
   d) The two days with the fewest number of riders were Saturday and Sunday.

3. The function $f(x) = 18x - 60$ represents the net profit, in dollars, of selling x plastic dinosaurs at Mega Toy Central. What is the total profit if Mega Toy Central sells 20 plastic dinosaurs?
   a) $300
   b) $250
   c) $200
   d) $155

4. In the figure below, AB = 2. What is the area of triangle ADC?

a) $\frac{\sqrt{3}}{8}$

b) $\frac{\sqrt{3}}{8}$

c) $\frac{1}{2}$

d) $\frac{\sqrt{3}}{2}$

5. In the xy-plane, the line $x - 2y = k$ passes through point $(4, -1)$. What is the value of k?

    a) 6
    b) 4
    c) 2
    d) −2

6. If $\frac{a^3}{b^2}$ is an integer, but $\frac{2a+9}{b}$ is not an integer, which of the following could be the values of a and b?

    a) $a = 5$, $b = 5$
    b) $a = 3$, $b = 2$
    c) $a = 6$, $b = 3$
    d) $a = 6$, $b = 4$

Questions 7 − 8 refer to the following information.

In 2014, quarterly sales for full-service restaurants and shoe stores in the United States each increased by a constant rate. For the first quarter of 2014, full-service restaurants had total sales of $60,083 (in millions), and each quarter their sales increased approximately $1,450 (in millions). For the first quarter of 2014, shoe stores had total sales of $8,005 (in millions), and each quarter their sales increased approximately $85 (in millions).

7. Of the following equations, which best models the linear relationship in 2014 between the total quarterly sales (in millions), y, for full-service restaurants and the number of quarters, x, since the first quarter of 2014?

    a) $y = 1450x + 60083$
    b) $y = -1450x - 60083$
    c) $y = 60083x + 1450$
    d) $y = -63083x - 1597$

8. If the same linear trend for shoe store sales continues, how many quarters after the first quarter of 2014 will the total quarterly sales, in millions, for shoe stores in the United States first exceed $10,000?

    a) 23
    b) 24
    c) 25
    d) 26

9. If $\frac{x+3}{2}$ is an integer, then x must be?

    a) a prime number
    b) a positive integer
    c) an odd number
    d) a multiple of 2

10. The quadratic function f is defined by $f(x) = 2(x + 2)^2 - 1$. In the xy-plane, which of the following could be the graph of $y = f(x)$ shifted 3 units to the right?

    a)

b)

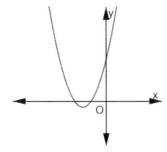

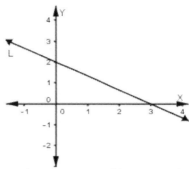

11. What is the equation of line L in the figure above?

    a) $y = 3x + 2$
    b) $y = -3x + 2$
    c) $y = -2x - 3$
    d) $y = -\frac{2}{3}x + 2$

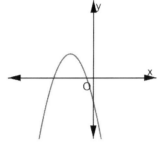

c)

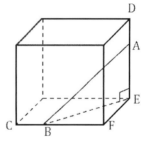

12. The cube shown above has edges of length 5. If $\overline{CB} = \overline{AD} = 2$, what is the length of $\overline{AB}$?

    a) $\sqrt{33}$
    b) $\sqrt{38}$
    c) $\sqrt{43}$
    d) $\sqrt{50}$

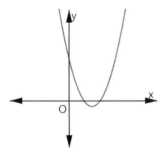

d)

13. If y is inversely proportional to x and y is equal to 12 when x is equal to 8, what is the value of y when $x = 24$?

    a) $\frac{1}{6}$
    b) $\frac{1}{4}$
    c) 4
    d) 2

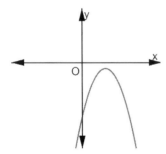

14. A printer that regularly sells for $150 is marked down to $100. What is the discount percentage?

    a) 33%
    b) 42%
    c) 45%
    d) 50%

15. The chart below shows the results of a swimming race. If all the students started at the same time, who finished second?

Swimming Race Results	
Student	Time (in seconds)
Grant	57.55
Robert	56.94
Larry	55.81
Adam	56.02
Chris	57.41

    a) Grant
    b) Robert
    c) Larry
    d) Adam

16. The figure above shows an indoor parking lot with the rectangular arrows indicating the different entrances and exits. What is the total number of distinct ways that a driver can enter and exit the parking lot?
    a) 9
    b) 5
    c) 4
    d) 20

17. The center of a circle is the origin of a rectangular coordinate plane. If (−4, 0), (0, 4), and (4, 0) are three points on the circumference of the circle, what is the probability that a randomly picked point inside the circle would fall inside the triangle formed by those three points?
    a) $\frac{1}{2}$
    b) $\frac{1}{3}$
    c) $\frac{1}{\pi}$
    d) $\frac{2}{\pi}$

$$2, 7, 14, 15, 26, 29, 32, 37, 41$$

18. Based on the sequence of numbers above, a second sequence is generated by increasing each odd-valued term by 5 and decreasing each even-valued term by 3. What is the difference between the total sum of the elements in the original sequence and the total sum of the second sequence?
    a) 4
    b) 6
    c) 10
    d) 13

19. ΔABC is an equilateral triangle with side length of 8. What is the area of ΔABC?
    a) 64
    b) 32
    c) $16\sqrt{3}$
    d) $16\sqrt{2}$

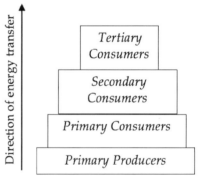

20. The energy pyramid above shows four trophic levels in an ecosystem and the direction of energy transfer between those levels. On average, 15% of the net energy of one trophic level is transferred to the next trophic level in an ecosystem. Based on the energy pyramid, if primary producers have 4,000 joules (J) of energy, approximately how much of this energy, in calories, is transferred to the secondary consumers in this ecosystem? (1 calorie = 4.18 J)
    a) 21.50
    b) 35.90
    c) 69.60
    d) 82.70

21. Which of the following CANNOT affect the value of the median in a set of nonzero

unique numbers with more than two elements?

a) Increase each number by 5
b) Double each number
c) Increase the smallest number only
d) Decrease the smallest number only

22. If $sin(x - \frac{\pi}{2}) = 0.2$, what is $cos\ x$?

a) 0.8
b) 0.98
c) −0.2
d) 0.2

Questions 23-24 refer to the following information

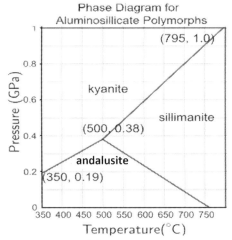

During mineral formation, the same chemical compound can become different minerals depending on the temperature and pressure at the time of formation. A phase diagram is a graph that shows the conditions that are needed to form each mineral. The graph above is a portion of the phase diagram for aluminosilicates, with the temperature T, in degrees Celsius (°C), on the horizontal axis, and the pressure P in gigapascals (GPa) on the vertical axis.

$$P = -0.0015T + 1.13$$

23. An equation of the boundary line between the andalusite and sillimanite regions is approximated by the equation above.

What is the meaning of the T-intercept of this line?

a) It is the maximum temperature at which sillimanite can form.
b) It is the temperature at which both andalusite and sillimanite can form when there is no pressure applied.
c) It is the increase in the number of degrees Celsius needed to remain on the boundary between andalusite and sillimanite if the pressure is reduced by 1 GPa.
d) It is the decrease in the number of gigapascals of pressure needed to remain on the boundary between andalusite and sillimanite if the temperature is increased by 1°C.

24. Which of the following systems of inequalities best descricbes the region where sillimanite can form?

a) $P \geq 0.0021T - 0.67$; $P \geq 0.0013T - 0.25$
b) $P \leq 0.0021T - 0.67$; $P \geq -0.0015T + 1.13$
c) $P \leq 0.0013T - 0.25$; $P \geq -0.0015T + 1.13$
d) $P \leq 0.0013T - 0.25$; $P \leq -0.0015T + 1.13$

25. If $sin(x^o) = a$, which of the following must be true for all values of x ?

a) $cos\ (x^o) = a$
b) $sin(90^o - x^o) = a$
c) $cos\ (90^o - x^o) = a$
d) $sin\ (x^2)° = a^2$

26. In the number line above, if 3 equally spaced points are drawn between A and B and point C is one of those points, which of the following is a possible coordinate for point C?
    a) −1
    b) 1
    c) 2
    d) 3

27. If $x^2 - y^2 = 15$, and $x - y = 3$, what is the value of $x + y$?
    a) 1
    b) 3
    c) 5
    d) 10

28. How many points do the graph of function, $f(x) = (x - 1)^2$, cross the x-axis?
    a) 0
    b) 1
    c) 2
    d) 3

29. The value of one particular copy machine decreases by 15 percent each year. If a new machine was purchased at $20,000, how many years from the date of purchase will the value of this machine be approaching to $12,200?
    a) One
    b) Two
    c) Three
    d) Four

30. Which of the following is the equation of the polynomial with roots at 0 and $3 - \sqrt{2}$?
    a) $x^3 + 6x^2 - 9x = 0$
    b) $x^3 - 6x^2 - 7x = 0$
    c) $x^3 + 6x^2 + 7x = 0$
    d) $x^3 - 6x^2 + 7x = 0$

Directions:

For questions 31-38, solve the problem and enter your answer in the grid, as described below, on the answer sheet.

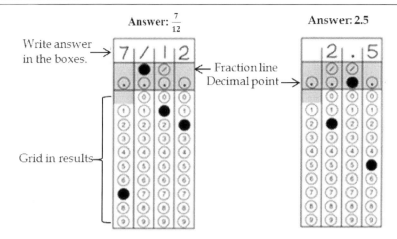

Answer: $\frac{7}{12}$

Write answer in the boxes.

← Fraction line

Decimal point →

Grid in results

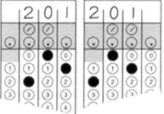

Answer: 2.5

Answer: 201
Either position is correct.

Note: You may start your answers in any column, space permitting. Columns not needed should be left blank.

- Mark no more than one circle in any column.
- Because the answer sheet will be machine-scored. **You will receive credit only if the circles are filled in correctly.**
- Although not required, it is suggested that you write your answer in the boxes at the top of the columns to help you fill in the circles accurately.
- Some problems may have more than one correct answer. In such case, grid only one answer.
- No question has a negative answer.
- **Mixed numbers** such as $3\frac{1}{2}$ must be

gridded as 3.5 or $\frac{7}{2}$. (If [3 1 / 2] is gridded, it will be interpreted as $\frac{31}{2}$, not $3\frac{1}{2}$.)

- **Decimal Answer:** If you obtain a decimal answer with more digits than the grid can accommodate, it may be either rounded or truncated, but it must fill the entire grid. The acceptable ways to grid $\frac{2}{3}$ are:

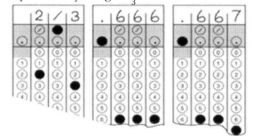

$$s(p) = 10000 - 4.4p$$

31. The function s above gives the remaining free space, in megabytes (MB), on a 10,000 MB memory card that is storing p photos, each with a size of 4.4 MB. If there are 1,200 photos on the card, how many MB of free space remain on the card?

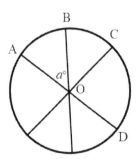

Note: Figure not drawn to scale.

32. In the figure above, O is the center of the circle, $\widehat{AB} = \widehat{BC}$, and $\widehat{AC} = \widehat{CD}$. What is the value of a, in degrees?

x	1	2	3	4	5
f(x)	−2	1	6	13	22

33. Some pairs of input and output values of the function *f* are shown above. The function *h* is defined by *h(x)* = *f* (2x − 1). What is the value of *h(3)*?

34. The area of a rectangle is 2,400 square meters. If the length of one side of the rectangle is 80 meters, what is the perimeter of the rectangle, in meters?

35. If the lengths of the edges of a cube are increased by 20%, the volume of the cube will increase by how many percent? (Round your answer to the nearest tenth)

36. In the figure below, if the area of the triangle is 20, what is the value of *k*?

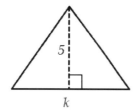

k

Questions 37 and 38 refer to the following information:

According to the combined ideal gas law, if the amount of gas stays constant, the relationship between pressure, volume, and temperature is as follows:
$$\frac{PV}{T} = constant$$
P is the pressure measured in atmospheres (atm), V is the volume measured in liters (L), and T is the temperature measured in Kelvin (K).
The relationship between Kelvin and Celsius is as follows:
$$K = 273 + °C$$
K is the temperature in Kelvin and °C is the temperature in Celsius.
The relationship between Celsius and Fahrenheit is as follows:
$$°C = (°F − 32) \times \frac{5}{9}$$
Where °C is the temperature in Celsius and °F is the temperature in Fahrenheit.

37. What will be the final volume, in liters, if the pressure of 10-liter sample of an ideal gas is changed from 2 atm to 3 atm and the temperature is changed from 273 K to 300 K? (Round your answer to the nearest tenth.)

38. If the initial volume of a gas is 10 liters and the pressure of 2 atm, what will be the approximate new volume, in liters, when the temperature is changed from 32 °F to 212 °F and the pressure remains unchanged? (Round your answer to the nearest tenth.)

SAT MATH PRACTICE TEST No. 3 ANSWER KEYS

Section 3

1. (C)	2. (B)	3. (C)	4. (C)	5. (D)	6. (C)	7. (C)	8. (B)	9. (C)	10. (C)
11. (A)	12. (C)	13. (D)	14. (D)	15. (C)	16. 1	17. 3	18. 10	19. 7	20. 67.5

Section 4

1. (A)	2. (D)	3. (A)	4. (A)	5. (A)	6. (A)	7. (A)	8. (B)	9. (C)	10. (C)
11. (D)	12. (C)	13. (C)	14. (A)	15. (D)	16. (D)	17. (C)	18. (D)	19. (C)	20. (A)
21. (D)	22. (C)	23. (B)	24. (B)	25. (C)	26. (C)	27. (C)	28. (B)	29. (C)	30. (D)
31. 4720	32. 45	33. 22	34. 220	35. 72.8	36. 8	37. 7.3	38. 13.7		

Section 3

1. Answer: (C)
$3x - 1 = 3$
$12x - 4 = 4(3x - 1) = 4 \times 3 = 12$

2. Answer: (B)
$3^{1-2x} = 243 = 3^5$
$1 - 2x = 5 \rightarrow x = -2$

3. Answer: (C)
$\frac{10(m + 10) - 10}{10}$
$= \frac{10(m + 10 - 1)}{10}$
$= m + 9$

4. Answer: (C)
$a + c = 180°$
$c = 180° - a$
$a + b = 180°$
$a = 180° - b$
$c = 180° - (180° - b)$
$b = c$

5. Answer: (D)
$x - 2y = 3$
$y = \frac{1}{2}x - 1.5$
Line l has a slope of $\frac{1}{2}$.
A line that is perpendicular to line l would have a slope of -2.

6. Answer: (C)
Substitute y with $5 - x$.
$x + 2(5 - x) = 6$
$x = 4$

7. Answer: (C)
If $x = y + 7$, then $y = z - 5$.
If $z = 5$, then $y = 0$.
$x = 0 + 7 = 7$

8. Answer: (B)
The slope of line $2x - y = b$ is 2.
Line l is perpendicular, so it have a slope of $-\frac{1}{2}$. We also know that it passes through the origin.
$y = -\frac{1}{2}x$
$a + 1 = -\frac{1}{2}(2a)$
$2a = -1, \quad a = -\frac{1}{2}$
Therefore, point $(-1, \frac{1}{2})$ passes through $2x - y = b$
$-2 - \frac{1}{2} = -\frac{5}{2} = b$

9. Answer: (C)
$Q = \sqrt{\frac{3dk}{h}}$
$Q^2 = \frac{3dk}{h} \rightarrow h = \frac{3dk}{Q^2}$

10. Answer: (C)
"True for all x" means the expressions on both sides need to be identical.
$(ax + 3)(5x^2 - bx + 4) = 20x^3 - 9x^2 - 2x + 12$
The coefficients of x^2 on both sides should be the same:
$-ab + 15 = -9$
$ab = 24$

11. Answer: (A)
$g(3) = f(\frac{3}{3}) - 2 = f(1) - 2$
From the graph above, $f(1) = 0$
$g(3) = 0 - 2 = -2$

12. *Answer: (C)*
$3x = a - 1$
$6x = 2 \times (3x) = 2 \times (a - 1) = 2a - 2$
$6x + 1 = 2a - 2 + 1 = 2a - 1$

13. *Answer: (D)*
You can multiply the numerator and denominator by the same factor to get an equivalent ratio.
$1.5 \times 2 : 1 \times 2 = 3 : 2$
Or just simply convert the ratios to decimals and compare, such as
$3 \div 2 = 1.5.$

14. *Answer: (D)*
$*x = x^2 + 4$
$x^2 + 4 = 3x^2$
$x^2 = 2 \rightarrow x = \pm\sqrt{2}$

15. *Answer: (C)*
The Average of a, b, and c is equal to the sum of a, b, and c divided by 3.
$a + b + c = 3m$
$a + b + c + d = 3m + d$
Average: $\frac{3m+d}{4}$

16. *Answer: 1*
Rationalize the denominator.
$\frac{2+i}{1+i} = \frac{(2+i)(1-i)}{(1+i)(1-i)} = \frac{3-i}{2} = \frac{3}{2} - \frac{1}{2}i = a + bi$
$a = \frac{3}{2}$ *and* $b = -\frac{1}{2}$
$a + b = \frac{3}{2} + \left(-\frac{1}{2}\right) = 1$

17. *Answer: 3*
The circle is tangent to the x-axis, since otherwise it would touch the axis at zero or two points (try drawing it out to see). Its radius is the distance from the center to the x-axis which is 3.

18. *Answer: 10*
Blue: White = 3: 1
Red : Blue = 2 : 1
Red : Blue : White = 6 : 3 : 1
The smallest possible number of marbles in the bag is 10.

19. *Answer: 7*
Draw a horizontal line y = 0.5 to find how many interceptions with the graph.
From the graph above, there are seven interceptions with line y = 0.5.

20. *Answer: 67.5*
$x + y = 180 - 90 = 90 \quad x = 90 \times \frac{3}{4} = 67.5$

Section 4

1. *Answer: (A)*
Divide both sides by 3.
$3(x + 5) = 18$
$x + 5 = 6$
$x = 1$

2. *Answer: (D)*
Based on the information in the table, the two days with the fewest number of riders were Saturday and Sunday.

3. *Answer: (A)*
Substitute x with 20.
$f(20) = 18 \times 20 - 60 = 300$

4. *Answer: (A)*
$2x + x = 90^o$
$x = 30^o$
These are two special 30−60−90 right triangles.
$AB = 2$
$AC = \frac{1}{2} \times 2 = 1$
$AD = \frac{\sqrt{3}}{2} \times AC = \frac{\sqrt{3}}{2}$
$DC = \frac{1}{2} \times AC = \frac{1}{2}$
Area of $\Delta ADC = \frac{1}{2} \times AD \times DC = \frac{1}{2} \times \frac{\sqrt{3}}{2} \times \frac{1}{2} = \frac{\sqrt{3}}{8}$

5. *Answer: (A)*
Plug in the values for x and y into the equation.
$4 - 2(-1) = k = 6$

6. *Answer: (A)*
Try out the values of a and b from answer choices.
a). $\frac{5^3}{5^2}, \frac{19}{5}$
b). $\frac{3^3}{2^2}, \frac{15}{2}$
c). $\frac{6^3}{3^2}, \frac{21}{3}$
d). $\frac{6^3}{4^2}, \frac{21}{4}$

7. *Answer: (A)*
This is a linear model.
The slope is 1450 and the initial value is 60083.
$y = 1450x + 60083$

8. *Answer: (B)*
$y = 85x + 8005 = 10000$
$x = 23.5 \rightarrow 24^{th}$ *quarter*

9. Answer: (C)
    $$\frac{x+3}{2} = n$$
    $x + 3 = 2n$
    $x = 2n + 3$
    $2n + 3$ is odd if n is an integer.

10. Answer: (C)
    $f(x) = 2(x + 2)^2 - 1$
    Vertex is at $(-2, -1)$.
    After shift 3 units to the right, the vertex is at $(1, -1)$, in the fourth quadrant.
    The answer is c)

11. Answer: (D)
    $$Slope = \frac{Rise}{Run} = \frac{0-2}{3-0} = -\frac{2}{3}$$
    y-intercept = 2
    $$y = -\frac{2}{3}x + 2$$

12. Answer: (C)
    $BF = 5 - 2 = 3$
    $EF = 5$
    $EA = 5 - 2 = 3$
    $AB = \sqrt{EA^2 + EB^2} = \sqrt{BF^2 + EF^2 + EA^2}$
    $AB = \sqrt{3^2 + 5^2 + 3^2} = \sqrt{43}$

13. Answer: (C)
    $8 \times 12 = y \times 24$
    $y = 4$

14. Answer: (A)
    Discount = \$150 - \$100 = \$50
    \$50 = \$150 × Discount Rate
    Discount Rate = $\frac{50}{150}$ = 0.33
    Changing 0.33 to percent gives you 33%.

15. Answer: (D)
    Adam has the 2nd shortest time listed.

16. Answer: (D)
    Because cars entering the parking lot will also exit, so use the Multiplication Principle.
    Total number of ways: $5 \times 4 = 20$

17. Answer: (C)
    Radius of the Circle = 4
    Area of the Circle = $\pi (4)^2 = 16\pi$
    Area of the Triangle = $\frac{1}{2} \times 4 \times 8 = 16$
    Probability = $\frac{16}{16\pi} = \frac{1}{\pi}$

18. Answer: (D)
    There are 5 odd-valued terms and 4 even-valued terms in this sequence.
    $5 \times 5 - 4 \times 3 = 13$

19. Answer: (C)
    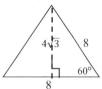
    30-60-90 special right triangle
    $\frac{1}{2} \times 8 \times 4\sqrt{3} = 16\sqrt{3}$

20. Answer: (A)
    It is two levels up from primary producers to secondary consumers.
    $(4000)(0.15)(0.15) \times \frac{1}{4.18}$
    = 21.5 calories

21. Answer: (D)
    The median of an odd-numbered set is the number in the middle when all numbers in the set have been sorted in numerical order. In an even-numbered set, it is the average of the two middle elements.
    We can change the median by:
    i.   Changing the value of the median
    ii. Changing order of numbers so that we have a new median
    Choices (a) and (b) change all values so the median will be changed. Choice (c) could result in a new median if the number changed becomes the new median. Choice (d) reduces the element that is already the smallest, and we know that there are more than 2 elements, so the median does not get changed.

22. Answer: (C)
    $$cos(x) = sin\left(\frac{\pi}{2} - x\right)$$
    $$= -sin\left(x - \frac{\pi}{2}\right) = -0.2$$

23. Answer: (B)
    "The T-intercept of the line" means when the pressure is zero.

24. *Answer: (B)*
The equation of the inequality between andalusite and sillimanite:
$P \geq -0.0015T + 1.13$
From two points of (500, 0.38) and (795, 1.0):
the slope is: $\frac{795-500}{1.0-0.38} = 0.0021$
y-intercept = −0.67
the equation of the inequality between kyanite and sillimanite:
$P \leq 0.0021T - 0.67$
Therefore, the answer is b).

25. *Answer: (C)*
$cos(90^o - x^o) = sin(x^o) = a$

26. *Answer: (C)*
Find the distance of $\overline{AB}$ *then divide it by 4.*
$\frac{AB}{4} = \frac{6-(-2)}{4} = 2$
The coordinate of point C could be (6 – 2) =4 or (−2 + 2) =0 or (4 – 2) =2.

27. *Answer: (C)*
$x^2 - y^2 = (x - y)(x + y)$
$3(x + y) = 15$
$x + y = 5$

28. *Answer: (B)*
The graph of f(x) intersects the x-axis when f(x) = 0.
$0 = (x - 1)^2 \quad \rightarrow \quad x = 1$

29. *Answer: (C)*
The price is decreasing by 15 percent each year, so the value of next year is 85% of the value of this year.
$12,200 = 20,000 \times (\frac{85}{100})^n$
$0.61 = (0.85)^n \rightarrow n = 3$

30. *Answer: (D)*
The equation should also have a root at $3 + \sqrt{2}$, *because all of the answer choices have rational coefficients. Therefore, the polynomial is* $x[x - (3 - \sqrt{2})][x - (3 + \sqrt{2})] = x[(x - 3)^2 - (\sqrt{2})^2] = (x^2 - 6x + 7) = x^3 - 6x^2 + 7x = 0$

31. *Answer: 4720*
$s = 10000 - 4.4(1200) = 4720\ MB$

32. *Answer: 45*
$\overset{\frown}{AB}$ *is half of* $\overset{\frown}{AC}$ *so it is* $\frac{1}{4}$ *of* $\overset{\frown}{AD}$.
$a = \frac{1}{4} \times 180^o$
$a = 45^o$

33. *Answer: 22*
$h(3) = f(2 \times 3 - 1) = f(5) = 22$

34. *Answer: 220*
Area of a Rectangle = Length × Width
$2400 = 80x$
$x = 30;\ Perimeter = (30 + 80) \times 2 = 220\ meters$

35. *Answer: 72.8*
If the original lengths of the edges of the cube are 1. After increasing by 20%, its lengths become 1.2. The volume of the cube is equal to (1.2)³ or 1.728. The volume of the cube increases 72.8%.

36. *Answer: 8*
$20 = \frac{1}{2} \times 5 \times k$
$k = 8$

37. *Answer: 7.3*
$\frac{PV}{T} = constant$
$\frac{P_1 V_1}{T_1} = constant = \frac{P_2 V_2}{T_2}$
$\frac{2 \times 10}{273} = \frac{3 \times V_2}{300}$
$v_2 = 7.3\ liters$

38. *Answer: 13.7*
$T_1 = (32 - 32) \times \frac{5}{9} = 0\ °C = 273 + 0 = 273\ K$
$T_2 = (212 - 32) \times \frac{5}{9} = 100\ °C = 273 + 100 = 373\ K$
$\frac{2 \times 10}{273} = \frac{2 \times V_2}{373} \quad \rightarrow \quad V_2 = 13.7\ liters$

SAT Math Practice Test No. 4

SECTION 3

Math Test — NO Calculator   25 MINUTES, 20 QUESTIONS

Directions:
For questions 1-15, solve each problem, choose the best answer from the choices provided, and fill in the corresponding circle on your answer sheet. **For questions 16-20,** solve the problem and enter your answer in the grid on the answer sheet. Please refer to the directions before question 16 on how to enter your answers in the grid. You may use any available space in your test booklet for scratch work.

Notes:
1. **No calculator** is allowed for this section. All numbers used are real numbers.
2. Figures that accompany problems in this test are intended to provide information useful in solving the problems. They are drawn as accurately as possible EXCEPT when it is stated in a specific problem that the figure is not drawn to scale. All figures lie in a plane unless otherwise indicated.
3. Unless otherwise specified, the domain of any function $f(x)$ assumed to be the set of all real numbers x for which $f(x)$ is a real number.

References:

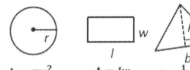   

$A = \pi r^2$ $A = lw$ $A = \frac{1}{2} bh$ $V = lwh$ $V = \pi r^2 h$ $c^2 = a^2 + b^2$ **Special Right Triangles**
$C = 2 \pi r$

The number of degrees of arc in a circle is 360; the number of radians of arc in a circle is 2π.
The sum of the degree measures of the angles in a triangle is 180.

1. Larry spent a total of $200 to lease snowboard equipment at Winter Mountain during his vacation. Each day of his vacation, he purchased a lift ticket for $44. If Larry purchased t lift tickets, how much money, in dollars, did Larry spend during his vacation at Winter Mountain on snowboard equipment and lift tickets?
   a) $44t$
   b) $44t - 200$
   c) $200 + 44t$
   d) $200 - 44t$

2. If $\sqrt{k + 3} - 6 = 0$, k is a constant. What is the value of k ?
   a) 1
   b) 3
   c) 9
   d) 33

3. If $a^2 + 11 = b^3$, and $3a = 12$, which of the following could be the value of b?
   a) 3
   b) 2
   c) 0
   d) −3

4. Alex has less money than Bob and Bob has less money than Chris. If a, b, and c represent the amounts of money that Alex, Bob, and Chris have, respectively, which of the following is true?
   a) a < b < c
   b) c < b < a
   c) b < a < c
   d) a < c < b

5. A parking lot charges $3.00 maintenance fee per day to use its parking space. In

addition, there is a charge of $1.25 per hour. Which of the following represents the total charge, in dollars, to park a car in the parking lot for m hours in one day?
a) $3 + 1.25m$
b) $3m + 1.25$
c) $(3 + 1.25)m$
d) $3 + 1.25 + m$

6. If $(3x + 6)(1 - x) = 0$, what are all the possible values of x?
a) 1 only
b) −2 only
c) 0 only
d) 1 and −2 only

7. A school choir consists of one row of singers, half of which are boys and the other half girls. Which of the following must be true?
a) The first person and the last person have different genders.
b) There are two girls next to each other.
c) If the last two are girls, there are at least two adjacent boys.
d) If there are two adjacent boys, there are also two adjacent girls.

8. The above design is to be painted using a different color for the face, the eyes (both of which have to be the same color), the nose, and the mouth. If 6 different colors are available, how many different designs are possible?
a) 120
b) 240
c) 360
d) 720

$$Q = \sqrt{\frac{3dk}{h}}$$

9. The formula above is used to estimate the ideal quantity, Q, of items a store manager needs to order, given the demand quantity, d, the setup cost per order, k, and the storage cost per item, h. Which of the following correctly expresses the storage cost per item in terms of the other variables?
a) $h = \sqrt{\frac{3dk}{Q}}$
b) $h = \frac{\sqrt{3dk}}{Q}$
c) $h = \frac{3dk}{Q^2}$
d) $h = \frac{Q^2}{3dk}$

10. A number a is multiplied by $\frac{1}{3}$. The product is then multiplied by 27, which results in 81. What is the value of a?
a) 3
b) 6
c) 9
d) 18

11. If x and y are positive integers and $(x^{\frac{1}{6}} y^{\frac{1}{6}})^3 = 8$, what is the value of xy?
a) 8
b) 32
c) 64
d) 128

$$\frac{x + 1}{x} = \frac{1}{x} - \frac{1}{x - 3}$$

12. What is the solution set of the equation above?
a) {1}
b) {0, 2}
c) {2}
d) {1, 2}

13. If $a^2 + b^2 = x$ and $2ab = y$, which of the following is equivalent to $4x + 4y$?
a) $(a + b)^2$
b) $(a + 2b)^2$

c) $(2a + 2b)^2$

d) $\left(\frac{1}{2}a + b\right)^2$

a) 0
b) 1
c) m^{-6}
d) m

14. If $x = 1$, what is $2y(6 - 5x)$ in terms of y?
   a) $2y - 10$
   b) $2y$
   c) $12y - 10$
   d) $12y$

15. If m is a positive number, which of the following is equal to $m^3 \times m^{-3}$?

Directions:

For questions 16-20, solve the problem and enter your answer in the grid, as described below, on the answer sheet.

Answer: $\frac{7}{12}$

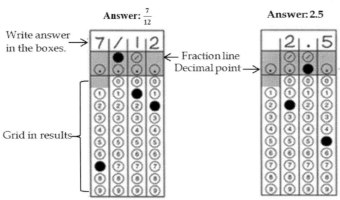

Answer: 2.5

Answer: 201
Either position is correct.

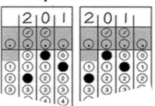

- Mark no more than one circle in any column.
- Because the answer sheet will be machine-scored. **You will receive credit only if the circles are filled in correctly.**
- Although not required, it is suggested that you write your answer in the boxes at the top of the columns to help you fill in the circles accurately.
- Some problems may have more than one correct answer. In such case, grid only one answer.
- No question has a negative answer.
- **Mixed numbers** such as $3\frac{1}{2}$ must be

Note: You may start your answers in any column, space permitting. Columns not needed should be left blank.

gridded as 3.5 or $\frac{7}{2}$. (If [3 1/2] is gridded, it will be interpreted as $\frac{31}{2}$, not $3\frac{1}{2}$.)

- **Decimal Answer:** If you obtain a decimal answer with more digits than the grid can accommodate, it may be either rounded or truncated, but it must fill the entire grid. The acceptable ways to grid $\frac{2}{3}$ are:

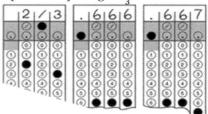

16. If $a - bi = i(3 - 7i)$, what is the value of $a + b$?

17. A car salesman's monthly pay consists of $1000 plus 2% of his sales. If he got paid $3,000 in a certain month, what was the dollar amount, in thousands, of his sales for that month?

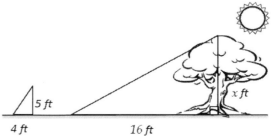

18. At a certain time of day, a tree casts a 16-foot shadow and a 5-foot stick casts a 4-foot shadow. What is the height, in feet, of the tree?

19. $4(p + 2) + 4(p - 1) = 10p$

What value of p is the solution of the equation above?

20. In the figure above, each square is one-fourth of the area of the square immediately larger than it. The area of the smallest square is what fraction of the area of the biggest square?

SECTION 4

Math Test — Calculator   55 MINUTES, 38 QUESTIONS

Directions:
For questions 1-30, solve each problem, choose the best answer from the choices provided, and fill in the corresponding circle on your answer sheet. **For questions 31-38**, solve the problem and enter your answer in the grid on the answer sheet. Please refer to the directions before question 31 on how to enter your answers in the grid. You may use any available space in your test booklet for scratch work.

Notes:
1. Acceptable calculators are allowed for this section. All numbers used are real numbers.
2. Figures that accompany problems in this test are intended to provide information useful in solving the problems. They are drawn as accurately as possible EXCEPT when it is stated in a specific problem that the figure is not drawn to scale. All figures lie in a plane unless otherwise indicated.
3. Unless otherwise specified, the domain of any function $f(x)$ assumed to be the set of all real numbers x for which $f(x)$ is a real number.

References:

$A = \pi r^2$ $A = lw$ $A = \frac{1}{2}bh$ $V = lwh$ $V = \pi r^2 h$ $c^2 = a^2 + b^2$ **Special Right Triangles**
$C = 2\pi r$

The number of degrees of arc in a circle is 360; the number of radians of arc in a circle is 2π.
The sum of the degree measures of the angles in a triangle is 180.

---

1. If $6 \cdot 2k = 72$, what is the value of $4k - 5$?
   a) 19
   b) 16
   c) 12
   d) 8

2. If 10 percent of 40 percent of a positive number is equal to 20 percent of y percent of the same positive number, find the value of y.
   a) 10
   b) 15
   c) 20
   d) 35

3. If 20 percent of x is 50, what is x percent of 40?

   a) 50
   b) 100
   c) 150
   d) 200

4. In $\triangle ABC$ below, $\angle ACB$ is 91°. Which of the following segments has the longest length?

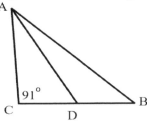

   a) Segment AD
   b) Segment AC
   c) Segment CB
   d) Segment AB

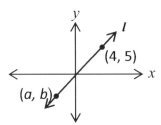

5. In the figure above, line l passes through the origin. What is the value of $\frac{b}{a}$?
    a) 1
    b) 1.25
    c) 1.33
    d) 1.5

6. If $5 \le x \le 7$ and $-3 \le y \le 1$, which of the following gives the set of all possible values of xy?
    a) $-15 \le xy \le 7$
    b) $0 \le xy \le 7$
    c) $-21 \le xy \le 5$
    d) $-21 \le xy \le 7$

Questions 7 − 8 refer to the following Information.

$$h = 3c$$

A wildlife biologist uses the formula above to estimate the height h, in centimeters, of an elephant from its feet to its shoulder, based on the circumference c, in centimeters, of the elephant's footprint.

7. If the wildlife biologist finds a circular elephant footprint that has a diameter of 30 centimeters (cm) while on a zoological study, which of the following is closest to the biologist's estimate of the elephant's height?
    a) 90.0 cm
    b) 94.2 cm
    c) 188.4 cm
    d) 282.6 cm

8. The circumference c of a mother elephant's circular footprint is 4 times the circumference of a baby elephant's circular footprint. What is the ratio of the height of the mother to the height of the baby?
    a) 1 to 4
    b) 1 to 3
    c) 4 to 1
    d) 4 to 3

$$2x\ ,\ y\ ,\ 2y$$
9. If the average (arithmetic mean) of the three numbers above is $3x$ and $x \ne 0$, what is y in terms of x?
    a) $2x$
    b) $3x$
    c) $\frac{5x}{2}$
    d) $\frac{7x}{3}$

10. In the xy-coordinate system, $(k, 7)$ is one of the points of intersection of the graphs $y = 2x^2 - 3$ and $y = -x^2 + m$, where m and k are constants. What is the value of m?
    a) 4
    b) 5
    c) 10
    d) 12

11. A rectangular box has dimensions 36 × 14 × 18. Without wasting any space, which of the following could be the dimensions of the smaller boxes which can be packed into the rectangular box?
    a) 2 × 5 × 6
    b) 7× 9 × 12
    c) 3 × 5 × 6
    d) 4 × 5 × 6

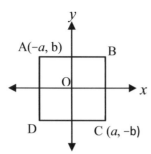

12. In the figure above, rectangle ABCD lies on the xy-coordinate plane. If the origin is located at the center of rectangle, which of the following could be the coordinates of point D?

   a) $(-a, b)$
   b) $(-a, -b)$
   c) $(-b, -a)$
   d) (b, a)

$$h(t) = -16t^2 + 320t + h_o$$

13. At time $t = 0$, a rocket was launched from a height of h_o feet above the ground. Until the rocket hit the ground, its height, in feet, after t seconds was given by the function h above. For which of the following values of t did the rocket have the same height as it did when $t = 5$.

   a) 10
   b) 15
   c) 18
   d) 20

14. Based on Mrs. Johnson's grading policies, if a student answers 90 to 100 percent of the questions correctly in a math test, she will receive a letter grade of A. If there are 60 questions on the final exam, what is the minimum number of questions the student would need to answer correctly to receive a grade of A?

   a) 34
   b) 38
   c) 42
   d) 54

15. Line m in the xy-plane contains the points $(2, 4)$ and $(0, 1)$. Which of the following is an equation of line ?

   a) $y = 2x + 3$
   b) $y = 2x + 4$
   c) $y = \frac{3}{2}x + 3$
   d) $y = \frac{3}{2}x + 1$

$$3xi + 2i^6 = 6i + 4i^{13} + 5y$$

16. In the equation above, x and y are real numbers and $i = \sqrt{-1}$. Which of the following ordered pair could be the solution for this equation?

   a) $(\frac{10}{3}, -\frac{2}{5})$
   b) $(-\frac{2}{5}, -\frac{10}{3})$
   c) $(\frac{10}{3}, \frac{2}{5})$
   d) $(-\frac{2}{5}, \frac{10}{3})$

Time(days)	Counts
0	5
1	50
2	500
3	5,000
4	50,000
5	500,000

17. The estimated counts of bacteria in a petri dish are over the course of five days, as shown in the table above. Which of the following best describes the relationship between time and the estimated counts of bacteria during the five-day period?

   a) Decreasing linear
   b) Increasing linear
   c) Exponential decay
   d) Exponential growth

18. A student folded many paper planes of different colors in the following order: red,

orange, yellow, green, blue, indigo and purple. If he finished 46 paper planes, and started with red, what color was the last paper plane?

  a) Yellow
  b) Green
  c) Blue
  d) Red

Questions 19 – 20 refer to the following information:

  The kinetic energy of an object is the energy that the object possesses due to its motion. Kinetic energy is equal to half of the product of the mass and the square of its velocity.
  The momentum is the quantity of the motion of a moving body, measured as a product of its mass and velocity.

19. If two bodies, A and B, have equal kinetic energies and the mass of A is nine times as much as the mass of B, what is the ratio of the momentum of A to that of B?

  a) $\frac{1}{3}$
  b) $\frac{3}{4}$
  c) 3
  d) 5

20. If two bodies A and B as described above have equal momentum, what is the ratio of the kinetic energy of A to that of B?

  a) $\frac{1}{9}$
  b) $\frac{1}{3}$
  c) 3
  d) 9

$$f(x) = 2^x - 1$$

21. The function f is defined by the equation above. Which of the following is the graph of in the xy-plane?

  a)

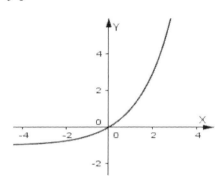

  b)

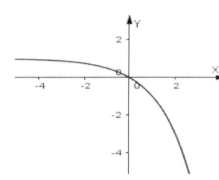

  c)

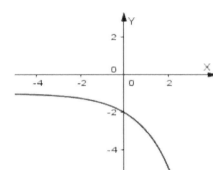

  d)

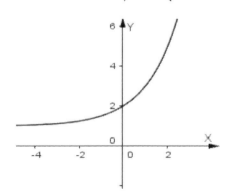

22. In June, 24 people enrolled in a cooking class. In July, the number of people who enrolled increased 150%. How many

people enrolled in the cooking class in July?

a) 30
b) 60
c) 70
d) 80

23. If $x > y > 0.1$, which of the following is less than $\frac{x}{y}$?

a) $\frac{x+0.1}{y+0.1}$
b) $\frac{2x}{2y}$
c) $\frac{x-0.1}{y-0.1}$
d) $(\frac{x}{y})^2$

24. In a sequence of numbers, each term after the first term is 4 greater than $\frac{1}{4}$ of the preceding term. If a_o is the first term and $a_o \neq 0$, which of the following represents the ratio of the third term to the second term?

a) $\frac{a_0+16}{4}$
b) $\frac{a_0+6}{4a_0}$
c) $\frac{a_0+4}{4a_0}$
d) $\frac{a_0+80}{4a_0+64}$

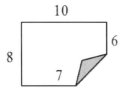

25. The figure above was originally a rectangle. What is the area of the figure after one corner was folded over as shown above?

a) 70
b) 72
c) 75
d) 77

26. Sam drove from home at an average speed of 40 miles per hour to her working place and then returned along the same route at an average speed of 30 miles per hour. If the entire trip took her 2.1 hours, what is

the entire distance, in miles, for the round trip?

a) 36
b) 72
c) 84
d) 90

27. A sample of seawater is 4% salt by mass and contains 1,000 grams of salt. Which of the following is closest to the mass, in grams, of the sample of seawater?

a) 27,500
b) 25,000
c) 19,600
d) 13,500

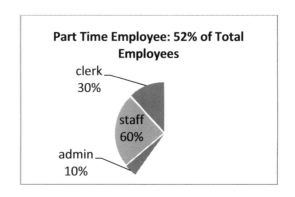

Full Time Employees

Full Time = 48% of Total Employees

28. According to the graphs above, how many part time administrators at Oak Town High School?
    a) 10
    b) 12
    c) 13
    d) 20

29. The ratio of 1.25 to 1 is equal to which of the following ratios?
    a) 2 to 1.5
    b) 3 to 2
    c) 4 to 3

d) 5 to 4

30. The scatterplot above shows a company's ice cream sales d, in dollars, and the high temperature, t, in degrees Celsius (°C), on 12 different days. A line of best fit for the data is also shown. Which of the following could be an equation of the line of best fit?
    a) $d = 0.03t + 402$
    b) $d = 10t + 402$
    c) $d = 33t + 300$
    d) $d = 33t + 84$

Directions:

For questions 31-38, solve the problem and enter your answer in the grid, as described below, on the answer sheet.

Answer: $\frac{7}{12}$

Write answer in the boxes. →

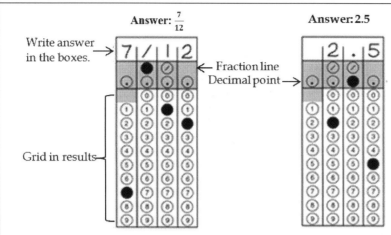

← Fraction line
Decimal point →

Grid in results →

Answer: 2.5

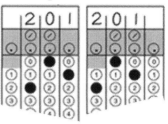

Answer: 201
Either position is correct.

Note: You may start your answers in any column, space permitting. Columns not needed should be left blank.

- Mark no more than one circle in any column.
- Because the answer sheet will be machine-scored. **You will receive credit only if the circles are filled in correctly.**
- Although not required, it is suggested that you write your answer in the boxes at the top of the columns to help you fill in the circles accurately.
- Some problems may have more than one correct answer. In such case, grid only one answer.
- No question has a negative answer.
- **Mixed numbers** such as $3\frac{1}{2}$ must be

gridded as 3.5 or $\frac{7}{2}$. (If $\boxed{3|1|/|2}$ is gridded, it will be interpreted as $\frac{31}{2}$, not $3\frac{1}{2}$.)

- **Decimal Answer:** If you obtain a decimal answer with more digits than the grid can accommodate, it may be either rounded or truncated, but it must fill the entire grid. The acceptable ways to grid $\frac{2}{3}$ are:

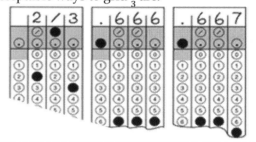

31. In the thirty days of June, for every day it rained, it did not rain for four days. The number of days it rained in June was how many days less than the number of days it did not rain?

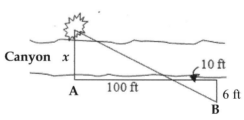

32. A bush fire is sighted on the other side of a canyon at points A and B as shown in the figure above. Find the width, in feet, of the canyon.

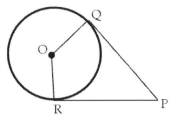

33. In the figure above, point O is the center of the circle, line segments PQ and PR are tangent to the circle at points Q and R, respectively, and the segments intersect at point P as shown. If the radius of the circle is 5 and the length of PQ is $5\sqrt{3}$, what is the area of minor sector $\widehat{RQ}$? (Round your answer to the nearest tenth.)

34. Jacob bought two types of pens: blue pens that cost $0.70 each and red pens that each cost m times as much as a blue pen. If the cost of 5 blue pens and 4 red pens was $13.30, what is the value of m?

35. If the lengths of the edges of a cube are increased by 20%, the volume of the cube will increase by how many percent? (Round your answer to the nearest tenth)

36. In the figure below, the area of the shaded region is 26 square units. What is the height of the smaller triangle?

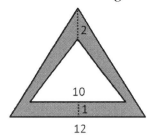

Questions 37 and 38 refer to the following information:

Survey Results of Households

Number of Children per Household	Frequency
0	x
1	3
2	2
3	5
4	2

37. In the table above, the median number of children per household is 2. What is minimum possible value of x?

38. What is the average number of children per household in this survey when the value of x is minimum?

SAT MATH PRACTICE TEST No. 4 ANSWER KEYS

Section 3

1. (C)	2. (D)	3. (A)	4. (A)	5. (A)	6. (D)	7. (C)	8. (C)	9. (C)	10. (C)
11. (C)	12. (C)	13. (C)	14. (B)	15. (B)	16. 4	17. 100	18. 20	19. 2	20. $\frac{1}{64}$

Section 4

1. (A)	2. (C)	3. (B)	4. (D)	5. (B)	6. (D)	7. (D)	8. (C)	9. (D)	10. (D)
11. (B)	12. (B)	13. (B)	14. (D)	15. (D)	16. (A)	17. (D)	18. (B)	19. (C)	20. (A)
21. (B)	22. (B)	23. (A)	24. (D)	25. (D)	26. (B)	27. (B)	28. (C)	29. (D)	30. (C)
31. 18	32. 60	33. 26.2	34. 3.5	35. 72.8	36. 8	37. 3	38. 2		

Section 3

1. Answer: (C)
   This is a linear model.
   $y = 44t + 200$

2. Answer: (D)
   $\sqrt{k + 3} - 6 = 0$
   $k + 3 = 36$
   $k = 33$

3. Answer: (A)
   $3a = 12, \ a = 4$
   $4^2 + 11 = b^3$
   $27 = b^3 = 3^3 \ \rightarrow \ b = 3$

4. Answer: (A)
   "Alex has less money than Bob" $\rightarrow a < b$
   "Bob has less money than Chris" $\rightarrow b < c$
   $a < b < c$

5. Answer: (A)
   Parking m hours costs $1.25 × m$ plus $3 maintenance fee per day, so the total charge would be $3 + 1.25m$.

6. Answer: (D)
   Solve for x by zero-product rule.
   $(3x + 6)(1 - x) = 0$
   $3x + 6 = 0$ or $1 - x = 0$
   $x = 1$ or -2

7. Answer: (C)
   There are no rules about how to arrange boys and girls, so (a) and (b) are incorrect.
   If there is one girl at each end, then two boys must be adjacent. Therefore, (d) is wrong.
   If the last two seated are girls, then two boys must be adjacent. (c) is correct.

8. Answer: (C)
   6 colors can be used to paint face, then 5 of the remaining colors can be used for the eyes, and 4 choices remain for the nose. There are 3 color left for the mouth. It doesn't matter in what order you paint the face, the number of color choices will always be 6, 5, 4, and 3 for the first, second, third, and fourth parts.
   $6 × 5 × 4 × 3 = 360$

9. Answer: (C)
   $Q = \sqrt{\dfrac{3dk}{h}}$
   $Q^2 = \dfrac{3dk}{h} \rightarrow h = \dfrac{3dk}{Q^2}$

10. Answer: (C)
    $a × \dfrac{1}{3} × 27 = 81$
    $a = 9$

11. Answer: (C)
    $(x^{1/6} \, y^{1/6})^3 \ = \ (xy)^{\frac{1}{2}}$
    $(xy)^{\frac{1}{2}} = 8$
    $xy = 64$

12. Answer: (C)
    $\dfrac{x+1}{x} = \dfrac{1}{x} - \dfrac{1}{x-3}$
    $1 + \dfrac{1}{x} = \dfrac{1}{x} - \dfrac{1}{x-3}$
    $-1 = \dfrac{1}{x-3}$
    $x - 3 = -1$
    $x = 2$

13. Answer: (C)
    $4x + 4y = 4(a^2 + b^2) + 4(2ab)$
    $= 4a^2 + 4b^2 + 8ab$
    $= (2a + 2b)^2$

14. Answer: (B)
Replace x with 1 in the equation.
$2y(6 - 5 \times 1) = 2y$

15. Answer: (B)
Except the number 0, any numbers raised to the power of 0 is equal to 1.
$m^3 \times m^{-3} = m^0 = 1$

16. Answer: 4
$a - bi = i(3 - 7i) = 3i - 7i^2$
$= 7 + 3i$
$a = 7$ and $b = -3 \rightarrow a + b = 4$

17. Answer: 100
Let his car sales be x, then
$3000 = 1000 + 0.02 \times x$
$3000 - 1000 = 0.02x$
$x = \$100,000$

18. Answer: 20
The corresponding sides of two similar triangles are proportional.
$\frac{5}{4} = \frac{x}{16} \rightarrow x = 20 \, ft$

19. Answer: 2
$4(p + 2) + 4(p - 1) = 10p$
$4p + 8 + 4p - 4 = 10p$
$8p + 4 = 10p$
$2p = 4 \rightarrow p = 2$

20. Answer: $\frac{1}{64}$
The Area of the Smallest Square $= \frac{1}{4} \times \frac{1}{4} \times \frac{1}{4} \times$ (the Area of the Biggest Square)
$\frac{1}{4^3} = \frac{1}{64}$

Section 4

1. Answer: (A)
$6 \cdot 2k = 72 \rightarrow k = 6$
$4k - 5 = 4 \times 6 - 5 = 19$

2. Answer: (C)
$\frac{10}{100} \times \frac{40}{100} \times A = \frac{20}{100} \times \frac{y}{100} \times A$
$\frac{10 \times 40}{100 \times 100} = \frac{20y}{100 \times 100}$
Therefore, $10 \times 40 = 20y$
$y = 20$.

3. Answer: (B)
Translate "20 percent of x is 50" into an algebraic equation: $\frac{20}{100} \times x = 50$
$x = \frac{100 \times 50}{20} = 250$
"x percent of 40" $= 40 \times \frac{250}{100} = 100$

4. Answer: (D)
In a triangle, bigger angles will always face bigger sides. No angle in ΔABC will have degree greater than 91, so the side facing $\angle ACB$ will be largest.
$\angle ADB > \angle ACD$ (by exterior angle theorem)
$AB > AD > AC$ and CD

5. Answer: (B)
$\frac{b-0}{a-0} = \frac{5-0}{4-0}$
$\frac{b}{a} = \frac{5}{4} = 1.25$

6. Answer: (D)
Try out different combinations of x and y.
$-21 \leq xy \leq 7$

7. Answer: (D)
Let D be the diameter of the elephant's footprint
$h = 3C = 3(\pi D)$
$h = 3(\pi)(30) = 282.6 \, cm$

8. Answer: (C)
$\frac{h_{mother}}{h_{baby}} = \frac{C_{mother}}{C_{baby}} = \frac{D_{mother}}{D_{baby}} = \frac{4}{1}$

9. Answer: (D)
$3x = \frac{2x+y+2y}{3}$
$9x = 2x + 3y$
$7x = 3y$
$y = \frac{7x}{3}$

10. Answer: (D)
Plug in the values for x and y into the equation.
$2(k)^2 - 3 = 7$
$k = \pm \sqrt{5}$
$7 = -(\pm\sqrt{5})^2 + m$
$7 = -5 + m; \, m = 12$

11. Answer: (B)
The number 5 is not a factor of 14, 36 or 18; therefore, answers (a), (c), (d) are not possible.
Only (b)'s dimensions could be packed into the rectangular box without wasting space.
$\frac{14}{7} \times \frac{36}{12} \times \frac{18}{9} = 12$

12. *Answer: (B)*
D is located in the quadrant III which has negative x and y coordinates.
$(-a, -b)$

13. *Answer: (B)*
$h(5) = -16(5)^2 + 320(5) + h_0 = -16t^2 + 320t + h_0$
divided by 16
$-25 + 100 = -t^2 + 20t$
$t^2 - 20t + 75 = 0$
$(t - 5)(t - 15) = 0$
$t = 5 \text{ or } 15$

14. *Answer: (D)*
$90\% = \frac{Correct\ Answers}{Total\ Questions}$
$\frac{x}{60} = \frac{90}{100}$ *(cross multiply)*
$x = \frac{90 \times 60}{100} = 54$

15. *Answer: (D)*
$Slope = \frac{4-1}{2-0} = \frac{3}{2}$
$y = \frac{3}{2}x + b$ *then plug in* $(0, 1)$
$b = 1$
The equation of line m:
$y = \frac{3}{2}x + 1$

16. *Answer: (A)*
$3xi + 2i^6 = 6i + 4i^{13} + 5y$
$3xi - 2 = 6i + 4i + 5y$
$3xi - 2 = 10i + 5y$
$-2 + (3x - 10)i = 5y + 0i$
$5y = -2$ *and* $3x - 10 = 0$
$y = -\frac{2}{5}$ *and* $x = \frac{10}{3}$

17. *Answer: (D)*
The number of bacteria counts is ten times more than the day before:
$f(t) = 5 \times 10^t$ *; t is the number of days.*
It is an exponential growth model.

18. *Answer: (B)*
The student used 7 colors in total. Divide the number of planes he made by 7 and use the remainder to find the color of the last plane.
$46 \div 7 = 6$ *with remainder 4*
The color for the 4th plane is green.

19. *Answer: (C)*
Let the mass of A be 9k and the mass of B be k.
$\frac{1}{2}(9k) \times (v_A)^2 = \frac{1}{2}(k) \times (v_B)^2$
$\frac{v_A}{v_B} = \frac{1}{3}$

$\frac{Momentum\ of\ A}{Momentum\ of\ B} = \frac{9k \times v_A}{k \times v_B} = 9 \times \frac{1}{3} = 3$

20. *Answer: (A)*
Momentum is measured as a product of mass and velocity.
$9k \times v_A = k \times v_B$
$\frac{v_A}{v_B} = \frac{1}{9}$
$\frac{K_e of\ A}{K_e of\ B} = \frac{\frac{1}{2} \times 9k \times v_A^2}{\frac{1}{2} \times k \times v_B^2} = \frac{1}{9}$

21. *Answer: (B)*
$y = -f(x) = -2^x + 1$
Answer b) is the graph of $y = -2^x + 1$
a) is the graph of $y = 2^x - 1$
c) is the graph of $y = -2^x - 1$
d) is the graph of $y = 2^x + 1$

22. *Answer: (B)*
$24(1 + 1.5) = 60$

23. *Answer: (A)*
$x > y > 0.1$
Plug in $x = 2$, *and* $y = 1$
Only answer (a), $\frac{2.1}{1.1}$, *less than 2.*

24. *Answer: (D)*
$1st\ Term = a_0$
$2nd\ Term = 4 + \frac{1}{4} \times a_0$
$3rd\ Term = 4 + \frac{1}{4}(4 + \frac{1}{4}a_0)$
$= 5 + \frac{1}{16}a_0$
$Ratio = \frac{5 + \frac{1}{16}a_0}{4 + \frac{1}{4}a_0} = \frac{a_0 + 80}{4a_0 + 64}$

25. *Answer: (D)*
Area of Original Rectangle − Area of Folded Triangle
$= 8 \times 10 - \frac{1}{2}(2 \times 3) = 77$

26. *Answer: (B)*
Let one trip have x miles.
$Time = 2.1 = t_1 + t_2 = \frac{x}{30} + \frac{x}{40}$
$2.1 = x(\frac{1}{30} + \frac{1}{40}) \rightarrow x = 36$
Entire Distance = 2 × 36 = 72

27. *Answer: (B)*
$\frac{4}{100} = \frac{1000}{x} \rightarrow x = 25,000$

28. *Answer: (C)*
Number of Full Time Employees = 15 + 45 + 60 = 120 employees.
Full time employees comprise of 48% of the total.
0.48 × Total Employees = 120 employees
Total Employees = 250 employees
Part Time Employees = 250 × 0.52 = 130 employees
130 × 0.1 = 13 part time administrators

29. *Answer: (D)*
You can multiply the numerator and denominator by the same factor to get an equivalent ratio.
1.25 × 4 : 1 × 4 = 5 : 4
Or just simply convert the ratios to decimals and compare, such as 5 ÷ 4 = 1.25.

30. *Answer: (C)*
Based on the graph, the slope of the line is 33 and its y-intercept is about 300.
The equation of this line: $d = 33t + 300$

31. *Answer: 18*
Rain Days : Dry Days = 1 : 4
$$\frac{The\ Number\ of\ Rain\ Days}{30\ Days} = \frac{1}{1+4}$$
Apply cross multiplication.
The Number of Rain Days = 6
30 − 6 = 24
The Number of Dry Days = 24
24 − 6 = 18

32. *Answer: 60*
The two triangles are similar; therefore, their corresponding sides are proportional.
$$\frac{x}{100} = \frac{6}{10} \rightarrow x = 60\ feet$$

33. *Answer: 26.2*

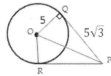

In the right triangle ΔOPQ, the ratio of $\frac{QP}{QO} = \sqrt{3}$;
therefore, $\angle QOP = 60^o$ and $\angle QOR = 120^o$
The area of the minor sector $\widehat{RQ} = \frac{120}{360} \times \pi \times 5^2 = 26.2$

34. *Answer: 3.5*
$5 \times 0.7 + 4 \times m \times 0.7 = 13.3$
$m = \frac{9.8}{2.8} = 3.5$

35. *Answer: 72.8*
If the original lengths of the edges of the cube are 1.
After increasing by 20%, its lengths become 1.2.
The volume of the cube is equal to $(1.2)^3$ or 1.728.
The volume of the cube increases 72.8%.

36. *Answer: 8*
If h is the height of smaller triangle, then the height of the big triangle is h + 3.
Area of Big Δ – Area of Small Δ = 26
$\frac{1}{2}(h + 3) \times 12 - \frac{1}{2}h \times 10 = 26$
$6h + 18 - 5h = 26$
$h = 8$

37. *Answer: 3*
If the median number of children per household is 2:
$(x + 3 + 2) = (5 + 2) + 1\ or$
$(x + 3 + 2) = (5 + 2) + 2\ or$
$(x + 3 + 2) = (5 + 2) + 3.$
$x = 3, 4\ or\ 5.$
The minimum value of x 3.

38. *Answer:2*
$x = 3$
$Average = \frac{0 \times x + 3 \times 1 + 2 \times 2 + 5 \times 3 + 2 \times 4}{3+3+2+5+2} = \frac{30}{15} = 2$

SAT Math Practice Test No. 5

SECTION 3

Math Test — NO Calculator   25 MINUTES, 20 QUESTIONS

Directions:
For questions 1-15, solve each problem, choose the best answer from the choices provided, and fill in the corresponding circle on your answer sheet. **For questions 16-20,** solve the problem and enter your answer in the grid on the answer sheet. Please refer to the directions before question 16 on how to enter your answers in the grid. You may use any available space in your test booklet for scratch work.

Notes:
1. **No calculator** is allowed for this section. All numbers used are real numbers.
2. Figures that accompany problems in this test are intended to provide information useful in solving the problems. They are drawn as accurately as possible EXCEPT when it is stated in a specific problem that the figure is not drawn to scale. All figures lie in a plane unless otherwise indicated.
3. Unless otherwise specified, the domain of any function $f(x)$ assumed to be the set of all real numbers x for which $f(x)$ is a real number.

References:

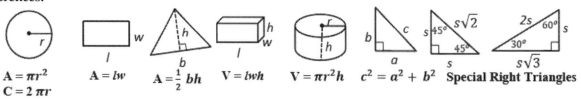

$A = \pi r^2$ $A = lw$ $A = \frac{1}{2} bh$ $V = lwh$ $V = \pi r^2 h$ $c^2 = a^2 + b^2$ **Special Right Triangles**
$C = 2\pi r$

The number of degrees of arc in a circle is 360; the number of radians of arc in a circle is 2π.
The sum of the degree measures of the angles in a triangle is 180.

---

1. A triangle has a perimeter of 27. The medium-length side is 3 more than the length of the shortest side, and the longest side is twice the length of the shortest side. Find the length of the shortest side?

    a) 5

    b) 6

    c) 7

    d) 8

2. Bob needs two 60" pieces of duct tape to protect each window in his house during hurricane season. There are 12 windows in the house. Bob had an m-foot roll of duct tape when he started. If no tape was wasted, which of the following represents the number of feet of duct tape left after he finished taping all of his windows?

    a) $m - 240$
    b) $m - 120$
    c) $m - 60$
    d) $m - 20$

3. Which of the following expressions must be negative if $x < 0$?

    a) $x^4 - 2$
    b) $x^3 - 3$
    c) $x^4 - 3x^2 - 1$
    d) $x^6 + 3x^2 + 1$

4. The front of a roller-coaster car is at the bottom of a hill and is 10 feet above the ground. If the front of the roller-coaster car rises at a constant rate of 8 feet per second, which of the following equations gives the height h, in feet, of the front of the roller-coaster car s seconds after it starts up the hill?

a) $h = 8s + 10$

b) $h = 10s + \frac{335}{8}$

c) $h = 8s + \frac{335}{15}$

d) $h = 10s + 8$

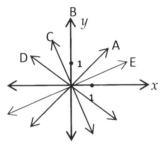

5. In the xy-coordinate system above, which of the following lines has a slope closest to 1?

a) A

b) B

c) C

d) D

6. If k is a constant and $2x + 5 = 3kx + 5$ for all values of x, what is the value of k?

a) 3

b) 2

c) 1

d) $\frac{2}{3}$

7. The value of $5n - 7$ is how much greater than the value of $5n - 8$?

a) 15

b) 1

c) $10n + 1$

d) $5n - 1$

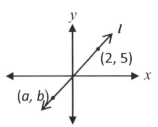

8. In the figure above, line l passes through the origin. What is the value of $\frac{b}{a}$?

a) 1

b) 1.5

c) 2

d) 2.5

9. Mary has the following scores on 7 quizzes in Algebra class: 84, 79, 83, 87, 81, 94, and 87. What was the median score of all of her Algebra quizzes?

a) 81

b) 84

c) 85

d) 86

10. Which of the following expressions is equivalent to $(3x^2 - 2) - (-5x^2 - 3x + 4)$?

a) $-2x^2 + 3x - 6$

b) $-2x^2 - 3x - 2$

c) $8x^2 - 3x + 2$

d) $8x^2 + 3x - 6$

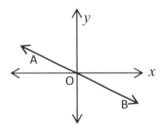

11. The coordinates of point A in the figure above are (a, b), where $|a| > |3b|$. Which of the following could be the slope of AB?

a) -1

b) $-\frac{1}{2}$

c) $-\frac{1}{3}$

d) $-\frac{1}{4}$

12. If $\sqrt{x} = 2$ then $x + 4 = ?$
   a) 2
   b) 4
   c) 8
   d) 80

13. The ratio of 1.5 to 1 is equal to which of the following ratios?
   a) 1 to 2
   b) 2 to 1
   c) 3 to 1
   d) 3 to 2

14. In the xy-plane, the graph of the equation $y = 4x - 3$ intersects the graph of the equation $y = x^2$ at two points. What is the sum of the x-coordinates of the two points?
   a) -4
   b) -3
   c) 3
   d) 4

15. If $xyz \neq 0$, then $\dfrac{x^2 y^4 z^8}{x^6 y^4 z^2} = ?$
   a) xyz
   b) $\dfrac{z^3}{x^3}$
   c) $\dfrac{z^4}{x^3}$
   d) $\dfrac{z^6}{x^4}$

Directions:

For questions 16-20, solve the problem and enter your answer in the grid, as described below, on the answer sheet.

Answer: $\frac{7}{12}$

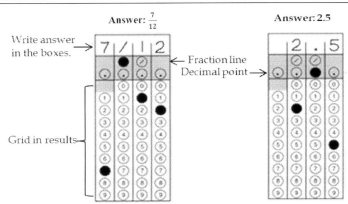

Write answer in the boxes. →

← Fraction line
Decimal point →

Grid in results →

Answer: 2.5

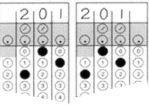

Answer: 201
Either position is correct.

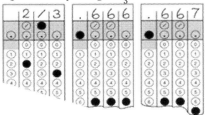

Note: You may start your answers in any column, space permitting. Columns not needed should be left blank.

- Mark no more than one circle in any column.
- Because the answer sheet will be machine-scored. **You will receive credit only if the circles are filled in correctly.**
- Although not required, it is suggested that you write your answer in the boxes at the top of the columns to help you fill in the circles accurately.
- Some problems may have more than one correct answer. In such case, grid only one answer.
- No question has a negative answer.
- **Mixed numbers** such as $3\frac{1}{2}$ must be

gridded as 3.5 or $\frac{7}{2}$. (If [grid] is gridded, it will be interpreted as $\frac{31}{2}$, not $3\frac{1}{2}$.)

- **Decimal Answer:** If you obtain a decimal answer with more digits than the grid can accommodate, it may be either rounded or truncated, but it must fill the entire grid. The acceptable ways to grid $\frac{2}{3}$ are:

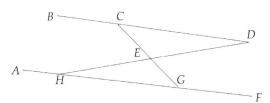

16. What is the value of $(2 - i)(2 + i)$?

17. If $x < 2$ and $a(x - 2)(x - 3) = 0$, what is the value of a?

18. If the sum of ten integers is odd, at most how many of these integers could be odd?

19. In the figure above, $\overline{AF} \parallel \overline{BD}$, and $\overline{CG}$ and $\overline{DH}$ intersect at E. If $HE = 16$, $ED = 24$ and $CG = 20$, what is the length of $\overline{EG}$?

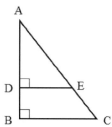

20. In the figure above, if $\overline{AC} = 15$, $\overline{DE} = 3$, and $\overline{AD} = 4$, then what is the length of $\overline{AC}$?

SECTION 4
Math Test — Calculator   55 MINUTES, 38 QUESTIONS

Directions:
For questions 1-30, solve each problem, choose the best answer from the choices provided, and fill in the corresponding circle on your answer sheet. For questions 31-38, solve the problem and enter your answer in the grid on the answer sheet. Please refer to the directions before question 31 on how to enter your answers in the grid. You may use any available space in your test booklet for scratch work.

Notes:
1. Acceptable calculators are allowed for this section. All numbers used are real numbers.
2. Figures that accompany problems in this test are intended to provide information useful in solving the problems. They are drawn as accurately as possible EXCEPT when it is stated in a specific problem that the figure is not drawn to scale. All figures lie in a plane unless otherwise indicated.
3. Unless otherwise specified, the domain of any function $f(x)$ assumed to be the set of all real numbers x for which $f(x)$ is a real number.

References:

$A = \pi r^2$ $A = lw$ $A = \frac{1}{2} bh$ $V = lwh$ $V = \pi r^2 h$ $c^2 = a^2 + b^2$ **Special Right Triangles**
$C = 2\pi r$

The number of degrees of arc in a circle is 360; the number of radians of arc in a circle is 2π.
The sum of the degree measures of the angles in a triangle is 180.

---

1. If $3(x + y)(x - y) = 30$ and $x - y = 5$, what is the value of $x + y$?
   a) 1
   b) 2
   c) 3
   d) −1

2. If 4 less than twice a number is equal to 20. What is 5 more than 3 times the number?
   a) 8
   b) 12
   c) 41
   d) 29

3. We start out with a set of 7 numbers. We subtract 3 from 3 of these numbers. If the average (arithmetic mean) of these seven numbers was 11 originally, what is the new average?
   a) 7.5
   b) 8
   c) 8.5
   d) 9.7

4. In the figure below, points D is the mid-point of $\overline{AB}$ and point E is the mid-point of $\overline{AC}$. If AB = 10, AC = 12, and DE = 7, what is the perimeter of quadrilateral DBCE?

a) 29
b) 30
c) 31
d) 32

5. What is the slope of a line that passes through the points (1, −1) and (−1, 5)?
   a) −3
   b) −2
   c) 0
   d) 2

6. The average score of John's 5 math tests is 80. If the teacher decides not to count his lowest score, which is 60, what will be John's new average score?
   a) 80
   b) 82
   c) 85
   d) 86

Questions 7 − 8 refer to the following information:
   The kinetic energy of an object is the energy that the object possesses due to its motion. Kinetic energy is equal to half of the product of the mass and the square of its velocity.
   The momentum is the quantity of the motion of a moving body, measured as a product of its mass and velocity.

7. If two bodies, A and B, have equal kinetic energies and the mass of A is four times as much as the mass of B, what is the ratio of the momentum of A to that of B?
   a) $\frac{1}{2}$
   b) $\frac{1}{4}$
   c) 2

d) 4

8. If two bodies A and B as described above have equal momentum, what is the ratio of the kinetic energy of A to that of B?
   a) $\frac{1}{2}$
   b) $\frac{1}{4}$
   c) 2
   d) 4

9. The Rockville Reservoir had an original storage capacity of 500,000 acre-feet at the end of 1950, the year in which it was built. Starting in 1951, sediment carried downstream by the Rockville River collected in the reservoir and began reducing the reservoir's storage capacity at the approximate rate of 1,000 acre-feet per year. What was the approximate storage capacity, in acre-feet, of the reservoir at the end of 2020?
   a) 300,000
   b) 400,000
   c) 430,000
   d) 450,000

10. If the sum of 7 numbers is between 41 and 43, then the average (arithmetic mean) of the 7 numbers could be which of the following?
   a) 5
   b) $5\frac{1}{2}$
   c) 6
   d) $6\frac{1}{2}$

11. If $f(x) = x^2 + x^{3/2}$, what is the value of $f(3) = ?$
   a) $3 \times (1 + 3\sqrt{3})$
   b) $(1 + 3\sqrt{3})$
   c) $3 \times (1 + 3\sqrt{3})$
   d) $3 \times (3 + \sqrt{3})$

Gender	Courses			Total
	Frenc h	Spani sh	Chine se	
Male	8	10	11	29
Female	12	14	15	41
Total	20	24	26	70

12. The table above represents the number of freshmen in Stoneville High School who currently enroll in three foreign language classes. Which of the following categories accounts for approximately 20 percent of all the students in those three foreign language classes?
    a) Males taking Chinese
    b) Females taking Spanish
    c) Males taking French
    d) Females taking Chinese

13. To make fruit punch, grapefruit juice, orange juice, and lemonade are mixed in with a ratio of 5:3:2 by volume, respectively. In order to make 5 liters of this drink, how much orange juice, in liters, is needed?
    a) 1
    b) 1.5
    c) 2
    d) 2.5

14. The 50 percent of 210 is the same as 35 percent of what number?
    a) 340
    b) 300
    c) 350
    d) 275

Auto Sales

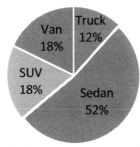

15. The pie graph above represents the automobiles that were sold by a dealer in 2010, according to their records. If the

dealer sold 50 more Sedans than all others combined, how many automobiles did it sell altogether?
    a) 1,000
    b) 1,150
    c) 1,250
    d) 1,500

16. If $x > y$, $w < z$, and $x < w$, which of the following must be true?
    $y < z$
    $w < y$
    $x < z$
    a) None
    b) II and III
    c) I and II
    d) I and III

17. In the xy-plane, line l passes through the origin and is perpendicular to the line $3x + 2y = 2b$, where b is a constant. If the two lines intersect at the point $(2a, a - 1)$, what is the value of b?
    a) –13
    b) –12
    c) –6
    d) 12

18. A "square-root-factor" is an integer greater than 1 with exactly three positive integer factors: itself, its square root, and 1. Which of the following is a square-root-factor?
    a) 128
    b) 81
    c) 64
    d) 49

5, 13, 29, 61, ...

19. The leading term in the sequence above is 5, and each successive term is formed by multiplying the preceding term by x and then adding y. What is the value of y?
    a) 1
    b) 2
    c) 3
    d) 4

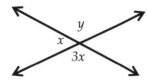

20. In the figure above, what is the value of 3x + 2y?
    a) 405
    b) 135
    c) 270
    d) 360

21. Of the following, which is the closest approximation of the cost per ticket when one purchases 8 tickets?

Bus Ticket Price	
Number of Bus Tickets	Price
1	7.5
Book of 6	40
Book of 12	75

    a) $6.67
    b) $6.70
    c) $6.80
    d) $6.90

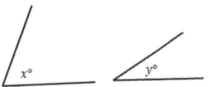

Note: Figures not drawn to scale.

22. The angles shown above are acute, and $sin(x°) = cos(y°)$. If $x = 3k − 11$ and $y = 2k − 9$, what is the value of k?
    a) 12
    b) 22
    c) 23.5
    d) 27.5

23. The table below, describing number of students who passed or failed the Algebra I final exam, is partially filled in. Based on the information in the table, how many females have failed?

Algebra I Final Exam Results			
	Pass	Fail	Total
Male	125		
Female			145
Total	230		305

a) 40
b) 50
c) 60
d) 80

Weights of New Born Babies (in ounces)							
96	95	98	101	110	100	91	88
112	70	89	97	99	101	105	112
130	132	101	97	160	101	100	105

24. The table above lists the weight, to the nearest ounce of a random sample of 24 new born babies. The outliers of 160 and 70 ounces are errors. Of the mean, median, and range of the values listed, which will NOT change if those two outliers are removed from the data?
    a) Median
    b) Range
    c) Standard deviation
    d) Mean

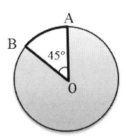

25. The circle above has an area of 16π. What is the perimeter of the shaded region?
    a) $8 − \frac{1}{3}π$
    b) $8 + 7π$
    c) $8 + \frac{2}{3}π$
    d) $8 + \frac{1}{3}π$

Questions 26 and 27 refer to the following information.

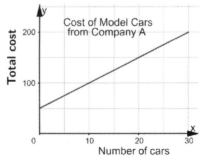

The manager of a toy store compares the cost of ordering model cars from two toy companies. Both companies charge a flat fee plus a fixed cost per car. The graph above shows the total cost that Company A charges for an order of cars. The total cost, in dollars, that Company B charges for an order of n cars is given by the function $B(n) = 4n + 90$, where $n > 0$.

26. The manager wants to order at least 15 cars from Company C but spend no more than \$300 on the order. Which of the following system of inequalities represents these constraints?

a) $n \geq 15, \ 4n + 90 \leq 300$

b) $n \geq 15, \ 4n + 90 \geq 300$

c) $n \leq 15, \ 4n + 90 \geq 300$

d) $n \leq 15, \ 4n + 90 \leq 300$

27. If the total cost of purchasing n cars from Company C is less than the total cost of purchasing n cars from Company A, which of the following inequalities represents all possible values of n?

a) $0 \leq n < 40$

b) $0 \leq n < 100$

c) $40 \leq n < 100$

d) $40 < n$

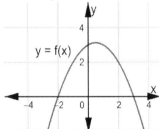

x	$g(x)$
-1	-2
0	2
1	0
2	-1
3	1

28. The graph of function f is shown in the xy–plane above, and selected values for the function g are shown in the table. For

which of the following values of x is $g(x) > f(x)$?

a) 0

b) 1

c) 2

d) 3

29. The efficiency of an engine is the proportion of its fuel energy that the engine can convert into motion energy. The equation $E = 1 - \dfrac{x}{p}$ relates an engine's efficiency, E, to its exhaust temperature x, in kelvins, and its operating temperature p, in kelvins. A particular automobile engine has an operating temperature of 480 kelvins and an exhaust temperature of 250 kelvins. Based on the engine's efficiency, about how many joules of motion energy can the engine obtain from 50,000,000 joules of fuel energy?

a) 15,200,000

b) 24,000,000

c) 64,600,000

d) 105,000,000

$$C = \frac{5}{9}(F - 32)$$

30. The equation above gives the relationship between the temperature measured in degrees Fahrenheit, F, and degrees Celsius, C. At what temperature, in degrees Fahrenheit, will the temperature measured in degrees Celsius be triple the value of the temperature measured in degrees Fahrenheit?

a) $\dfrac{-160}{32}$

b) $\frac{-160}{22}$

c) 160

d) 320

Directions:

For questions 31-38, solve the problem and enter your answer in the grid, as described below, on the answer sheet.

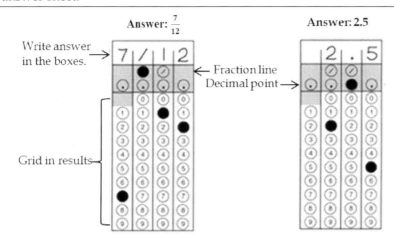

Answer: $\frac{7}{12}$

Write answer in the boxes.

← Fraction line
Decimal point →

Grid in results

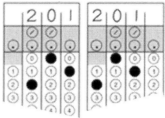

Answer: 2.5

Answer: 201
Either position is correct.

Note: You may start your answers in any column, space permitting. Columns not needed should be left blank.

- Mark no more than one circle in any column.
- Because the answer sheet will be machine-scored. **You will receive credit only if the circles are filled in correctly.**
- Although not required, it is suggested that you write your answer in the boxes at the top of the columns to help you fill in the circles accurately.
- Some problems may have more than one correct answer. In such case, grid only one answer.
- No question has a negative answer.
- **Mixed numbers** such as $3\frac{1}{2}$ must be

gridded as 3.5 or $\frac{7}{2}$. (If [3 1/2] is gridded, it will be interpreted as $\frac{31}{2}$, not $3\frac{1}{2}$.)

- **Decimal Answer:** If you obtain a decimal answer with more digits than the grid can accommodate, it may be either rounded or truncated, but it must fill the entire grid. The acceptable ways to grid $\frac{2}{3}$ are:

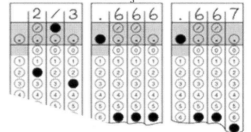

$$\frac{1}{2}(2ax - 5) = 5$$

31. Based on the equation above, what is the value of $4ax$?

32. What is one possible integer length of $\overline{AC}$ if $\angle A > \angle B > \angle C$?

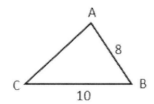

x	1	2	3	4	5
$f(x)$	−2	1	6	13	22

33. Some pairs of input and output values of the function f are shown above. The function h is defined by $h(x) = f(2x − 1)$. What is the value of $h(3)$?

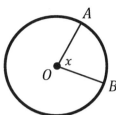

34. In the figure above, the circle has center O and radius 5. If the area of the minor sector $\widehat{AB}$ is between 9 and 14, what is one possible integer value of arc length s?

35. In a toy factory production line, every 9th toy has their electronic parts checked and every 12th toy will have their safety features checked. In the first 180 toys, what is the probability that a toy will have both its electronic parts and safety features checked?

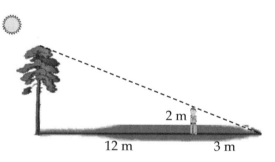

36. Sam walked 12 meters away from the base of a tree as shown in the figure above. At the point he was standing, he noticed that his shadow reached the same spot on the ground as the shadow of the tree. If Sam is 2 meters tall and his shadow is 3 meters long, how high is the tree, in meters?

Questions 37 and 38 refer to the following information.

International Tourist Arrivals, in millions

Countries	2012	2013
France	83.0	84.7
United State	66.7	69.8
Spain	57.5	60.7
China	57.7	55.7
Italy	46.4	47.7
Turkey	35.7	37.8
Germany	30.4	31.5
United Kingdom	26.3	32.2
Russia	24.7	28.4

The table above shows the number of international tourist arrivals, rounded to the nearest tenth of a million, to the top nine tourist destinations in both 2012 and 2013.

37. Based on the information given in the table, how much greater, in millions, was the median number of international tourist arrivals to the top nine tourist destinations in 2013 than the median number in 2012, to the nearest tenth of a million?

38. The number of international tourist arrivals in Russia in 2012 was 13.5% greater than in 2011. The number of international tourist arrivals in Russia was k million more in 2012 than in 2011. What is the value of k to the nearest tenth?

SAT MATH PRACTICE TEST No. 5 ANSWER KEYS

Section 3

1. (B)	2. (B)	3. (B)	4. (A)	5. (A)	6. (D)	7. (B)	8. (D)	9. (B)	10. (D)
11. (D)	12. (C)	13. (D)	14. (D)	15. (D)	16. 5	17. 0	18. 9	19. 8	20. 25

Section 4

1. (B)	2. (C)	3. (D)	4. (D)	5. (A)	6. (C)	7. (C)	8. (B)	9. (C)	10. (C)
11. (D)	12. (B)	13. (B)	14. (B)	15. (C)	16. (D)	17. (A)	18. (D)	19. (C)	20. (A)
21. (D)	22. (B)	23. (A)	24. (A)	25. (B)	26. (A)	27. (D)	28. (D)	29. (B)	30. (B)
31. 30	32. 9	33. 22	34. 4 or 5	35. $\frac{1}{36}$	36. 10	37. 1.3	38. 2.9		

Section 3

1. Answer: (B)
   Let the length of the shortest side be x.
   $27 = x + x + 3 + 2x$
   $x = 6$

2. Answer: (B)
   Every window needs 2 pieces of tape and each piece of tape is 60 inches long, so $60 \times 2 = 120$ inches needed for each window.
   Twelve windows, in total, would need 12×120 inches of tape.
   12×120 inches = 120 feet
   $(m - 120)$ feet left after the use.

3. Answer: (B)
   If $x < 0$, then the result of an odd power of x is negative and the result of an even power of x is positive.

4. Answer: (A)
   A linear model: $h = 8s + 10$

5. Answer: (A)
   Line A has the slope closest to 1.

6. Answer: (D)
   Because the equation is true for all values of x, the two expressions have the same coefficients for corresponding terms.
   $3k = 2, \quad k = \frac{2}{3}$

7. Answer: (B)
   Find the difference between the two expressions.
   $(5n - 7) - (5n - 8) = 1$

8. Answer: (D)
   $\frac{b - 0}{a - 0} = \frac{5 - 0}{2 - 0}$
   $\frac{b}{a} = \frac{5}{2} = 2.5$

9. Answer: (B)
   Sort the scores in order.
   79, 81, 83, 84, 87, 87, 94
   The median is 84.

10. Answer: (D)
    $(3x^2 - 2) - (-5x^2 - 3x + 4)$
    $= 3x^2 - 2 + 5x^2 + 3x - 4$
    $= 8x^2 + 3x - 6$

11. Answer: (D)
    A line with a negative slope descends from left to right; therefore, the slope of the line in the graph is negative.
    $|a| > |3b| \rightarrow \frac{1}{3} > |\frac{b}{a}|$

12. Answer: (C)
    Square both sides of the radical equation.
    $\sqrt{x} = 2$
    $(\sqrt{x})^2 = 2^2$
    $x = 4$
    $x + 4 = 8$

13. Answer: (D)
    You can multiply the numerator and denominator by the same factor to get an equivalent ratio.
    $1.5 \times 2 : 1 \times 2 = 3 : 2$
    Or just simply convert the ratios to decimals and compare, such as
    $3 \div 2 = 1.5$.

14. Answer: (D)
$4x - 3 = x^2$
$x^2 - 4x + 3 = 0$
$(x - 1)(x - 3) = 0$
$x = 1 \ or \ 3$
$1 + 3 = 4$

15. Answer: (D)
Apply exponent rules.
$\frac{x^2 y^4 z^8}{x^6 y^4 z^2} = \left(\frac{x^2}{x^6}\right)\left(\frac{y^4}{y^4}\right)\left(\frac{z^8}{z^2}\right) = \frac{z^6}{x^4}$

16. Answer: 5
$(2 - i)(2 + i) = 2^2 - (i)^2 = 4 - (-1) = 5$

17. Answer: 0
Solve for x by zero-product rule.
$a(x - 2)(x - 3) = 0$
One of the terms a, (x− 2), and (x − 3) must be equal to zero.
Given that x < 2, only a can be equal to zero.

18. Answer: 9
Sum of odd number of odd integers is odd. So there are 9 odd integers at most.

19. Answer: 8
$\Delta CED \sim \Delta GEH$
$\frac{HE}{EG} = \frac{ED}{CE}$
$\frac{16}{EG} = \frac{24}{20 - EG}$
$320 - 16EG = 24EG$
$320 = 40EG$
$EG = 8$

20. Answer: 25

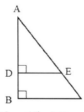

Since $\overline{DE} \parallel \overline{BC}$, $BC = 15$, $DE = 3$, and $AD = 4$
$AE = \sqrt{3^2 + 4^2} = 5$
$\frac{AE}{AC} = \frac{DE}{C}$
$\frac{5}{AC} = \frac{3}{15} \ \rightarrow \ AC = 25$

Section 4

1. Answer: (B)
$3 \times 5 \times (x + y) = 30$
$x + y = 2$

2. Answer: (C)
Let the number be x.
$2x - 4 = 20$
$x = 12$
$3x + 5 = 36 + 5 = 41$

3. Answer: (D)
$Average: \frac{Sum \ of \ Terms}{Number \ of \ Terms}$
$\frac{7 \times 11 - 3 \times 3}{7} = 9.7$

4. Answer: (D)
Point D is the mid-point of $\overline{AB}$ and point E is the mid-point of $\overline{AC}$, so $\frac{AD}{AB} = \frac{AE}{AC} = \frac{1}{2}$
Therefore, $\Delta ADE \sim \Delta ABC$ by SAS Similarity theorem
$AB = 10$
$DB = 5$
$\frac{1}{2} = \frac{DE}{BC}$
$DE = 7$
$BC = 14$
$EC = \frac{1}{2} AC = 6$
Perimeter of DBCE = 5 + 7 + 14 + 6 = 32

5. Answer: (A)
$Slope = \frac{Rise}{Run} = \frac{5 - (-1)}{-1 - 1} = -3$

6. Answer: (C)
John's original average is 80 for 5 tests.
$5 \times 80 = 400$ (sum for 5 tests)
$400 - 60 = 340$ (sum for 4 tests)
$\frac{340}{4} = 85$ (average of 4 tests)

7. Answer: (C)
Let the mass of A be 4k and the mass of B be k.
$\frac{1}{2}(4k) \times (v_A)^2 = \frac{1}{2}(k) \times (v_B)^2$
$\frac{v_A}{v_B} = \frac{1}{2}$
$\frac{Momentum \ of \ A}{Momentum \ of \ B} = \frac{4k \times v_A}{k \times v_B} = 4 \times \frac{1}{2} = 2$

8. Answer: (B)
Momentum is measured as a product of mass and velocity.
$4k \times v_A = k \times v_B$
$\frac{v_A}{v_B} = \frac{1}{4}$
$\frac{K_e of \ A}{K_e of \ B} = \frac{\frac{1}{2} \times 4k \times v_A^2}{\frac{1}{2} \times k \times v_B^2} = \frac{4}{16} = \frac{1}{4}$

9. Answer: (C)
$y = -1000x + 500000$
$x = 2020 - 1950 = 70$
$y = (-1000)(70) + 500000 = 430,000$

10. Answer: (C)
$Average = \frac{Sum}{7}$
$\frac{41}{7} < Average < \frac{43}{7}$
$5.85 < Average < 6.1$

11. Answer: (D)
The value of f(3) is calculated by replacing x with 3 in the function.
$3^2 + 3^{3/2} = 9 + 3\sqrt{3} = 3(3 + \sqrt{3})$

12. Answer: (B)
$70 \times 0.2 = 14$
There are 14 female students taking Spanish.

13. Answer: (B)
Every 10 liters, (2 + 3 + 5), of drink, 3 liters of orange juice will be needed. So 5 liters of this drink, we need $\frac{3}{10} \times 5$ of orange juice.
Orange Juice = $0.3 \times 5 = 1.5$ liters

14. Answer: (B)
This sentence can be translated into: $\frac{50}{100} \times 210 = \frac{35}{100} \times A$
$A = \frac{50}{35} \times 210 = 300$

15. Answer: (C)
Solve this problem using proportions.
There were 4% (52% − 48%) more Sedans sold than all other cars combined.
$4\% : 50 = 100\% : x$
$x = 1,250$ cars

16. Answer: (D)
Draw a number line and locate w, x, y and z on the line.
Only (I) and (III) are correct.

17. Answer: (A)
The line of $3x + 2y = 2b$ has a slope of $\frac{-3}{2}$.
Line l is perpendicular, so it should have a slope of $\frac{2}{3}$.
We also know that it passes through the origin.
$y = \frac{2}{3}x$
$a - 1 = \frac{2}{3}(2a)$

$3a - 3 = 4a \quad \rightarrow a = -3$
point (−6 , −4) passing through $3x + 2y = 2b \rightarrow$
$-6 \times 3 - 4 \times 2 = -26 = 2b$
$b = -13$

18. Answer: (D)
The square root of the number must be a prime number.
Only $\sqrt{49}$ is a prime number.

19. Answer: (C)
$13 - 5 = 8$
$29 - 13 = 16$
$61 - 29 = 32$
So each successive term is multiplying the proceeding term by 2 and adding 3.
$13 = 2 \times 5 + 3$, so $y = 3$
$61 = 29 \times 2 + 3$ (double check the answer)

20. Answer: (A)
$3x + x = 180°$ and $y = 3x$
$4x = 180°$
$x = 45°$
$3x = 135° = y$
$2y = 135 \times 2 = 270°$
$3x + 2y = 135 + 270 = 405°$

21. Answer: (D)
$\frac{\$40 + 2 \times 7.5}{8 \text{ tickets}} = \$6.875$ per ticket

22. Answer: (B)
$(3k - 11) + (2k - 9) = 90$
$k = 22$

23. Answer: (A)
The Number of Students Passing = the Number of Males Passing + the Number of Females Passing
$230 = 125 +$ the Number of Females Passing
The Number of Females Passing = 105
Total Number of Females = Number of Females Passing + Number of Females Failing
The Number of Females Failing = $145 - 105 = 40$

24. Answer: (A)
Only median will not change when the highest and the lowest data are removed.

25. Answer: (B)
The perimeter of the shaded region is equal to the major arc length plus twice the radius.
Perimeter = Major Arc Length + 2 × Radius
To find the radius, we solve:
$$\pi r^2 = 16\pi \rightarrow r = 4$$
Arc Length of Shaded Region $= \frac{2 \times \pi \times (360^o - 45^o)}{360^o} = 7\pi$
Perimeter of Shaded Region $= 7\pi + 8$

26. Answer: (A)
$n \geq 15, 4n + 90 \leq 300$

27. Answer: (D)
It is a linear model for company A.
Pick two points from the graph, (0, 50) and (10, 100)
The slope is 5, and the y-intercept: 50
$y = 5n + 50$
$4n + 90 < 5n + 50$
$n > 40$

28. Answer: (D)
$g(3) = 1$ and $f(3) = 0$
$g(3) > f(3)$

29. Answer: (B)
$E = 1 - \frac{x}{p} = 1 - \frac{250}{480} = 0.48$
Motion energy: $50000000 \times 0.48 = 24,000,000$

30. Answer: (B)
$C = 3F = \frac{5}{9}(F - 32)$
$27F - 5F = -160$
$= -\frac{160}{22}$

31. Answer: 30
$\frac{1}{2}(2ax - 5) = 5$
$2ax - 5 = 10$
$2ax = 15$
$4ax = 30$

32. Answer: 9
The longest side of a triangle is opposite the largest angle.
Since $\angle A > \angle B > \angle C$,
$\overline{BC} > \overline{AC} > \overline{AB}$, and so
$10 > \overline{AC} > 8$. The only possible integer is 9.

33. Answer: 22
$h(3) = f(2 \times 3 - 1) = f(5) = 22$

34. Answer: 4 or 5
Area of the Sector $= \frac{1}{2}r^2\theta$
$9 < \frac{1}{2}5^2\theta < 14$
$\frac{18}{25} < \theta < \frac{28}{25}$
$s = r\theta$
$3.6 < s < 5.6$
$s = 4$ or 5

35. Answer: $\frac{1}{36}$
The LCM of 9 and 12 is 36.
The every 36th toy will have both of their electronic parts and safety features checked.
There are 5 such toys (180 divided by 36).
$\frac{5}{180} = \frac{1}{36}$

36. Answer: 10
Let the height of the tree be x.
The two triangles are similar; therefore, their corresponding sides are proportional.
$\frac{3}{12 + 3} = \frac{2}{x}$
$x = 10\ m$

37. Answer: 1.3
Median number in 2013: 47.7 million
Median number in 2012: 46.4 million
The difference: $47.7 - 46.4 = 1.3$ million

38. Answer: 2.9
Let x be the number of international tourist arrivals in Russia in 2011:
$24.4 = (1 + 0.135)x$
$x = 21.5$
The difference $24.4 - 21.5 = 2.9$ million

SAT Math Practice Test No. 6

SECTION 3

Math Test — NO Calculator   25 MINUTES, 20 QUESTIONS

Directions:

For questions 1-15, solve each problem, choose the best answer from the choices provided, and fill in the corresponding circle on your answer sheet. **For questions 16-20,** solve the problem and enter your answer in the grid on the answer sheet. Please refer to the directions before question 16 on how to enter your answers in the grid. You may use any available space in your test booklet for scratch work.

Notes:
1. **No calculator** is allowed for this section. All numbers used are real numbers.
2. Figures that accompany problems in this test are intended to provide information useful in solving the problems. They are drawn as accurately as possible EXCEPT when it is stated in a specific problem that the figure is not drawn to scale. All figures lie in a plane unless otherwise indicated.
3. Unless otherwise specified, the domain of any function $f(x)$ assumed to be the set of all real numbers x for which $f(x)$ is a real number.

References:

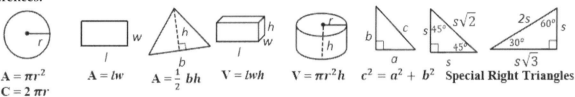

$A = \pi r^2$ $A = lw$ $A = \frac{1}{2}bh$ $V = lwh$ $V = \pi r^2 h$ $c^2 = a^2 + b^2$ **Special Right Triangles**
$C = 2\pi r$

The number of degrees of arc in a circle is 360; the number of radians of arc in a circle is 2π.
The sum of the degree measures of the angles in a triangle is 180.

---

1. If $\frac{j}{6} = 2$ and $5k = 35$, what is the value of $\frac{k}{j}$?
   a) $\frac{7}{12}$
   b) $\frac{7}{6}$
   c) $\frac{6}{7}$
   d) $\frac{12}{7}$

$$f(x) = \frac{x+3}{2}$$

2. For the function f above, what is the value of (1) ?
   a) $\frac{2}{3}$
   b) $\frac{2}{5}$
   c) 1
   d) 2

3. What is the sum of the complex numbers $3 - 2i$ and $4 + 5i$, where $i = \sqrt{-1}$?
   a) $7 - 7i$
   b) $7 + 3i$
   c) $14i$
   d) 14

4. In the figure below, $l_1 \parallel l_2$. Which of the following statements must be true?

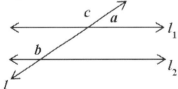

Note: Figure not drawn to scale.
   I. $a + c = 180°$
   II. $b + c = 180°$
   III. $a + b = 180°$
   a) I only
   b) I and II only
   c) I and III only
   d) I, II, and III

5. Which of the following represents the graph of the equation $x + y = 2$ in the xy-plane?

a)

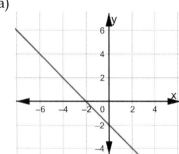

b)

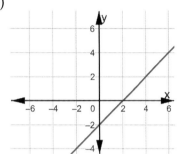

c)

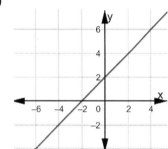

d)

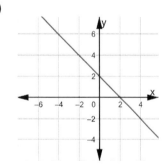

6. If $x > 0$ and $x^y x^{\frac{1}{2}} = x^{\frac{1}{4}}$, what is the value of y?

   a) $\frac{1}{2}$

   b) $\frac{1}{4}$

   c) $-\frac{1}{4}$

   d) $-\frac{1}{2}$

7. If $y = x\sqrt{5}$ and $x \neq 0$, what does x^2 equal in terms of y?

a) $\frac{y^2}{5}$

b) $5y^2$

c) $\frac{25}{y^2}$

d) $\frac{y^2}{25}$

8. If a linear function passes through the points $(1, s)$, $(3, t)$ and $(5, 10)$, what is the value of $2t - s$?

   a) 2

   b) 8

   c) 10

   d) 12

$$x^{16} - x^{14} = k(x^{15} - x^{14}) \qquad x > 1$$

9. Based on the two conditions listed above, what is k in terms of x?

   a) $x + 1$

   b) $x - 1$

   c) $\frac{1}{x-1}$

   d) $\frac{1}{x+1}$

$$wxy + xyz = wx + yz$$

10. In the equation above, w, x, and z are each greater than 1. Which of the following is equivalent to y?

   a) $-x$

   b) $-\frac{1}{x}$

   c) $\frac{1}{xz-z}$

   d) $\frac{wx}{wx+xz-z}$

11. If $x^2 - 2x = 8$, which of the following is a possible value of $x^2 - x =$?

   a) 12

   b) 9

   c) −6

   d) −9

12. How old was William c years ago if a years later he will b years old (given that $b > a + c$)?

   a) $a + b$

   b) $a + b + c$

c) $a - b - c$
d) $b - a - c$

13. By 7 AM, $\frac{1}{4}$ of all students were in school. Half an hour later, 100 more students arrived, raising the attendance to $\frac{3}{4}$ of the total students. How many students are in this school?
    a) 240
    b) 220
    c) 200
    d) 180

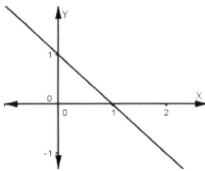

14. The figure above shows the graph of the line $y = mx + b$, where m and b are constants. Which of the following best represents the graph of the line $y = -2mx - b$?

a)

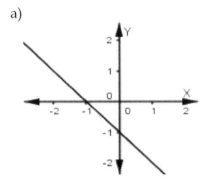

b)

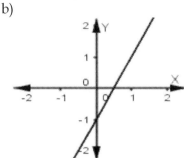

c)

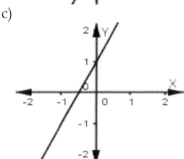

d)

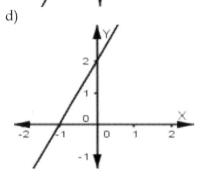

15. What is the least value of integer x such that the value of $2x + 1$ is greater than 13?
    a) 7
    b) 6
    c) 5
    d) 4

Directions:

For questions 16-20, solve the problem and enter your answer in the grid, as described below, on the answer sheet.

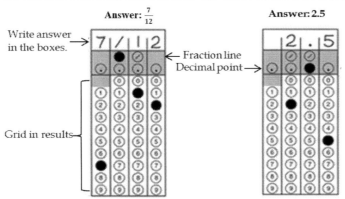

Answer: $\frac{7}{12}$

Write answer in the boxes.

← Fraction line
Decimal point →

Grid in results

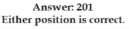

Answer: 2.5

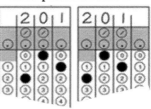

Answer: 201
Either position is correct.

Note: You may start your answers in any column, space permitting. Columns not needed should be left blank.

- Mark no more than one circle in any column.
- Because the answer sheet will be machine-scored. **You will receive credit only if the circles are filled in correctly.**
- Although not required, it is suggested that you write your answer in the boxes at the top of the columns to help you fill in the circles accurately.
- Some problems may have more than one correct answer. In such case, grid only one answer.
- No question has a negative answer.
- **Mixed numbers** such as $3\frac{1}{2}$ must be

gridded as 3.5 or $\frac{7}{2}$. (If [3│1│/│2] is gridded, it will be interpreted as $\frac{31}{2}$, not $3\frac{1}{2}$.)

- **Decimal Answer:** If you obtain a decimal answer with more digits than the grid can accommodate, it may be either rounded or truncated, but it must fill the entire grid. The acceptable ways to grid $\frac{2}{3}$ are:

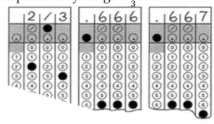

16. A rectangular storage room has a volume of 7350 cubic feet. If its length is 70 feet and its height is 5 feet, what is the width of the room, in feet?

17. For a service visit, a technician charges a $40 dollars fee plus an additional $15 for every $\frac{1}{4}$ hour of work. If the technician's total charge was $160, for how much time, in hours, did the technician charge?

18. For a function f, $f(-1) = 5$ and $f(1) = 9$. If the graph of $y = f(x)$ is a line in the xy-plane, what is the slope of the line?

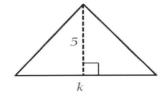

19. In the figure above, if the area of the triangle is 15, what is the value of k?

20. If $\frac{x+y}{x-y} = 4$ and $y \neq 0$, what is the value of $\frac{x}{y}$?

SECTION 4

Math Test — Calculator   55 MINUTES, 38 QUESTIONS

Directions:

For questions 1-30, solve each problem, choose the best answer from the choices provided, and fill in the corresponding circle on your answer sheet. **For questions 31-38**, solve the problem and enter your answer in the grid on the answer sheet. Please refer to the directions before question 31 on how to enter your answers in the grid. You may use any available space in your test booklet for scratch work.

Notes:

1. Acceptable calculators are allowed for this section. All numbers used are real numbers.
2. Figures that accompany problems in this test are intended to provide information useful in solving the problems. They are drawn as accurately as possible EXCEPT when it is stated in a specific problem that the figure is not drawn to scale. All figures lie in a plane unless otherwise indicated.
3. Unless otherwise specified, the domain of any function $f(x)$ assumed to be the set of all real numbers x for which $f(x)$ is a real number.

References:

 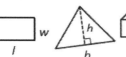   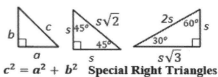

$A = \pi r^2$ $A = lw$ $A = \frac{1}{2} bh$ $V = lwh$ $V = \pi r^2 h$ $c^2 = a^2 + b^2$ **Special Right Triangles**
$C = 2\pi r$

The number of degrees of arc in a circle is 360; the number of radians of arc in a circle is 2π.
The sum of the degree measures of the angles in a triangle is 180.

---

1. If $\frac{10x^4}{ax^2} = 5x^b$, what is the value of $a - b$?
   a) 0
   b) 1
   c) 2
   d) 3

2. After 20 customers entered a deli store and 4 customers left, there were 3 times as many customers as there were at the beginning. How many customers were in that deli store at the very beginning?
   a) 6
   b) 7
   c) 8
   d) 12

3. If the product of 0.6 and a number is equal to 1, what is the number?

   a) 2
   b) $\frac{3}{5}$
   c) 1
   d) $\frac{2}{5}$

4. In the figure below, if ABCD is a square with area of 16, what is the area of triangle BEF?

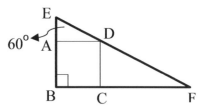

   a) 12
   b) 18
   c) $16(1 + \frac{2\sqrt{3}}{3})$
   d) $16\sqrt{3}$

5. A teacher has signed up for a program that automatically delivers books for the

classroom library. The classroom library currently consists of 40 books. If the program delivers 10 books a month, how many books will the classroom library consist of after 5 months?

a) 90
b) 100
c) 110
d) 120

6. Which of the following conditions would make $2x - y < 0$?

a) $2x = y$
b) $x > 0$
c) $y > 0$
d) $2x < y$

Questions 7 – 8 refer to the following information:

The Doppler effect is the change in frequency of a wave while its source is moving. The Doppler effect formulas shown below are used to calculate the frequency of sound as a result of relative motion between the source and the observer.

If the source is moving toward an observer at rest, the change of observed frequency can be calculated by:

$$f_{observed} = f_{original} \left(\frac{v_{sound}}{v_{sound} - v_{source}} \right)$$

If the observer is moving toward the sound and the source moving closer to the observer, the change of frequency can be calculated by:

$$f_{observed} = f_{original} \left(\frac{v_{sound} + v_{observer}}{v_{sound} - v_{source}} \right)$$

$f_{observed}$ = observed frequency
$f_{original}$ = frequency of the original wave
v_{sound} = speed of the sound
$v_{observer}$ = speed of the observer
v_{source} = speed of the source

7. Standing on the side walk, you observe an ambulance moving toward you. As the ambulance passes by with its siren blaring, you hear the pitch of the siren change. If the ambulance is approaching at the speed of 50 miles/hour and the siren's pitch sounds at a frequency of 340 Hertz, what is the observed frequency, in Hertz? Assume that the speed of sound in air is 760 miles/hour.

a) 332
b) 364
c) 399
d) 409

8. If you are driving a car at the speed of 50 miles/hour while an ambulance is approaching to you at the speed of 70 miles/hour, what is the observed frequency of the siren, in Hertz? Assume that the ambulance sounds at a frequency of 340 Hertz and the speed of sound in air is 760 miles/hour.

a) 332
b) 364
c) 399
d) 409

		Zoos		
Animal Types	Phila-delphia	National	Phoenix	Total
Amphibians	8	20	4	32
Birds	25	71	57	153
Fish	12	39	3	54
Mammals	71	84	50	205
Reptiles	20	50	19	89
Total	136	264	113	533

9. The table above shows the number of animals in three different zoos, categorized by type. If an animal is to be selected at random from the Philadelphia zoo for observation, what is the probability that the animal will be an amphibian?

a) $\frac{8}{253}$

b) $\frac{8}{136}$

c) $\frac{32}{553}$

d) $\frac{8}{32}$

10. If the average (arithmetic mean) of 12, 16 and x is equal to x, what is the value of x?

a) 9
b) 10
c) 14
d) 16

11. $\frac{1}{5}$ of 80 is equal to what percent of 200?

a) 5 %
b) 8 %
c) 10 %
d) 16 %

12. If $10^{xy} = 1,000$, where x and y are positive integers and $x > y$, what is one possible value of x?

a) 3
b) 4
c) 5
d) 7

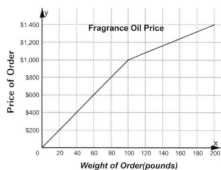

13. The graph above shows the price that a chemical company charges for an order of fragrance oil, depending on the weight of the order. Based on the graph, which of the following statements must be true?

a) The company charges more per pound for orders greater than 100 pounds than for orders less than 100 pounds.

b) The company charges less per pound for orders greater than 100 pounds than for orders less than 100 pounds.

c) The company charges less per pound for orders greater than 1,000 pounds than for orders less than 1,000 pounds.

d) The company charges the same price per pound, regardless of order size.

14. According to the circle graph above, how many types of automobiles show less than 30 percent of the total sales?

a) 0
b) 1
c) 2
d) 3

15. A bike traveled 80 miles in 5 hours. At this rate, how many miles would the bike travels in 6 hours?

a) 64
b) 90
c) 96
d) 100

16. For a salad dish, each customer can choose from 5 types of vegetables and 4 types of dressings. How many distinct salad dishes containing one type of vegetable and one dressing are there?
    a) 20
    b) 16
    c) 14
    d) 8

17. If the area of an equilateral triangle equals the area of a square multiplied by $\sqrt{3}$, what is the ratio of the length of a side of the triangle to the length of a side of the square?
    a) 2 : 1
    b) 2 : 3
    c) 1 : 2
    d) 4 : 3

18. The table below, describing number of students who passed or failed the Algebra I final exam, is partially filled in. Based on the information in the table, how many females have failed?

Algebra I Final Exam Results			
	Pass	Fail	Total
Male	120		
Female			140
Total	220		300

    a) 35
    b) 40
    c) 45
    d) 50

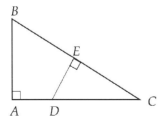

Note: Figure not drawn to scale.

19. In the figure above, triangle *ABC* and triangle *EDC* are right triangles. If *EC* =

$6\sqrt{3}$ and the cosine of angle *ABC* is $\frac{1}{2}$, what is the length of segment E*D*?
    a) 6
    b) $6\sqrt{3}$
    c) 12
    d) 18

20. Helen threw a fair six sided dice 5 times. Each throw showed a different number according to the rules:
    The first roll was greater than 5.
    The second roll was less than 3.
    The third roll was 4.
    The fourth roll was the same as the first roll.
    The fifth roll was an even number.
    Which of the following must be true?
    a) Helen could have rolled a 6 more than three times.
    b) Helen could have rolled a 5 only one time.
    c) Helen rolled more even numbers than odd numbers.
    d) Helen rolled 3 at least once.

21. The number of books that have been checked out of the town public library in a particular week was recorded in the table below. If the median number of books checked out for the whole week was 93, which of the following could have been the number of books checked out on Saturday and Sunday, respectively, of the same week?

Town Library Checkout Records	
Day of the Week	Number of Books Checked Out

Monday	87
Tuesday	91
Wednesday	92
Thursday	93
Friday	96

    a) 88 and 92
    b) 89 and91
    c) 90 and 97
    d) 94 and 97

22. If $x^2 - y^2 = 24$, and $x - y = 4$, what is the value of $x + 2y$?
    a) 1
    b) 3
    c) 5
    d) 7

Questions 23-24 refer to the following information

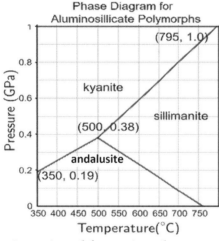

During mineral formation, the same chemical compound can become different minerals depending on the temperature and pressure at the time of formation. A phase diagram is a graph that shows the conditions that are needed to form each mineral. The graph above is a portion of the phase diagram for aluminosilicates, with the temperature T, in degrees Celsius (°C), on the horizontal axis, and the pressure P in gigapascals (GPa) on the vertical axis.

$$P = -0.0015T + 1.13$$

23. An equation of the boundary line between the andalusite and sillimanite regions is approximated by the equation above. What is the meaning of the T-intercept of this line?
    a) It is the maximum temperature at which sillimanite can form.
    b) It is the temperature at which both andalusite and sillimanite can form when there is no pressure applied.
    c) It is the increase in the number of degrees Celsius needed to remain on the boundary between andalusite and sillimanite if the pressure is reduced by 1 GPa.
    d) It is the decrease in the number of gigapascals of pressure needed to remain on the boundary between andalusite and sillimanite if the temperature is increased by 1°C.

24. Which of the following systems of inequalities best descricbes the region where sillimanite can form?
    a) $P \geq 0.0021T - 0.67$; $P \geq 0.0013T - 0.25$
    b) $P \leq 0.0021T - 0.67$; $P \geq -0.0015T + 1.13$
    c) $P \leq 0.0013T - 0.25$; $P \geq -0.0015T + 1.13$
    d) $P \leq 0.0013T - 0.25$; $P \leq -0.0015T + 1.13$

$$y = 2x + 4$$
$$y = (x - 3)(x + 2)$$

25. The system of equations above is graphed in the xy-plane. At which of the following points do the graphs of the equations intersect?
    a) $(-2, 0)$
    b) $(0, -2)$
    c) $(5, -14)$
    d) $(-5, 14)$

26. If w is a positive number and $w > w^2$, which of the following statements is true?

$$w^2 > w^3$$
$$w > \frac{w}{3}$$
$$w > w^3$$

a) I, II
b) II, III
c) I, II, and III
d) I only

27. Among the 12 colleges Helen applied to, 3 are her top schools. How many admissions would Helen have to receive to guarantee that she can get into at least one of her top schools?

   a) 8
   b) 9
   c) 10
   d) 11

28. The front row of an auditorium has 15 seats. There are 50 rows in total. If each row has 2 more seats than the row before it, which expression gives the total number of seats in the last row?

   a) $15 + 2(50 - 1)$
   b) $15 + 2(50)$
   c) $50(15 + 2)$
   d) $15 + 50^2$

29. The fruits provided in the student lounge contain pears, apples, and oranges. The ratio of the numbers of pears to apples is $3 : 5$ and the ratio of the numbers of apples to oranges is $3 : 5$. Find the ratio of the numbers of pears to oranges?

   a) $9 : 25$
   b) $25 : 9$
   c) $3 : 5$
   d) $5 : 3$

30. If the equation $x^3 - 9x^2 + px - q = 0$ has 3 equal roots, then

   a) each root = 2
   b) each root = -3
   c) $q = 27$
   d) $q = 3$

Directions:

For questions 31-38, solve the problem and enter your answer in the grid, as described below, on the answer sheet.

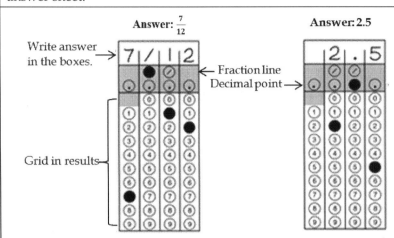

Answer: $\frac{7}{12}$

Write answer in the boxes.

← Fraction line

Decimal point →

Grid in results

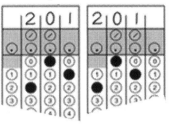

Answer: 2.5

Answer: 201

Either position is correct.

- Mark no more than one circle in any column.
- Because the answer sheet will be machine-scored. **You will receive credit only if the circles are filled in correctly.**
- Although not required, it is suggested that you write your answer in the boxes at the top of the columns to help you fill in the circles accurately.
- Some problems may have more than one correct answer. In such case, grid only one answer.
- No question has a negative answer.
- **Mixed numbers** such as $3\frac{1}{2}$ must be

Note: You may start your answers in any column, space permitting. Columns not needed should be left blank.

gridded as 3.5 or $\frac{7}{2}$. (If [3|1|/|2] is gridded, it will be interpreted as $\frac{31}{2}$, not $3\frac{1}{2}$.)

- **Decimal Answer:** If you obtain a decimal answer with more digits than the grid can accommodate, it may be either rounded or truncated, but it must fill the entire grid. The acceptable ways to grid $\frac{2}{3}$ are:

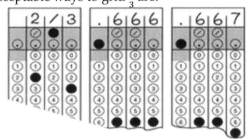

$$\frac{1}{2}(2ax - 5) = 5$$

31. Based on the equation above, what is the value of $4ax$?

32. In the xy-plane below, O is the center of the circle with a radius of 2, and the measure of $\angle\theta$ is $\frac{\pi}{3}$ radians. What is the value of $x + y$? (Round your answer to the nearest tenth.)

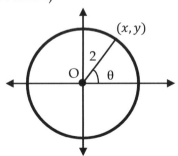

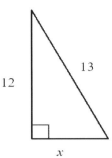

33. In the right triangle above, what is the value of x?

34. If the sum of all consecutive integers from -41 to x, inclusive, is 42, what is the value of x?

35. The first term of the sequence above is 1, and every term after the first term is -2 times the preceding term. How many of the first 100 terms of this sequence are less than 100?

$$(1 - i)(3 + i) = a + bi$$

36. In the equation above, a and b are two real numbers. What is the value of $a + b$?

Questions 37 and 38 refer to the following information:

A new machine in a manufacturing factory is depreciated approximately 20% for the first 5 years and 8% for the next 10 years. If this machine costs $10,000 brand new, the following equations are used to model its value for the first 15 years:

$$\begin{cases} V_t = \$10{,}000 \times r_1^t & when\ 0 < t \le 5 \\ V_t = V_5 \times r_2^{t-5} & when\ 5 < t \le 15 \end{cases}$$

V_t is the value of the machine at time t, the number of years after purchasing.

37. What is the value of $r_1 + r_2$?

38. After how many years will a brand new machine be worth less than $2,000?

SAT MATH PRACTICE TEST No. 6 ANSWER KEYS

Section 3

1. (A)	2. (D)	3. (B)	4. (C)	5. (D)	6. (C)	7. (A)	8. (C)	9. (A)	10. (D)
11. (A)	12. (D)	13. (C)	14. (B)	15. (A)	16. 21	17. 2	18. 2	19. 6	20. $\frac{5}{3}$

Section 4

1. (A)	2. (C)	3. (B)	4. (C)	5. (A)	6. (D)	7. (B)	8. (C)	9. (B)	10. (C)
11. (B)	12. (A)	13. (B)	14. (C)	15. (C)	16. (A)	17. (A)	18. (B)	19. (A)	20. (C)
21. (D)	22. (D)	23. (B)	24. (B)	25. (A)	26. (C)	27. (C)	28. (A)	29. (A)	30. (C)
31. 30	32. 2.73	33. 5	34. 42	35. 54	36. 2	37. 1.72	38. 11		

Section 3

1. Answer: (A)
$\frac{j}{6} = 2 \rightarrow j = 12$
$5k = 35 \rightarrow k = 7$
$\frac{k}{j} = \frac{7}{12}$

2. Answer: (D)
$f(1) = \frac{1+3}{2} = 2$

3. Answer: (B)
$3 - 2i + 4 + 5i = 7 + 3i$

4. Answer: (C)
$a + c = 180°$
$c = 180° - a$
$a + b = 180°$
$a = 180° - b$
$c = 180° - (180° - b)$
$b = c$

5. Answer: (D)
$x + y = 2$
$y = -x + 2$
Slope = −1 and y-intercept = 2
The answer is d).

6. Answer: (C)
$x^y x^{\frac{1}{2}} = x^{(y+\frac{1}{2})} = x^{\frac{1}{4}}$
$y + \frac{1}{2} = \frac{1}{4} \rightarrow y = -\frac{1}{4}$

7. Answer: (A)
Divide by $\sqrt{5}$ on both sides of the equation $y = x\sqrt{5}$.
$x = \frac{y}{\sqrt{5}}$ (Then square both sides.)
$x^2 = \frac{y^2}{5}$

8. Answer: (C)
The line segment connecting the first two points must have the same slope as the line segment connecting the last two points.
$\frac{10-s}{5-1} = \frac{10-t}{5-3} \rightarrow \frac{10-s}{4} = \frac{10-t}{2}$
$40 - 4t = 20 - 2s \rightarrow 2t - s = 10$

9. Answer: (A)
$k = \frac{x^{16}-x^{14}}{x^{15}-x^{14}} = \frac{x^{14}(x^2-1)}{x^{14}(x-1)} = \frac{(x+1)(x-1)}{x-1} = x + 1$

10. Answer: (D)
Grouping all terms with y and factoring out y:
$y(wx + xz - z) = wx$
$y = \frac{wx}{wx+xz-z}$

11. Answer: (A)
Factor $x^2 - 2x - 8$.
$(x - 4)(x + 2) = 0$
$x = 4 \ or \ -2$
Plug $x = 4$ and -2 into the expression.
$x^2 - x = (4)^2 - 4 = 12 \ \ or$
$x^2 - x = (-2)^2 - (-2) = 6$

12. Answer: (D)
Find the current age first, and then subtract c. Let x be the current age.
$x + a = b$
$x = b - a$
Current Age = b − a
William's Age c Years Ago = b − a − c

13. *Answer: (C)*
Let m be the total number of students in the school.
$(\frac{1}{4} \times m)$ *students arrive by 7 AM and 100 students*
arrive half an hour later. The total number of students
that have arrived would be
$\frac{1}{4} \times m + 100 = \frac{3}{4} \times m.$
m = 200 students

14. *Answer: (B)*
From the graph, slope equals −1 and y-intercept is 1.
m = −1, b = 1
y = −2mx − b = 2x − 1   (with positive slope and
negative y-intercept)

15. *Answer: (A)*
2x + 1 > 13
2x > 12   →   x > 6
The least value of integer is 7.

16. *Answer: 21*
Volume = Length × Height × Width
7350 = 70 × 5 × Width
Width = 21 feet

17. *Answer: 2*
A linear model with initial value of 40 and slope of
15(4) = 60 per hour.
y = 60x + 40 = 160
x = 2 hours

18. *Answer: 2*
$Slope = \frac{9-5}{1-(-1)} = 2$

19. *Answer: 6*
$15 = \frac{1}{2} \times 5 \times k$
k = 6

20. *Answer: $\frac{5}{3}$*
Cross multiply and then divide both sides by y.
$\frac{x+y}{x-y} = 4 \rightarrow x + y = 4(x - y)$
$\frac{x}{y} + 1 = 4(\frac{x}{y} - 1) = 4\frac{x}{y} + 4$
$\frac{x}{y} = \frac{5}{3}$

Section 4

1. *Answer: (A)*
To divide terms with same base, divide the coefficients
of the terms and subtract the exponents.
$\frac{10x^4}{ax^2} = \frac{10x^4}{2x^2} = 5x^{4-2} = 5x^2$
a = 2 and b = 2
a − b = 2 − 2 = 0

2. *Answer: (C)*
Let x be the original number of customers, then x + 20
− 4 = 3x.
x = 8

3. *Answer: (B)*
0.6a = 1
$a = \frac{1}{0.6} = \frac{10}{6} = \frac{5}{3} = 1.667 \text{ or } 1.67$

4. *Answer: (C)*
Each of these triangles is a 30–60–90 triangle.
The Area of Large Triangle $= \frac{1}{2} \times \overline{BE} \times \overline{BF}$
Side of Square $= \sqrt{16} = 4$
$\overline{BE}$ *(faces 30° angle)* $= 4 + \frac{4}{\sqrt{3}}$
$\overline{BF}$ *(faces 60° angle)* $= 4 + 4\sqrt{3}$
Area $= \frac{1}{2} \times (4 + 4\sqrt{3})(4 + \frac{4}{\sqrt{3}}) = 16(1 + \frac{2\sqrt{3}}{3})$

5. *Answer: (A)*
40 + (10) × 5 = 90

6. *Answer: (D)*
If 2x − y < 0, then 2x < y.

7. *Answer: (B)*
The source is moving toward an observer at rest.
$f_{observed} = f_{original}\left(\frac{v_{sound}}{v_{sound} - v_{source}}\right)$
$v_{observer} = 0 \text{ miles/hour}$
$v_{source} = 50 \text{ miles/hour}$
$v_{sound} = 760 \text{ miles/hour}$
$f_{observed} = 340 \times \left(\frac{760}{760 - 50}\right) = 364 \text{ Hertz}$

8. *Answer: (C)*
The observer is moving toward the sound.
$f_{observed} = f_{original}\left(\frac{v_{sound} + v_{observer}}{v_{sound} - v_{source}}\right)$
$v_{observer} = 50 \text{ miles/hour}$
$v_{source} = 70 \text{ miles/hour}$
$v_{sound} = 760 \text{ miles/hour}$
$f_{observed} = 340 \times \left(\frac{760 + 50}{760 - 70}\right) = 399.1 \text{ Hertz}$

9. Answer: (B)
    $$p = \frac{Amphibian\ In\ philadelphia}{Total\ in\ Philadelphia}$$
    $$= \frac{8}{136}$$

10. Answer: (C)
    Average: $\frac{12 + 16 + x}{3} = x$
    $28 + x = 3x$
    $28 = 2x$
    $x = 14$

11. Answer: (B)
    $\frac{1}{5}$ of $80 \rightarrow \frac{1}{5} \times 80 = 16$
    $16 = \frac{x}{100} \times 200$
    $16 = 2x$
    $x = 8$
    Therefore, $\frac{1}{5} \times 80 = 16$, which is equal to $200 \times 8\% = 16$

12. Answer: (A)
    Change both sides to the base 10.
    $10^{xy} = 10^3 \rightarrow xy = 3$
    Since both x and y are positive integers, both x and y can only be equal to 1 or 3.
    $x > y \rightarrow x = 3$

13. Answer: (B)
    After ordering 100 pounds of fragrance oil, the slope of the line becomes smaller. The answer is b).

14. Answer: (C)
    30% is slightly more than $\frac{1}{4}$ (25%) of the whole graph. From the graph above, two types of automobiles make up less than $\frac{1}{4}$ of the whole graph.

15. Answer: (C)
    This is a ratio problem.
    $\frac{80}{5} = \frac{x}{6}$ (cross multiply)
    $x = 96$

16. Answer: (A)
    For one vegetable AND one dressing, use the Multiplication Principle.
    $5 \times 4 = 20$

17. Answer: (A)
    Let the length of the side of the triangle be x and the length of the side of the square be y.
    Area of an equilateral triangle= $\frac{\sqrt{3}}{4} x^2$
    Area of a square = y^2
    $\frac{\sqrt{3}}{4} x^2 = \sqrt{3}\, y^2$
    $x^2 = 4 y^2$
    $x : y = 2 : 1$

18. Answer: (B)
    The number of students passing = The number of males passing + The number of females passing
    $220 = 120 +$ The number of females passing
    The number of females passing = 100
    Total number of females = The number of females passing + The number of females failing
    The number of females failing: $140 - 100 = 40$

19. Answer: (A)
    $\Delta ABC \sim \Delta EDC$
    $cos(\angle ABC) = cos(\angle EDC) = \frac{1}{2} = \frac{ED}{DC} = \frac{1}{2} \rightarrow ED = \frac{1}{2} DC$
    $\frac{EC}{DC} = \frac{\sqrt{3}}{2} = \frac{6\sqrt{3}}{DC} \rightarrow DC = 12$
    $ED = \frac{1}{2} DC = 6$

20. Answer: (C)
    List of results: 6, less than 3, 4, 6, even.
    Only (c) could meet all the conditions.

21. Answer: (D)
    If the median number of books checked out for the whole week was 93, the number of books checked out on both Saturday and Sunday should be more than 93.

22. Answer: (D)
    $x^2 - y^2 = (x - y)(x + y)$
    $4(x + y) = 24$,
    $x + y = 6$
    $x - y = 4$
    Solve above system equations:
    $x = 5$ and $y = 1$
    $x + 2y = 7$

23. Answer: (B)
    "The T-intercept of the line" means when the pressure is zero.

24. Answer: (B)

The equation of the inequality between andalusite and sillimanite: $P \geq -0.0015T + 1.13$
From two points of (500, 0.38) and (795, 1.0):
the slope is: $\frac{795-500}{1.0-0.38} = 0.0021$
y-intercept = -0.67
the equation of the inequality between kyanite and sillimanite:
$P \leq 0.0021T - 0.67$
Therefore, the answer is b).

25. Answer: (A)
$2x + 4 = (x - 3)(x + 2)$
$x^2 - 3x - 10 = 0$
$(x + 2)(x - 5) = 0$
$x = -2$ and $y = 0$ or
$x = 5$ and $y = 14$
Therefore, $(-2, 0)$ or $(5, 14)$

26. Answer: (C)
w is a positive number and $w < w^2$.
$w^2 - w > 0$
$w(1 - w) > 0 \rightarrow w > 0$ and $1 - w > 0$
$-w > -1$, $w < 1$ So $0 < w < 1$.
If $0 < w < 1$, then any number multiplied by w produces a number smaller than the original number.
Therefore, $w^2 > w^3$, $w^3 > w^4$, and so on.
I, II, III are all correct.

27. Answer: (C)
$12 - 3 = 9$
She applied to 9 schools that are not her top choices. If all 9 of these schools accept Helen, then the 10th school which accepts her must be one of her top schools.
$9 + 1 = 10$

28. Answer: (A)
Arithmetic sequence
$a_n = a_1 + (n - 1) \times d$
$a_{50} = 15 + (50 - 1) \times 2$

29. Answer: (A)
Use the same ratio number to compare
Pear : Apple = $3:5$ = $9:15$
Pear: Orange = $3:5$ = $15:25$
Apple : Orange = $9:25$

30. Answer: (C)
Let each root be r, then
$(x - r)^3 = x^3 - 3x^2r + 3xr^2 - r^3$
Therefore, $3r = 9$ (sum of roots = 9)
$r = 3, q = 27,$ and $p = 27$

31. Answer: 30
$\frac{1}{2}(2ax - 5) = 5$
$2ax - 5 = 10$
$2ax = 15 \rightarrow 4ax = 30$

32. Answer: 2.73
$x = r cos(\theta) = 2 \times cos\left(\frac{\pi}{3}\right) = 1$
$y = r sin(\theta) = 2 \times sin\left(\frac{\pi}{3}\right) = 1.73$
$x + y = 2.73$

33. Answer: 5
Use the Pythagorean Theorem.
$x^2 + 12^2 = 13^2 \rightarrow x = 5$

34. Answer: 42
The sum of all integers from –41 to +41 is 0. The next term is 42.
Therefore, $x = 42$

35. Answer: 54
Among the first 100 terms, there are 50 negative numbers and 4 positive numbers less than 100: 1, 4, 16, and 64.
Total numbers less than 100 is 50 + 4 = 54

36. Answer: 2
$(1 - i)(3 + i) = 4 - 2i = a + bi$
$a = 4$ and $b = -2$
$a + b = 2$

37. Answer: 1.72
The machine depreciates 20% each year for the first 5 years:
$V_t = 10,000 \times (1 - 0.2)^t$
$r_1 = 0.8$
The machine depreciates 8% each year for the next 10 years:
$V_t = V_5 \times (1 - 0.08)^{t-5}$
$r_2 = 0.92$
$r_1 + r_2 = 0.8 + 0.92 = 1.72$

38. Answer: 11
After the first five years:
$V_5 = 10,000 \times (0.8)^5 = 3276.8$
$3276.8(0.92)^{t-5} < 2000$
$0.92^{t-5} < 0.61$
With calculator, the first whole number value of t that satisfies the above inequality is 11.
After 11 years, the value of the machine will be less than $2,000

SAT Math Practice Test No. 7

Directions:
For questions 1-15, solve each problem, choose the best answer from the choices provided, and fill in the corresponding circle on your answer sheet. **For questions 16-20,** solve the problem and enter your answer in the grid on the answer sheet. Please refer to the directions before question 16 on how to enter your answers in the grid. You may use any available space in your test booklet for scratch work.

Notes:
1. **No calculator** is allowed for this section. All numbers used are real numbers.
2. Figures that accompany problems in this test are intended to provide information useful in solving the problems. They are drawn as accurately as possible EXCEPT when it is stated in a specific problem that the figure is not drawn to scale. All figures lie in a plane unless otherwise indicated.
3. Unless otherwise specified, the domain of any function $f(x)$ assumed to be the set of all real numbers x for which $f(x)$ is a real number.

References:

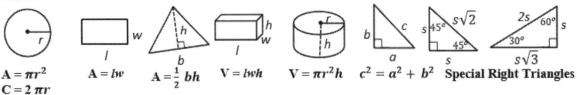

$A = \pi r^2$ $A = lw$ $A = \frac{1}{2}bh$ $V = lwh$ $V = \pi r^2 h$ $c^2 = a^2 + b^2$ **Special Right Triangles**
$C = 2\pi r$

The number of degrees of arc in a circle is 360; the number of radians of arc in a circle is 2π.
The sum of the degree measures of the angles in a triangle is 180.

1. If $x + y = 13$ and $x < 7$, then which of the following must be true?
   a) $y > 0$
   b) $y < 13$
   c) $y = 6$
   d) $y > 6$

2. If $2x + 1 = 9$, what is the value of $\sqrt{5x - 4}$?
   a) 4
   b) –4
   c) 3
   d) –3

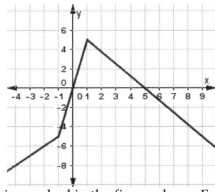

3. $f(x)$ is graphed in the figure above. For what values of x does $f(x)$ have a negative slope?
   a) $x > -1$
   b) $-1 < x < 1$
   c) $x > 1$
   d) $0 < x$

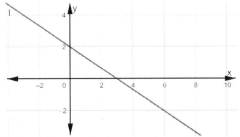

4. Line l is shown in the xy-plane above. Line m (not shown) is parallel to line l and passes through the point $(0, 3)$. Which of the following is an equation of line m ?

    a) $y = -\frac{2}{3}x + 3$

    b) $y = -\frac{3}{2}x + 3$

    c) $y = \frac{2}{3}x + 3$

    d) $y = \frac{3}{2}x + 3$

5. Mary has the following scores on 7 quizzes in Algebra class: 84, 79, 85, 87, 81, 94, and 87. What is the median score of all of her Algebra quizzes?

    a) 81
    b) 84
    c) 85
    d) 86

6. What number decreased by 5 is equal to 21 increased by 3?

    a) 13
    b) 29
    c) 19
    d) 23

7. If x and y are non-zero integers, what is x percent of y percent of 2500?

    a) xy
    b) $4xy$
    c) $10xy$
    d) $\frac{1}{4}xy$

$$2ax - 15 = 3(x + 5) + 5(x - 1)$$

8. In the equation above, a is a constant. If no value of x satisfies the equation, what is the value of ?

    a) 1
    b) 2
    c) 3
    d) 4

9. Mary has the following scores on 7 quizzes in Algebra class: 84, 79, 83, 87, 81, 94, and 87. What was the median score of all of her Algebra quizzes?

    a) 81
    b) 84
    c) 85
    d) 86

10. Which of the following expressions is equivalent to $(3x^2 - 2) - (-5x^2 - 3x + 4)$?

    a) $-2x^2 + 3x - 6$
    b) $-2x^2 - 3x - 2$
    c) $8x^2 - 3x + 2$
    d) $8x^2 + 3x - 6$

11. At West Hill High School, some members of the Key Club are on the math team and no members of the math team are freshmen. Which of the following must also be true?

    a) No members of the Key Club are freshmen.
    b) Some members of the Key Club are freshmen.
    c) Some members of the Key Club are not freshmen.
    d) More tenth graders are on the math team than are on the Key Club.

12. Set X has x elements and set Y has y elements. If they have exactly w elements in common, how many elements are in set X or set Y but not in both set X and Y?

    a) $x + y$
    b) $x + y - w$
    c) $x + y - 2w$
    d) $x + y + 2w$

13. Point Q lies on the line with equation $y - 3 = 2(x - 3)$. If the x-coordinate of Q is 2, what is the y-coordinate of Q?

    a) 2
    b) 1
    c) 0
    d) −1

$$P = 205(1.005)^{\left(\frac{t}{5}\right)}$$

14. The equation above can be used to model the population, in thousands, of a certain city t years after 2000. According to the model, the population is predicted to increase by 0.5% every n year(s). What is the value of n?

    a) 3
    b) 5
    c) 10
    d) 205

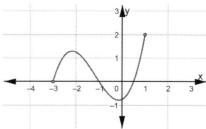

15. The entire graph of $y = f(x)$ is shown in the xy-plane above. Which of the following could be the product of all the values of x for which $f(x) = 0$?

    a) $-\frac{3}{2}$
    b) 0
    c) $\frac{3}{2}$
    d) $\frac{2}{3}$

Directions:

For questions 16-20, solve the problem and enter your answer in the grid, as described below, on the answer sheet.

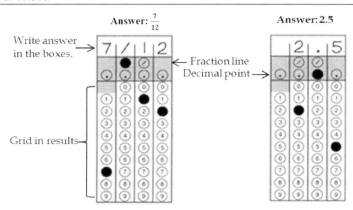

Answer: $\frac{7}{12}$

Write answer in the boxes. →

← Fraction line
Decimal point →

Grid in results →

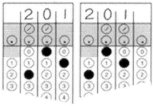

Answer: 2.5

Answer: 201
Either position is correct.

Note: You may start your answers in any column, space permitting. Columns not needed should be left blank.

- Mark no more than one circle in any column.
- Because the answer sheet will be machine-scored. **You will receive credit only if the circles are filled in correctly.**
- Although not required, it is suggested that you write your answer in the boxes at the top of the columns to help you fill in the circles accurately.
- Some problems may have more than one correct answer. In such case, grid only one answer.
- No question has a negative answer.
- **Mixed numbers** such as $3\frac{1}{2}$ must be

gridded as 3.5 or $\frac{7}{2}$. (If [3|1|/|2] is gridded, it will be interpreted as $\frac{31}{2}$, not $3\frac{1}{2}$.)

- **Decimal Answer:** If you obtain a decimal answer with more digits than the grid can accommodate, it may be either rounded or truncated, but it must fill the entire grid. The acceptable ways to grid $\frac{2}{3}$ are:

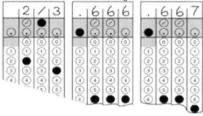

16. If a solution of iodine and alcohol contains 3 ounces of iodine and 13.5 ounces of alcohol, how many ounces of alcohol need to evaporate so that the ratio of iodine to alcohol is 2 to 5?

17. If $x = 7 + (6 \times 5^3 + 1)$, Find the value of x.

18. If the sum of ten integers is odd, at most how many of these integers could be odd?

19. What is the hundredths digit in the number 123.987?

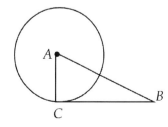

Note: Figure not drawn to scale.
20. In the figure above, the circle has center A, and line segment CB is tangent to the circle at point C. If $AB = 1.0$ and $CB = 0.6$, what is the length of the diameter of the circle?

SECTION 4
Math Test — Calculator   55 MINUTES, 38 QUESTIONS

Directions:

For questions 1-30, solve each problem, choose the best answer from the choices provided, and fill in the corresponding circle on your answer sheet. **For questions 31-38**, solve the problem and enter your answer in the grid on the answer sheet. Please refer to the directions before question 31 on how to enter your answers in the grid. You may use any available space in your test booklet for scratch work.

Notes:

1. Acceptable calculators are allowed for this section. All numbers used are real numbers.
2. Figures that accompany problems in this test are intended to provide information useful in solving the problems. They are drawn as accurately as possible EXCEPT when it is stated in a specific problem that the figure is not drawn to scale. All figures lie in a plane unless otherwise indicated.
3. Unless otherwise specified, the domain of any function $f(x)$ assumed to be the set of all real numbers x for which $f(x)$ is a real number.

References:

   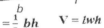

$A = \pi r^2$ $A = lw$ $A = \frac{1}{2} bh$ $V = lwh$ $V = \pi r^2 h$ $c^2 = a^2 + b^2$ **Special Right Triangles**
$C = 2\pi r$

The number of degrees of arc in a circle is 360; the number of radians of arc in a circle is 2π.
The sum of the degree measures of the angles in a triangle is 180.

---

1. If $n > 0$, what is the value of $4^n + 4^n + 10 \times 4^n + 4^{n+1}$?
    a) 4^{4n}
    b) $4^{(n+4)}$
    c) $4^{(n+1)}$
    d) $4^{(n+2)}$

2. If a number was rounded to 20.3, which of the following could have been the original number?
    a) 20.24
    b) 20.249
    c) 20.35
    d) 20.25

3. If $\frac{y}{y-3} = \frac{4}{3}$, then what does y equal to?
    a) 4
    b) 8
    c) –8
    d) 12

4. A supermarket has brand A juice smoothie on sale every 8 days and has brand B juice smoothie on sale every 5 days. Within a year (365 days), how many times does this supermarket have both brands of juice smoothie on sale on the same day?
    a) 9
    b) 10
    c) 12
    d) 24

$$w, x, y, z$$

5. In the sequence above, if each term after the first is d more than the preceding term, what is the sum of w, x, y, and z in terms of w and d?
    a) $3w + 6d$
    b) $4w + 3d$
    c) $6w + 6d$
    d) $2(2w + 3d)$

6. If $0 > x > y$, which of the following is less than $\frac{x}{y}$?

a) 1
b) 2
c) xy
d) $\frac{x}{2y}$

Questions 7 − 8 refer to the following information:

The unemployment rate is officially defined as the percentage of unemployed individuals divided by all individuals currently willing to work. To count as unemployed, a person must be 16 or older and have not held a job during the week of the survey.

According to the Bureau of Labor Statistics, below is a comparison of the seasonally adjusted unemployment rates for certain states and the percent change from August 2015 to September 2015.

State	Rate (August 2015)	Monthly % Change from August 2015 to September 2015
New York	5.2	↓ 2%
Pennsylvania	5.4	↓ 2%
South Carolina	6.0	↓ 5%
California	6.1	↓ 3%
Arizona	6.3	− 0%
New Mexico	6.7	↑ 1%

7. The unemployment rate in South Carolina has dropped from August to September. According to the data shown in the table, what was the unemployment rate in September 2015 for the state of South Carolina?
   a) 5.9
   b) 5.8
   c) 5.7
   d) 5.6

8. If about 530,000 residents of New York were unemployed in August 2015, approximately how many New York residents were willing to work in August 2015?
   a) 9,900,000
   b) 10,200,000
   c) 99,000
   d) 102,000

9. Rachel has either blue or black pens in her pencil case. If the ratio of the number of blue pens to the number of black pens is $\frac{1}{5}$, Rachel could have the following number of pens in her pencil case EXCEPT?
   a) 12
   b) 18
   c) 34
   d) 36

10. Which of the following is the graph of $y = -(x+3)^2 - 2$
   a)

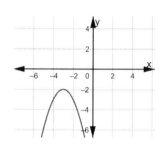

   b)

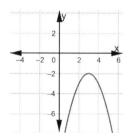

   c)

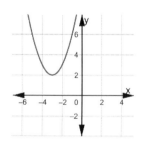

   d)

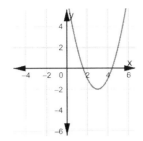

11. If $3 - 2i$ is a root of $2x^2 + ax + b = 0$, then the value of b is
   a) 7.5
   b) –7.5
   c) 26
   d) It cannot be determined.

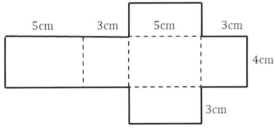

12. If the figure above is folded along the dashed lines, a rectangular box will be formed. What is the volume of the box in cubic centimeters?
   a) 45
   b) 60
   c) 72
   d) 81

13. If $x = y^2$ for any positive integer x, and if $z = x^3 + x^4$, what is z in terms of y?
   a) $y^2 + y^3$
   b) y^3
   c) $y^6 + y^3$
   d) $y^6 + y^8$

14. If John earns \$3,000 a month and he saves \$600 out of his salary, what percent of John's earnings is his monthly savings?
   a) 15%
   b) 20%
   c) 25%
   d) 30%

15. A car rental company calculates the price of renting a car by adding the fixed rental fee with an additional charge for every 10 miles traveled. If the charge to rent a car and drive 50 miles is \$120 and the charge to rent a car and drive 200 miles is \$165, what would be the price, in dollars, to rent a car and travel 300 miles?
   a) 178
   b) 186
   c) 195
   d) 225

$$(4x + 4)(ax - 1) - x^2 + 4$$

16. In the expression above, a is a constant. If the expression is equivalent to bx, where b is a constant, what is the value of b?
   a) -5
   b) -3
   c) 0
   d) 12

17. In a high school pep rally, a student is to be chosen at random. The probability of choosing a freshman is $\frac{1}{8}$. Which of the following cannot be the total number of students in the pep rally?
   a) 20
   b) 24
   c) 32
   d) 80

$$1, 5, 17, t, 161, \dots$$

18. In the sequence above, what is the value of t?
   a) 34
   b) 51
   c) 53
   d) 68

Questions 19 and 20 refer to the following Information.

$$d = 2,565 - 500t$$

An airplane flies directly from a city in Pennsylvania to a city in Ecuador. The equation above estimates the distance, d, in miles, from the city in Ecuador of the airplane t hours after taking off from the city in Pennsylvania.

19. Which of the following is the best interpretation of the number 2,565 in this equation?
    a) The speed, in miles per hour, of the airplane
    b) The distance, in miles, the airplane travels in one hour
    c) The distance, in miles, the airplane travels between the two cities
    d) The time, in minutes, it takes the airplane to reach the city in Ecuador

20. According to the equation, approximately how many hours will it take the airplane to travel between the two cities?
    a) 6.2
    b) 5.8
    c) 5.3
    d) 5.1

$$\sqrt[3]{x^b}$$
21. Which of the following is equivalent to the expression above for all $x > 0$, where a and b are positive integers?
    a) x^{3b}

b) $x^{\frac{3}{b}}$
c) $x^{\frac{b}{3}}$
d) x^{3-b}

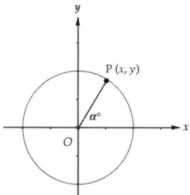

Note: Figure not drawn to scale.
22. On the unit circle above, if the values of sine and cosine of the angle $\alpha°$ are equal, what is the sum $x + y$?
    a) $2\sqrt{2}$
    b) $\sqrt{2}$
    c) $\frac{\sqrt{2}}{2}$
    d) $\frac{\sqrt{2}}{3}$

23. Jenn had to pay off her student loan $24,000 on a twelve-year payment plan. The amount she paid each year for the first six years is three times as much as the amount she paid each of her remaining years. How much did she pay the first year?
    a) $3,000
    b) $2,000
    c) $1,500
    d) $1,000

$$s = 9.8t$$
24. The equation above can be used to approximate the speed s, in meters per second (m/s), of an object t seconds after being dropped into a free fall. Which of the

following is the best interpretation of the number 9.8 in this context?

    a) The speed, in m/s, of the object when it hits the ground

    b) The increase in speed, in m/s, of the object for each second after it is dropped

    c) The speed, in m/s, of the object t seconds after it is dropped

    d) The initial speed, in m/s, of the object when it is dropped

25. If the perimeter of an equilateral triangle equals the perimeter of a square, what is the ratio of the length of a side of the square to the length of a side of the triangle?

    a) $1:1$

    b) $2:3$

    c) $3:4$

    d) $4:3$

26. How many positive factors does the number 24 have?

    a) 4

    b) 5

    c) 7

    d) 8

27. The cost of a long-distance call using phone company A is $1.00 for the first three minutes and $.10 for each additional minute. The same call using the phone company B is charged flat rate at $0.15 per minute for any amount of time. For a call that lasts t minutes, the cost using company A is the same as the cost using the company B, what is the value of t?

    a) 15

    b) 14

    c) 12

    d) 10

28. If x is a positive integer and $3^{2x} + 3^{(2x+1)} = y$, what is $3^{(2x+2)}$ in terms of y?

    a) $\frac{y-1}{3}$

    b) $4y$

    c) $9y$

    d) $\frac{9}{4}y$

29. Five erasers cost as much as 3 pencils. If Matt bought one eraser and one pencil for $1.60, how much does one pencil cost in dollars?

    a) 0.50

    b) 0.60

    c) 1.00

    d) 1.10

30. Earth's outer core can be modeled by a spherical shell that extends from a distance of approximately 1,200 kilometers from Earth's center to approximately 3,400 kilometers from Earth's center. Which of the following is closest to the volume of Earth's outer core, in cubic kilometers?

    a) 1.52×10^7

    b) 3.18×10^7

    c) 4.46×10^{10}

    d) 1.57×10^{11}

Directions:

For questions 31-38, solve the problem and enter your answer in the grid, as described below, on the answer sheet.

Answer: $\frac{7}{12}$

Write answer in the boxes.

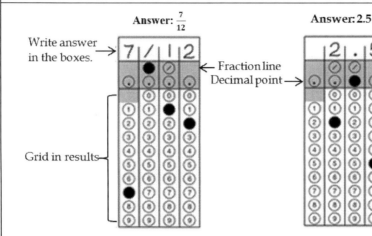

Grid in results

Fraction line

Decimal point

Answer: 2.5

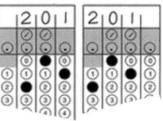

Answer: 201
Either position is correct.

- Mark no more than one circle in any column.
- Because the answer sheet will be machine-scored. **You will receive credit only if the circles are filled in correctly.**
- Although not required, it is suggested that you write your answer in the boxes at the top of the columns to help you fill in the circles accurately.
- Some problems may have more than one correct answer. In such case, grid only one answer.
- No question has a negative answer.
- **Mixed numbers** such as $3\frac{1}{2}$ must be

Note: You may start your answers in any column, space permitting. Columns not needed should be left blank.

gridded as 3.5 or $\frac{7}{2}$. (If [3 1 / 12] is gridded, it will be interpreted as $\frac{31}{2}$, not $3\frac{1}{2}$.)

- **Decimal Answer:** If you obtain a decimal answer with more digits than the grid can accommodate, it may be either rounded or truncated, but it must fill the entire grid. The acceptable ways to grid $\frac{2}{3}$ are:

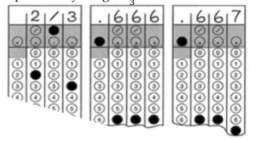

31. If $f(x) = 2x - 1$ and $g(x) = \sqrt{x^2 - 8}$, what is the value of $f(g(3))$?

32. The three interior angle measures of a triangle have the ratio 3 : 4 : 5. What is the sum of the measures, in degrees, of the smallest and largest angles?

33. There are 12 red boxes, 18 blue boxes, and 20 white boxes. If a blue marble is

randomly placed into one of these boxes, what is the probability that it will be placed in a box that is the same color as it?

34. Monday morning, Jason starts out with a certain amount of money that he plans to spend throughout the week. Every

morning after that, he spends exactly $\frac{1}{3}$ the amount he has left. 6 days later, on Sunday morning, he finds that he has \$64 left. How many dollars did Jason originally have on Monday morning?

35. Gina drove at an average of 40 miles per hour from her house to a bookstore. Along the same route, she returned at an average of 60 miles per hour. If the entire trip took her 1 hour, how many miles did Gina drive in total?

36. In the figure below, if the area of the triangle is 20, what is the value of k?

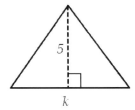

Questions 37 and 38 refer to the following information:

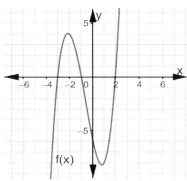

37. The function $f(x) = x^3 + bx^2 - cx - d$ as graphed in the xy-plane above. What is value of $b + c + d =$?

38. How many real solutions are there if $f(x) = x$?

SAT MATH PRACTICE TEST No. 7 ANSWER KEYS

Section 3

1. (D)	2. (A)	3. (C)	4. (A)	5. (C)	6. (B)	7. (D)	8. (D)	9. (B)	10. (D)
11. (C)	12. (C)	13. (B)	14. (B)	15. (C)	16. 6	17. 758	18. 9	19. 8	20. 1.6

Section 4

1. (D)	2. (D)	3. (D)	4. (A)	5. (D)	6. (D)	7. (C)	8. (B)	9. (C)	10. (A)
11. (C)	12. (B)	13. (D)	14. (B)	15. (C)	16. (B)	17. (A)	18. (C)	19. (C)	20. (D)
21. (C)	22. (B)	23. (A)	24. (B)	25. (C)	26. (D)	27. (B)	28. (D)	29. (C)	30. (D)
31. 1	32. 120	33. 0.36 or $\frac{9}{25}$	34. 729	35. 48	36. 8	37. 13	38. 3		

Section 3

1. Answer: (D)
Substitute x with $(13 - y)$.
$x < 7$
$13 - y < 7$
$13 - 7 < y$
$6 < y$

2. Answer: (A)
$2x + 1 = 9$
$x = 4$
$5(4) - 4 = 16$
$\sqrt{16} = 4$

3. Answer: (C)
A line with a negative slope descends from left to right.
According to the graph above, only when $x > 1$ does the line have a negative slope.

4. Answer: (A)
$\frac{2-0}{0-3} = -\frac{2}{3}$
Slope of line m = Slope of line l = $-\frac{2}{3}$
Line m passes through $(0, 3)$.
y-intercept of line m: 3
The equation of line m is $y = -\frac{2}{3}x + b \rightarrow b = 3$
$y = -\frac{2}{3}x + 3$

5. Answer: (C)
Sort the scores in order.
79, 81, 84, 85, 87, 87, 94
The median is 85.

6. Answer: (B)
$x - 5 = 21 + 3 \rightarrow x = 29$

7. Answer: (D)
x percent of y percent of 2500 $\rightarrow$
$\frac{x}{100} \times \frac{y}{100} \times 2500 = \frac{xy}{4}$

8. Answer: (D)
$2ax - 15 = 3(x + 5) + 5(x - 1)$
$2ax - 15 = 8x + 10$
If $a = 4$, then the equation has no solution because
$-15 \neq 10$. The answer is d).

9. Answer: (B)
Sort the scores in order.
79, 81, 83, 84, 87, 87, 94
The median is 84.

10. Answer: (D)
$(3x^2 - 2) - (-5x^2 - 3x + 4)$
$= 3x^2 - 2 + 5x^2 + 3x - 4$
$= 8x^2 + 3x - 6$

11. Answer: (C)
Some students on Key Club also on math team in which there are no freshmen.

12. Answer: (C)
There are $(x - w)$ members belong to X only and $(y - w)$ members belong to Y only.
$(x - w) + (y - w) = x + y - 2w$

13. Answer: (B)
$y - 3 = 2(2 - 3) \rightarrow y = 1$

14. *Answer: (B)*
An exponential model:
$P = P_0 (1 + r)^k$
Where P_0 is the initial value, r is the fraction of the increase and k is the number of period.
$P = 205(1.005)^{\left(\frac{t}{5}\right)} = 205\left(1 + \frac{0.5}{100}\right)^{\frac{t}{5}}$
The population is predicted to increase by 0.5% every 5 years.

15. *Answer: (C)*
The x-intercepts are the roots of $y = f(x)$, which are $-3, -1$ and 0.5, according to the graph.
$(-3)(-1)(0.5) = \frac{3}{2}$

16. *Answer: 6*
Only alcohol can evaporate.
Let x be the amount of alcohol evaporated in ounces.
$\frac{3}{13.5 - x} = \frac{2}{5}$ *(cross multiply)*
$15 = 27 - 2x$
$x = 6$

17. *Answer: 758*
Apply PEMDAS.
$x = 7 + (6 \times 125 + 1) = 7 + (750 + 1) = 7 + 751 = 758$

18. *Answer: 9*
Sum of odd number of odd integers is odd. So there are 9 odd integers at most.

19. *Answer: 8*
Thousands digit: 1
Hundreds digit: 2
Units digit: 3
Tenths digit: 9
Hundredths digit: 8
Thousandths digit: 7

20. *Answer: 1.6*
AC is perpendicular to CB.
ΔABC is a right triangle.
$(AC)^2 = (AB)^2 - (CB)^2$
$(AC)^2 = (1)^2 - (0.6)^2$
$(AC)^2 = 0.64$
$(AC) = 0.8$
Diameter = 2(AC) = 1.6

2. *Answer: (D)*
According to the rounding rules, the original number can be in the range: $25.25 \le x \le 25.34$

3. *Answer: (D)*
$\frac{y}{y - 3} = \frac{4}{3} \rightarrow cross\ multiply$
$3y = 4(y - 3) = 4y - 12$
$y = 12$

4. *Answer: (A)*
The LCM of 8 and 5 is 40.
Every 40 days, A and B will be on sale on the same day.
$\frac{365}{40} = 9.125$

5. *Answer: (D)*
The four terms can be rewritten as w, w+d, w+2d, and w+3d
The Sum of the Sequence = $w + w + d + w + 2d + w + 3d = 4w + 6d = 2(2w + 3d)$

6. *Answer: (D)*
If $0 > x > y$, then $\frac{y}{x} > 1 > \frac{x}{y} > 0$.

7. *Answer: (C)*
Let the unemployment rate in September be x.
$\frac{x - 6.0}{6.0} = -0.05$
$x = 5.7$

8. *Answer: (B)*
Let the number of residents who were willing to work be x.
$\frac{530,000}{x} = 5.2\%$
$5.2x = 53,000,000$
$x = 10,192,308 \approx 10,200,000$

9. *Answer: (C)*
The total number of pens is a whole number and a multiple of (1 + 5).
34 is not a multiple of 6.

10. *Answer: (A)*
The vertex at $(-3, -2)$ and the graph is an open-downward parabolic.
The answer is a).

Section 4

1. *Answer: (D)*
$4^n + 4^n + 10 \times 4^n + 4 \times 4^n = 16 \times 4^n = 4^{(n+2)}$

11. *Answer: (C)*
    The product of the roots is $\frac{b}{2}$. *The sum of the roots is*
    $-\frac{b}{a}$.
    $(3 - 2i)(3 + 2i) = 13 = \frac{b}{2}$
    $b = 26$

12. *Answer: (B)*
    After folding, the height of the box will be 3 cm, the length will be 5 cm, and the width will be 4cm.
    Volume = 3 cm × 4 cm × 5 cm = 60 cm³

13. *Answer: (D)*
    Replace x with y².
    $z = (y^2)^3 + (y^2)^4 = y^6 + y^8$

14. *Answer: (B)*
    $Percent = \frac{Part}{Whole} \times 100$
    $\frac{600}{3000} \times 100 = 20$

15. *Answer: (C)*
    Let initial charge be $x, and the fee for every 10 miles be $y.
    $x + 5y = 120$
    $x + 20y = 165$
    $15y = 45, \quad y = 3, \quad x = 105$
    For traveling 300 miles, the total charge is
    $105 + 30 \times 3 = 195$.

16. *Answer: (B)*
    $(4x + 4)(ax - 1) - x^2 + 4 = 4ax^2 - 4x + 4ax - 4 - x^2 + 4 = x^2(4a - 1) + x(4a - 4) = bx$
    $(4a - 1)x^2 = 0 \rightarrow a = \frac{1}{4}$
    $x(4a - 4) = -3x = bx$
    $b = -3$

17. *Answer: (A)*
    The total number of students must be a multiple of 8. Note that the number of students must be a whole number.
    Only (a) is not a multiple of 8.

18. *Answer: (C)*
    Examine the first few terms to figure out the pattern. This is a sequence constructed by multiplying the previous term by 3 and then adding 2 to the product each time to get the next term.
    $1 \times 3 + 2 = 5; 5 \times 3 + 2 = 17;$
    $17 \times 3 + 2 = 53; t = 53$

19. *Answer: (C)*
    When $t = 0 \rightarrow d = 2656$
    It is the distance between two cities.

20. *Answer: (D)*
    The plane arrives when d = 0.
    $0 = 2565 - 500t \rightarrow t = 5.1$

21. *Answer: (C)*
    $\sqrt[3]{x^b} = x^{\frac{b}{3}}$

22. *Answer: (B)*
    In the first Quadrant, the values of sine and cosine are only equal at $\alpha = 45$. *Here,* $cos(\alpha°) = sin(\alpha°) = \frac{\sqrt{2}}{2}$,
    so $x = y = \frac{\sqrt{2}}{2}$ *and* $x + y = \sqrt{2}$

23. *Answer: (A)*
    Let the first year payment be $x and each of her last 6 years be $y.
    $x = 3y$ *and* $6x + 6y = 24000$
    $18y + 6y = 24000$
    $y = 1000$
    $x = 3000$
    The first year payment is $3000.

24. *Answer: (B)*
    "The slope of 9.8" means speed increase 9.8 per second. The answer is b).

25. *Answer: (C)*
    Let the length of the side of the triangle be x and the length of the side of the square be y.
    $3x = 4y$
    $y : x = 3 : 4$

26. *Answer: (D)*
    $24 = 2^3 \times 3^1$
    Number of positive factors:
    $(3 + 1) \times (1 + 1) = 8$

27. *Answer: (B)*
    $1 + (t - 3) \times 0.1 = 0.15t \quad \rightarrow \quad t = 14$

28. *Answer: (D)*
    $3^{2x} + 3^{(2x+1)} = 4 \times 3^{2x}$
    $4 \times 3^{2x} = y$
    $3^{2x} = \frac{y}{4}$
    $3^{(2x+2)} = 9 \times 3^{2x} = 9 \times \frac{y}{4} = \frac{9y}{4}$

29. *Answer: (C)*
    Let the price of one eraser be x and the price of one pencil be y. The price of 6 erasers = The price of 3 pencils.
    $5x = 3y, x = \frac{3}{5}y$
    $x + y = 1.60$
    $\frac{3}{5}y + y = 1.60$
    Solve for y to get the price of one pencil $1.00.

30. *Answer: (D)*
    The volume of outer core of Earth;
    $\frac{4}{3}\pi[3400^3 - 1200^3] = 1.57 \times 10^{11}$

31. *Answer: 1*
    $g(3) = \sqrt{3^2 - 8} = \sqrt{1} = 1$
    $f(g(3)) = f(1) = 2(1) - 1 = 1$

32. *Answer: 120*
    We can define the measures of the three angles to be 3x, 4x, and 5x.
    $3x + 4x + 5x = 180°$
    $x = 15°$
    $3x + 5x = 8x = 8 \times 15 = 120°$

33. *Answer: 0.36 or $\frac{9}{25}$*
    $Probability = \frac{Number\ of\ Successful\ Events}{Total\ Number\ of\ Possible\ Events}$
    $\frac{18}{12 + 18 + 20} = 0.36$

34. *Answer: 729*
    Jason spends $\frac{1}{3}$ of his money each day, so he has $\frac{2}{3}$ of his money left next morning.
    Let Jason have $x on Monday. On Sunday, he will have:$(\frac{2}{3} \times \frac{2}{3} \times \frac{2}{3} \times \frac{2}{3} \times \frac{2}{3} \times \frac{2}{3})x$ dollars left.
    $\frac{2^6 x}{3^6} = 64$
    $x = 3^6 = 729$ *dollars*

35. *Answer: 48*
    Let one trip have x miles
    Total Time = $t_{go} + t_{back}$
    $1 = \frac{x}{40} + \frac{x}{60} = x(\frac{1}{40} + \frac{1}{60}) \rightarrow x = 24$
    Total miles: $2 \times 24 = 48$ miles

36. *Answer: 8*
    $20 = \frac{1}{2} \times 5 \times k$
    $k = 8$

37. *Answer: 13*
    There are three roots of f(x):
    $f(x) = (x + 3)(x + 1)(x - 2)$
    $= x^3 + 2x - 5x - 6$
    $b = 2; c = 5; d = 6$
    $b + c + d = 13$

38. *Answer: 3*
    There are three intersections between $y = x$ and $y = x^3 + 2x - 5x - 6$

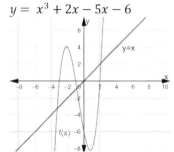

SAT Math Practice Test No. 8

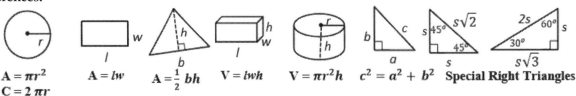
1. The average (arithmetic mean) of 10, 14, and x is 18. What is the value of x?
   a) 25
   b) 26
   c) 27
   d) 30

2. If x, y, and z are positive numbers and $xyz = x^2$, which of the following must equal x?
   a) yz
   b) xy
   c) xz
   d) 1

3. When the number 13 is divided by the positive integer p, the remainder is 1. For how many different values of p is this true?
   a) Six
   b) Five
   c) Four
   d) Three

4. Points A, B, C, D, E lie on a line from left to right. The length of AC is 4, the length of BE is 6 and the length of BC is 3. What is the length of AE?
   a) 10
   b) 9
   c) 8
   d) 7

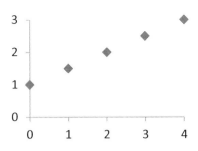

5. Which of the lines described by the following equations best fits those points above?

 a) $y = 0.5x - 1$
 b) $y = 0.5x + 1$
 c) $y = -0.5x - 1$
 d) $y = -0.5x + 1$

$$\begin{cases} 8x - 5y = 17 \\ 7x + 5y = 15 \end{cases}$$

6. For the solution (x, y) to the system of equations above, what is the value of ?

 a) 1
 b) $\frac{2}{5}$
 c) $-\frac{3}{5}$
 d) -1

7. If $y = x\sqrt{3}$ and $x \neq 0$, what does x^2 equal in terms of y?

 a) $\frac{y^2}{3}$
 b) $3y^2$
 c) $\frac{9}{y^2}$
 d) $\frac{y^2}{9}$

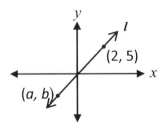

8. In the figure above, line l passes through the origin. What is the value of $\frac{b}{a}$?

 a) 1
 b) 1.5
 c) 2
 d) 2.5

9. If $\frac{6x}{\sqrt{x+1}} = 3\sqrt{2}$, what is one possible value of x?

 a) -7
 b) -1
 c) 0
 d) 1

$$(ax + 3)(5x^2 - bx + 4) = 20x^3 - 9x^2 - 2x + 12$$

10. The equation above is true for all x, where a and b are constants. What is the value of ab ?

 a) 18
 b) 20
 c) 24
 d) 40

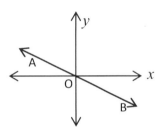

11. The coordinates of point A in the figure above are (a, b), where $|a| > |3b|$. Which of the following could be the slope of AB?

 a) -1
 b) $-\frac{1}{2}$
 c) $-\frac{1}{3}$
 d) $-\frac{1}{4}$

12. Which of the following equations has a graph in the xy-plane with no x-intercepts?

 a) $y = x^2 + 3x + 4$
 b) $y = x^2 - 5x - 6$
 c) $y = 3x^2$
 d) $y = 2x - 5$

13. If $g(x) = 3x - 6$, then at what value of x does the graph of $g(x)$ cross the x-axis?

 a) -6
 b) -3
 c) 0
 d) 2

14. Let $*m$ be defined as $*m = m^2 + 4$ for all values of m. If $*x = 3x^2$, which of the following could be the value of x?
   a) -2
   b) 1
   c) 2
   d) $-\sqrt{2}$

15. If m is a positive number, which of the following is equal to $m^3 \times m^{-3}$?
   a) 0
   b) 1
   c) m^{-6}
   d) m

Directions:
For questions 16-20, solve the problem and enter your answer in the grid, as described below, on the answer sheet.

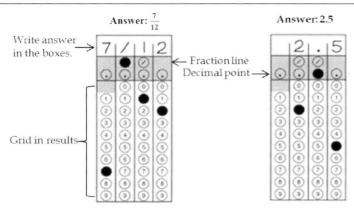

Answer: $\frac{7}{12}$

Write answer in the boxes.

← Fraction line
Decimal point →

Grid in results

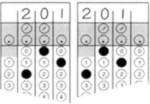

Answer: 2.5

Answer: 201
Either position is correct.

Note: You may start your answers in any column, space permitting. Columns not needed should be left blank.

- Mark no more than one circle in any column.
- Because the answer sheet will be machine-scored. **You will receive credit only if the circles are filled in correctly.**
- Although not required, it is suggested that you write your answer in the boxes at the top of the columns to help you fill in the circles accurately.
- Some problems may have more than one correct answer. In such case, grid only one answer.
- No question has a negative answer.
- **Mixed numbers** such as $3\frac{1}{2}$ must be

gridded as 3.5 or $\frac{7}{2}$. (If [3 1 / 2] is gridded, it will be interpreted as $\frac{31}{2}$, not $3\frac{1}{2}$.)

- **Decimal Answer:** If you obtain a decimal answer with more digits than the grid can accommodate, it may be either rounded or truncated, but it must fill the entire grid. The acceptable ways to grid $\frac{2}{3}$ are:

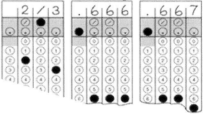

16. A rectangular storage room has a volume of 7350 cubic feet. If its length is 70 feet and its height is 5 feet, what is the width of the room, in feet?

17. Positive integers x, y, and z satisfy the equations $x^{-\frac{1}{2}} = \frac{1}{2}$ and $y^z = 8$, $z > y$, what is the value of $x + y + z$?

18. A bag contains only red, white, and blue marbles. If randomly choosing a blue marble is three times as likely as randomly choosing a white marble, and randomly choosing a red marble is twice as likely as randomly choosing a blue marble, then what is the smallest possible number of marbles in the bag?

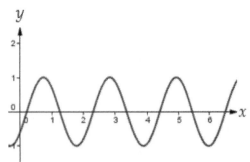

19. According to the graph shown above, how many distinct positive values of x are there on the graph when $y = 0.5$?

20. Ms. DePietro provides some markers to her Arts class. If each student takes 3 markers, there will be 1 marker left. If 5 students take 4 markers each and the rest of students take 2 markers each, there will be no markers left. How many students are in Ms. DePietro's Arts class?

SECTION 4
Math Test — Calculator   55 MINUTES, 38 QUESTIONS

Directions:
For questions 1-30, solve each problem, choose the best answer from the choices provided, and fill in the corresponding circle on your answer sheet. **For questions 31-38**, solve the problem and enter your answer in the grid on the answer sheet. Please refer to the directions before question 31 on how to enter your answers in the grid. You may use any available space in your test booklet for scratch work.

Notes:
1. Acceptable calculators are allowed for this section. All numbers used are real numbers.
2. Figures that accompany problems in this test are intended to provide information useful in solving the problems. They are drawn as accurately as possible EXCEPT when it is stated in a specific problem that the figure is not drawn to scale. All figures lie in a plane unless otherwise indicated.
3. Unless otherwise specified, the domain of any function $f(x)$ assumed to be the set of all real numbers x for which $f(x)$ is a real number.

References:

  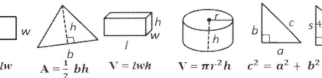

$A = \pi r^2$ $A = lw$ $A = \frac{1}{2}bh$ $V = lwh$ $V = \pi r^2 h$ $c^2 = a^2 + b^2$ **Special Right Triangles**
$C = 2\pi r$

The number of degrees of arc in a circle is 360; the number of radians of arc in a circle is 2π.
The sum of the degree measures of the angles in a triangle is 180.

1. Which of the lines described by the following equations best fits those points above?

   a) $y = \frac{1}{4}x + \frac{1}{2}$
   b) $y = \frac{1}{4}x + 1$
   c) $y = -\frac{1}{4}x - \frac{1}{2}$
   d) $y = -\frac{1}{2}x + \frac{1}{2}$

2. If $f(x) = \frac{x^3 - 5}{x^2 - 2x + 8}$, then what is $f(3)$?

a) 0
b) 2
c) 4
d) 6

3. N students have an average of K scores on a math test. Another 3 students were absent and received zeroes on the test. What is the average score of this math test in terms of N and K, taking into accounts all of the students?

   a) $\frac{NK}{3}$
   b) $\frac{NK}{K+3}$
   c) $\frac{NK}{N+3}$
   d) $\frac{N-3}{K}$

4. In the figure below, triangles A and B are isosceles right triangles and C is a square. If the area of A is 8 and the area of B is 18, what is the area of C?

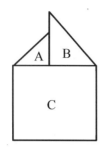

a) 64
b) 81
c) 100
d) 144

5. What is the slope of a line that passes through the points (1, −1) and (−1, 5)?
   a) −3
   b) −2
   c) 0
   d) 2

6. Which of the following is the expression $x^2 + 3xy + 5x^3 + 15x^2y$ in fully factored form?
   a) $xy(1 + 5x)(x + 3)$
   b) $(x + 5x^2)(x + 3y)$
   c) $x(1 + 5x)(x + 3y)$
   d) $(1 + 5x)(x + 3y)$

Questions 7 − 8 refer to the following information:

The kinetic energy of an object is the energy that the object possesses due to its motion. Kinetic energy is equal to half of the product of the mass and the square of its velocity.
The momentum is the quantity of the motion of a moving body, measured as a product of its mass and velocity.

7. If two bodies, A and B, have equal kinetic energies and the mass of A is four times as much as the mass of B, what is the ratio of the momentum of A to that of B?
   a) $\frac{1}{2}$
   b) $\frac{1}{4}$
   c) 2

d) 4

8. If two bodies A and B as described above have equal momentum, what is the ratio of the kinetic energy of A to that of B?
   a) $\frac{1}{2}$
   b) $\frac{1}{4}$
   c) 2
   d) 4

9. How many positive three-digit integers have the hundreds digit equal to the multiple of 3 and the units digit (ones digit) is an even digit?
   a) 150
   b) 160
   c) 162
   d) 180

10. Washington High School randomly selected freshman, sophomore, junior, and senior students for a survey about potential changes to next year's schedule. Of students selected for the survey, $\frac{1}{4}$ were freshmen and $\frac{1}{3}$ were sophomores. Half of the remaining selected students were juniors. If 336 students were selected for the survey, how many were seniors?
    a) 65
    b) 70
    c) 90
    d) 120

11. If $f(x) = x^2 + x^{3/2}$, what is the value of $f(3) =$?
    a) $3 \times (1 + 3\sqrt{3})$
    b) $(1 + 3\sqrt{3})$
    c) $3 \times (1 + 3\sqrt{3})$
    d) $3 \times (3 + \sqrt{3})$

12. Find the equation of a circle that has a diameter with the endpoints given by the points (3, 5) and (−1, 1).
    a) $(x − 1)^2 + (y − 3)^2 = 8$
    b) $(x + 1)^2 + (y + 3)^2 = 8$
    c) $(x − 1)^2 + (y − 3)^2 = 4$

d) $(x + 1)^2 + (y - 3)^2 = 8$

c) 6.4

d) 12.5

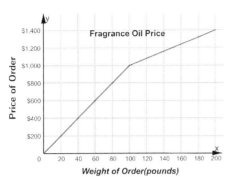

Fragrance Oil Price

Weight of Order(pounds)

13. The graph above shows the price that a chemical company charges for an order of fragrance oil, depending on the weight of the order. Based on the graph, which of the following statements must be true?

   a) The company charges more per pound for orders greater than 100 pounds than for orders less than 100 pounds.

   b) The company charges less per pound for orders greater than 100 pounds than for orders less than 100 pounds.

   c) The company charges less per pound for orders greater than 1,000 pounds than for orders less than 1,000 pounds.

   d) The company charges the same price per pound, regardless of order size.

14. If x and y are positive integers and $2^{2x} + 2^{(2x+2)} = y$, what is 2^x in terms of y?

   a) $\dfrac{y}{5}$

   b) $\dfrac{\sqrt{y}}{\sqrt{5}}$

   c) $\dfrac{y}{12}$

   d) $\dfrac{\sqrt{y}}{5}$

15. The load capacity of a certain washing machine is 14 pounds. What is the approximate load capacity of the same washing machine, in kilograms? (1 kilogram = 2.2046 pounds)

   a) 2.6

   b) 5.8

$$\frac{6}{x^2 - 9} = \frac{2}{x - 3} + \frac{1}{x + 3}$$

16. Which statement describes the solution to the equation above?

   a) 1 is the only solution.

   b) -1 is the only solution.

   c) 1 and -1 are both solutions.

   d) There are no solutions.

Time(days)	Counts
0	5
1	50
2	500
3	5,000
4	50,000
5	500,000

17. The estimated counts of bacteria in a petri dish are over the course of five days, as shown in the table above. Which of the following best describes the relationship between time and the estimated counts of bacteria during the five-day period?

   a) Decreasing linear

   b) Increasing linear

   c) Exponential decay

   d) Exponential growth

Questions 18-20 refer to the following information.

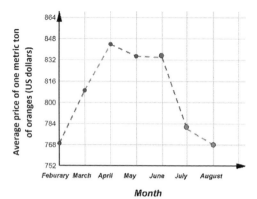

The line graph above shows the average price of one metric ton of oranges, in dollars, for each of seven months in 2018.

18. Between which two consecutive months shown did the average price of one metric ton of oranges decrease the most?
    a) March to April
    b) May to June
    c) June to July
    d) July to August

19. Which of the following is closest to the mean price, in dollars, of the seven recorded prices of one metric ton of oranges?
    a) 835
    b) 806
    c) 782
    d) 769

20. In 2018, the average price of one metric ton of oranges decreased by 2.36% from January (not shown) to February. Which of the following is closest to the price of one metric ton of oranges in January 2018?
    a) 710
    b) 772
    c) 786
    d) 829

21. How much money was originally in Sue's checking account if she withdrew m dollars, deposited n dollars, and now has l dollars in her checking account?
    a) $l + m - n$

b) $l - m - n$
c) $m + n - l$
d) $m + n + l$

$$p(t) = 1000 \times (3)^{\frac{t}{2}}$$

22. The growth of certain kind of bacterial is observed and its population growth, p, t days from the first observation, is modeled by the function above. By how much does the bacterial population increase from $t = 4$ to $t = 6$?
    a) 18,000
    b) 16,000
    c) 15,000
    d) 14,000

23. The figure below shows a top view of a container with a square-shaped opening and which is divided into 5 smaller compartments. The side of the overall square is double the length of the side of the center square and the areas of compartments A, B, C, and D are all equal. If a baseball is thrown into the box at random, what is the probability that the baseball is found in compartment A?

    a) $\frac{1}{4}$
    b) $\frac{2}{15}$
    c) $\frac{3}{16}$
    d) $\frac{1}{8}$

2, 2, 4, 4, 4, 4, 6, 6, 6, 6, 6, 6, ...

24. The sequence above is made up of a list of positive even numbers. Each even number n appears in the sequence n times. On which term in the sequence does the number 10 first appear?

a) 18
b) 21
c) 24
d) 30

25. In the figure below, circle O is tangent to a square at points A and B. If the area of △ABC is 8, what is the area of the circle?

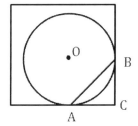

a) 4π
b) 6π
c) $6\sqrt{2}\pi$
d) 16π

$$(3x + 4a) + 2(ax - 3) = 7x + 2$$

26. In the equation above, a is a constant. If the equation holds true for all value of x. What is the value of a?

a) 6
b) 4
c) 2
d) 0

27. The cost of a long-distance call using phone company A is $1.00 for the first three minutes and $.10 for each additional minute. The same call using the phone company B is charged flat rate at $0.15 per minute for any amount of time. For a call that lasts t minutes, the cost using company A is the same as the cost using the company B, what is the value of t?

a) 15
b) 14
c) 12
d) 10

28. If $12\sqrt{12} = x\sqrt{y}$ where x and y are positive integers and $x > y$, which of the following could be the value of xy?

a) 32
b) 48
c) 72
d) 102

29. If $7 = m^x$, then $7m^2 = ?$

a) m^{2x}
b) m^{7x}
c) m^{x+2}
d) m^{x+7}

30. Which of the following is the equation of the polynomial with roots at 0 and $3 - \sqrt{2}$?

a) $x^3 + 6x^2 - 9x = 0$
b) $x^3 - 6x^2 - 7x = 0$
c) $x^3 + 6x^2 + 7x = 0$
d) $x^3 - 6x^2 + 7x = 0$

Directions:

For questions 31-38, solve the problem and enter your answer in the grid, as described below, on the answer sheet.

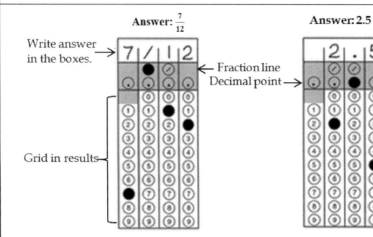

Answer: $\frac{7}{12}$

Write answer in the boxes.

← Fraction line
Decimal point →

Grid in results

Answer: 2.5

Answer: 201
Either position is correct.

Note: You may start your answers in any column, space permitting. Columns not needed should be left blank.

- Mark no more than one circle in any column.
- Because the answer sheet will be machine-scored. **You will receive credit only if the circles are filled in correctly.**
- Although not required, it is suggested that you write your answer in the boxes at the top of the columns to help you fill in the circles accurately.
- Some problems may have more than one correct answer. In such case, grid only one answer.
- No question has a negative answer.
- **Mixed numbers** such as $3\frac{1}{2}$ must be

gridded as 3.5 or $\frac{7}{2}$. (If 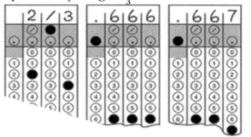 is gridded, it will be interpreted as $\frac{31}{2}$, not $3\frac{1}{2}$.)

- **Decimal Answer:** If you obtain a decimal answer with more digits than the grid can accommodate, it may be either rounded or truncated, but it must fill the entire grid. The acceptable ways to grid $\frac{2}{3}$ are:

31. If $|2x + 3| = 5$ and $|3y - 3| = 6$, what is one possible value of $|x + y|$?

32. If 8 out of 24 students in a math class get a perfect score, then the class average (arithmetic mean) on this test will be 91 points out of 100. What was the average score for the remaining students?

33. Seven different surveys of the daily commuting time, in minutes, of Chicago-based employees yielded the values 30, 15, 42, 32, 55, 22, 40. Seven different surveys of the daily commuting time, in minutes, of San Francisco-based employees yielded the values 44, 31, 20, 32, 46, x, 39. If these two data sets have the same mean, what is the value of x?

34. In the figure below, point O is the center of the circle, line segments PQ and PR are tangent to the circle at points Q and R, respectively, and the segments intersect at point P as shown. If the radius of the circle is 6 and the length of PQ is $6\sqrt{3}$, what is the area of minor sector $\overarc{RQ}$?

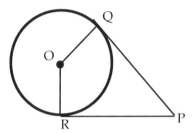

35. What is the area of the figure below?

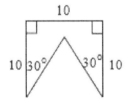

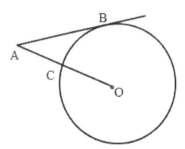

36. In the diagram above, AB is tangent to circle O at point B. AB = 2AC and the radius has length 3. What is the length of $\overline{AO}$?

Questions 37 and 38 refer to the following information.

Amount of Electricity Generated from Renewable Sources

State	Amount (billions of kWh)
California	42
Massachusetts	12
Wisconsin	6

The table above shows the amount of electricity, in billions of kilowatt-hours (kWh), generated from renewable sources in three states in the United States in 2008.

37. The amount of electricity generated from renewable sources in California was 10% of the total amount of electricity generated from renewable sources in the United States. What fraction of the total amount of electricity generated from renewable sources in the United States was generated in Wisconsin?

38. In 2008, 15% of all electricity generated in Massachusetts came from renewable sources. Massachusetts plans that by 2024, the amount of electricity, x, in billions of kWh, from renewable sources will be 25% of all electricity generated in the state. In Massachusetts, if the total amount of electricity generated in 2024 is the same as the total amount generated in 2008, what is the value of x?

SAT MATH PRACTICE TEST No. 8 ANSWER KEYS

Section 3

1. (D)	2. (A)	3. (B)	4. (D)	5. (B)	6. (B)	7. (A)	8. (D)	9. (D)	10. (C)
11. (D)	12. (A)	13. (D)	14. (D)	15. (B)	16. 21	17. 9	18. 10	19. 7	20. 9

Section 4

1. (A)	2. (B)	3. (C)	4. (C)	5. (A)	6. (C)	7. (C)	8. (B)	9. (A)	10. (B)
11. (D)	12. (A)	13. (B)	14. (B)	15. (C)	16. (A)	17. (D)	18. (C)	19. (B)	20. (C)
21. (A)	22. (A)	23. (C)	24. (B)	25. (D)	26. (C)	27. (B)	28. (C)	29. (C)	30. (D)
31. 0, 1, 4, or 5	32. 86.5	33. 22	34. 37.7	35. 56.6 or 56.7	36. 5	37. $\frac{1}{70}$	38. 20		

Section 3

1. Answer: (D)
   The average of these three numbers is 18, so the sum will be 3 × 18 =54.
   $10 + 14 + x = 54 \rightarrow x = 54 - 24 = 30$

2. Answer: (A)
   Divide both sides by x.
   $xyz = x^2$
   $yz = x$

3. Answer: (B)
   Find all the factors of (13 − 1) that are greater than 1. The factors of 12 that are greater than 1 are 2, 3, 4, 6 and 12. 5 different values of p.

4. Answer: (D)
   $AE = AC + BE - BC$
   $4 + 6 - 3 = 7$

5. Answer: (B)
   $Slope = \frac{Rise}{Run} = \frac{2-1}{2-0} = 0.5$
   y-intercept = 1
   $y = 0.5x + 1$

6. Answer: (B)
   $\begin{cases} 8x - 5y = 15 \ - - - -(1) \\ 7x + 5y = 15 \ - - - -(2) \end{cases}$
   $(1) + (2) \rightarrow 15x = 30$
   $x = 2$
   $7(2) + 5y = 15 \rightarrow y = \frac{1}{5}$
   $xy = 2 \times \frac{1}{5} = \frac{2}{5}$

7. Answer: (A)
   Divide by $\sqrt{3}$ on both sides of the equation $y = x\sqrt{3}$.
   $x = \frac{y}{\sqrt{3}}$ (Then square both sides.)
   $x^2 = \frac{y^2}{3}$

8. Answer: (D)
   $\frac{b - 0}{a - 0} = \frac{5 - 0}{2 - 0}$
   $\frac{b}{a} = \frac{5}{2} = 2.5$

9. Answer: (D)
   Take square on both sides of the equation: $(\frac{6x}{\sqrt{x+1}})^2 = (3\sqrt{2})^2$
   $\frac{36x^2}{x + 1} = 18$
   $36x^2 = 18x + 18$
   $2x^2 = x + 1 \rightarrow x = 1 \ or \ -\frac{1}{2}$

10. Answer: (C)
    "True for all x" means the expressions on both sides need to be identical.
    $(ax + 3)(5x^2 - bx + 4) = 20x^3 - 9x^2 - 2x + 12$
    The coefficients of x^2 on both sides should be the same:
    $-ab + 15 = -9$
    $ab = 24$

11. Answer: (D)
    A line with a negative slope descends from left to right; therefore, the slope of the line in the graph is negative.
    $|a| > |3b| \rightarrow \frac{1}{3} > |\frac{b}{a}|$

12. Answer: (A)
    "with no x-intercepts"→ No real solution → $b^2 - 4ac < 0$
    $3^3 - 4(1)(4) < 0$
    The answer is a)

13. *Answer: (D)*
The value of x where g(x) crosses the x-axis is the value of x where g(x) is equal to 0.
$0 = 3x - 6$
$x = 2$

14. *Answer: (D)*
$*x = x^2 + 4$
$x^2 + 4 = 3x^2$
$x^2 = 2 \rightarrow x = \pm\sqrt{2}$

15. *Answer: (B)*
Except the number 0, any numbers raised to the power of 0 is equal to 1.
$m^3 \times m^{-3} = m^0 = 1$

16. *Answer: 21*
Volume = Length × Height × Width
$7350 = 70 \times 5 \times Width$
Width = 21 feet

17. *Answer: 9*
$x^{-\frac{1}{2}} = \frac{1}{2}, \quad x = \left(\frac{1}{2}\right)^{-2} = 2^2 = 4$
$8 = 2^3 = y^z$
$y = 2$ and $z = 3$
$x + y + z = 2 + 3 + 4 = 9$

18. *Answer: 10*
Blue: White = 3: 1
Red : Blue = 2 : 1
Red : Blue : White = 6 : 3 : 1
The smallest possible number of marbles in the bag is 10.

19. *Answer: 7*
Draw a horizontal line y = 0.5 to find how many interceptions with the graph.
From the graph above, there are seven interceptions with line y = 0.5.

20. *Answer: 9*
Let x be the number of students in Ms. DePietro's Arts class.
$3x + 1 = 5 \times 4 + (x - 5) \times 2$
$x = 9$

Section 4

1. *Answer: (A)*
$Slope = \frac{Rise}{Run} = \frac{1-\frac{1}{2}}{2-0} = \frac{1}{4}$
$y\text{-}intercept = \frac{1}{2}$
$y = \frac{1}{4}x + \frac{1}{2}$

2. *Answer: (B)*
$f(3) = \frac{3^3 - 5}{3^2 - 2(3) + 8} = \frac{22}{11} = 2$

3. *Answer: (C)*
$Average = \frac{Total\ Score}{Number\ of\ Students}$
$Average = \frac{K \times N}{N + 3}$

4. *Answer: (C)*
The area of each of the right isosceles triangles is $\frac{1}{2} \times$ (length of leg)^2.
Let x be the length of triangle A's legs
$\frac{1}{2}x^2 = 8 \rightarrow x = 4$
Let y be the length of triangle B's legs
$\frac{1}{2}y^2 = 18 \rightarrow y = 6$
Thus, the square C has a side of 10 and its area is 100.

5. *Answer: (A)*
$Slope = \frac{Rise}{Run} = \frac{5-(-1)}{-1-1} = -3$

6. *Answer: (C)*
$x^2 + 3xy + 5x^3 + 15x^2y$
$= x(x + 3y) + 5x^2(x + 3y)$
$= (x + 5x^2)(x + 3y)$
$= x(1 + 5x)(x + 3y)$

7. *Answer: (C)*
Let the mass of A be 4k and the mass of B be k.
$\frac{1}{2}(4k) \times (v_A)^2 = \frac{1}{2}(k) \times (v_B)^2$
$\frac{v_A}{v_B} = \frac{1}{2}$
$\frac{Momentum\ of\ A}{Momentum\ of\ B} = \frac{4k \times v_A}{k \times v_B} = 4 \times \frac{1}{2} = 2$

8. *Answer: (B)*
Momentum is measured as a product of mass and velocity.
$4k \times v_A = k \times v_B$
$\frac{v_A}{v_B} = \frac{1}{4}$
$\frac{K_e of\ A}{K_e of\ B} = \frac{\frac{1}{2} \times 4k \times v_A^2}{\frac{1}{2} \times k \times v_B^2} = \frac{4}{16} = \frac{1}{4}$

9. Answer: (A)
    The hundreds has 3 choices (3, 6, 9) and the units digit
    has 5 choices (2, 4, 6, 8, 0). There are 10 possible values
    of tens digit (0 – 9).
    Total = 3 × 5 × 10 = 150

10. Answer: (B)
    $Juniors = \dfrac{1-\frac{1}{4}-\frac{1}{3}}{2} = \dfrac{\frac{5}{12}}{2} = \dfrac{5}{24}$
    $Seniors = 1 - \dfrac{1}{3} - \dfrac{1}{4} - \dfrac{5}{24} = \dfrac{5}{24}$
    $336 \times \dfrac{5}{24} = 70$

11. Answer: (D)
    The value of $f(3)$ is calculated by replacing x with 3 in
    the function.
    $3^2 + 3^{3/2} = 9 + 3\sqrt{3} = 3(3 + \sqrt{3})$

12. Answer: (A)
    $Center: \left(\dfrac{3-1}{2}, \dfrac{5+1}{2}\right) = (1, 3)$
    $Radius: \sqrt{(3-1)^2 + (5-3)^2} = \sqrt{8}$
    $Equation: (x-1)^2 + (y-3)^2 = 8$

13. Answer: (B)
    After ordering 100 pounds of fragrance oil, the slope of
    the line becomes smaller. The answer is b).

14. Answer: (B)
    $2^{2x} + 2^{(2x+2)} = 5 \times 2^{2x}$
    $5 \times 2^{2x} = y \quad \rightarrow \quad 2^{2x} = \dfrac{y}{5}$
    $(2^x)^2 = \dfrac{y}{5} \quad \rightarrow \quad 2^x = \dfrac{\sqrt{y}}{\sqrt{5}}$

15. Answer: (C)
    $x = \dfrac{14}{2.2064} = 6.345$

16. Answer: (A)
    $\dfrac{2}{x-3} + \dfrac{1}{x+3} = \dfrac{2x+6+x-3}{(x+3)(x-3)} = \dfrac{3x+3}{x^2-9}$
    $\dfrac{3x+3}{x^2-9} = \dfrac{6}{x^2-9}$
    $6 = 3x + 3 \rightarrow x = 1$

17. Answer: (D)
    The number of bacteria counts is ten times more than
    the day before:
    $f(t) = 5 \times 10^t$; t is the number of days.
    It is an exponential growth model.

18. Answer: (C)
    Based on the graph, the two consecutive months that
    the average price of one metric ton of oranges decreases
    the most is between June to July.

19. Answer: (B)
    $\dfrac{768+808+844+835+835+768+782}{7} = 805.7$

20. Answer: (C)
    $x(1 - 0.0236) = 768$
    $x = 786.56$

21. Answer: (A)
    If there were x dollars in the account originally, then
    the total dollars now is:
    $l = x - m + n$
    $x = l + m - n$

22. Answer: (A)
    Plug in the two different values of t and find their
    difference.
    $p(6) – p(4) = 27,000 – 9,000 = 18,000$

23. Answer: (C)
    Find the ratio of the total area to the area of A.
    If the total area is 1, the small square area in the middle
    will be $\dfrac{1}{4}$.
    $Area\ of\ A = \dfrac{1-\frac{1}{4}}{4} = \dfrac{3}{16}$
    $Probability = \dfrac{3}{16}$

24. Answer: (B)
    The number 2 appears twice, the number 4 appears
    four times, and so on. The number of terms up to
    integer 8 appears $2 + 4 + 6 + 8 = 20$ times. The
    number 10 first appears in the sequence right after the
    last 8. $20 + 1 = 21$

25. Answer: (D)
    Since CB = CA, $\triangle ABC$ is an isosceles right triangle.
    $Area\ of\ \triangle ABC = \dfrac{1}{2} \times AC^2 = 8$
    $AC = 4$
    Since OB is a radius of the circle and it is equal to AC,
    the radius of the circle has length 4.
    $Area\ of\ Circle = \pi \times 4^2 = 16\pi$

26. Answer: (C)
    Just plug in any value of x:
    When $x = 0$, $4a - 6 = 2 \rightarrow a = 2$

27. Answer: (B)
    $1 + (t - 3) \times 0.1 = 0.15t \quad \rightarrow \quad t = 14$

28. Answer: (C)
    $12\sqrt{12} = 12 \times 2\sqrt{3} = 24\sqrt{3}$
    $x = 24$ and $y = 3$
    $xy = 24 \times 3 = 72$

29. *Answer: (C)*
$7m^2 = m^x \times m^2 = m^{(x+2)}$

30. *Answer: (D)*
The equation should also have a root at $3 + \sqrt{2}$, because all of the answer choices have rational coefficients. Therefore, the polynomial is $x[x - (3 - \sqrt{2})][x - (3 + \sqrt{2})] = x\left[(x-3)^2 - (\sqrt{2})^2\right] = (x^2 - 6x + 7) = x^3 - 6x^2 + 7x = 0$

31. *Answer: 0, 1, 4, or 5*
$2x + 3 = 5 \rightarrow x = 1$
or
$2x + 3 = -5 \rightarrow x = -4$
$3y - 3 = 6 \rightarrow y = 3$
or
$3y - 3 = -6 \rightarrow y = -1$
$|x + y| = 0, 1, 4, 5$

32. *Answer: 86.5*
To find the average score for the remaining students, we need to find the total score of all the remaining students and divide that by the number of remaining students.
There are 24 – 8 = 16 remaining students who did not get a perfect score. The sum of all scores is 24× 91 (which includes the test scores for the 8 that got a perfect score).
$24 \times 91 - 8 \times 100 = 1384$
Average: $\frac{1384}{24 - 8} = 86.5$

33. *Answer: 22*
If these two data sets have the same mean,
$$\frac{30+15+42+32+55+22+40}{7} = \frac{46+31+20+32+46+x+39}{7}$$
$x = 22$

34. *Answer: 37.7*

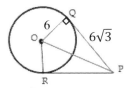

In the right triangle ΔOPQ, the ratio of $\frac{QP}{QO} = \sqrt{3}$; therefore, $\angle QOP = 60^\circ$ and $\angle QOR = 120^\circ$
The area of the minor sector $\widehat{RQ} = \frac{120}{360} \times \pi \times 6^2 = 12\pi = 37.7$

35. *Answer: 56.6 or 56.7*

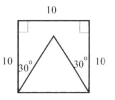

The triangle above has 60º - 60º - 60º interior angles, which makes it an equilateral triangle with side length 10. To find the area, find the area of the square and subtract the area of the triangle.
$10 \times 10 - \frac{\sqrt{3}}{4} \times 10 \times 10 = 56.7$

36. *Answer: 5*
ΔOAB is a right triangle with hypotenuse $\overline{OA}$, so use the Pythagorean Theorem.
$OB = OC = 3$
$AC = x \quad AB = 2x \quad AO = 3 + x$
$(2x)^2 + 3^2 = (3 + x)^2$
$4x^2 + 9 = x^2 + 6x + 9 \quad 3x^2 = 6x \rightarrow x = 2 \quad so\ AO = 5$

37. *Answer:* $\frac{1}{70}$
Use proportion to solve.
$\frac{10\%}{42} = \frac{x}{6}$
$x = \frac{10}{7}\% = \frac{1}{70}\ (fraction)$

38. *Answer: 20*
Use proportion to solve.
$\frac{15\%}{12} = \frac{25\%}{x} \rightarrow x = 20\ kWh$

SAT Math Practice Test No. 9

Directions:
For questions 1-15, solve each problem, choose the best answer from the choices provided, and fill in the corresponding circle on your answer sheet. **For questions 16-20**, solve the problem and enter your answer in the grid on the answer sheet. Please refer to the directions before question 16 on how to enter your answers in the grid. You may use any available space in your test booklet for scratch work.

Notes:
1. **No calculator** is allowed for this section. All numbers used are real numbers.
2. Figures that accompany problems in this test are intended to provide information useful in solving the problems. They are drawn as accurately as possible EXCEPT when it is stated in a specific problem that the figure is not drawn to scale. All figures lie in a plane unless otherwise indicated.
3. Unless otherwise specified, the domain of any function $f(x)$ assumed to be the set of all real numbers x for which $f(x)$ is a real number.

References:

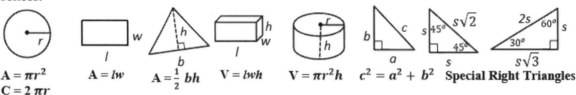

$A = \pi r^2$ $A = lw$ $A = \frac{1}{2}bh$ $V = lwh$ $V = \pi r^2 h$ $c^2 = a^2 + b^2$ **Special Right Triangles**
$C = 2\pi r$

The number of degrees of arc in a circle is 360; the number of radians of arc in a circle is 2π.
The sum of the degree measures of the angles in a triangle is 180.

---

1. If $x^{\frac{1}{4}} = \sqrt{3}$, then what is the value of x?
    a) 1
    b) 3
    c) 9
    d) 27

2. Bob needs two 60″ pieces of duct tape to protect each window in his house during hurricane season. There are 12 windows in the house. Bob had an m-foot roll of duct tape when he started. If no tape was wasted, which of the following represents the number of feet of duct tape left after he finished taping all of his windows?
    a) $m - 240$
    b) $m - 120$
    c) $m - 60$
    d) $m - 20$

3. If 3 times a number is the same as the number itself. What is the number?

    a) $\frac{1}{2}$
    b) 0
    c) 1
    d) 2

4. A, B, and C are three points on a line in that order. If $\overline{AB} = 25$ and $\overline{BC}$ is 10 less than $\overline{AB}$, what is the length of $\overline{AC}$?
    a) 40
    b) 38
    c) 35
    d) 32

5. Which of the following is equivalent to $(2x + 4)^2 - 4x^2$?
    a) $16(x + 1)$

b) $12(x + 1)$

c) $8(2x + 1)$

d) $4(4x + 1)$

6. If $| x | < 1$, which of the following is the greatest?

    a) 2

    b) $1 - x$

    c) $1 + x$

    d) $2x$

7. The value of $5n - 7$ is how much greater than the value of $5n - 8$?

    a) 15

    b) 1

    c) $10n + 1$

    d) $5n - 1$

8. It takes between 6 and 8 minutes for Joe to run one mile up to the hill during a marathon. The amount of time it takes for him to run a mile down the hill is 2 to 3 minutes shorter than the time it takes him to run up the hill. What is the range of possible times it would take Joe to run one mile down the hill?

    a) 4 and 5 minutes

    b) 3 and 6 minutes

    c) 5 and 7 minutes

    d) 6 and 8 minutes

9. There are 12 more men than women enrolled in a cooking class. If there are M men enrolled, then, in terms of M, what percent of those enrolled are men?

    a) $\frac{100M}{M+12}\%$

    b) $\frac{100M}{M-12}\%$

    c) $\frac{100M}{2M+12}\%$

    d) $\frac{100M}{2M-12}\%$

10. In a toy factory production line, every 10th toy has their electronic parts checked and every 5th toy will have their safety features checked. In the first 150 toys, what is the probability that a toy will have both its electronic parts and safety features checked?

    a) $\frac{1}{10}$

    b) $\frac{1}{5}$

    c) $\frac{1}{3}$

    d) $\frac{1}{2}$

11. At what value(s) of x does the function $f(x) = x^2 - 9$ cross the x-axis?

    a) 0 only

    b) 3 only

    c) –3 only

    d) –3 and 3

12. What is the intersection of X and Y if X is the set of positive multiples of 3 and Y is the set of positive multiples of 4?

    a) the set of all positive integers

    b) the set of all positive real numbers

    c) the set of positive multiples of 12

    d) the set of positive multiples of 4

$$x = 2y - 5$$
$$y = -2x + 5$$

13. The ordered pair (x, y) satisfies the system of equations above. What is the value of $x + y$?

    a) $-\frac{2}{5}$

    b) 0

    c) 3

    d) 4

$$P = 205(1.005)^{\left(\frac{t}{5}\right)}$$

14. The equation above can be used to model the population, in thousands, of a certain city t years after 2000. According to the model, the population is predicted to

increase by 0.5% every n year(s). What is the value of n?

   a) 3
   b) 5
   c) 10
   d) 205

b) 2
c) 4
d) 8

15. If x and y are positive integers and $5^2x + 5^2y = 100$, what is the value of $x + y$?

   a) 1

Directions:
For questions 16-20, solve the problem and enter your answer in the grid, as described below, on the answer sheet.

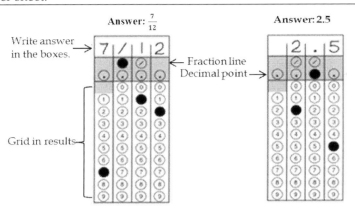

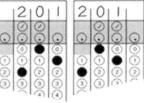

Answer: 201
Either position is correct.

Note: You may start your answers in any column, space permitting. Columns not needed should be left blank.

- Mark no more than one circle in any column.
- Because the answer sheet will be machine-scored. **You will receive credit only if the circles are filled in correctly.**
- Although not required, it is suggested that you write your answer in the boxes at the top of the columns to help you fill in the circles accurately.
- Some problems may have more than one correct answer. In such case, grid only one answer.
- No question has a negative answer.
- **Mixed numbers** such as $3\frac{1}{2}$ must be

gridded as 3.5 or $\frac{7}{2}$. (If ⬛ is gridded, it will be interpreted as $\frac{31}{2}$, not $3\frac{1}{2}$.)

- **Decimal Answer:** If you obtain a decimal answer with more digits than the grid can accommodate, it may be either rounded or truncated, but it must fill the entire grid. The acceptable ways to grid $\frac{2}{3}$ are:

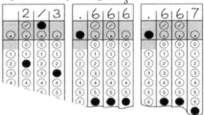

16. The ratio of action movies to dramas in Albert's DVD collection is 4 to 3. If the total number of DVDs in the collection is greater than 20 but less than 30, what could be a possible number of DVDs in his collection?

17. Bella sells only rings and necklaces on her website. Rings sell for $50 each, and necklaces sell for $30 each. If Bella sold 25 pieces of jewelry and her sales totaled $1,050, how many necklaces did Bella sell?

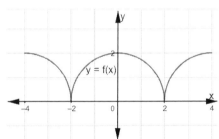

18. The figure above shows the complete graph of the function f in the xy-plane. The function g (not shown) is defined by $g(x) = f(x) + 6$. What is the maximum value of the function ?

19. In the figure below, two circles with centers A and B are tangent to each other and both tangent to the x-axis in the xy-coordinate system. If circle A has a radius of 1 and circle B has a radius of 4, what is the slope of the segment that connects both centers?

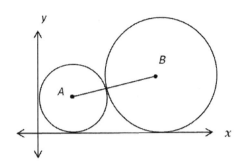

Note: Figure not drawn to scale.

$$(5 - 4i)(1 + 3i) = a + bi$$

20. In the equation above, a and b are real numbers and $i = \sqrt{-1}$. What is the value of a ?

SECTION 4

Math Test — Calculator   55 MINUTES, 38 QUESTIONS

Directions:
For questions 1-30, solve each problem, choose the best answer from the choices provided, and fill in the corresponding circle on your answer sheet. For questions 31-38, solve the problem and enter your answer in the grid on the answer sheet. Please refer to the directions before question 31 on how to enter your answers in the grid. You may use any available space in your test booklet for scratch work.

Notes:
1. Acceptable calculators are allowed for this section. All numbers used are real numbers.
2. Figures that accompany problems in this test are intended to provide information useful in solving the problems. They are drawn as accurately as possible EXCEPT when it is stated in a specific problem that the figure is not drawn to scale. All figures lie in a plane unless otherwise indicated.
3. Unless otherwise specified, the domain of any function $f(x)$ assumed to be the set of all real numbers x for which $f(x)$ is a real number.

References:

  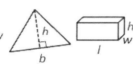   

$A = \pi r^2$ $A = lw$ $A = \frac{1}{2} bh$ $V = lwh$ $V = \pi r^2 h$ $c^2 = a^2 + b^2$ **Special Right Triangles**
$C = 2\pi r$

The number of degrees of arc in a circle is 360; the number of radians of arc in a circle is 2π.
The sum of the degree measures of the angles in a triangle is 180.

---

1. If $6 \cdot 2k = 72$, what is the value of $4k - 5$?
   a) 19
   b) 16
   c) 12
   d) 8

2. If 10 percent of 40 percent of a positive number is equal to 20 percent of y percent of the same positive number, find the value of y.
   a) 10
   b) 15
   c) 20
   d) 35

3. Number of Flight Arrivals at Kennedy
   Airport in a Month

	On time	Delayed	Total
Airline A	2,029	861	2,890
Airline B	1,150	700	1,850
Airline C	3,179	1,561	4,740

   Based on the table above, what fraction of the flights for Airline A were delayed?
   a) $\frac{861}{1561}$

   b) $\frac{861}{2029}$

   c) $\frac{861}{2890}$

   d) $\frac{2029}{2890}$

4. In the figure below, $\overline{EB} = 3$, $\overline{DC} = 5$, and $\overline{BC} = 4$. What is the value of AB?

   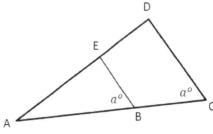

   a) 4
   b) 5
   c) 6
   d) 8

   $$x(x^2 + 2) + (2x^2 - 2x)$$

5. Which of the following expressions is equivalent to the expression above?
   a) $4x^2$
   b) $x^3 + 2x^2$
   c) $x^3 + x^2$
   d) $x^3 + 2x^2 - 4x$

6. There are 15 boxes of apples in the storage room. Each box has at least 21 apples, and at most 28 apples. Which of the following could be the total number of apples in the storage room?
   a) 200
   b) 250
   c) 300
   d) 350

Questions 7 − 8 refer to the following information:

Jenny has a summer job at an ice cream shop. She needs to order a few boxes of small cups and a few boxes of large cups. The storage room can hold up to 20 boxes. Each box of small cups costs $25 and each box of large cups costs $40. A maximum of $600 is budgeted for cups.

7. If x represents the number of boxes of small cups and y represents the number of boxes of large cups that Jenny can order, which of the following systems of equations represents the number of each she could order?

   a) $\begin{cases} x \geq 0 \\ y \geq 0 \\ x + y \leq 20 \\ 25x + 40y \leq 600 \end{cases}$

   b) $\begin{cases} x \geq 0 \\ y \geq 0 \\ x + y < 20 \\ 25x + 40y < 600 \end{cases}$

   c) $\begin{cases} x \geq 0 \\ y \geq 0 \\ x + y > 20 \\ 25x + 40y > 600 \end{cases}$

   d) $\begin{cases} x \geq 0 \\ y \geq 0 \\ x + y \geq 20 \\ 25x + 40y \leq 600 \end{cases}$

8. Which of the following graphs represents the number of boxes of each type of cup she could order?

   a)
   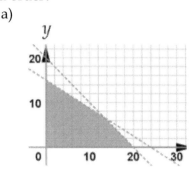

   b)
   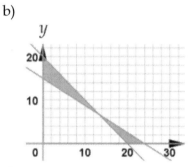

   c)
   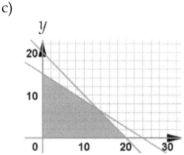

   d)
   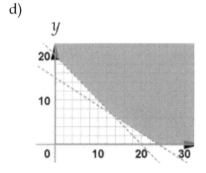

9. The sum of two different numbers x and y is 70, and the difference when the smaller number is subtracted from the larger number is 30. What is the value of xy?
   a) 100
   b) 210
   c) 1,000
   d) 2,100

10. If the sum of 7 numbers is between 41 and 43, then the average (arithmetic mean) of the 7 numbers could be which of the following?
    a) 5
    b) $5\frac{1}{2}$
    c) 6
    d) $6\frac{1}{2}$

11. What is the remainder when $2x^4 - 3x^3 + 4x^2 - 5x + 6$ is divided by $x - 3$?
    a) 108
    b) 96
    c) 87
    d) 75

12. Biologists found a new species of pale shrimp at the world's deepest undersea vent, the Beebe Vent Field. The vent is 3.1 miles below the sea's surface. Approximately how many kilometers below the sea's surface is the vent? (1 kilometer ≈ 0.6214 miles)
    a) 2
    b) 3
    c) 4
    d) 5

13. Sam drove from home at an average speed of 50 miles per hour to her working place and then returned along the same route at an average speed of 40 miles per hour. If the entire trip took her 2.25 hours, what is the entire distance, in miles, for the round trip?
    a) 90
    b) 100
    c) 120

d) 125

14. If 60 percent of 30 percent of a number is 36.54, what is the number?
    a) 104
    b) 153
    c) 203
    d) 406

15. Which of the following scatterplots is the best representation of a function, $f(x) = mx + b$, where m is a negative number and b is a positive number?
    a)

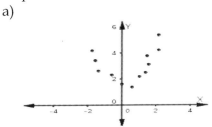

    b)

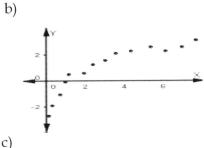

    c)

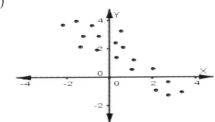

    d)

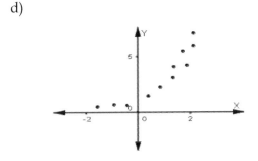

16. The figure above shows an indoor parking lot with the rectangular arrows indicating the different entrances and exits. What is the total number of distinct ways that a driver can enter and exit the parking lot?
    a) 9
    b) 5
    c) 4
    d) 20

17. If the area of an equilateral triangle equals the area of a square multiplied by $\sqrt{3}$, what is the ratio of the length of a side of the triangle to the length of a side of the square?
    a) 2 : 1
    b) 2 : 3
    c) 1 : 2
    d) 4 : 3

18. The first term of a sequence of numbers is −1. If each term after is the product of −3 and the preceding term, what is the 5th term of the sequence?
    a) 27
    b) −27
    c) −81
    d) 81

19. For all numbers m and n, let $m!!n$ be defined by $m!!n = m^2 - n^2$. If p and q are different positive integers, which of the following can be negative?
    I. $p!!q$
    II. $(p + q) !!p$
    III. $p!! (p + q)$
    a) II only
    b) III only
    c) I and III only
    d) I, II, III

20. If Planet X is 20,000 billion meters away from the Sun, what is its orbital period, in

Earth years? (Round your answer to the nearest whole number.)
    a) 1224
    b) 1360
    c) 1546
    d) 2016

21. A pump can be set to extract water from a pool at one of three different rates: 1 gallon per minute, 4 gallons per minute, or 8 gallons per minute. The graph below shows the amount of water left in the pool from the time the pump was turned on. How many minutes after being turned on was the pump switched to a rate of 8 gallons per minute?

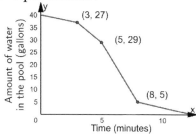

    a) 3
    b) 5
    c) 8
    d) 29

22. The budget for a school band was $5,000 in 2013. The budget decreased by 10% from 2013 to 2014 and then increased by 20% from 2014 to 2015. Which of the following expressions represents the budget, in dollars, for the school band in 2015?
    a) (1.1)(1.2)(5,000)
    b) (0.9)(0.8)(5,000)
    c) (1.1)(0.8)(5,000)
    d) (0.9)(1.2)(5,000)

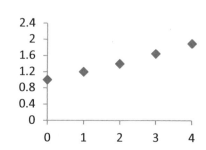

23. Which of the lines described by the following equations best fits those points above?
    a) $y = 0.2x - 1$
    b) $y = 0.2x + 1$
    c) $y = -0.2x - 1$
    d) $y = -0.2x + 1$

2012 Graduates' Plans
Total Number of Graduates:400

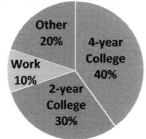

24. In 2012, how many graduates from Paterson High School chose to go to 2 or 4 years of college to continue their education?
    a) 250
    b) 260
    c) 270
    d) 280

25. The perimeter of square X is 5 times the perimeter of square Y. If the area of square Y is 36, then what is the length of the side of square X?
    a) 18
    b) 24
    c) 28
    d) 30

Treatments	Number of Plants		
	Regressed	Thrived	Total
A	60	150	210
B	160	50	210

26. The table above shows the results of an experiment involving the effect of two treatments, A and B, on plants. Based on the results, what fraction of the plants that thrived received treatment A?

a) $\frac{2}{3}$
b) $\frac{1}{2}$
c) $\frac{3}{4}$
d) $\frac{2}{5}$

27. Among the 12 colleges Helen applied to, 3 are her top schools. How many admissions would Helen have to receive to guarantee that she can get into at least one of her top schools?
    a) 8
    b) 9
    c) 10
    d) 11

28. If $f\left(\frac{3x}{x-4}\right) = x^2 + x + 1$, what is the value of $f(5)$?
    a) 18
    b) 55
    c) 100
    d) 111

Questions 29 – 30 refer to the following information:
    The function $f(x) = 2x^4 - 13x^3 + 28x^2 - 23x + 6$ is graphed in the xy-plane below.

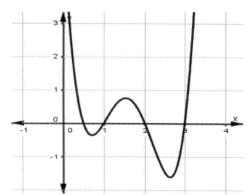

a) 1
b) 2
c) 3
d) 4

29. If c is a constant such that the equation
    $f(x) = c$ has four real solutions, which of
    the following could be the value of c?
        a) 2
        b) 1
        c) 0
        d) −1

30. How many real solutions are there
    if $f(x) = x$?

Directions:

For questions 31-38, solve the problem and enter your answer in the grid, as described below, on the answer sheet.

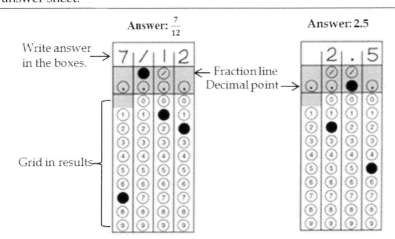

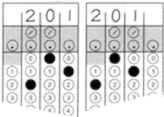

- Mark no more than one circle in any column.
- Because the answer sheet will be machine-scored. **You will receive credit only if the circles are filled in correctly.**
- Although not required, it is suggested that you write your answer in the boxes at the top of the columns to help you fill in the circles accurately.
- Some problems may have more than one correct answer. In such case, grid only one answer.
- No question has a negative answer.
- **Mixed numbers** such as $3\frac{1}{2}$ must be

Note: You may start your answers in any column, space permitting. Columns not needed should be left blank.

gridded as 3.5 or $\frac{7}{2}$. (If [3 1 / 2] is gridded, it will be interpreted as $\frac{31}{2}$, not $3\frac{1}{2}$.)

- **Decimal Answer:** If you obtain a decimal answer with more digits than the grid can accommodate, it may be either rounded or truncated, but it must fill the entire grid. The acceptable ways to grid $\frac{2}{3}$ are:

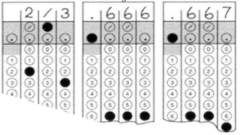

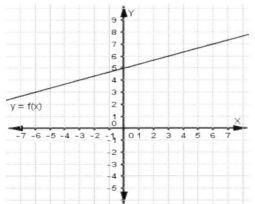

31. The graph of the linear function f is shown in the xy-coordinate plane above. If the slope of the graph g is 6 times the slope of the graph of f, and the graph of g passes through the point $(0, -3)$, what is the value of $g(10)$?

$$p(x) = \frac{17}{200} x^2 - 8x - c$$

32. The function above calculates the profit P, in dollars, from growing and selling x units of corn. c is a constant. If 200 units were sold for a total profit of $1,400, what is the value of c?

33. If $sin(\frac{\pi}{2} - x) = 0.55$, what is $cos\, x$?

Questions 37 and 38 refer to the following information:

Median Ages of Populations of Selected Nine Countries, 2018

Country	Median Age of Population (years)
Brazil	29.6
China	35.9
Germany	45.7
India	26.5
Indonesia	28.5
Nigeria	18.0
Philippines	23.1
Russia	38.8
United States	37.1

$$\frac{1}{2}x = a$$
$$x + y = 5a$$

34. In the system of equations above, a is a constant such that $0 < a < \frac{1}{3}$. If (x, y) is a solution to the system of equations, what is one possible value of y ?

35. What is the area of the figure below?

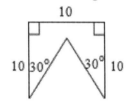

37. What is the range, in years, of the median ages of the populations for the countries in the table above?

38. What is the median of those nine countries' median age of population in the table?

$$(1 - i)(3 + i) = a + bi$$

36. In the equation above, a and b are two real numbers. What is the value of $a + b$?

SAT MATH PRACTICE TEST No. 9 ANSWER KEYS

Section 3

1. (C)	2. (B)	3. (B)	4. (A)	5. (A)	6. (A)	7. (B)	8. (B)	9. (D)	10. $\frac{1}{10}$
11. (D)	12. (C)	13. (D)	14. (B)	15. (C)	16. 21, 28	17. 10	18. 8	19. $\frac{3}{4}$ or .75	20. 17

Section 4

1. (A)	2. (C)	3. (C)	4. (C)	5. (B)	6. (D)	7. (A)	8. (C)	9. (C)	10. (C)
11. (A)	12. (D)	13. (B)	14. (C)	15. (D)	16. (D)	17. (A)	18. (C)	19. (C)	20. (C)
21. (B)	22. (D)	23. (B)	24. (D)	25. (D)	26. (C)	27. (C)	28. (D)	29. (C)	30. (B)
31. 17	32. 400	33. 0.55	34. $0 < y < 1$	35. 56.6 or 56.7	36. 2	37. 27.7	38. 29.6		

Section 3

1. Answer: (C)
    $(x^{\frac{1}{4}})^4 = x$
    $(\sqrt{3})^4 = 9$

2. Answer: (B)
    Every window needs 2 pieces of tape and each piece of tape is 60 inches long, so $60 \times 2 = 120$ inches needed for each window.
    Twelve windows, in total, would need 12×120 inches of tape.
    12×120 inches $= 120$ feet
    $(m - 120)$ feet left after the use.

3. Answer: (B)
    Let the number be a.
    $3a = a$
    $3a - a = 0 \rightarrow a = 0$

4. Answer: (A)
    $BC = 25 - 10 = 15$
    $AC = AB + BC = 25 + 15 = 40$
    Given that the points A, B, C are in order.

5. Answer: (A)
    $(2x + 4)^2 - 4x^2$
    $= 4x^2 + 16x + 16 - 4x^2$
    $= 16x + 16$
    $= 16(x + 1)$

6. Answer: (A)
    $|x| < 1 \rightarrow -1 < x < 1 \rightarrow$
    $-1 < -x < 1$; therefore,
    b). $0 < 1 - x < 2$
    c). $0 < 1 + x < 2$
    d). $-2 < 2x < 2$
    So among those answer choices the number 2 is the greatest value.
    Shortcuts: Plug $x = 0.5$ into each answer choice and compare the results. This method works better when you try different values to verify your answer.

7. Answer: (B)
    Find the difference between the two expressions.
    $(5n - 7) - (5n - 8) = 1$

8. Answer: (B)
    Running down the hill saves 2 to 3 minutes. Therefore, the minimum amount of time would be $6 - 3 = 3$ minutes and the maximum amount of time would be $8 - 2 = 6$ minutes.

9. Answer: (D)
    There are $(M - 12)$ women in the class.
    Percent of Men in Class $= (\frac{M}{Total}) \times 100\%$
    $= \frac{100M}{M + M - 12}\% = \frac{100M}{2M - 12}\%$

10. Answer: $\frac{1}{10}$
    The LCM of 10 and 5 is 10.
    The every 10th toy will have both of their electronic parts and safety features checked.
    There are 15 such toys (150 divided by 10).
    $\frac{15}{150} = \frac{1}{10}$

11. *Answer: (D)*
    "f(x) crosses the x-axis" means f(x) = 0.
    $x^2 - 9 = 0, \quad x = \pm 3$

12. *Answer: (C)*
    The common multiples of 3 and 4 will be the multiples of 12.

13. *Answer: (D)*
    Solve the system of equations.
    $x = 2y - 5 - -(1)$
    $y = -2x + 5 - -(2)$
    $(1) + 2 \times (2) \rightarrow x + 2y = (2y - 5) + 2(-2x + 5)$
    $x + 2y = 2y - 4x + 5$
    $5x = 5 \rightarrow x = 1$
    Then $y = 3 \rightarrow x + y = 4$

14. *Answer: (B)*
    An exponential model:
    $P = P_0 (1 + r)^k$
    Where P_0 is the initial value, r is the fraction of the increase and k is the number of period.

    $P = 205(1.005)^{\left(\frac{t}{5}\right)} = 205 \left(1 + \frac{0.5}{100}\right)^{\frac{t}{5}}$
    The population is predicted to increase by 0.5% every 5 years.

15. *Answer: (C)*
    $5^2 x + 5^2 y = 25(x + y) = 100$
    $x + y = 4$

16. *Answer: 21, 28*
    The total number should be a multiple of (4 + 3).
    The numbers between 20 and 30 and a multiple of 7 are 21, and 28.

17. *Answer: 10*
    Number of necklaces sold = x
    Number of ring sold = y
    $x + y = 25$
    $30x + 50y = 1050$
    Solve the system of the equations above: x = 10 and y = 15

18. *Answer: 8*
    The maximum value of f(x) is 2; therefore, the maximum value of g(x) is:
    $g(x) = f(x) + 6 = 2 + 6 = 8$

19. *Answer:* $\frac{3}{4}$ *or* .75

    $Slope = \frac{Rise}{Run}$
    Rise = Difference of Radii = 4−1= 3
    AB = 4 + 1 = 5
    The triangle is a right triangle, so we use the Pythagorean Theorem to solve for the run.
    $Run^2 + Rise^2 = 5^2$
    $Run = \sqrt{5^2 - 3^2} = 4$ *and Slope* $= \frac{3}{4}$

20. *Answer: 17*
    $(5 - 4i)(1 + 3i) = 5 + 15i - 4i - 12i^2$
    $17 + 11i = a + bi$
    $a = 17$

Section 4

1. *Answer: (A)*
   $6 \cdot 2k = 72 \rightarrow k = 6$
   $4k - 5 = 4 \times 6 - 5 = 19$

2. *Answer: (C)*
   $\frac{10}{100} \times \frac{40}{100} \times A = \frac{20}{100} \times \frac{y}{100} \times A$
   $\frac{10 \times 40}{100 \times 100} = \frac{20y}{100 \times 100}$
   Therefore, $10 \times 40 = 20y$
   $y = 20.$

3. *Answer: (C)*
   $\frac{Delay\ of\ Airline\ A}{Total\ of\ Airline\ A} = \frac{861}{2890}$

4. *Answer: (C)*
   Since ∠B and ∠C have the same angle degree, $\overline{EB}$ ∥ $\overline{DC}$. Thus, ΔABE is similar to ΔACD.
   $\frac{AB}{AC} = \frac{EB}{DC} = \frac{AB}{AB+BC} = \frac{3}{5}$
   $\frac{AB}{AB+4} = \frac{3}{5}$
   $AB = 6$

5. *Answer: (B)*
   $x(x^2 + 2) + (2x^2 - 2x) = x^3 + 2x + 2x^2 - 2x = x^3 + 2x^2$

6. *Answer: (D)*
    Set up the inequality for the number of apples and then multiply the inequality by 15.
    $(21 < x < 28) \times 15$
    $315 < 15x < 420$

7. *Answer: (A)*
    The number of boxes must be greater or equal than zero.
    The storage room can hold up to 20 boxes and the maximum of $600 can be spent; therefore, the answer is a).
    $$\begin{cases} x \geq 0 \\ y \geq 0 \\ x + y \leq 20 \\ 25x + 40y \leq 600 \end{cases}$$

8. *Answer: (C)*
    Only answer c) depicts the correct system of equations of the previous question.
    $$\begin{cases} x \geq 0 \\ y \geq 0 \\ x + y \leq 20 \\ 25x + 40y \leq 600 \end{cases}$$

9. *Answer: (C)*
    $x + y = 70$
    $x - y = 30$
    $x = 50 \ and \ y = 20 \rightarrow xy = 1,000$

10. *Answer: (C)*
    $Average = \frac{Sum}{7}$
    $\frac{41}{7} < Average < \frac{43}{7}$
    $5.85 < Average < 6.1$

11. *Answer: (A)*
    The remainder theorem states that if polynomial $P(x)$ is divided by $x - r$, its remainder is $P(r)$.
    $P(3) = 2 \times 3^4 - 3 \times 3^3 + 4 \times 3^2 - 5(3) + 6 = 108$

12. *Answer: (D)*
    $\frac{1 \ km}{0.6214 \ miles} = \frac{x \ km}{3.1}$
    $x = 5$

13. *Answer: (B)*
    Let one trip have x miles.
    $Time = 2.25 = t_1 + t_2 = \frac{x}{50} + \frac{x}{40}$
    $2.25 = x(\frac{1}{50} + \frac{1}{40})$
    $x = 50$
    $Total \ Distance = 2 \times 50 = 100$

14. *Answer: (C)*
    This can be translated into $0.6 \times 0.3 \times A = 36.54$.
    $A = \frac{36.54}{0.6 \times 0.3} = 203$

15. *Answer: (D)*

    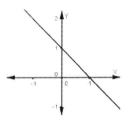

    The graph of $f(x) = -x + 1$:
    So, answer is (d).

16. *Answer: (D)*
    Because cars entering the parking lot will also exit, so use the Multiplication Principle.
    Total number of ways: $5 \times 4 = 20$

17. *Answer: (A)*
    Let the length of the side of the triangle be x and the length of the side of the square be y.
    Area of an equilateral triangle $= \frac{\sqrt{3}}{4} x^2$
    Area of a square $= y^2$
    $\frac{\sqrt{3}}{4} x^2 = \sqrt{3} \ y^2$
    $x^2 = 4 \ y^2$
    $x : y = 2 : 1$

18. *Answer: (C)*
    $-1, 3, -9, 27, -81$

19. *Answer: (C)*
    $p!!q = p^2 - q^2$
    When $p < q$, $p!!q < 0$
    $(p + q) !! p = (p + q)^2 - p^2 > 0$
    $p!! (p + q) = p^2 - (p + q)^2 < 0$
    Only (I) and (III) can be negative.

20. *Answer: (C)*
    $\frac{(Orbital \ Period)^2}{20000^3} = \frac{1^2}{149.6^3}$
    $Orbital \ Period = 1546 \ Earth \ years$

21. *Answer: (B)*
    The slope of the line between two points,
    $(5, 29) \ and \ (8, 5)$ is $\frac{29-5}{5-8} = -8$.
    The rate of the pump is 8 gallons from the 5th minute.
    The answer is b).

22. *Answer: (D)*
    $5000 \times (1 - 10\%)(1 + 20\%) = 5000 \times 90\% \times 120\% = 5000 \times 0.9 \times 1.2$

23. *Answer: (B)*
$Slope = \frac{Rise}{Run} = 0.2$
y-intercept = 1
$y = 0.2x + 1$

24. *Answer: (D)*
30% + 40% = 70% of the total number of graduates go to 2 or 4 years of college.
0.7 × 400 = 280 students

25. *Answer: (D)*
Area of a Square = Side²
Side of X : Side of Y = 5 : 1
Area of X : Area of Y = 25 : 1
Area of X = 25 × 36 = 900
$Side of X = \sqrt{900} = 30$

26. *Answer: (C)*
Total that thrived:
150 + 50 = 200
Thrived from A: 150
$Fraction = \frac{150}{200} = \frac{3}{4}$

27. *Answer: (C)*
12 − 3 = 9
She applied to 9 schools that are not her top choices. If all 9 of these schools accept Helen, then the 10th school which accepts her must be one of her top schools.
9 + 1 = 10

28. *Answer: (D)*
$\frac{3x}{x-4} = 5 \rightarrow x = 10$
$f\left(\frac{3x}{x-4}\right) = f(5) = x^2 + x + 1$
$= 100 + 10 + 1$
$= 111$

29. *Answer: (C)*

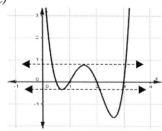

According to the graph above, there will be four intersection points when the value of c is roughly between −0.3 and 0.7.

30. *Answer: (B)*

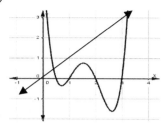

According to the graph above, there are two intersection points between the lines $f(x) = x$ and $f(x) = 2x^4 − 13x^3 + 28x^2 − 23x + 6$.

31. *Answer: 17*
The graph of f passes through the points (0, 5) and (3, 6)
$Slope of f = \frac{6-5}{3-0} = \frac{1}{3}$
$y - 5 = \frac{1}{3}x$
$y = f(x) = \frac{1}{3}x + 5$
$g(x) = \frac{6}{3}x - 3 = 2x - 3$
$g(10) = 20 - 3 = 17$

32. *Answer: 400*
Plug in the values of x and y to solve for c.
$1400 = \frac{17}{200} \times 200^2 - 8 \times 200 - c$
$c = 400$

33. *Answer: 0.55*
Cofuntion: The value of a trigonometric function of an angle is equal to the value of the cofunction of the complement of that angle.
$sin(\theta) = cos(90° - \theta)$
$cos(\theta) = sin(90° - \theta)$

34. *Answer: $0 < y < 1$*
Solve the system of equations:
$x = 2a$
$y = 3a$
$0 < a < \frac{1}{3} \rightarrow 0 < 3a < 1$
$0 < y < 1$

35. *Answer: 56.6 or 56.7*

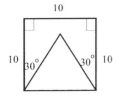

The triangle above has 60⁰ - 60⁰ - 60⁰ interior angles, which makes it an equilateral triangle with side length 10. To find the area, find the area of the square and subtract the area of the triangle.

$$10 \times 10 - \frac{\sqrt{3}}{4} \times 10 \times 10 = 56.7$$

36. *Answer: 2*
$$(1 - i)(3 + i) = 4 - 2i = a + bi$$
$$a = 4 \text{ and } b = -2$$
$$a + b = 2$$

37. *Answer: 27.7*
$$Range = Max - Min$$
$$= 45.7 - 18.0 = 27.7$$

38. *Answer:29.6*
The median should be in the middle when data is sorted:
Sorted data: 18.0, 23.1, 26.5, 28.5, 29.6, 35.9, 37.1, 38.8, 45.7
Median: 29.6

SAT Math Practice Test No. 10

SECTION 3

Math Test — NO Calculator   25 MINUTES, 20 QUESTIONS

Directions:

For questions 1-15, solve each problem, choose the best answer from the choices provided, and fill in the corresponding circle on your answer sheet. **For questions 16-20,** solve the problem and enter your answer in the grid on the answer sheet. Please refer to the directions before question 16 on how to enter your answers in the grid. You may use any available space in your test booklet for scratch work.

Notes:

1. **No calculator** is allowed for this section. All numbers used are real numbers.
2. Figures that accompany problems in this test are intended to provide information useful in solving the problems. They are drawn as accurately as possible EXCEPT when it is stated in a specific problem that the figure is not drawn to scale. All figures lie in a plane unless otherwise indicated.
3. Unless otherwise specified, the domain of any function $f(x)$ assumed to be the set of all real numbers x for which $f(x)$ is a real number.

References:

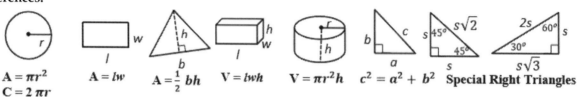

$A = \pi r^2$ $A = lw$ $A = \frac{1}{2}bh$ $V = lwh$ $V = \pi r^2 h$ $c^2 = a^2 + b^2$ **Special Right Triangles**
$C = 2\pi r$

The number of degrees of arc in a circle is 360; the number of radians of arc in a circle is 2π.
The sum of the degree measures of the angles in a triangle is 180.

---

1. If $x \times y = x$ for all values of x, what is the value of y?
   a) $-x$
   b) -1
   c) 0
   d) 1

2. If $(x + y)^2 = 49$ and $(x - y)^2 = 29$, what is the value of xy?
   a) 2
   b) 5
   c) 6
   d) 10

3. Which of the following expressions must be negative if $x < 0$?
   a) $x^4 - 2$
   b) $x^3 - 3$
   c) $x^4 - 3x^2 - 1$
   d) $x^6 + 3x^2 + 1$

$$y \geq -2x + 11$$
$$y > 3x - 9$$

4. In the xy-plane, point A is contained in the graph of the solution set of the system of inequalities above. Which of the following could be the coordinates of point A?
   a) (2, 1)
   b) (4, 1)
   c) (4, 5)
   d) (6, 6)

$$c = 80h + 100$$

5. The equation above gives the amount c, in dollars, an electrician charges for a job that

takes h hours. Ms. Sanchez and Mr. Roland each hired this electrician. The electrician worked 2 hours longer on Ms. Sanchez's job than on Mr. Roland's job. How much more did the electrician charge Ms. Sanchez than Mr. Roland?

    a) $80
    b) $140
    c) $160
    d) $200

$$\frac{1}{2}(x-1) = x - 3$$

6. What value of x satisfies the equation above?

    a) $\frac{4}{3}$
    b) 3
    c) 5
    d) $\frac{16}{3}$

7. Which of the following could be the sum of 9 numbers if the average of these 9 numbers is greater than 9 and less than 10?

    a) 91
    b) 90
    c) 85
    d) 81

8. Which of the following is the graph of a linear function with a positive slope and a negative y-intercept?

a)

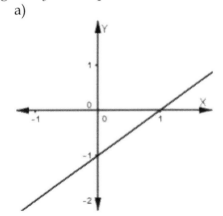

b)

.

c)

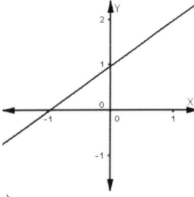

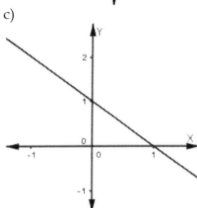

d)

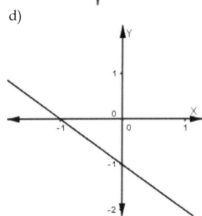

9. If x is the greatest prime factor of 34 and y is the greatest prime factor of 49, what is the value of $x - y$?

    a) 8
    b) 9
    c) 10
    d) 15

10. A supermarket has brand A juice smoothie on sale every 7 days and has brand B juice

smoothie on sale every 4 days. Within a year (365 days), how many times does this supermarket have both brands of juice smoothie on sale on the same day?
- a) 9
- b) 12
- c) 13
- d) 24

11. If $x^2 > 9$, which of the following must be true?
- a) $x > 3$
- b) $x < 3$
- c) $x < -3$
- d) $x > 3$ or $x < -3$

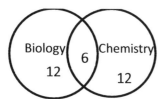

12. The Venn diagram above shows the distribution of 30 students in a class who took biology, chemistry, or both. If there are total 30 students in this class, what percent of the students studied chemistry?
- a) 30%
- b) 40%
- c) 50%
- d) 60%

13. The price of green tea leaves is D dollars for 5 ounces and each ounce makes x bottles of green tea drink. In terms of D and x, which of the following expressions shows the cost of making 1 bottle of green tea drink?
- a) $5Dx$
- b) $\frac{5D}{x}$
- c) $\frac{5x}{D}$
- d) $\frac{D}{5x}$

14. Which of the following is the fraction $\frac{1}{2-i}$ equivalent to?
- a) $-2i$
- b) $2 + i$
- c) $\frac{2-i}{3}$
- d) $\frac{2+i}{5}$

15. In Bridgetown High School, each class period is 1 hour and 25 minutes long, each break in between periods is 5 minutes long and lunch (between 2nd and 3rd period) is 45 minutes long. If 4th period is to end at 2:00, what time should the school day begin?
- a) 7:00
- b) 7:15
- c) 7:25
- d) 7:45

Directions:

For questions 16-20, solve the problem and enter your answer in the grid, as described below, on the answer sheet.

Answer: $\frac{7}{12}$

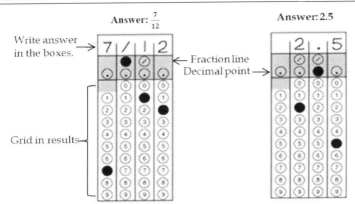

Write answer in the boxes.

← Fraction line
Decimal point →

Answer: 2.5

Grid in results

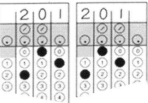

Answer: 201
Either position is correct.

Note: You may start your answers in any column, space permitting. Columns not needed should be left blank.

- Mark no more than one circle in any column.
- Because the answer sheet will be machine-scored. **You will receive credit only if the circles are filled in correctly.**
- Although not required, it is suggested that you write your answer in the boxes at the top of the columns to help you fill in the circles accurately.
- Some problems may have more than one correct answer. In such case, grid only one answer.
- No question has a negative answer.
- **Mixed numbers** such as $3\frac{1}{2}$ must be

gridded as 3.5 or $\frac{7}{2}$. (If 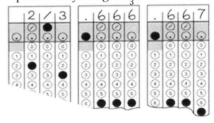 is gridded, it will be interpreted as $\frac{31}{2}$, not $3\frac{1}{2}$.)

- **Decimal Answer:** If you obtain a decimal answer with more digits than the grid can accommodate, it may be either rounded or truncated, but it must fill the entire grid. The acceptable ways to grid $\frac{2}{3}$ are:

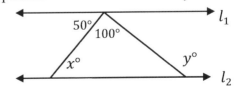

$$3s + t = 10$$

16. In the equation above, what is the value of s when $= -1$?

17. If $5x = 4y^2 = 20$, what is the value of xy^2?

18. A square and an equilateral triangle have equal perimeter. If the square has an area of 36 square feet, what is the length of one side of the triangle, in feet?

19. Find the radius of the circle given by the equation $x^2 + y^2 + 4x + 4y - 1 = 0$.

20. In the figure below, lines l_1 and l_2 are parallel. What is the value of y?

SECTION 4
Math Test — Calculator   55 MINUTES, 38 QUESTIONS

Directions:

For questions 1-30, solve each problem, choose the best answer from the choices provided, and fill in the corresponding circle on your answer sheet. **For questions 31-38**, solve the problem and enter your answer in the grid on the answer sheet. Please refer to the directions before question 31 on how to enter your answers in the grid. You may use any available space in your test booklet for scratch work.

Notes:

1. Acceptable calculators are allowed for this section. All numbers used are real numbers.
2. Figures that accompany problems in this test are intended to provide information useful in solving the problems. They are drawn as accurately as possible EXCEPT when it is stated in a specific problem that the figure is not drawn to scale. All figures lie in a plane unless otherwise indicated.
3. Unless otherwise specified, the domain of any function $f(x)$ assumed to be the set of all real numbers x for which $f(x)$ is a real number.

References:

$A = \pi r^2$
$C = 2\pi r$

$A = lw$

$A = \frac{1}{2} bh$

$V = lwh$

$V = \pi r^2 h$

$c^2 = a^2 + b^2$ **Special Right Triangles**

The number of degrees of arc in a circle is 360; the number of radians of arc in a circle is 2π.
The sum of the degree measures of the angles in a triangle is 180.

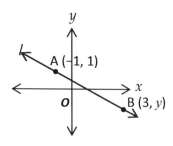

1. In the figure above, the slope of line l is $-\frac{1}{2}$. What is the value of y?
   a) $\frac{1}{2}$
   b) 1
   c) $-\frac{1}{2}$
   d) -1

2. At her summer job, Paula earns the same amount of money for each hour she works. If she earns $240 for working 20 hours, how much does she earn for 5 hours?
   a) $12
   b) $50
   c) $60
   d) $100

3. If $(0.10) \times y = 10^2$, then $y =$?
   a) 0.01
   b) 0.001
   c) 100
   d) 1000

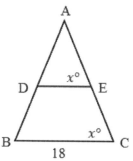

4. In the figure above, if $\overline{AD} = \overline{DB}$, what is the length of $\overline{DE}$?
   a) 6
   b) 9
   c) $9\sqrt{2}$
   d) 12

5. In the figure above, two congruent circles are inscribed in a rectangle. If the area of one circle is 4π, what is the area of the rectangle?
   a) 24
   b) 27
   c) 32
   d) 36

6. A development company is advertising that the mean area of the apartments in a new complex is 1,500 square feet. The complex consists of 10 buildings with a total of 1,000 apartments. A sample of 100 apartments will be selected from the complex to test the company's statement about the mean apartment area. Which of the following is an unbiased sampling method?
   a) Select the first 100 apartments built.
   b) Select the first 100 apartments that are occupied.
   c) Select at random 5 top-floor apartments from each of the buildings.
   d) Select at random 100 apartments from all the apartments in the 10 buildings.

Questions 7 – 8 refer to the following Information.
$$h = 3c$$
A wildlife biologist uses the formula above to estimate the height h, in centimeters, of an elephant from its feet to its shoulder, based on the circumference c, in centimeters, of the elephant's footprint.

7. If the wildlife biologist finds a circular elephant footprint that has a diameter of 30 centimeters (cm) while on a

zoological study, which of the following is closest to the biologist's estimate of the elephant's height?
   a) 90.0 cm
   b) 94.2 cm
   c) 188.4 cm
   d) 282.6 cm

8. The circumference c of a mother elephant's circular footprint is 4 times the circumference of a baby elephant's circular footprint. What is the ratio of the height of the mother to the height of the baby?
   a) 1 to 4
   b) 1 to 3
   c) 4 to 1
   d) 4 to 3

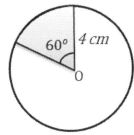

9. In the figure above, the circle has a center O and radius of 4 cm. What is the area of the shaded portion, in square centimeters?
   a) $\frac{1}{2}\pi$
   b) $2\frac{2}{3}\pi$
   c) $2\frac{3}{4}\pi$
   d) 3π

10. If the average (arithmetic mean) of 12, 16 and x is equal to x, what is the value of x?
    a) 9
    b) 10
    c) 14
    d) 16

11. A right circular cylinder with radius 3 and height 7 has a volume v, In terms of v, what

is the volume of the right circular cylinder with radius 3 and height 14?
- a) $v + 7$
- b) $7v$
- c) $5v$
- d) $2v$

12. What is the perimeter of a triangle that has vertices (–2, 0), (4, 0), and (1, 4) on the *xy*-coordinates plane?
- a) 16
- b) 14
- c) $6 + 2\sqrt{6}$
- d) 10

13. If water enters a certain type of garden hose with a diameter of 1.5 cm at a speed of 5 m/s, calculate the speed of water when it travels to the nozzle, which has diameter 0.7 cm.
- a) 30.66 m/s
- b) 22.96 m/s
- c) 17.23 m/s
- d) 14.21 m/s

14. If John gives Sally $5, Sally will have twice the amount of money that John will have. Originally, there was a total of $45 between the two of them. How much money did John initially have?
- a) 25
- b) 20
- c) 18
- d) 15

15. Which of the following is closest to the decrease in sales in millions between 2004 and 2005 according to the graph above?
- a) 10
- b) 12
- c) 15
- d) 20

16. If $x > y$, $w < z$, and $x < w$, which of the following must be true?
$$y < z$$
$$w < y$$
$$x < z$$
- a) None
- b) II and III
- c) I and II
- d) I and III

17. If $(x^{24})^a = (x^2)^4$, and $x > 1$, what is the value of a ?
- a) $\frac{1}{4}$
- b) $\frac{1}{3}$
- c) $\frac{1}{2}$
- d) 2

$$1, 5, 17, t, 161, ...$$

18. In the sequence above, what is the value of t?
- a) 34
- b) 51
- c) 53
- d) 68

19. Let *m be defined as *$m = m^2 + 4$ for all values of m. If *$x = 2x^2$, which of the following could be the value of x?
- a) –2
- b) 1
- c) $\sqrt{2}$
- d) $-\sqrt{2}$

20. Helen threw a fair six sided dice 5 times. Each throw showed a different number according to the rules:

Sales graph showing Sales (in Millions) on the y-axis (0, 20, 40, 60, 80) versus Years on the x-axis (2001, 2002, 2003, 2004, 2005).

The first roll was greater than 5.
The second roll was less than 3.
The third roll was 4.
The fourth roll was the same as
the first roll.
The fifth roll was an even
number.

Which of the following must be true?
  a) Helen could have rolled a 6 more than three times.
  b) Helen could have rolled a 5 only one time.
  c) Helen rolled more even numbers than odd numbers.
  d) Helen rolled 3 at least once.

$$f(x) = \sqrt{x^2 - 1}$$

21. Which of the following values of x makes $f(x)$ undefined?
  a) −2
  b) 0
  c) 2
  d) 1

22. If $x^2 - y^2 = 24$, and $x - y = 4$, what is the value of $x + 2y$?
  a) 1
  b) 3
  c) 5
  d) 7

23. If $f(x) = \frac{2 - x^2}{x}$ for all nonzero x, then $f(2) =$?
  a) 1
  b) 2
  c) 3
  d) −1

24. How many positive factors does the number 72 have?
  a) 5
  b) 6
  c) 12
  d) 9

25. If $sin(x^o) = a$, which of the following must be true for all values of x ?
  a) $\cos (x^o) = a$
  b) $sin(90^o - x^o) = a$
  c) $\cos (90^o - x^o) = a$

  d) $sin (x^2)^o = a^2$

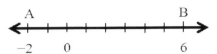

26. In the number line above, if 3 equally spaced points are drawn between A and B and point C is one of those points, which of the following is a possible coordinate for point C?
  a) −1
  b) 1
  c) 2
  d) 3

27. Which of the following is a factor of $2x^2 + 5x - 12$?
  a) $2x - 3$
  b) $2x - 4$
  c) $x - 4$
  d) $x - 6$

Questions 28 − 29 refer to the following information:

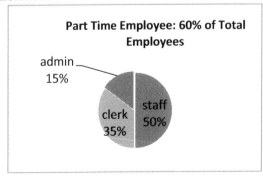

Part Time Employee: 60% of Total Employees

admin 15%
clerk 35%
staff 50%

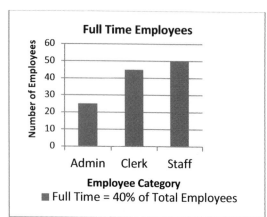

Full Time Employees

Number of Employees

Admin   Clerk   Staff

Employee Category

■ Full Time = 40% of Total Employees

28. According to the graphs above, the total number of part-time employees is how many more than the total number of full-time employees at Oak Town High School?
   a) 20
   b) 40
   c) 50
   d) 60

29. According to the graphs above, how many part-time staff members are at Oak Town High School?
   a) 100
   b) 90

c) 80
d) 60

30. The graph of $h(x)$ is a line. If $h(-2) = 7$ and $h(4) = 3$, then an equation of $h(x)$ is
   a) $\frac{2}{3}x - \frac{17}{3}$
   b) $-\frac{2}{3}x + \frac{17}{3}$
   c) $\frac{2}{3}x + \frac{17}{3}$
   d) $-\frac{3}{2}x + \frac{17}{3}$

Directions:

For questions 31-38, solve the problem and enter your answer in the grid, as described below, on the answer sheet.

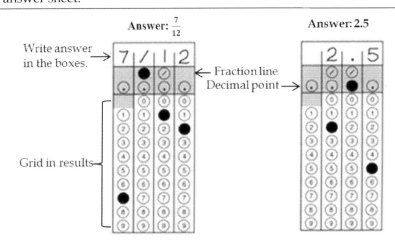

Answer: $\frac{7}{12}$

Write answer in the boxes. →

← Fraction line

Decimal point →

Answer: 2.5

Answer: 201
Either position is correct.

Grid in results →

Note: You may start your answers in any column, space permitting. Columns not needed should be left blank.

- Mark no more than one circle in any column.
- Because the answer sheet will be machine-scored. **You will receive credit only if the circles are filled in correctly.**
- Although not required, it is suggested that you write your answer in the boxes at the top of the columns to help you fill in the circles accurately.
- Some problems may have more than one correct answer. In such case, grid only one answer.
- No question has a negative answer.
- **Mixed numbers** such as $3\frac{1}{2}$ must be

gridded as 3.5 or $\frac{7}{2}$. (If $3 1/2$ is gridded, it will be interpreted as $\frac{31}{2}$, not $3\frac{1}{2}$.)

- **Decimal Answer:** If you obtain a decimal answer with more digits than the grid can accommodate, it may be either rounded or truncated, but it must fill the entire grid. The acceptable ways to grid $\frac{2}{3}$ are:

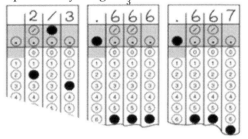

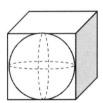

31. In the figure above, a cube has a volume of 64 cubic units. What is the length of the diameter of a sphere that is inscribed in the cube?

32. What is the remainder when $2x^4 - 3x^3 + 4x^2 - 5x + 6$ is divided by $x - 3$?

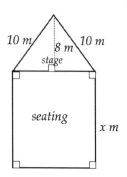

33. The figure above is the floor plan drawn
    by an architect for a small concert hall. The
    stage has depth 8 meters (m) and two walls
    each of length 10 m. If the seating portion
    of the hall has an area of 180 square
    meters, what is the value of x?

34. How many cups, each with a capacity of 8
    fluid ounces, can be filled with water from
    a cooler that contains 10 gallons of water?
    (1 gallon = 128 fluid ounces)

35. Gina drove at an average of 40 miles per
    hour from her house to a bookstore. Along
    the same route, she returned at an average
    of 60 miles per hour. If the entire trip took
    her 1 hour, how many miles did Gina drive
    in total?

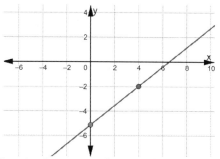

36. A line is shown in the xy-plane above. A
    second line (not shown) is perpendicular to
    the line shown and passes through the
    points $(1,1)$ and $(0,d)$, where d is a
    constant. What is the value of d ?

Questions 37 and 38 refer to the following
information:

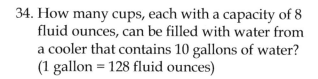

37. The figure above represents eight chairs
    that will be assigned randomly to eight
    students, one student per chair. If Sam and
    Chris are two of the eight students, what is
    the probability, in fraction, that each will
    be assigned a chair indicated by an X?

38. what is the probability, after simplifying in
    fraction, that Chris and Sam sit together?

SAT MATH PRACTICE TEST No. 10 ANSWER KEYS

Section 3

1. (D)	2. (B)	3. (B)	4. (C)	5. (C)	6. (C)	7. (C)	8. (A)	9. (C)	10. (C)
11. (D)	12. (D)	13. (D)	14. (D)	15. (C)	16. $\frac{11}{3}$	17. 20	18. 8	19. 3	20. 150

Section 4

1. (D)	2. (C)	3. (D)	4. (B)	5. (C)	6. (D)	7. (D)	8. (C)	9. (B)	10. (C)
11. (D)	12. (A)	13. (B)	14. (B)	15. (C)	16. (D)	17. (B)	18. (C)	19. (A)	20. (C)
21. (B)	22. (D)	23. (D)	24. (C)	25. (C)	26. (C)	27. (A)	28. (D)	29. (B)	30. (B)
31. 4	32. 108	33. 15	34. 160	35. 48	36. $\frac{7}{3}$	37. $\frac{1}{28}$	38. $\frac{1}{4}$		

Section 3

1. Answer: (D)
Divide by x on both sides.
$y = 1$

2. Answer: (B)
$(x + y)^2 - (x - y)^2 = (x^2 + y^2 + 2xy) - (x^2 + y^2 - 2xy) = 4xy$
$49 - 29 = 4xy$
$xy = 5$

3. Answer: (B)
If $x < 0$, then the result of an odd power of x is negative and the result of an even power of x is positive.

4. Answer: (C)
Plug in: a) $(2, 1)$ to 1st equation.
$1 \geq -2(2) + 11$ (wrong)
Plug in: b) $(4, 1)$ to 1st equation.
$1 \geq -2(4) + 11$ (wrong)
Plug in: c) $(4, 5)$ to 1st eq.
$5 \geq -2(4) + 11$ (ok)
Plug in: c) $(4, 5)$ to 2nd eq.
$5 \geq -2(4) + 11$ (ok)
The answer is c)

5. Answer: (C)
It costs $80 for every one additional hour of work.
$2 \times 80 = \$160$

6. Answer: (C)
$x - 1 = 2x - 6 \rightarrow x = 5$

7. Answer: (C)
Sum = Number of Elements × Average
$9 \times 9 < \text{Sum} < 10 \times 9$
$81 < \text{Sum} < 90$

8. Answer: (A)
A line with a positive slope increases from left to right.
(a) has a positive slope and a negative y-intercept.

9. Answer: (C)
The greatest prime factor of 34 is 17 and the greatest prime factor of 49 is 7.
$x - y = 17 - 7 = 10$

10. Answer: (C)
The LCM of 7 and 4 is 28.
Every 28 days, A and B will be on sale on the same day.
$\frac{365}{28} = 13.035$

11. Answer: (D)
$x^2 > 9 \rightarrow x^2 - 9 > 0$
$(x - 3)(x + 3) > 0$
The terms $(x - 3)$ and $(x + 3)$ must be both positive or both negative for the term
$(x - 3)(x + 3)$ to be greater than 0.
$x > 3$ or $x < -3$

12. Answer: (D)
Among the total 30 students, there were $(6 + 12)$ students studied chemistry.
$\frac{18}{30} = 0.6 = 60\%$

13. Answer: (D)
$D = 5 \text{ ounces} \times \frac{x \text{ Bottles}}{Ounce} \times \text{Price of One Bottle}$
$\text{Price of One Bottle} = \frac{D}{5x}$

14. *Answer: (D)*
    Rationalize the denominator.
    $\frac{1}{2-i} \times \frac{2+i}{2+i} = \frac{2+i}{4-i^2} = \frac{2+i}{5}$

15. *Answer: (C)*
    The total time spent in school is 4 periods + lunch + 2 breaks (between periods 1 and 2, and periods 3 and 4). Total Time = 4 × (1 hour 25 minutes) + 45 minutes + 2 × 5 minutes= 6 hours 35 minutes
    6 hours 35 minutes before 2:00PM is 7:25 AM.

16. *Answer:* $\frac{11}{3}$
    $3s + (-1) = 10$
    $s = \frac{11}{3}$

17. *Answer: 20*
    $x = \frac{20}{5} = 4$; $y^2 = \frac{20}{4} = 5$
    $xy^2 = 4 \times 5 = 20$

18. *Answer: 8*
    The length of a side of the square: $\sqrt{36} = 6$. *The perimeter of this square is 4 × 6 = 24.*
    Let x be the length of one side of the triangle. The perimeter of the triangle is 3x.
    $3x = 24 \rightarrow x = 8$

19. *Answer: 3*
    Rewrite the equation in standard form.
    $x^2 + 4x + 4 + y^2 + 4y + 4 = 1 + 8$
    $(x + 2)^2 + (y + 2)^2 = 3^2$
    The center of the circle is $(-2, -2)$ *and the radius is 3.*

20. *Answer: 150*
    $x = 50$
    $180 - 100 - 50 = 30$
    $y = 180 - 30 = 150$

Section 4

1. *Answer: (D)*
   $slope = \frac{y-1}{3-(-1)} = -\frac{1}{2}$
   $y - 1 = -2 \rightarrow y = -1$

2. *Answer: (C)*
   $\frac{\$240}{20\ hours} = \frac{\$x}{5\ hours}$
   $20x = 240 \times 5$
   $x = 60$

3. *Answer: (D)*
   Divide both sides by 0.1.
   $(0.10) \times y = 100$
   $y = \frac{100}{0.1} = 1000$

4. *Answer: (B)*
   $\triangle ABC$ *and* $\triangle ADE$ *are similar by the AA Similarity Thoerem.*
   $\frac{AD}{AB} = \frac{1}{2} = \frac{DE}{BC}$
   $\frac{1}{2} = \frac{DE}{18}$
   $DE = 9$

5. *Answer: (C)*
   The length of the rectangle is 4r and its width is 2r.
   $\pi r^2 = 4\pi$
   $r = 2$
   Area of Rectangle = 4r × 2r = 8 × 4 = 32

6. *Answer: (D)*
   It needs to select samples randomly in order to be unbiased.

7. *Answer: (D)*
   Let D be the diameter of the elephant's footprint
   $h = 3C = 3(\pi D)$
   $h = 3(\pi)(30) = 282.6\ cm$

8. *Answer: (C)*
   $\frac{h_{mother}}{h_{baby}} = \frac{C_{mother}}{C_{baby}} = \frac{D_{mother}}{D_{baby}} = \frac{4}{1}$

9. *Answer: (B)*
   The area of the shaded portion is $\frac{60}{360}$ *of the area of the whole circle.*
   Shaded Area $= \frac{60}{360} \times \pi \times 4^2 = \frac{8}{3}\pi = 2\frac{2}{3}\pi$

10. *Answer: (C)*
    Average: $\frac{12 + 16 + x}{3} = x$
    $28 + x = 3x$
    $28 = 2x$
    $x = 14$

11. *Answer: (D)*
    $v = \pi(3)^2 \times 7$
    $v_2 = \pi(3)^2 \times 14$
    $\frac{v}{v_2} = \frac{\pi(3)^2 \times 7}{\pi(3)^2 \times 14} = \frac{1}{2}$
    $v_2 = 2v$

12. *Answer: (A)*
Without using the distance formula, we can tell that the points (–2, 0) and (4, 0) are 6 units apart. Use the distance formula to find the lengths for the other two sides.
Perimeter = $6 + \sqrt{(-2-1)^2 + (0-4)^2} +$
$\sqrt{(4-1)^2 + (0-4)^2} = 6 + 5 + 5$
$= 16$

13. *Answer: (B)*
$A_1V_1 = A_2V_2$
$\pi\left(\frac{1.5}{2}\right)^2 \times 5 = \pi\left(\frac{0.7}{2}\right)^2 \times V_2$
$V_2 = 22.96\ m/s$

14. *Answer: (B)*
Let J be the amount of money John initially had and S be the amount of money Sally initially had. Together, they originally had $45.
$J + S = 45$
$J = 45 - S$
After John gives Sally $5, John will have J – 5 dollars and Sally will have S + 5 dollars. Therefore, S + 5 = 2(J – 5).
$S + 5 = 2(45 - S - 5) = 80 - 2S$
$S = 25$
Plug J = 45 – S into the equation above to get J = $20.

15. *Answer: (C)*
2004 Sales = 60 million units
2005 Sales = 45 million units
$60 - 45 = 15$ *million units*

16. *Answer: (D)*
Draw a number line and locate w, x, y and z on the line.
Only (I) and (III) are correct.

smaller $\longleftarrow$ y x w z $\longrightarrow$ larger

17. *Answer: (B)*
$(x^{24})^a = (x^2)^4 = x^{24a} = x^8$
$24a = 8 \rightarrow a = \frac{1}{3}$

18. *Answer: (C)*
Examine the first few terms to figure out the pattern. This is a sequence constructed by multiplying the previous term by 3 and then adding 2 to the product each time to get the next term.
$1 \times 3 + 2 = 5; 5 \times 3 + 2 = 17;$
$17 \times 3 + 2 = 53; t = 53$

19. *Answer: (A)*
$*x = x^2 + 4$, $x^2 + 4 = 2x^2$
$x^2 = 4$
$x = \pm 2$

20. *Answer: (C)*
List of results: 6, less than 3, 4, 6, even.
Only (c) could meet all the conditions.

21. *Answer: (B)*
The value under the square root must be greater than or equal to zero.

22. *Answer: (D)*
$x^2 - y^2 = (x - y)(x + y)$
$4(x + y) = 24,$
$x + y = 6$
$x - y = 4$
Solve above system equations:
$x = 5$ and $y = 1$
$x + 2y = 7$

23. *Answer: (D)*
Plug x = 2 into the function.
$f(2) = \frac{2-(2)^2}{2} = \frac{-2}{2} = -1$

24. *Answer: (C)*
$72 = 2^3 \times 3^2$
Number of positive factors of 72:
$(3 + 1) \times (2 + 1) = 12$

25. *Answer: (C)*
$cos(90^o - x^o) = sin(x^o) = a$

26. *Answer: (C)*
Find the distance of $\overline{AB}$ then divide it by 4.
$\frac{AB}{4} = \frac{6-(-2)}{4} = 2$
The coordinate of point C could be (6 – 2) =4 or (–2 + 2) =0 or (4 – 2) =2.

27. *Answer (a)*
First, find two numbers whose product is –24 and sum is 5. These two numbers are –3 and 8.
$2x^2 + 5x - 12 = 2(x + \frac{8}{2})(x - \frac{3}{2}) \rightarrow 2(x + 4)(x - \frac{3}{2})$
$= (x + 4)\left(2x - 2 \times \frac{3}{2}\right)$
$= (x + 4)(2x - 3)$

28. *Answer: (D)*
    Number of Full Time Employees = 25 + 45 + 50 =120
    employees.
    Full time employees comprise of 40% of the total.
    0.4 × Number of Employees = 120.
    Number of Employees = 300.
    Part Time Employees = 300 × 0.6= 180.
    Part Time Employees − Full Time Employees = 180 −
    120 = 60 employees

29. *Answer: (B)*
    Number of Part time staff = number of Part Time
    Employees × 0.5 = 180 × 0.5 = 90.

30. *Answer: (B)*
    Either use the substitution method or find the slope of
    the line.
    Slope $= \frac{3-7}{4-(-2)} = \frac{-4}{6} = -\frac{2}{3}$
    y-intercept: $7 = -\frac{2}{3} \times (-2) + b$
    $b = \frac{17}{3}$

31. *Answer: 4*
    Diameter of Sphere = Length of Side of Cube
    Length of Side of Cube $= \sqrt[3]{64} = 4$

32. *Answer: 108*
    Remainder Theorem: If polynomial P(x)is divided
    by x − r, its remainder is P(r).
    $P(3) = 2 \times 3^4 - 3 \times 3^3 + 4 \times 3^2 - 5(3) + 6 = 108$

33. *Answer: 15*

    $a^2 + 8^2 = 10^2$
    $a = 6$
    The width of the seating portion is $2 \times 6 = 12$
    $12x = 180 \rightarrow x = 15$

34. *Answer: 160*
    $10(128)\left(\frac{1}{8}\right) = 160$

35. *Answer: 48*
    Let one trip have x miles
    Total Time = $t_{go} + t_{back}$
    $1 = \frac{x}{40} + \frac{x}{60} = x(\frac{1}{40} + \frac{1}{60}) \rightarrow x = 24$
    Total miles: $2 \times 24 = 48$ *miles*

36. *Answer:* $\frac{7}{3}$

    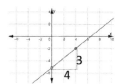

    The equation of the line in the graph is $y = \frac{3}{4}x - 5$.
    The equation of the second line is $y = -\frac{4}{3}x + b$.
    Plug in (1, 1),
    $1 = -\frac{4}{3}(1) + b \rightarrow b = \frac{7}{3}$
    $y = -\frac{4}{3}x + \frac{7}{3}$
    $f(0) = -\frac{4}{3} \times 0 + \frac{7}{3} = \frac{7}{3}$

37. *Answer:* $\frac{1}{28}$
    The arrangement that we want is an arrangement
    where six students choose from 6 chairs and two
    students (Sam and Chris) choose from the 2 chairs
    marked with an X. Then we will divide the number of
    special arrangements by the number of possible
    arrangements, where Sam and Chris are not
    constrained to the two chairs with Xs.
    Probability $= \frac{Special\ Arrangements}{Total\ Arrangemens}$
    Total Arrangements = 8!
    Special Arrangements = 6! × 2!
    $P = \frac{6! \times 2!}{8!} = \frac{2}{8 \times 7} = \frac{1}{28}$

38. *Answer:* $\frac{1}{4}$
    Total arrangement: = 8!
    Special Arrangements:
    Consider Chris and Sam tie together as one person:
    The number of this arrangement:
    7! × 2!
    $p = \frac{7! \times 2!}{8!} = \frac{1}{4}$

Index

MORE BOOKS BY DR. JANG:

Dr. Jang's SAT 800 Series:

Dr. Jang's SAT 800 Math Workbook
Dr. Jang's SAT 800 Chemistry Subject Test
Dr. Jang's SAT 800 Physics Subject Test
Dr. Jang's SAT 800 Math Subject Test Level 2
Dr. Jang's SAT 800 Math Ten Practice Tests

Dr. Jang's AP 5 Series:

Dr. Jang's AP 5 Physics 1 Workbook
Dr. Jang's AP 5 Chemistry Workbook

Dr. Jang's ACT:
Dr. Jang's ACT 36 Math Workbook

Visit Our Website for More Services and More Practice Questions:
www.DrJang800.com

The Goals of Dr. Jang's Books:

~For students:
To help you study based on your skill level.

~For teachers:
To help you plan lessons based on students' needs.

"Giving instruction based on each student's characteristics and ability will achieve the best educational results."
~ *Confucius*

Made in the USA
Las Vegas, NV
16 September 2022

55396585R10227